# CliffsNotes®

## Praxis® Middle School Mathematics (5169)

# CliffsNotes®

# Praxis® Middle School Mathematics (5169)

## 2ND EDITION

*by*
*Sandra Luna McCune, Ph.D.*

Houghton Mifflin Harcourt
Boston • New York

*About the Author*

**Sandra Luna McCune, Ph.D.,** is professor emeritus and a former Regents professor in the Department of Elementary Education at Stephen F. Austin State University, where she received the Distinguished Professor Award. She now is a full-time author and consultant and resides near Austin, Texas.

*Author Acknowledgments*

Sandra Luna McCune wishes to thank her late husband Donice for his brilliant understanding of mathematics that made this book possible.

*Dedication*

With much love, this book is dedicated to my grandchildren: Richard, Rose, Jude, Sophia, Josephine, and Myla.

*Editorial*

**Executive Editor:** Greg Tubach

**Senior Editor:** Christina Stambaugh

**Production Editor:** Erika West

**Copy Editor:** Lynn Northrup

**Technical Editors:** Mary Jane Sterling and Tom Page

**Proofreader:** Susan Moritz

**CliffsNotes® Praxis® Middle School Mathematics (5169), 2nd Edition**

Copyright © 2016 by Houghton Mifflin Harcourt Publishing Company

All rights reserved.

Cover image © Shutterstock / Mavrick

Library of Congress Control Number: 2016935915
ISBN: 978-0-544-62825-0 (pbk)

Printed in the United States of America
DOO 10 9 8 7 6 5 4 3 2     4500701160

For information about permission to reproduce selections from this book, write to trade.permissions@hmhco.com or to Permissions, Houghton Mifflin Harcourt Publishing Company, 3 Park Avenue, 19th Floor, New York, New York 10016.

www.hmhco.com

# Table of Contents

# Introduction

## General Description

The Praxis Middle School Mathematics test (test code 5169, Praxis MS Math) is designed to assess the mathematical knowledge and skills that are believed necessary for competent professional practice by entry-level teachers of middle school mathematics. According to the *Praxis Study Companion* for the Praxis Middle School Mathematics test (available at www.ets.org/s/praxis/pdf/5169.pdf), the test addresses two broad content categories:

I. Arithmetic and Algebra

II. Geometry and Data

The computer-delivered test consists of 55 questions. Of the 55 questions, 10 are pretest items that do not count toward your score. No penalty is imposed for wrong answers (you merely score a 0 for that test question). You are given 2 hours to complete the test.

To get up-to-date information about the Praxis MS Math test, go to www.ets.org/praxis/prepare/materials/5169 on the ETS website. If new information on the test becomes available, it will be posted on this site.

## Allocation of the Test Content

According to the *Praxis Study Companion* for the Praxis MS Math test (see "General Description" above for the Internet address), the approximate number of questions and percentage of the test for each content category are as follows:

### Allocation of the Test Content

| Content Category | Approximate Number of Questions | Approximate Percentage of Test |
|---|---|---|
| Arithmetic and Algebra | 34 | 62% |
| Geometry and Data | 21 | 38% |

## Question Types

The Praxis MS Math test has several different question types. You may be asked to choose one correct answer choice from among four options, select all correct answer choices from a list of options presented, select a response from a drop-down menu, drag and drop an answer choice to an on-screen area where it belongs, or fill in a numeric response in an answer box. There is no set number for each question type, nor do the question types appear in a specific order. For each question, you select a single answer choice unless written instructions preceding the question state otherwise.

This section presents examples of the three main question types you can expect to see on the Praxis MS Math test: multiple-choice (select one answer), multiple-choice (select one or more answers), and numeric entry (fill in a numeric response in an answer box).

Read the directions carefully before you answer each question. If a question has answer choices with **ovals,** then you must select a single answer choice. If a question has answer choices with **square boxes,** then you must select one or more answer choices. If a question presents no answer choices, you are provided with a **blank rectangular box** (or two stacked boxes, for answers with fractions) and you must manually enter your answer.

| Ovals | $\bigcirc$ | Multiple-choice question (select one answer choice) |
|---|---|---|
| Square Boxes | $\square$ | Multiple-choice question (select one or more answer choices) |
| Rectangular Box | ▭ | Numeric-entry question (fill in your answer) |
| Two Stacked Boxes | ⊟ | Numeric-entry question (fill in your fraction answer) |

**Note: The example questions and practice tests in this book label each multiple-choice answer choice with a letter for clarity. These letters do not appear on the computer screen when you take the actual test. Instead, you will click on the oval or square(s) next to the answer you choose.**

## Multiple-Choice (Select One Answer Choice) Questions

The multiple-choice (select one answer choice) questions require you to choose one correct answer choice from among four options.

Example

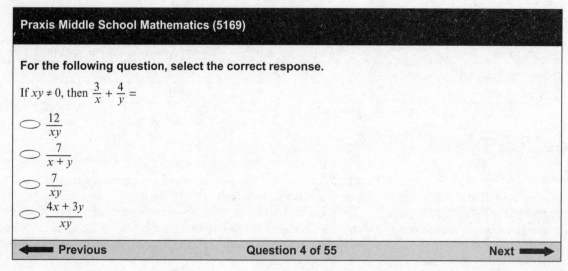

# Multiple-Choice (Select One or More Answer Choices) Questions

The multiple-choice (select one or more answer choices) questions require you to choose ALL of the correct answer choices and *no others* from among a list of options presented. The correct answer might be just one of the answer choices or it could be as many as all of the answer choices. The question is scored as incorrect unless you select all of the correct choices and no others. There is no partial credit.

Example

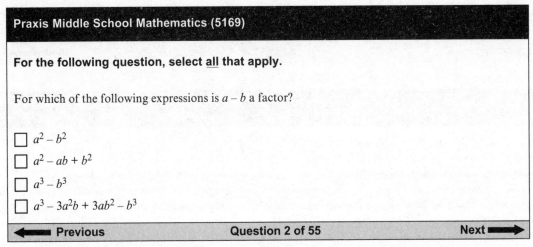

# Numeric-Entry (Fill in a Numeric Answer) Questions

Numeric-entry (fill in a numeric answer) questions do not present answer choices. Instead, you are required to fill in a numeric answer to the question. Here are guidelines.

- If you are answering a question that shows a single rectangular box for the answer, click on the box and use the keyboard to type in your answer.
- If a question asks specifically for the answer as a fraction, there will be two boxes—a numerator box and a denominator box. Click on the upper box and use the keyboard to type in the numerator of your answer. Then click on the lower box to type in the denominator of your answer. Do NOT use decimals in fractions.
- Type in the exact answer unless the question requires you to round the answer.
- For a decimal point, type a period.
- For a negative sign, type a hyphen.
- Use the backspace key to erase.
- Equivalent forms of an answer in decimal notation are all correct. For example, if the answer is 45, then answers such as 45, 45., or 45.0 are all correct. If the answer is 3.7, then answers such as 3.7, 3.70, or 03.7 are all correct.
- Fractions do not have to be reduced to lowest terms (although you might have to reduce a fraction so that it fits in the answer boxes). For example, if the answer is $\frac{2}{5}$, then fractions that are equivalent to $\frac{2}{5}$, such as $\frac{4}{10}$ and $\frac{20}{50}$, are also correct.

Examples

---

**Praxis Middle School Mathematics (5169)**

**For the following question, enter your numeric answer in the box below the question.**

A length of cable is attached to the top of a 15-foot pole. The cable is anchored 8 feet from the base of the pole. What is the length, in feet, of the cable?

⬚ feet

⬅ **Previous**      **Question 17 of 55**      **Next** ➡

---

**Praxis Middle School Mathematics (5169)**

**For the following question, enter your fractional answer in the boxes below the question.**

The enrollment at a small community college for the fall semester is 10% higher than the enrollment in the fall semester a year ago. The number of female students increased by 5%, and the number of male students increased by 20%. Female students make up what fraction of the current enrollment at the community college? Give your answer as a fraction.

⬚
⬚

⬅ **Previous**      **Question 52 of 55**      **Next** ➡

---

# ETS On-Screen Graphing Calculator

While you are taking the Praxis MS Math test, an on-screen graphing calculator will be available to you. Practice using the ETS on-screen graphing calculator while working through this CliffsNotes book. You can download a 90-day free trial version at www.infinitysw.com/ets. Online tutorials are available on the website, and the downloadable calculator manual is available at http://infinitysw.s3.amazonaws.com/ets/ets_calculator_manual.pdf. *Note:* Hereafter in this book, the ETS on-screen graphing calculator that you will be allowed to access when you are taking the Praxis MS Math test is referred to simply as "the ETS graphing calculator."

# Scoring of the Test

Educational Testing Service (ETS) does not release the exact details of the way the Praxis MS Math test is scored. For each question you answer correctly you get 1 raw point, and your total raw score is the number of questions you answer correctly out of the 45 questions on the test that count.

Your raw point score is converted to a scaled score that adjusts for the difficulty level of the particular edition of the test that you took. Your score report for the test will show a scaled score ranging from 100 to 200. Read *Understanding Your Praxis Scores* (available at www.ets.org/s/praxis/pdf/uyps_1516.pdf) for more information about the scoring of the test.

The recommended passing score is 31 out of a possible 45 raw-score points. The scaled score corresponding to a raw score of 31 (69% correct) is 165 on a 100–200 scale.

Note: For the practice tests in this study guide, you are provided a guideline for converting your raw score to a percent-correct score. A percent-correct score of 69% (38 correct out of 55 questions) or higher should roughly equate to a passing scaled score.

# The Role of the Praxis MS Math Test in Teacher Certification

The Praxis MS Math test is one of the Praxis Subject Assessment tests designed by Educational Testing Service (ETS). The Praxis Subject Assessment tests are part of a national teacher assessment program and are used as part of the certification or licensing requirements in states across the U.S. You should be able to transfer your score on the Praxis MS Math test from state to state for those states that use the Praxis Subject Assessment tests.

If your state has selected the Praxis MS Math test to assess middle school teacher candidates' mathematical knowledge and skills, then this CliffsNotes book is a valuable resource to help you achieve the passing score for your state. Test scores needed to obtain certification vary from state to state because each state sets its own passing score. ETS maintains a list of passing scores by state for the Praxis MS Math test at www.ets.org/s/praxis/pdf/passing_scores.pdf. Here is a current listing of state passing scores (as of January 2016):

| | | |
|---|---|---|
| Alabama—148 | Kentucky—165 | Pennsylvania—165 |
| Alaska—165 | Louisiana—165 | Rhode Island—165 |
| Arkansas—165 | Maine—165 | South Carolina—165 |
| Connecticut—165 | Maryland—165 | South Dakota—165 |
| Delaware—165 | Mississippi—165 | Tennessee—165 |
| District of Columbia—165 | Nevada—165 | Utah—165 |
| Hawaii—164 | New Hampshire—165 | Vermont—165 |
| Idaho—165 | New Jersey—165 | Virginia—165 |
| Iowa—151 | North Carolina—165 | West Virginia—165 |
| Kansas—157 | North Dakota—165 | Wyoming—165 |

State testing requirements are subject to change. For the most up-to-date score requirements, visit your state department of education or your state page on the Praxis website, at www.ets.org/praxis/states.

100 to 200

45    31

# Studying for the Praxis MS Math Test

When you read through the descriptions of the Praxis MS Math test content category topics, you may feel overwhelmed by the task of preparing for the test. Here are some suggestions for developing an effective study program using this book.

1. Set up a regular schedule of study sessions. Try to set aside approximately 2 hours for each session. If you complete one session per day (including weekends), it should take you about 4 to 6 weeks to work your way through the review and practice material provided in this book. Of course, if your test date is coming up soon, you might need to lengthen your study time per day.

2. Reserve a place for studying where you will have few distractions, so that you can concentrate. Make sure that you have adequate lighting and a room temperature that is comfortable—not too warm or too cold. Be sure that you have an ample supply of water to keep your brain hydrated, and you might also want to have some light snacks available. To improve mental alertness, choose snacks that are high in protein and low in carbohydrates. Gather all the necessary study aids (paper, pencils, note cards, and so on) beforehand. Let your voicemail answer your phone during your study time.

3. Take Practice Test 1 (Chapter 9) before you begin reading the review material to help you discover your strengths and weaknesses. Read the answer explanations for all the questions, not just the ones you missed, because you might have gotten some of your correct answers by guessing. Make a list of the content categories with which you had the most problems. Plan your study program so that you can spend more time on content topics that your Practice Test 1 results indicate are weak areas for you. For example, if you did very well in numbers and operations, but poorly in algebra and functions, then you should plan to spend more time studying the review material on algebra and functions.

4. Carefully study the review material in chapters 1–8 of this book to refresh your memory about the key ideas for each of the content topics, being sure to concentrate as you go through the material. Work through the examples and make sure you understand them thoroughly.

5. Make flashcards to aid you in memorizing key definitions and formulas and keep them with you at all times. When you have a few spare minutes, take out the flashcards and go over the information you've recorded on them.

6. Take several brief 2- to 3-minute breaks during your study sessions to give your mind time to absorb the review material you just read. According to brain research, you remember the first part and last part of something you've read more easily than you remember the middle part. Taking several breaks will allow you to create more beginnings and endings to maximize the amount of material you remember. It's best not to leave your study area during a break. Try stretching or simply closing your eyes for a few minutes.

7. Periodically review material you have already studied to reinforce what you have learned and to help you identify topics you might need to restudy.

8. When you complete your first review, take Practice Test 2 (Chapter 10). Use a timer and take the test under the same conditions you expect for the actual test, being sure to adhere to the 2-hour time limit for the test. When you finish taking the test, as you did for Practice Test 1, carefully study the answer explanations for *all* the questions. Then, go back and review again any topics in which you performed unsatisfactorily.

9. When you complete your second review, take Practice Test 3 (Chapter 11) under the same conditions you expect for the actual test, adhering to the 2-hour time limit. When you finish taking the test, carefully study the answer explanations for *all* the questions and do additional study, if needed.

10. Organize a study group, if possible. A good way to learn and reinforce the material is to discuss it with others. If feasible, set up a regular time to study with one or more classmates or friends. Take turns explaining how to work problems. This strategy will help you not only to clarify your own understanding of the underlying mathematics, but also to discover new insights into how to approach various problems.

After completing your study program, you should find yourself prepared and confident to achieve a passing score on the Praxis MS Math test.

# How to Prepare for the Day of the Test

There are several things you can do to prepare yourself for the day of the test.

1. Know how to get to the test center and how to get into the room where you will be testing.

2. Make sure you have dependable transportation to get to the test center and know where you should park (if you plan to go by car).

3. Keep all the materials you will need to bring to the test center—especially, your admission ticket and identification—in a secure place so you easily can find them on the day of the test.

4. The night before the test, try to get a good night's rest. Avoid taking nonprescription drugs or consuming alcohol, as the use of these products might impair your mental faculties on test day.

5. On the day of the test, get to the test center early—at least 30 minutes before your test is scheduled to begin.

6. Dress in comfortable clothing and wear comfortable shoes. Even if it is warm outside, wear layers of clothing that can be removed or put on, depending on the temperature in the test center.

7. Eat a light meal. Select foods that give you the most energy and stamina.

8. Drink plenty of water to make sure that your brain remains hydrated for optimal thinking during the test.

9. Make a copy of this list and post it in a strategic location. Check it before you leave for the test center.

Tip: Go to http://www.ets.org/s/praxis/flash/prometric/18204_praxis-prometric-video.html for a video tutorial of what to expect at the test center on test day.

# Test-Taking Strategies for the Praxis MS Math Test

Here are some general test-taking strategies to help maximize your score on the test.

1. When you receive the test, take several deep, slow breaths before you begin, exhaling slowly while mentally visualizing yourself performing successfully on the test.

2. During the test, follow all the directions, including the test center administrator's (TCA) oral directions and the written directions on the computer screen. If you do not understand something in the directions, raise your hand and ask the TCA for clarification.

3. Move through the test at a steady pace. The test consists of 55 questions. When you get to questions 27 and 28, check the on-screen timer to see how much time has passed. If more than 1 hour has gone by, you will need to pick up the pace. Otherwise, continue to work as rapidly as you can without being careless, *but do not rush.*

4. Try to work the problems in order. However, if a question is taking too much time, use the Mark button to mark the question to review later, and move on.

5. Read each question entirely. Skimming to save time can cause you to misread a question or miss important information.

6. For multiple-choice (select one answer choice) questions, read all the answer choices before you select an answer. You might find an answer that immediately strikes you as correct, but this determination might have occurred because you jumped to a false conclusion or made an incorrect assumption. Also, eliminate as many wrong choices as you can. When applicable, estimate the answer to help you decide which answers are unreasonable.

7. For multiple-choice (select one or more answer choices) questions, systematically assess each answer choice one by one and either select it or eliminate it.

8. For numeric-entry questions, give the exact answer unless the question tells you to round your answer. If you must round your answer, do not round until you have completed all your calculations. For answers that must be given as fractions, save time by not reducing to lowest terms.

9. Don't read too much into a question. For example, don't presume a geometric figure is drawn accurately or to scale.

10. With application problems, always double-check to be sure you are answering the question asked.

11. Use the on-screen calculator, but use it wisely. Keep in mind that graphing calculators are powerful tools, but they can make errors. See the discussion about graphing calculators that follows this section.

12. Change an answer only if you have a good reason to do so.

13. If you are trying to recall information during the test, close your eyes and try to visualize yourself in your study place. This may trigger your memory.

14. Use the on-screen Help button as often as needed. But do keep in mind that the timer for the test does not pause when you are using the Help feature.

15. Before ending your test, be sure you have answered every test question. You are not penalized for a question you answered incorrectly (you merely score a 0 for that test question), so even if you have no clue about the correct response, make a guess.

16. Remain calm during the test. If you find yourself getting anxious, stop and take several deep, slow breaths and exhale slowly, while mentally visualizing yourself in a peaceful place, to help you relax. Keep your mind focused on the task at hand—completing your test. Trust yourself. You should not expect to know the correct response to every question on the test. Think only of doing your personal best.

As you work through the practice tests provided in this book, consciously use the strategies suggested in this section as preparation for the actual Praxis MS Math test. Try to reach a point where the strategies are automatic for you.

> **Tip:** Go to https://www.ets.org/s/praxis/flash/cbt/praxis_cdt_demo_web1.html for an interactive Praxis computer-delivered testing demonstration. The demonstration explains main features that are common to all Praxis computer-delivered tests, including how to log in and how to navigate through a test.

# Graphing Calculators and the Praxis MS Math Test

Graphing calculators are very powerful tools, but you should be aware that they can make errors!

One situation in which errors might occur is when the calculator is finding the roots or zeros of a high-degree polynomial (for example, a polynomial of degree 8). The algorithm that the calculator uses to find the roots of the polynomial forces the calculator to round numbers to a certain number of decimal places before the final result is obtained, thus yielding inaccurate answers.

Errors can also occur when the calculator is drawing the graph of a function. Your choice of viewing window dimensions can give results that are visually very misleading. For example, you can be led to believe that a function has only two zeros when, in fact, it has three zeros. Changing the dimensions for the viewing window can clear up the problem in most cases; however, not every time. Most notably, for some graphing calculators, the graph of $y = \sin\left(\dfrac{1}{x}\right)$ at values near $x = 0$ will never be correct no matter what window dimensions you select.

The point of this discussion is to make you aware that such mistakes can happen. Therefore, you should use your mathematical expertise to evaluate all calculator results for reliability and accuracy.

You will benefit greatly from this CliffsNotes book. By using the recommendations in this chapter as you complete your study program, you will be prepared to walk into the testing room with confidence. Good luck on the test and in your future career as a middle school mathematics teacher!

# Chapter 1

# Numbers and Operations

This chapter provides a review of key ideas and formulas of arithmetic and basic number concepts that are important for you to know for the Praxis MS Math test. Sample questions, comparable to what might be presented on the test, are given at the end of the chapter. The answer explanations for the sample questions are provided immediately after the questions.

## Arithmetic Operations

**Addition, subtraction, multiplication,** and **division** are the four basic arithmetic operations. Each of the operations has special symbolism and terminology associated with it. The following table shows the terminology and symbolism you are expected to know.

### Terminology and Symbolism for the Four Basic Arithmetic Operations

| Operation | Symbols(s) Used | Name of Parts | Example |
|---|---|---|---|
| Addition | + (plus sign) | addend + addend = sum | $5 + 9 = 14$ |
| Subtraction | − (minus sign) | minuend − subtrahend = difference | $14 - 5 = 9$ |
| Multiplication | × (times sign) | factor × factor = product | $10 \times 6 = 60$ |
| Multiplication | · (raised dot) | factor · factor = product | $10 \cdot 6 = 60$ |
| Multiplication | ( )( ) parentheses | (factor)(factor) = product | $(10)(6) = 60$ |
| Division | ÷ (division sign) | dividend ÷ divisor = quotient | $60 \div 10 = 6$ |
| Division | $\overline{)}$ (long division symbol) | $\text{divisor}\overline{)\text{dividend}}^{\text{quotient}}$ | $10\overline{)60}^{\,6}$ |
| Division | / (slash or fraction bar) | dividend/divisor = quotient | $60/10 = 6$ |
| Division | stacked fraction bar | $\dfrac{\text{dividend}}{\text{divisor}} = \text{quotient}$ | $\dfrac{60}{10} = 6$ |

The examples in the preceding table show that addition and subtraction "undo" each other. Mathematicians express this relationship by saying that addition and subtraction are **inverses** of each other. Similarly, multiplication and division are **inverses** of each other; they "undo" each other, *provided division by 0 is not involved.*

Be *very* careful when division involves zero. Zero can be a dividend; that is, you can divide a nonzero number into zero. However, 0 *cannot* be a divisor, which means that you *cannot* divide by 0. The quotient of any number divided by zero has no meaning; that is, *division by zero is undefined—you can't do it!* Even zero divided by zero is undefined. Following is a summary of division involving zero.

### Division Involving Zero

| Rule | Meaning | Examples |
|---|---|---|
| You *cannot* divide by zero. Zero cannot be the divisor! | $\dfrac{\text{any number}}{0}$ is undefined. $\dfrac{0}{0}$ is undefined. | $\dfrac{21}{0}$ is undefined. $0 \div 0$ is undefined. |
| You can divide zero by a nonzero number. Zero can be the dividend as long as the divisor is not zero. | $\dfrac{0}{\text{any nonzero number}} = 0$ | $\dfrac{0}{27} = 0$ |

# Integers

For this topic, you must understand the structure of the integers and their properties.

## Subsets of the Integers

The **integers** = {..., −3, −2, −1, 0, 1, 2, 3, ...}.

*Note:* Read the braces,{ }, around the numbers as "The set consisting of." Interpret the three dots, ..., in this context to mean that the pattern continues without end.

The **counting numbers** (or **natural numbers**) = {1, 2, 3, ...}.

The **whole numbers** = {0, 1, 2, 3, ...}.

A **prime number** is an integer greater than 1 that has exactly two distinct factors: itself and 1. The first 10 primes are 2, 3, 5, 7, 11, 13, 17, 19, 23, and 29.

The integers greater than 1 that are *not* prime are the **composite numbers.** The first 10 composites are 4, 6, 8, 9, 10, 12, 14, 15, 16, and 18.

The integer 1 is neither prime nor composite.

The **integers** are either **positive** {1, 2, 3, ...} or **negative** {..., −3, −2, −1} or **zero.** Negative numbers have a small horizontal line (−) attached to the left of the number.

> **Tip: You do not have to write the + sign on positive numbers (although it's not wrong to do so). If no sign is written with a nonzero number, then you know that it is a positive number. The number zero is neither positive nor negative.**

Integers that divide evenly by 2 are **even.** The even integers = {..., −6, −4, −2, 0, 2, 4, 6, ...}. *Tip:* Note that 0 is an even integer.

Integers that do *not* divide evenly by 2 are **odd.** The odd integers = {..., −5, −3, −1, 1, 3, 5, ...}.

If $ab = n$, where $a$, $b$, and $n$ are integers, then $a$ and $b$ are **factors,** or **divisors,** of $n$, and $n$ is a **multiple** of $a$ (and of $b$) and is **divisible** by $a$ (and by $b$). Here are some useful facts.

- Every integer has a finite number of distinct factors (see "Divisibility Rules and Factoring" below for a formula).
- Every nonzero integer has an infinite number of multiples.
- The number 1 is a factor (or divisor) of every integer, but it is a multiple of only 1 and −1.
- The number 0 is a multiple of every integer, but it is a factor of only 0.

*Tip:* The terms *factor, divisor,* and *divisible* apply only to integers. However, the term *multiple* can be used with any number $x$, as in $nx$, provided $n$ is an integer.

## Mathematical Induction, Fundamental Theorem of Arithmetic, and Division Algorithm

**Principle of Mathematical Induction:** Any set of counting numbers that contains the number 1 and $(k + 1)$, whenever it contains the counting number $k$, contains all the counting numbers.

**Fundamental Theorem of Arithmetic:** Every integer greater than or equal to 2 is either a prime or can be factored into a product of primes in one and only one way, except for the order in which the factors appear. The result is the unique **prime factorization** of the integer. Here is an example of using a factor tree to find the prime factorization of the number 36.

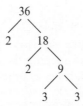

The numbers at the tips of the "branches" are prime factors—you cannot factor them any further. So the prime factors of 36 are 2 and 3, and its prime factorization is $2 \cdot 2 \cdot 3 \cdot 3 = 2^2 \cdot 3^2$.

**Division Algorithm:** If an integer $m$ is divided by a positive integer $d$, the result is a unique integer $q$ (the **quotient**) and unique integer $r$ (the **remainder**), where $0 \leq r < d$ and $m = dq + r$. In addition, $r = 0$ if and only if $m$ is a multiple of $d$. Here are examples.

When 21 is divided by 5, the quotient is 4 and the remainder is 1; and $21 = (5)(4) + 1$. On the number line, 21 is 1 unit to the right of $(5)(4) = 20$.

When 30 is divided by 5, the quotient is 6 and the remainder is 0; and $30 = (5)(6)$.

## Divisibility Rules and Factoring

Divisibility rules can help with factoring numbers. You write $a|b$ to mean $a$ divides $b$ evenly or, equivalently, $b$ is **divisible by** $a$. For example $3|36$ means 36 is divisible by 3. Therefore, 3 is a factor of 36. The following table shows some common divisibility rules that are helpful to know.

### Some Common Divisibility Rules

| Divisibility by | Rule | Example |
|---|---|---|
| 2 | The last digit of the number is even. | $2|2,347,854$ because 4 (the last digit) is even. |
| 3 | The sum of the number's digits is divisible by 3. | $3|151,515$ because 3 divides $(1 + 5 + 1 + 5 + 1 + 5) = 18$ (the sum of the digits). |
| 4 | The last two digits form a number that is divisible by 4. | $4|47,816$ because 4 divides 16 (the number formed by the last two digits). |
| 5 | The last digit of the number is 0 or 5. | $5|42,115$ because the last digit is 5. |
| 6 | The number is divisible by both 2 and 3. | $6|18,122,124$ because $2|18,122,124$ (the last digit is even) and $3|18,122,124$ (21, the sum of the digits, is divisible by 3). |
| 7 | Double the last digit and subtract the product from the number formed by the remaining digits. If the result is a number divisible by 7, the original number is also divisible by 7. | $7|875$ because $(87 - 2 \cdot 5) = (87 - 10) = 77$, which is divisible by 7. |
| 8 | The last three digits form a number that is divisible by 8. | $8|55,864$ because 8 divides 864 (the number formed by the last three digits). |
| 9 | The sum of the number's digits is divisible by 9. | $9|151,515$ because 9 divides $(1 + 5 + 1 + 5 + 1 + 5) = 18$ (the sum of the digits). |
| 10 | The last digit of the number is 0. | $10|66,660$ because the last digit is 0. |
| 11 | Alternately add and subtract the digits. If the result is a number divisible by 11, the original number is also divisible by 11. | $11|2,574$ because 11 divides $(2 - 5 + 7 - 4) = 0$ (the alternating sum and difference of the digits). |

Here is useful information to know about divisibility and factors.

- If an integer divides evenly into an integer *n,* then it divides evenly into any multiple of *n.* For example, 3|36, so 3|13(36) = 468.
- If an integer divides evenly into both of the integers *m* and *n,* then it divides evenly into *am* + *bn,* for any integers *a* and *b.* For example, 9|36 and 9|81, so 9|(2 · 36 + 5 · 81); that is, 9|477.
- If the prime factorization of a positive integer *z* is $p_1^{k_1} p_2^{k_2} \cdots p_n^{k_n}$, where the *p*s are distinct positive prime numbers and the *k*s are their corresponding exponents, then the number of positive factors (or divisors) of *z* is the product $(k_1 + 1)(k_2 + 1) \ldots (k_n + 1)$. Here are examples.

    The number of positive factors (or divisors) of $z = a^3bc^2d^5$, where *a, b, c,* and *d* are prime numbers, is (3 + 1)(1 + 1)(2 + 1)(5 + 1) = (4)(2)(3)(6) = 144.

> **Tip: Recall that if no exponent is written on a variable or number, the exponent is understood to be 1 (for example, $b = b^1$).**

    The number of factors (positive and negative) of 18 is 12. The number of positive factors of 18, which equals $(2)(3^2)$, is (1 + 1)(2 + 1) = (2)(3) = 6. Because the negatives of the positive factors are factors of 18 as well, the number of factors of 18 is 2(6) = 12.

# Greatest Common Factor and Least Common Multiple

The **greatest common factor** of two or more numbers is the greatest number that will divide evenly into each of the numbers. It can be obtained by writing the prime factorization of each number and building a product consisting of each factor the *highest* number of times it appears as a *common* factor of the numbers in the set. The greatest common factor of two numbers *m* and *n* is denoted gcf (*m, n*). For example, $24 = 2 \cdot 2 \cdot 2 \cdot 3 = 2^3 \cdot 3$ and $36 = 2 \cdot 2 \cdot 3 \cdot 3 = 2^2 \cdot 3^2$ implies gcf (24, 36) = $2^2 \cdot 3 = 12$.

Another way to find the gcf of two numbers is to list all the factors of the two numbers and then select the greatest factor common to both. For example, the factors of 24 are 1, 2, 3, 4, 6, 8, 12 , and 24, and the factors of 36 are 1, 2, 3, 4, 6, 9, 12 , 18, and 36. The greatest factor common to both is 12. Thus, gcf (24, 36) = 12.

> **Tip: The gcf of two numbers *m* and *n* is also known as their greatest common divisor, denoted gcd (*m, n*). This terminology is logical because the gcf is the greatest number that will divide evenly into both numbers.**

Use the gcf for word problems in which you must find the greatest common number, the greatest common measure, the greatest common size, and so forth that could be used to divide or distribute objects or things evenly from unequal-size sets so that *none are left over*. Here is an example.

> A high school club has 18 boys and 12 girls as members. For a presentation activity, the club's faculty sponsor wants to evenly divide the boys and girls into groups, so that each group has the same number of boys and the same number of girls as the other groups, and no one is left out. What is the greatest number of groups the sponsor can make?

The greatest number of groups is the gcf (18, 12) = 6. Each of the 6 groups will have 5 students in it, 3 boys (18 ÷ 6) and 2 girls (12 ÷ 6). Notice that 5 × 6 = 30, which is the total number of student members (18 + 12 = 30).

The **least common multiple** of a set of numbers is the least number that is a multiple of each of the numbers. It can be obtained by writing the prime factorization of each number and building a product consisting of each factor the *most* number of times it appears as a factor in any *one* of the numbers in the set. The least common multiple of two numbers *m* and *n* is denoted lcm (*m, n*). For example, $24 = 2 \cdot 2 \cdot 2 \cdot 3 = 2^3 \cdot 3$ and $36 = 2 \cdot 2 \cdot 3 \cdot 3 = 2^2 \cdot 3^2$ implies lcm (24, 36) = $2^3 \cdot 3^2 = 72$.

You also can find the lcm of two numbers by listing, in order, multiples of the greater number until you obtain a multiple that is also a multiple of the other number. This multiple will be the lcm of the two numbers. For example, the multiples of 36 are 36, 72, and so on. Because 72 is a multiple of 24, lcm (24, 36) = 72.

> **Tip:** The least common multiple of a set of numbers is the least number that is divisible by each of the numbers in the set.

Use the lcm for word problems in which you must find the minimum common number, the minimum common measure, the minimum common time, and so forth between multiple events or items. Here is an example.

> At the entrance to a concert, every 75th person gets a coupon for a free music download and every 100th person gets a coupon for an autographed picture of the performer. What is the minimum number of people who must enter for a person to receive both coupons?

The minimum number of people is the lcm (75, 100) = 300. The 300th person will be the first person to receive both coupons.

The product of two integers $m$ and $n$ equals their greatest common factor times their least common multiple; that is, $mn = \text{gcf } (m, n) \cdot \text{lcm } (m, n)$. For example, $24 \cdot 36 = 864$, which equals gcf $(24, 36) \cdot$ lcm $(24, 36) = 12 \cdot 72 = 864$.

Thus, a quick way to compute the lcm of two numbers is to divide their product by their gcf. For example, in the previous example, $\text{lcm } (75, 100) = \dfrac{(75)(100)}{\text{gcf } (75,100)} = \dfrac{(75)(100)}{25} = \dfrac{\left(\overset{3}{\cancel{75}}\right)(100)}{\underset{1}{\cancel{25}}} = 300.$

# Rational Numbers

The rational numbers are the numbers that you are familiar with from school and from your everyday experiences with numbers. The rational numbers include the counting numbers, whole numbers, integers, and positive and negative fractions, decimals, and percents.

The **rational numbers** $= \left\{ \dfrac{p}{q}, \text{where } p \text{ and } q \text{ are integers with } q \neq 0 \right\}$. For example, $\dfrac{3}{4}, -\dfrac{2}{5}, \dfrac{325}{1,000}, \dfrac{15}{7},$ and $-\dfrac{75}{100}$ are rational numbers.

All integers are rational numbers because you can write each as a ratio whose denominator is 1, as shown here.

$$\cdots, -3 = \frac{-3}{1}, -2 = \frac{-2}{1}, -1 = \frac{-1}{1}, 0 = \frac{0}{1}, 1 = \frac{1}{1}, 2 = \frac{2}{1}, 3 = \frac{3}{1}, \cdots$$

Rational numbers can be expressed as fractions, decimals, or percents.

# Fractions

A **fraction** $\dfrac{n}{d}$ has three parts. The number $n$ is the **numerator,** the number $d$ is the **denominator,** and the horizontal line between $n$ and $d$ is the **fraction bar.** Even though it takes two numerical components—the numerator and denominator—to make a fraction, the fraction itself is just one number. Specifically, it is a rational number.

The fraction $\dfrac{n}{d}$ means $n \div d$. **Remember:** The denominator of a fraction cannot be zero because division by zero is undefined.

The **reciprocal** of the fraction $\dfrac{p}{q}$ is the fraction $\dfrac{q}{p}$, provided $p \neq 0$ and $q \neq 0$.

A fraction has three signs: the sign of the fraction, the sign of the numerator, and the sign of the denominator. You can change the signs in pairs without changing the value of the fraction. For example, $\frac{3}{4} = -\frac{-3}{4} = -\frac{3}{-4} = \frac{-3}{-4}$.

**Fundamental Rule of Fractions:** If both the numerator and denominator of a fraction are multiplied (or divided) by the same nonzero number, the value of the fraction is unchanged. The resulting fraction and the original fraction are **equivalent.** Equivalent fractions have the same value. For example, $\frac{3}{4}$ and $\frac{3 \cdot 25}{4 \cdot 25} = \frac{75}{100}$ are equivalent fractions. Similarly, $\frac{24}{36}$ and $\frac{24 \div 12}{36 \div 12} = \frac{2}{3}$ are equivalent fractions.

When a fraction's numerator and denominator have one or more common factors (other than 1), to **reduce** (or **simplify**) the fraction to an equivalent fraction in **lowest terms,** divide the numerator and denominator by their greatest common factor, as in $\frac{75 \div 25}{100 \div 25} = \frac{3}{4}$. In this case, gcf (75, 100) = 25.

To write a fraction as an equivalent fraction with a larger denominator, multiply the numerator and denominator by the same whole number (greater than 1). For example, $\frac{2 \cdot 12}{3 \cdot 12} = \frac{24}{36}$. To write two fractions as equivalent fractions with the same denominator, you can use the least common multiple as the common denominator. For example, $\frac{1}{4}$ and $\frac{2}{3}$ are equivalent to $\frac{3}{12}$ and $\frac{8}{12}$, respectively.

A **proper fraction** is one in which the numerator is less than the denominator. For example, $\frac{1}{2}$, $\frac{9}{10}$, and $\frac{24}{36}$ are proper fractions. An **improper fraction** is one in which the numerator is greater than or equal to the denominator. For example, $\frac{3}{2}$, $\frac{29}{10}$, and $\frac{36}{36}$ are **improper fractions.** Any improper fraction has a value greater than or equal to 1.

A **mixed number** is the sum of an integer part and a fractional part, written together like these examples: $1\frac{1}{2}$, $2\frac{9}{10}$.

When you read a mixed number, say the word *and* between the integer and the fraction. For example, $2\frac{9}{10}$ is read as "two and nine-tenths." In a negative mixed number, the negative sign applies to both parts of the mixed number. For example, $-1\frac{1}{2}$ means $-\left(1 + \frac{1}{2}\right) = -\frac{3}{2}$.

To change an improper fraction to a mixed number or to a whole number, divide the numerator by the denominator and write the remainder, if any, like this: $\frac{\text{remainder}}{\text{denominator}}$. For example, $\frac{29}{10} = 10\overline{)29} \begin{array}{r} 2 \\ \underline{-20} \\ 9 \end{array} = 2\frac{9}{10}$.

Even though you are allowed to use a calculator on the Praxis MS Math test, you still need to know and understand how to perform computations with fractions. Understanding the process will make it less likely that you will make an error when performing a calculation and will also help you evaluate the reasonableness of the result of your computation.

The following table summarizes rules for addition and subtraction of fractions.

**Rules for Addition and Subtraction of Fractions**

| Operation | Rule | Examples |
|---|---|---|
| Addition/Subtraction—Like Denominators | Add/subtract the numerators of the fractions to obtain the numerator of the answer, which is placed over the common denominator. Reduce to lowest terms, if needed. | $\frac{5}{8} + \frac{1}{8} = \frac{5+1}{8} = \frac{6}{8} = \frac{6 \div 2}{8 \div 2} = \frac{3}{4}$; $\frac{5}{8} - \frac{1}{8} = \frac{5-1}{8} = \frac{4}{8} = \frac{4 \div 4}{8 \div 4} = \frac{1}{2}$ |

*(Continued)*

**Rules for Addition and Subtraction of...**

| Operation | Rule |
|-----------|------|
| Addition/Subtraction—Unlike Denominators | Write the fractions as equiv... fractions with the same denominator, using the l... common multiple as th... denominator. Add/su... numerators of the frac... obtain the numerator of the answer, which is placed over the common denominator. Reduce to lowest terms, if needed. |

The following table summarizes rules for multiplication and division with fractions.

**Rules for Multiplication and Division of Fractions**

| Operation | Rule | Example |
|-----------|------|---------|
| Multiplication—Proper Fractions or Improper Fractions | Multiply the numerators to obtain the numerator of the product and multiply the denominators to obtain the denominator of the product. Reduce to lowest terms, if needed. | $\dfrac{1}{3} \times \dfrac{3}{4} = \dfrac{1 \times 3}{3 \times 4} = \dfrac{3}{12} = \dfrac{3 \div 3}{12 \div 3} = \dfrac{1}{4}$ |
| Multiplication—Proper Fraction and Whole Number | Write the whole number as an equivalent fraction with denominator 1 and then multiply as with proper fractions. | $\dfrac{3}{4} \times 12 = \dfrac{3}{4} \times \dfrac{12}{1} = \dfrac{3 \times 12}{4 \times 1} = \dfrac{36}{4} = \dfrac{36 \div 4}{4 \div 4} = \dfrac{9}{1} = 9$ |
| Multiplication—One or More Mixed Numbers | Change the mixed numbers to improper fractions and then multiply as with proper fractions. | $2\dfrac{3}{4} \times 1\dfrac{1}{3} = \dfrac{11}{4} \times \dfrac{4}{3} = \dfrac{11 \times 4}{4 \times 3} = \dfrac{44}{12} = \dfrac{44 \div 4}{12 \div 4} = \dfrac{11}{3}$ or $3\dfrac{2}{3}$ |
| Division—Proper Fractions or Improper Fractions | Multiply the first fraction by the *reciprocal* of the second fraction. | $\dfrac{4}{3} \div \dfrac{1}{2} = \dfrac{4}{3} \times \dfrac{2}{1} = \dfrac{4 \times 2}{3 \times 1} = \dfrac{8}{3}$ or $2\dfrac{2}{3}$ |
| Division—Whole Number Divisor | Write the whole number as an equivalent fraction with denominator 1 and then multiply the first fraction by the *reciprocal* of the whole number fraction. | $\dfrac{4}{5} \div 3 = \dfrac{4}{5} \div \dfrac{3}{1} = \dfrac{4}{5} \times \dfrac{1}{3} = \dfrac{4 \times 1}{5 \times 3} = \dfrac{4}{15}$ |
| Division—One or More Mixed Numbers | Change the mixed numbers to improper fractions and then multiply the first fraction by the *reciprocal* of the second fraction. | $2\dfrac{1}{3} \div 1\dfrac{1}{2} = \dfrac{7}{3} \div \dfrac{3}{2} = \dfrac{7}{3} \times \dfrac{2}{3} = \dfrac{7 \times 2}{3 \times 3} = \dfrac{14}{9}$ or $1\dfrac{5}{9}$ |

**Tip:** Here is a mnemonic to help you remember division of fractions: "Keep, change, flip," meaning "*Keep* the first fraction, *change* division to multiplication, and then *flip* the second fraction to its reciprocal."

lying fractions easier by reducing to lowest terms before any multiplication is performed. Simply
ommon to a numerator and denominator (as in reducing) before multiplying. For example,

$$2\frac{3}{4} \times 1\frac{1}{3} = \frac{11}{\cancel{4}} \times \frac{\cancel{4}^{1}}{3} = \frac{11}{3} \text{ or } 3\frac{2}{3}$$

## mals

nals are rational numbers that are written using a base-10 place-value system. The value of a number is
ed on the placement of the decimal point in the number, as shown below.

| Thousands | Hundreds | Tens | Ones | **Decimal Point** | Tenths | Hundredths | Thousandths |
|---|---|---|---|---|---|---|---|
| 3, | 5 | 4 | 7 | . | 6 | 1 | 2 |

The value of the number is 3 thousands + 5 hundreds + 4 tens + 7 ones + 6 tenths + 1 hundredth + 2 thousandths,
which is the same as $3,000 + 500 + 40 + 7 + \dfrac{6}{10} + \dfrac{1}{100} + \dfrac{2}{1,000}$.

In a decimal number, the number of digits to the right of the decimal point up to and including the final digit is
the number of decimal places in the number. For example, a whole number such as 376 has zero decimal places,
the number 37.6 has one decimal place, the number 3.76 has two decimal places, and the number 3.760 has three
decimal places.

**Tip: If no decimal point is shown in a number, the decimal point is understood to be to the immediate right of
the rightmost digit.**

The decimal equivalent of a rational number either **terminates** in 0s or eventually **repeats** a block of one or more
of the same digits.

To obtain the decimal representation of a rational number that is in fractional form, divide the numerator by the
denominator. Insert a decimal point in the numerator and zeros to the right of the decimal point to complete the
division. For example,

$$\frac{3}{5} = 0.6 \text{ because } 5\overline{)3.0}^{\,0.6}$$

In this case, the decimal **terminates** in zeros (eventually has a zero remainder). You needed to insert only one zero
after the decimal point for the division to reach a zero remainder. Inserting additional zeros would lead to
repeated 0s to the right of 0.6 (like this: 0.6000…).

For some rational numbers, the decimal keeps going, but eventually in a block of one or more digits that repeats
over and over again. These decimals are **repeating**. Here is an example of a repeating decimal.

$$\frac{2}{3} = 3\overline{)2.000...}^{\,0.666...}$$
$$\begin{array}{r} -18 \\ \hline 20 \\ -18 \\ \hline 20 \\ -18 \\ \hline \vdots \end{array}$$

No matter how long you continue to insert zeros and divide, the 6s in the quotient continue without end. Put a bar over the repeating digit (or digits when more than one digit repeats) to indicate the repetition. Thus, $\frac{2}{3} = 0.\overline{6}$. Or you can stop the division at some point and write the remainder as a fraction whose denominator is the divisor. For example,

$$\frac{2}{3} = 3\overline{)\begin{array}{l} 0.66 \\ 2.00 \\ \underline{-18} \\ \phantom{0}20 \\ \underline{-18} \\ \phantom{00}2 \end{array}} = 0.66\frac{2}{3}$$

Either form is correct. That is, $\frac{2}{3} = 0.\overline{6} = 0.66\frac{2}{3}$.

***Tip:*** It is incorrect to write $\frac{2}{3} = 0.6$ or $\frac{2}{3} = 0.66$. Still, when decimals repeat, they are usually rounded to a specified degree of accuracy. For example, $0.666... \approx 0.67$ when rounded to two decimal places. The symbol "$\approx$" is read "is approximately equal to."

All terminating and repeating decimals are rational numbers. To change a terminating decimal fraction to its equivalent fractional representation, place the digits that are to the right of the decimal point over the power of 10 corresponding to the rightmost place value of the number. Reduce the resulting fraction as needed. For example,

$$0.375 = \frac{375}{1,000} = \frac{375 \div 125}{1,000 \div 125} = \frac{3}{8}$$

Here is a procedure for determining the fractional form of a repeating decimal fraction.

Let $x = 0.4545...$. Determine its fractional form.

Do three steps. First, multiply both sides of the equation $x = 0.4545...$ by $10^r$, where $r$ is the number of digits in the repeating block of digits in the decimal expansion. Next, subtract the original equation from the new equation. Then divide both sides of the resulting equation by the coefficient of $x$.

*Step 1.* Multiply both sides of the equation $x = 0.4545...$ by $10^2 = 100$ (because two digits repeat).

$$x = 0.4545...$$
$$100 \cdot x = 100(0.4545...)$$
$$100x = 45.4545...$$

*Step 2.* Subtract the original equation from the new equation.

$$\begin{array}{r} 100x = 45.4545... \\ \underline{-x = -0.4545...} \\ 99x = 45.0000... \end{array}$$

*Step 3.* Solve for $x$ by dividing both sides of the resulting equation by the coefficient of $x$.

$$99x = 45$$
$$\frac{99x}{99} = \frac{45}{99}$$
$$\frac{\cancel{99}x}{\cancel{99}} = \frac{45 \div 9}{99 \div 9}$$
$$x = \frac{5}{11}$$

Thus, $0.4545\ldots = \dfrac{5}{11}$.

**Tip:** Notice when you multiply $0.4545\ldots$ by 100, you can write the product as $45.4545\ldots$. You can do this because there are infinitely many 45s to the right of the decimal point, so you can write as many as you please.

Here is an example of converting a mixed decimal fraction to its equivalent fractional form.

> Let $x = 3.666\ldots$. Determine its fractional form.

*Step 1.* Multiply both sides of the equation $x = 3.666\ldots$ by $10^1 = 10$ (because one digit repeats).

$$x = 3.666\ldots$$
$$10 \cdot x = 10(3.666\ldots)$$
$$10x = 36.666\ldots$$

*Step 2.* Subtract the original equation from the new equation.

$$\begin{array}{r} 10x = 36.666\ldots \\ -x = -3.666\ldots \\ \hline 9x = 33.000\ldots \end{array}$$

*Step 3.* Solve for $x$ by dividing both sides of the resulting equation by the coefficient of $x$.

$$9x = 33$$
$$\frac{9x}{9} = \frac{33}{9}$$
$$\frac{\cancel{9}x}{\cancel{9}} = \frac{33 \div 3}{9 \div 3}$$
$$x = \frac{11}{3}$$

Thus, $3.666\ldots = \dfrac{11}{3}$ or $3\dfrac{2}{3}$.

You should do your decimal computations with the ETS graphing calculator when you take the Praxis MS Math test. Just for review, the following table summarizes rules for decimal computations.

### Rules for Computations with Decimals

| Operation | Rule | Example(s) |
|---|---|---|
| Addition/ subtraction | Line up the decimal points vertically. Add/ subtract as you would with whole numbers. Place the decimal point in the answer directly under the decimal points in the problem. | $65.3 + 0.34 = 65.30$;  $65.3 - 0.34 = 65.30$ <br> $\underline{+0.34} \quad\quad\quad \underline{-0.34}$ <br> $65.64 \quad\quad\quad\quad 64.96$ |
| **Tip: Fill in empty decimal places with zeros.** | | |
| Multiplication | Multiply the numbers as whole numbers. Place the decimal point in the proper place in the product. The number of decimal places in the product is the sum of the number of decimal places in the numbers being multiplied. If there are not enough places, insert one or more zeros at the *left* end of the number. | $0.002 \times 0.0003 = \begin{array}{r} 0.002 \\ \underline{\times\ 0.0003} \\ 0.0000006 \end{array}$ |

*(Continued)*

**Rules for Computations with Decimals**

| Operation | Rule | Example(s) |
|-----------|------|------------|
| Division | Rewrite the problem as an equivalent problem with a whole number divisor. Do this by multiplying the divisor and dividend by the power of 10 that makes the divisor a whole number, inserting additional zeros after the dividend, if needed. Divide as with whole numbers. Place the decimal point in the quotient directly above the decimal point in the dividend. | $2.04 \div 0.002 = 0.002\overline{)2.040} = 0002\overline{)2040.} = 1{,}020$ |

# Percents

*Percent* means "per hundred." The percent sign is a short way to write $\frac{1}{100}$ or 0.01. When you see a percent sign, you can substitute multiplying by $\frac{1}{100}$ or by 0.01 for the percent sign.

A **percent** is a way of writing a fraction as an equivalent fraction in which the denominator is 100. Thus, $25\%$ $= 25 \cdot \frac{1}{100} = \frac{25}{100} = 0.25$. Think of percents as special ways to write ordinary decimals or fractions. For example, $100\%$ is just a special way to write the number 1—because $100\% = 100 \cdot \frac{1}{100} = \frac{100}{100} = 1$. If you have $100\%$ of something, you have all of it. A percent that is less than $100\%$ is less than 1. When you have less than $100\%$ of something, you have less than all of it. A percent that is greater than $100\%$ is greater than 1. When you have more than $100\%$ of something, you have more than all of it. Here are examples.

$100\%$ of \$200 is \$200.

$50\%$ of \$200 is \$100.

$150\%$ of \$200 is \$300.

Write a percent as an equivalent fraction by writing the number immediately to the left of the percent sign as the numerator of a fraction in which the denominator is 100. The resulting fraction may then be reduced to lowest terms. Here are examples.

$$50\% = \frac{50}{100} = \frac{50 \div 50}{100 \div 50} = \frac{1}{2}; \ 75\% = \frac{75}{100} = \frac{75 \div 25}{100 \div 25} = \frac{3}{4}; \ 1\% = \frac{1}{100}; \ 125\% = \frac{125}{100} = \frac{125 \div 25}{100 \div 25} = \frac{5}{4} = 1\frac{1}{4}$$

When percents contain decimal fractions, multiply the numerator and denominator by 10, 100, or 1,000, and so on, to remove the decimal in the numerator, and then reduce the resulting fraction, if possible. Here are examples.

$$12.5\% = \frac{12.5}{100} = \frac{12.5 \times 10}{100 \times 10} = \frac{125}{1{,}000} = \frac{125 \div 125}{1{,}000 \div 125} = \frac{1}{8}; \ 0.2\% = \frac{0.2}{100} = \frac{0.2 \times 10}{100 \times 10} = \frac{2}{1{,}000} = \frac{2 \div 2}{1{,}000 \div 2} = \frac{1}{500}$$

If a percent contains a simple common fraction, replace the percent sign with multiplying by $\frac{1}{100}$, and then reduce, if possible. Here are examples.

$$\frac{1}{2}\% = \frac{1}{2} \times \frac{1}{100} = \frac{1}{200}; \ \frac{3}{4}\% = \frac{3}{4} \times \frac{1}{100} = \frac{3}{400}; \ \frac{5}{8}\% = \frac{5}{8} \times \frac{1}{100} = \frac{5}{800} = \frac{5 \div 5}{800 \div 5} = \frac{1}{160}$$

*Tip:* $\frac{1}{2}\%$, $\frac{3}{4}\%$, and $\frac{5}{8}\%$ are each less than $1\%$.

When percents contain mixed fractions, change the mixed fraction to an improper fraction, replace the percent sign with multiplying by $\frac{1}{100}$, and then reduce, if possible. Here are examples.

$$12\frac{1}{2}\% = \frac{25}{2} \times \frac{1}{100} = \frac{25}{200} = \frac{25 \div 25}{200 \div 25} = \frac{1}{8}; \ 33\frac{1}{3}\% = \frac{100}{3} \times \frac{1}{100} = \frac{100}{300} = \frac{100 \div 100}{300 \div 100} = \frac{1}{3}$$

Write a percent as an equivalent decimal by changing it to an equivalent fraction in which the denominator is 100 and then dividing by 100. For example, $75\% = \dfrac{75}{100} = 100\overline{)75.00}^{\,0.75}$. A shortcut for this process is to move the decimal point two places to the left (which is the same as dividing by 100) and discard the percent sign. Here are examples.

$25\% = 0.25$; $32\% = 0.32$; $45.5\% = 0.455$; $8\% = 0.08$; $200\% = 2.00 = 2$

Conversely, to write a decimal in percent form, move the decimal point two places to the right (which is the same as multiplying by 100) and attach the percent sign (%) at the end of the resulting number. Why does this make sense?

Recall that the percent sign is a short way to write $\dfrac{1}{100}$, which means 1 divided by 100. Because the percent sign has division by 100 built into it, when you put the percent sign at the end of the number, you undo the multiplication by 100 that you did earlier. Thus, the value of the original number does not change. Here are examples.

$0.45 = 45\%$; $0.01 = 1\%$; $0.125 = 12.5\%$; $2 = 2.00 = 200\%$; $0.0025 = 0.25\%$

To write a fraction in percent form, first write the fraction as an equivalent decimal by performing the indicated division and then change the resulting decimal to a percent. When the quotient is a repeating decimal, carry the division to two decimal places and then write the remainder as a fraction, like this: $\dfrac{\text{remainder}}{\text{divisor}}$. Here are examples.

$$\frac{1}{4} = 4\overline{)1.00}^{\,0.25} = 0.25; \quad \frac{3}{5} = 5\overline{)3.00}^{\,0.60} = 60\%; \quad \frac{1}{3} = 3\overline{)1.00}^{\,0.33} = 0.33\frac{1}{3} = 33\frac{1}{3}\%$$

Before you take the Praxis MS Math test, it would be to your advantage to memorize the following list of common percents with their fraction and decimal equivalents. Make a set of flashcards to carry with you and drill on these when you have spare time.

| | | | |
|---|---|---|---|
| $100\% = 1.00 = 1$ | $33\frac{1}{3}\% = 0.33\frac{1}{3} = \frac{1}{3}$ | $20\% = 0.20 = 0.2 = \frac{1}{5}$ | $10\% = 0.10 = 0.1 = \frac{1}{10}$ |
| $75\% = 0.75 = \frac{3}{4}$ | $66\frac{2}{3}\% = 0.66\frac{2}{3} = \frac{2}{3}$ | $40\% = 0.40 = 0.4 = \frac{2}{5}$ | $30\% = 0.30 = 0.3 = \frac{3}{10}$ |
| $50\% = 0.50 = 0.5 = \frac{1}{2}$ | | $60\% = 0.60 = 0.6 = \frac{3}{5}$ | $5\% = 0.05 = \frac{1}{20}$ |
| $25\% = 0.25 = \frac{1}{4}$ | | $80\% = 0.80 = 0.8 = \frac{4}{5}$ | |

**Tip: Pay attention to percent signs. For example, do not confuse 0.25% with 25%. These two percents are not equal: 0.25% = 0.0025, while 25% = 0.25, which is 100 times larger than 0.0025.**

# Irrational Numbers

Irrational numbers are numbers that *cannot* be written as the ratio of two integers. They have nonterminating, nonrepeating decimal representations. There are infinitely many decimals that are neither terminating nor repeating decimals. For example, 0.343344333444... is such a decimal. Even though you can predict that if the pattern in the digits to the right of the decimal point continues, four 3s followed by four 4s would come next in the decimal representation, the number is not a repeating decimal because a *block of the same digits* does not repeat. Therefore, 0.343344333444... is an irrational number. Other examples of irrational numbers are $\sqrt{6}$ (the square root of 6), $\sqrt[3]{-75}$ (the cube root of −75), $e$ (Euler's number), and $-\pi$ (negative pi). With these numbers, there is no discernible repeating pattern in the decimal representation. You can use an ellipsis (...) to indicate digits are missing, as shown here.

$$\sqrt{6} = 2.449490\ldots,\ \sqrt[3]{-75} = -4.217163\ldots,\ e = 2.718281\ldots,\ -\pi = -3.141593\ldots$$

**Tip: Some roots of rational numbers are rational, and others are not. For example, $\sqrt{6}$ is irrational; but $\sqrt{4}$ is 2, a rational number. $\sqrt[3]{-75}$ is irrational; but $\sqrt[3]{-8}$ is –2, a rational number. Furthermore, be cautious with *even* roots of rational numbers. When working with real numbers, be aware that taking the square root, fourth root, eighth root, and so forth of a *negative* number will *not* yield a real number.**

For computational purposes, you can only approximate irrational numbers. For example, if you want to use $\sqrt{6}$, $\sqrt[3]{-75}$, $e$, or $-\pi$ in computations, you can obtain an approximate value for each using a preselected number of decimal places. For example, their decimal representations to three places are as follows:

$$\sqrt{6} \approx 2.449,\ \sqrt[3]{-75} \approx -4.217,\ e \approx 2.718,\ -\pi \approx -3.142$$

**Tip: Use the ETS graphing calculator to estimate irrational numbers. Use the $\boxed{\sqrt{x}}$ key under the math menu to estimate square roots; use the $\boxed{\sqrt[x]{y}}$ key under the math menu to estimate cube roots and so forth; use the $\boxed{\pi}$ key under the trig menu to estimate $\pi$.**

However, it is important to remember that if the *exact* value of an irrational root is desired, the radical symbol must be retained. For example, if the area of a square is 6 cm$^2$, then the exact length of each side of the square is $\sqrt{6}$ cm. *Note:* See "Roots and Radicals" later in this chapter for an additional discussion of roots.

# Real Numbers

The real numbers, denoted $R$, are made up of all the rational numbers plus all the irrational numbers. The counting numbers, whole numbers, integers, rational numbers, and irrational numbers are all subsets of the real numbers. The relationship of the subsets of the real numbers is illustrated in the following figure. Each set in the figure contains those sets below it to which it is connected.

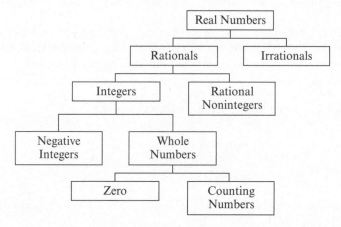

The real numbers can be represented on a number line. Every real number corresponds to a point on the number line, and every point on the number line corresponds to a real number. Positive numbers are located to the right of zero, and negative numbers are to the left of zero. Here are examples.

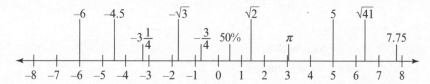

# Absolute Value

The **absolute value** of a real number is its distance from zero on the number line. The absolute value is indicated by two vertical bars (| |), one on either side of the number. As shown below, |6| = |−6| = 6 because each is 6 units from zero on the number line.

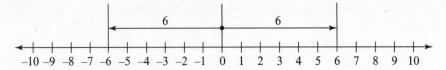

Distance always has a *nonnegative* (*positive* or *zero*) value. So, absolute value is always *nonnegative*. The absolute value of zero is zero; and, for any *nonzero* number, the absolute value is positive. This is true whether the nonzero number is positive or negative. Here are examples.

$$\left|-15\right| = 15, \quad \left|\frac{3}{4}\right| = \frac{3}{4}, \quad \left|0\right| = 0, \quad \left|-4.5\right| = 4.5, \quad \left|-100\right| = 100, \quad \left|100\right| = 100$$

As you can see, the absolute values of the numbers in the examples are the values of the numbers with no signs attached. Obviously, the absolute value of a specific number (whose numerical value you know) is just the value of the number with no sign attached. However, when you don't know the numerical value of an unknown number $x$, its absolute value could be $x$ or it could be $x$'s opposite. Therefore, **absolute value** is defined as follows:

$$\text{For any real number } x, \text{ the absolute value of } x \text{ is } \left|x\right| = \begin{cases} x, & \text{if } x \geq 0 \\ -x, & \text{if } x < 0 \end{cases}.$$

Remember, $-x$ can be a positive number. Don't be confused by the $-$ symbol to the left of $x$ in the lower portion of the definition. The $-$ symbol to the immediate left of $x$ is the symbol for the operation of **negation.** It tells you to change the sign of $x$. When $x$ itself is *nonnegative* (positive or zero), $|x|$ is the *nonnegative* number $x$; but when $x$ is *negative,* $|x|$ is the *positive* number $-x$.

Thus, for every real number $x$, its absolute value, denoted $|x|$, is either $x$ or $-x$, whichever is a *nonnegative* number (that is, whichever one is farther to the right on the number line). The definition says that for a positive number or zero ($x \geq 0$), the absolute value is the same as the number, but for a negative number ($x < 0$), the absolute value is the same as the number's opposite.

Absolute value has the following properties for all real numbers $x$ and $y$.

$$\left|x\right| \geq 0$$

$$\left|0\right| = 0$$

$$\left|x\right| = \left|-x\right|$$

$$\left|xy\right| = \left|x\right|\left|y\right|$$

$$\left|\frac{x}{y}\right| = \frac{\left|x\right|}{\left|y\right|}, \text{ provided } y \neq 0$$

$$\left|x + y\right| \leq \left|x\right| + \left|y\right|$$

$$\sqrt{x^2} = \left|x\right|$$

If $c$ is any positive number,

$|x| = c$ if and only if $x = c$ or $x = -c$.

$|x| < c$ if and only if $-c < x < c$ (**conjunction**).

$|x| > c$ if and only if $x < -c$ or $x > c$ (**disjunction**).

*Note:* Properties involving < and > hold if you replace < with ≤ and > with ≥.

See "Absolute Value Functions" in Chapter 3 for an additional discussion of absolute value.

# Roots and Radicals

You **square** a number by multiplying the number by itself. The reverse of squaring a number is finding the **square root.** Every positive number has two square roots that are equal in absolute value and opposite in sign. For example, $(5)^2 = 25$ and $(-5)^2 = 25$ implies 5 and −5 are square roots of 25. The positive square root is the **principal square root.** The **square root radical** $\left(\sqrt{\phantom{x}}\right)$ denotes the principal square root. Thus, $\sqrt{(5)(5)} = \sqrt{25} = 5$ and $\sqrt{(-5)(-5)} = \sqrt{25} = 5$. In general, $\sqrt{x^2} = |x|$. Zero has only one square root, namely 0. The principal square root of 0 is 0.

> **Tip:** The square root radical $\left(\sqrt{\phantom{x}}\right)$ always returns one number as the answer, and that number is nonnegative (positive or 0). For example, $\sqrt{25} = 5$, not ±5, and $\sqrt{(-5)^2} = |-5| = 5$, not −5.

> **Tip:** On the ETS graphing calculator, use the $\boxed{\sqrt{x}}$ key under the math menu to find square roots.

A number that is an exact square of another number is a **perfect square.** Here is a list of principal square roots of some perfect squares.

| | | | | |
|---|---|---|---|---|
| $\sqrt{1} = 1$ | $\sqrt{25} = 5$ | $\sqrt{81} = 9$ | $\sqrt{169} = 13$ | $\sqrt{289} = 17$ |
| $\sqrt{4} = 2$ | $\sqrt{36} = 6$ | $\sqrt{100} = 10$ | $\sqrt{196} = 14$ | $\sqrt{400} = 20$ |
| $\sqrt{9} = 3$ | $\sqrt{49} = 7$ | $\sqrt{121} = 11$ | $\sqrt{225} = 15$ | $\sqrt{625} = 25$ |
| $\sqrt{16} = 4$ | $\sqrt{64} = 8$ | $\sqrt{144} = 12$ | $\sqrt{256} = 16$ | |

> **Tip:** On the Praxis MS Math test, don't try to find square roots of negative numbers because no real number will multiply by itself to give a negative number.

You **cube** a number by using it as a factor three times. The inverse of cubing a number is finding the **cube root.** Every real number has exactly one real cube root, called its **principal cube root.** The **cube root radical** $\left(\sqrt[3]{\phantom{x}}\right)$ denotes the principal cube root. The small 3 in the radical indicates to find the cube root. The principal cube root of a negative number is negative, and the principal cube root of a positive number is positive. For example, $\sqrt[3]{8} = 2$ and $\sqrt[3]{-8} = -2$.

A number that is an exact cube of another number is a **perfect cube.** Here is a list of principal cube roots of some positive perfect cubes.

$$\sqrt[3]{0} = 0 \qquad \sqrt[3]{1} = 1 \qquad \sqrt[3]{8} = 2 \qquad \sqrt[3]{27} = 3 \qquad \sqrt[3]{64} = 4 \qquad \sqrt[3]{125} = 5 \qquad \sqrt[3]{1{,}000} = 10$$

In general, if $a^n = x$ where $n$ is a positive integer, $a$ is called an **$n$th root** of $x$, written $a = \sqrt[n]{x}$. The expression $\sqrt[n]{x}$ is called a **radical,** $x$ is called the **radicand,** $n$ is called the **index** and indicates which root is desired. If no index is written, it is understood to be 2, and the radical expression indicates the principal square root of the radicand.

Here are some facts about roots.

A positive real number has exactly one real positive $n$th root whether $n$ is even or odd.

When $n$ is odd, every real number has exactly one real $n$th root.

When $n$ is even, the $n$th root of a negative number is undefined in the real number system.

The $n$th root of zero is zero, whether $n$ is even or odd.

Here are examples.

$$\sqrt{36} = 6 \qquad \sqrt[3]{125} = 5 \qquad \sqrt[3]{-64} = -4 \qquad \sqrt{-64} \text{ Not a real number} \qquad \sqrt[4]{-16} \text{ Not a real number}$$

**Tip: On the ETS graphing calculator, use the $\boxed{\sqrt[x]{y}}$ key under the math menu to find *n*th roots.**

Following are rules for radicals when $x$ and $y$ are real numbers, $m$ and $n$ are positive integers, and the radical expression denotes a real number.

$$\sqrt[n]{0} = 0 \qquad \sqrt[n]{x^n} = x \text{ if } n \text{ is odd} \qquad \sqrt[n]{x^n} = |x| \text{ if } n \text{ is even} \qquad \sqrt[n]{x^m} = \left(\sqrt[n]{x}\right)^m \qquad \sqrt[pn]{x^{pm}} = \sqrt[n]{x^m}$$

$$\left(\sqrt[n]{x}\right)\left(\sqrt[n]{y}\right) = \sqrt[n]{xy} \qquad \frac{\sqrt[n]{x}}{\sqrt[n]{y}} = \sqrt[n]{\frac{x}{y}}, (y \neq 0) \qquad \sqrt[m]{\sqrt[n]{x}} = \sqrt[mn]{x} \qquad a\left(\sqrt[n]{x}\right) + b\left(\sqrt[n]{x}\right) = (a+b)\left(\sqrt[n]{x}\right)$$

These rules form the basis for simplifying radical expressions. (See Appendix A for a discussion on simplifying radicals.)

# Exponents

In mathematical expressions, **exponentiation** is indicated by a small raised number, called the **exponent,** written to the upper right of a quantity, which is the **base** for the exponential expression. Common types of exponents are summarized in the following table.

**Common Types of Exponents**

| Type of Exponent | Definition | Examples |
|---|---|---|
| Positive Integer | If $x$ is any real number and $n$ is a positive integer, then $x^n = \underbrace{x \cdot x \cdot x \cdot \cdots \cdot x}_{n \text{ factors of } x}$, where $x^n$ is read "$x$ to the $n$th power" or as "$x$ to the $n$." *Tip:* The exponent 2 on a number is usually read "squared" rather than "to the second power." Likewise, the exponent 3 is usually read "cubed" rather than "to the third power." | $12^2 = 12 \cdot 12 = 144$; $(-3)^3 = (-3)(-3)(-3)$ $= -27$; $2^5 = 2 \cdot 2 \cdot 2 \cdot 2 \cdot 2 = 32$ |
| Zero | For any real number $x$ (except 0), $x^0 = 1$. | $(-128.75)^0 = 1$; $\left(5^{100}\right)^0 = 1$ |
| Positive Rational Number | If $x$ is any real number and $m$ and $n$ are positive integers, then $x^{\frac{1}{n}} = \sqrt[n]{x}$ and $x^{\frac{m}{n}} = \left(\sqrt[n]{x}\right)^m$ or $\sqrt[n]{x^m}$, provided, in all cases, that $x \geq 0$ when $n$ is even. | $16^{\frac{1}{2}} = \sqrt{16} = 4$; $64^{\frac{4}{3}} = \left(\sqrt[3]{64}\right)^4 = (4)^4 = 256$; $(-32)^{\frac{3}{5}} = \left(\sqrt[5]{-32}\right)^3 = (-2)^3 = -8$ |
| Negative Rational Number | If $x$ is any real number (except 0) and $m$ and $n$ are positive integers so that $-n$ and $-\frac{m}{n}$ are negative numbers, then $x^{-n} = \frac{1}{x^n}$; $\frac{1}{x^{-n}} = x^n$, $x^{-\frac{m}{n}} = \frac{1}{x^{\frac{m}{n}}} = \frac{1}{\left(\sqrt[n]{x}\right)^m}$, and $\frac{1}{x^{-\frac{m}{n}}} = x^{\frac{m}{n}} = \left(\sqrt[n]{x}\right)^m$, provided, in all cases, $x > 0$ when $n$ is even. | $5^{-3} = \frac{1}{5^3} = \frac{1}{125}$; $\frac{1}{5^{-3}} = 5^3 = 125$; $(-64)^{-\frac{2}{3}} = \frac{1}{(-64)^{\frac{2}{3}}} = \frac{1}{\left(\sqrt[3]{-64}\right)^2} = \frac{1}{(-4)^2} = \frac{1}{16}$ |

**Tip: On the ETS graphing calculator, use the $\boxed{x^y}$ key under the math menu to perform exponentiation.**

The following rules for exponents hold.

**Rules for Exponents**

| Rule | Example(s) |
|---|---|
| $b^m b^n = b^{m+n}$ (product rule) | $2^3 2^4 = 2^{3+4} = 2^7$ |
| $\dfrac{b^m}{b^n} = b^{m-n} = \dfrac{1}{b^{n-m}}$, $b \neq 0$ (quotient rule) | $\dfrac{3^6}{3^2} = 3^{6-2} = 3^4$; $\dfrac{5^4}{5^7} = 5^{4-7} = \dfrac{1}{5^{7-4}} = \dfrac{1}{5^3}$ |
| $\left(b^m\right)^p = b^{mp}$ (power of a power) | $\left(5^3\right)^2 = 5^{3 \cdot 2} = 5^6$ |
| $(ab)^p = a^p b^p$ (power of a product) | $(5 \cdot 2)^3 = 5^3 2^3$ |
| $\left(\dfrac{a}{b}\right)^p = \dfrac{a^p}{b^p}$, $b \neq 0$ (power of a quotient) | $\left(\dfrac{10}{2}\right)^3 = \dfrac{10^3}{2^3}$ and $\dfrac{10^3}{2^3} = \left(\dfrac{10}{2}\right)^3$ |
| $\left(\dfrac{a}{b}\right)^{-p} = \left(\dfrac{b}{a}\right)^p$, $a \neq 0$, $b \neq 0$ (reciprocal rule) | $\left(\dfrac{3}{4}\right)^{-2} = \left(\dfrac{4}{3}\right)^2$ |
| $(a+b)^n = \underbrace{(a+b)(a+b) \cdots (a+b)}_{n \text{ times}}$, for $n$ a positive integer (power of a binomial) | $(a+b)^2 = (a+b)(a+b) = a^2 + 2ab + b^2$ <br> **Tip:** Expand the product using rules for multiplying binomials. |
| If $a^m = a^n$, then $m = n$, provided $a \neq 1$ (one-to-one property). | $2^x = 2^9$ implies $x = 9$. |

Here is clarification about exponents.

- The product and quotient rules for exponential expressions can be used only when the exponential expressions have exactly the same base. For example, $x^2 x^3 = x^{2+3} = x^5$ and $\dfrac{x^5}{x^3} = x^{5-3} = x^2$, but $x^2 y^3$ and $\dfrac{x^5}{y^3}$ cannot be simplified further.
- Exponentiation is not "commutative." For example, $2^5 \neq 5^2$; $2^5 = 32$, but $5^2 = 25$.
- Parentheses take precedence over exponentiation. For example, $(3+2)^3 \neq 3^3 + 2^3$; $(3+2)^3 = 5^3 = 125$, but $3^3 + 2^3 = 27 + 8 = 35$. In other words, exponentiation does not distribute over addition (or subtraction).
- An exponent applies only to the base to which it is attached. For example, $3 \cdot 5^2 \neq 3^2 \cdot 5^2$; $3 \cdot 5^2 = 3 \cdot 25 = 75$, but $3^2 \cdot 5^2 = 9 \cdot 25 = 225$.
- Exponentiation takes precedence over negation. For example, $-5^2 \neq (-5)^2$; $-5^2 = -(5 \cdot 5) = -25$, but $(-5)^2 = -5 \cdot -5 = 25$.
- Use parentheses around the factors for which the exponent applies. For example, $(3 \cdot 5)^2 = 3^2 \cdot 5^2 = 9 \cdot 25 = 225$.
- A negative number raised to an even power yields a positive product. For example, $(-2)^4 = -2 \cdot -2 \cdot -2 \cdot -2 = 16$.
- A negative number raised to an odd power yields a negative product. For example, $(-2)^5 = -2 \cdot -2 \cdot -2 \cdot -2 \cdot -2 = -32$.
- A negative exponent means to write a reciprocal, not to make your answer negative. For example, $2^{-6} = \dfrac{1}{2^6} = \dfrac{1}{64}$, not $-\dfrac{1}{64}$.
- A nonzero number or mathematical expression raised to the 0 power is 1; that is, (nonzero numerical quantity)$^0 = 1$.

In general, when you have zero or negative exponents in a mathematical expression, you should rewrite it as an equivalent expression that no longer contains zero or negative exponents. For example,

$$\frac{x^3 y^{-4} z^{-1}}{u^0 x^{-2} y^3 z^{-3}} = \frac{x^3 x^2 z^3}{1 y^4 y^3 z} = \frac{x^5 z^2}{y^7}$$

Be careful with this process. Only exponential expressions that are *factors* can be moved from the numerator to the denominator (or from the denominator to the numerator) of a fraction simply by changing the sign of the exponent. For example,

$$\frac{1}{2^{-1}3^{-1}} = \frac{2 \cdot 3}{1} = \frac{6}{1} = 6, \text{ but } \frac{1}{2^{-1}+3^{-1}} = \frac{1}{\frac{1}{2}+\frac{1}{3}} = \frac{1}{\frac{5}{6}} = 1\frac{1}{5}; \ \frac{1}{2^{-1}+3^{-1}} \neq \frac{2+3}{1} = \frac{5}{1} = 5$$

# Comparing and Ordering Real Numbers

When you are comparing two real numbers, think of their relative locations on the number line. The number that is farther to the right is the greater number. For example, $-3.25 < -0.5$ because, as shown on the number line below, $-0.5$ lies to the right of $-3.25$.

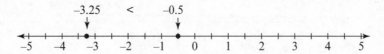

When you compare decimals, compare the digits in each place value from left to right. If the decimals do not have the same number of decimal places, insert or delete zeros after the last digit to the right of the decimal point to make the number of decimal places the same. Remember, inserting or deleting zeros after the last digit to the right of the decimal point does not change the value of a decimal. For example, $2.5 = 2.50 = 2.500 = 2.5000$ and so on. Thus, $2.28 < 2.5$ because $2.28 < 2.50$.

When comparing fractions that have the same denominator, compare the numerators. For example, $\frac{7}{8} > \frac{5}{8}$ because $7 > 5$.

If the denominators of the fractions are not the same, you can write the fractions as equivalent fractions using a common denominator and then compare the numerators. For example, $\frac{3}{4} < \frac{7}{8}$ because $\frac{6}{8} < \frac{7}{8}$. You also could change each of the fractions to a decimal and then make the comparison. For example, $\frac{3}{4} < \frac{7}{8}$ because $0.750 < 0.875$.

**Tip: Change fractions to decimals by performing the division on the ETS graphing calculator.**

To compare a mixture of decimals and fractions, change the fractions to decimals. Round them off if they repeat. When you are instructed to order a list of numbers, put them in order from least to greatest or from greatest to least, depending on how the question is stated.

Here is an example.

> Order the numbers $\frac{7}{8}$, 0.35, 4.8, and $\frac{2}{3}$ from least to greatest.

Before proceeding, change $\frac{7}{8}$ to 0.875, and $\frac{2}{3}$ to 0.667 (rounding to 3 places). Write 0.35 as 0.350 and 4.8 as 4.800. Next, compare the transformed numbers and put them in order as follows: 0.350, 0.667, 0.875, 4.800. Lastly, substitute the original numbers for their stand-ins to obtain the final answer: 0.35, $\frac{2}{3}$, $\frac{7}{8}$, 4.8.

Here are some tips for handling situations that might occur in problems that involve comparing and ordering real numbers.

- If negative numbers are involved, they will be less than all the positive numbers and 0.
- If percents are involved, change the percents to decimals.

- If the problem contains exponential expressions, evaluate them before making comparisons.
- If you have square roots that are rational numbers, find the square roots before making comparisons.
- If you have irrational square roots, use the ETS graphing calculator to estimate the square roots before comparing them to other numbers.

Here is an example.

> Order the following numbers from least to greatest: $\sqrt{37}, 2^3, 4.39, -4, \dfrac{9}{2}$

You do not have to proceed in the order the numbers are listed. Clearly, $-4$ is less than all the other numbers. Evaluate $2^3$ to obtain 8. Change $\dfrac{9}{2}$ to 4.50, which is greater than 4.39. In order from least to greatest, these four numbers are $-4, 4.39, 4.50, 8$. Estimate $\sqrt{37}$ to be approximately 6.08, which puts it between 4.50 and 8 in the list. Thus, the final answer is $-4, 4.39, \dfrac{9}{2}, \sqrt{37}, 2^3$.

# Intervals and Interval Notation

**Intervals** show sets of numbers on the real number line. **Open intervals** do not include the endpoints. **Closed intervals** include both endpoints. **Half-open** (or half-closed) intervals include only one endpoint. Finite intervals are **bounded intervals**. Intervals that extend indefinitely to the right or left or both are **unbounded intervals**.

To graph an interval on the number line, shade the number line to show the numbers included in the interval. Use a solid circle to indicate an endpoint is included and an open circle to indicate an endpoint is not included. The following table summarizes intervals and interval notation.

| Interval | Notation and Type | Graph |
|----------|-------------------|-------|
| $x < b$ | $(-\infty, b)$, unbounded, open | |
| $x > a$ | $(a, \infty)$, unbounded, open | |
| $x \leq b$ | $(-\infty, b]$, unbounded, half-open | |
| $x \geq a$ | $[a, \infty)$, unbounded, half-open | |
| $a < x < b$ | $(a, b)$, bounded, open | |
| $a \leq x < b$ | $[a, b)$, bounded, half-open | |
| $a < x \leq b$ | $(a, b]$, bounded, half-open | |
| $a \leq x \leq b$ | $[a, b]$, bounded, closed | |

# Operations with Real Numbers

On the Praxis MS Math test, you will need to know how to perform addition, subtraction, multiplication, and division of real numbers. These operations are performed by using the absolute values, which are always positive or zero, of the numbers.

# Addition and Subtraction of Real Numbers

For sums and differences of real numbers, use the following rules.

**Rules for Addition and Subtraction of Real Numbers**

| Rule | Examples |
|---|---|
| **Rule 1:** The sum of 0 and any number is the number. | $-6 + 0 = -6$; $0 + 5 = 5$ |
| **Rule 2:** The sum of a number and its opposite is 0. | $-4 + 4 = 0$; $8 + (-8) = 0$ |
| **Rule 3:** To add two numbers that have the same sign, add their absolute values and give the sum their common sign. | $4 + 6 = 10$; $-4 + (-6) = -10$ |
| **Rule 4:** To add two numbers that have opposite signs, subtract the lesser absolute value from the greater absolute value and give the result the sign of the number with the greater absolute value. | $-5 + 13 = 8$; $4 + (-16) = -12$ |
| **Rule 5:** To subtract one number from another, add the opposite of the second number to the first. | $28 - (-2) = 28 + (2) = 30$; $-36 - 16 = -36 + (-16) = -52$ |

If you have three or more real numbers to add together, you may find it convenient to first add all the positive numbers; second, add all the negative numbers; and then add the resulting two answers. Here is an example.

$$14 + -35 + 6 + -25 = 20 + (-60) = -40$$

Other times, you might look for opposites that sum to zero. Here is an example.

$$1,200 + (-450) + 5 + (-1,200) + 450 = 1,200 + (-1,200) + (-450) + 450 + 5 = 0 + 0 + 5 = 5$$

# Multiplication and Division of Real Numbers

For products and quotients of real numbers, use the following rules.

**Rules for Multiplication and Division of Real Numbers**

| Rule | Examples |
|---|---|
| **Rule 1:** Zero times any number is 0. | $0 \cdot 8 = 0$; $-7 \cdot 0 = 0$ |
| **Rule 2:** To multiply two nonzero numbers that have the same sign, multiply their absolute values and make the product positive. | $2 \cdot 5 = 10$; $-2 \cdot -5 = 10$ |
| **Rule 3:** To multiply two nonzero numbers that have opposite signs, multiply their absolute values and make the product negative. | $-2 \cdot 5 = -10$; $2 \cdot -5 = -10$ |
| **Rule 4:** When 0 is one of the factors, the product is always 0; otherwise, products with an even number of negative factors are positive, whereas those with an odd number of negative factors are negative. | $(-2)(6)(0)(-1) = 0$; $(-2)(6)(5)(-1) = 60$; $(-2)(6)(-5)(-1) = -60$ |
| **Rule 5:** To divide by a nonzero number, follow the same rules for the signs as for multiplication, except divide the absolute values of the numbers instead of multiplying. | $\dfrac{45}{9} = 5$; $\dfrac{-15}{5} = -3$; $\dfrac{50}{-25} = -2$; $\dfrac{-24}{-6} = 4$ |
| **Rule 6:** The quotient is 0 when the dividend is 0 and the divisor is a nonzero number. | $\dfrac{0}{100} = 0$; $\dfrac{0}{-100} = 0$ |
| **Rule 7:** The quotient is undefined when the divisor is 0. | $\dfrac{100}{0}$ is undefined; $\dfrac{0}{0}$ is undefined |

> **Tip:** Unlike addition, for multiplication/division when the signs are the same, it doesn't matter what the common sign is—the product/quotient is positive no matter what. Similarly, unlike addition, for multiplication/division when the signs are different, it doesn't matter which number has the greater absolute value—the product/quotient is negative no matter what.

The rules for addition, subtraction, multiplication, and division apply to all real numbers. Here are examples.

$$-\frac{5}{8}+\left(-\frac{1}{8}\right)=-\frac{6}{8}=-\frac{3}{4}$$

$$\frac{2}{3}-\frac{3}{4}=\frac{8}{12}-\frac{9}{12}=-\frac{1}{12}$$

$$24.5+134.28=158.78$$

$$-18.5+7.25=-11.25$$

$$\frac{3}{4}\times-12=\frac{3}{\cancel{4}}\times-\frac{\cancel{12}^{3}}{1}=-\frac{9}{1}=-9$$

$$\left(-2\frac{3}{4}\right)\left(-1\frac{1}{3}\right)=\left(-\frac{11}{\cancel{4}}\right)\left(-\frac{\cancel{4}^{1}}{3}\right)=\frac{11}{3}\text{ or }3\frac{2}{3}$$

$$(-0.75)(400)=-300$$

$$(-125.43)(-0.005)=0.62715$$

$$\frac{-0.6}{0.125}=-4.8$$

## Sums, Differences, and Products of Even and Odd Integers

Here is helpful information to know about sums, differences, and products of even and odd integers.

- The sum or difference of two even integers is even. Examples: $24+8=32$; $(-30)+(-4)=-34$; $100-56=44$
- The sum or difference of two odd integers is even. Examples: $27+9=36$; $(-41)+(-5)=-46$; $95-53=42$
- The product of two even numbers is even. Examples: $(4)(-28)=-112$; $(18)(12)=216$
- The sum or difference of an even integer and an odd integer is odd. Examples: $24+7=31$; $(-15)+(-4)=-19$; $101-70=31$
- The product of an even integer and an odd integer is even. Examples: $(4)(-25)=-100$; $(18)(3)=54$
- If $n$ is an integer, and $n^2$ is even, then $n$ is even. Examples: If $n^2=36$, then $n=6$ or $n=-6$. If $n^2=64$, then $n=8$ or $-8$.
- If $n$ is an integer, and $n^2$ is odd, then $n$ is odd. Examples: If $n^2=81$, then $n=9$ or $-9$. If $n^2=625$, then $n=25$ or $-25$.

> **Tip:** An even integer can be written as **2n**, where **n** is an integer. An odd integer can be written as **2m + 1**, where **m** is an integer.

## Sums, Differences, and Products of Rational and Irrational Numbers

Here is helpful information to know about sums, differences, and products of rational and irrational numbers.

- The sum or difference of two rational numbers is rational. Examples: $1.75+\frac{3}{2}=3.25$; $-\frac{1}{3}-\left(-\frac{5}{6}\right)=\frac{1}{2}$
- The product of two rational numbers is rational. Examples: $(2.5)(-1.1)=-2.75$; $\left(\frac{3}{4}\right)(90.8)=68.1$

- The sum or difference of a rational number and an irrational number is irrational. Examples: $\sqrt{2}+9$; $1\frac{3}{4}-\sqrt{41}$

- The product of a nonzero rational number and an irrational number is irrational. Examples: $(0.5)\left(\sqrt{2}\right)=0.5\sqrt{2}$; $(-1)\left(-\sqrt{23}\right)=\sqrt{23}$

- The sum or difference of two irrational numbers can be rational or irrational. Examples: $4\sqrt{5}-4\sqrt{5}=0$; $4\sqrt{5}+2\sqrt{5}=6\sqrt{5}$

- The product of two irrational numbers can be rational or irrational. Examples: $\left(4\sqrt{3}\right)\left(-5\sqrt{3}\right)=-60$; $\left(7\sqrt{2}\right)\left(3\sqrt{8}\right)=84$; $\left(5\sqrt{2}\right)\left(\sqrt{3}\right)=5\sqrt{6}$

- For any positive real number $a$, $\left(\sqrt[n]{a}\right)^{n}=a$ and $\sqrt[n]{a^{n}}=a$. Examples: $\left(\sqrt[4]{81}\right)^{4}=81$ and $\sqrt[5]{2^{5}}=2$

# The Order of Operations

When more than one operation is involved in a numerical expression, you must follow the **order of operations** to evaluate the expression. A commonly used mnemonic is "Please Excuse My Dear Aunt Sally"—abbreviated as PEMDAS. The first letters of the words remind you of the following:

First, operations enclosed in **P**arentheses (or other grouping symbols, if present)

Next, **E**xponentiation

Then, **M**ultiplication and **D**ivision in the order in which they occur from left to right

Last, **A**ddition and **S**ubtraction in the order in which they occur from left to right

**Tip: Note that multiplication does not have to be done before division, or addition before subtraction. You multiply and divide in the order in which these operations occur in the problem. Similarly, you add and subtract in the order in which these operations occur in the problem.**

Here are examples of using the order of operations to simplify numerical expressions.

Simplify: $90-5\cdot3^{2}+42\div(5+2)$

$$
\begin{aligned}
90-5\cdot3^{2}+42\div(5+2) &= 90-5\cdot3^{2}+42\div(7) &&\text{First, do computations inside parentheses.}\\
&= 90-5\cdot9+42\div(7) &&\text{Next, evaluate exponents.}\\
&= 90-45+6 &&\text{Then, multiply and divide from left to right.}\\
&= 51 &&\text{Finally, add and subtract from left to right.}
\end{aligned}
$$

When simplified, the numerical expression $90-5\cdot3^{2}+42\div(5+2)=51$.

Simplify: $-50+40\div2^{3}-5(4+6)$

$$
\begin{aligned}
-50+40\div2^{3}-5(4+6) &= -50+40\div2^{3}-5(10) &&\text{First, do computations inside parentheses.}\\
&= -50+40\div8-5(10) &&\text{Next, evaluate exponents.}\\
&= -50+5-50 &&\text{Then, multiply and divide from left to right.}\\
&= -95 &&\text{Finally, add and subtract from left to right.}
\end{aligned}
$$

When simplified, the numerical expression $-50+40\div2^{3}-5(4+6)=-95$.

---

Simplify: $8 - 4 \div (7 - 5) - (7 + 3) \div 2$

---

| | |
|---|---|
| $8 - 4 \div (7 - 5) - (7 + 3) \div 2 = 8 - 4 \div 2 - 10 \div 2$ | First, do computations inside parentheses. |
| $= 8 - 4 \div 2 - 10 \div 2$ | Next, evaluate exponents—none, so skip this step. |
| $= 8 - 2 - 5$ | Then, divide from left to right. |
| $= 1$ | Finally, subtract from left to right. |

When simplified, the numerical expression $8 - 4 \div (7 - 5) - (7 + 3) \div 2 = 1$.

Sometimes, you might find it convenient to transform exponential expressions by applying the rules of exponents *before* proceeding through the order of operations.

Here is an example.

---

Evaluate $(3 \cdot 10)^2 - \dfrac{5^7}{5^4}$ .

---

| | |
|---|---|
| $(3 \cdot 10)^2 - \dfrac{5^7}{5^4} = 3^2 \cdot 10^2 - \dfrac{5^7}{5^4}$ | Transform $(3 \cdot 10)^2$ instead of multiplying inside the parentheses first. |
| $= 3^2 \cdot 10^2 - 5^3$ | Transform $\dfrac{5^7}{5^4}$ instead of doing the exponentiation first. |
| $= 9 \cdot 100 - 125$ | |
| $= 900 - 125$ | |
| $= 775$ | |

**Tip: If you decide to apply the rules of exponents before proceeding through the order of operations, only transform products or quotients, not sums or differences. Otherwise, errors could result.**

# Properties of Number Systems

The set of real numbers has the following **properties** under the operations of addition and multiplication.

**Field Properties**

| Property | Explanation |
|---|---|
| **Closure property:** $a + b$ and $ab$ are real numbers. | The sum or product of any two real numbers is a real number. |
| **Commutative property:** $a + b = b + a$ and $ab = ba$. | You can switch the order of any two numbers when you add or multiply without changing the answer. |
| **Associative property:** $(a + b) + c = a + (b + c)$ and $(ab)c = a(bc)$. | The way the addends or factors are grouped does not affect the final sum or product. |
| **Additive identity property:** There exists a real number, denoted 0, such that $a + 0 = a$ and $0 + a = a$. | This property ensures that zero is a real number and that its sum with any real number is the number. |
| **Multiplicative identity property:** There exists a real number, denoted 1, such that $a \cdot 1 = a$ and $1 \cdot a = a$. | This property ensures that 1 is a real number and that its product with any real number is the number. |
| **Additive inverse property:** For every real number $a$, there exists a real number, denoted $-a$, such that $a + (-a) = 0$ and $(-a) + a = 0$. | This property ensures that for every real number, there is another real number, opposite to it in sign, which, when added to the number, gives 0. |

*(Continued)*

## Field Properties

| Property | Explanation |
|---|---|
| **Multiplicative inverse property:** For every nonzero real number $a$, there exists a real number, denoted $a^{-1}$, such that $a \cdot a^{-1} = 1$ and $a^{-1} \cdot a = 1$. | This property ensures that for every real number, *except zero,* there is another real number, which, when multiplied by the number, gives 1. |
| **Distributive property:** $a(b + c) = ab + ac$ and $(b + c)a = ba + ca$. | When you have a factor times a sum, you can either add first and then multiply, or multiply first and then add. Either way, the answer works out to be the same. |
| **Zero product property:** If $ab = 0$, then $a = 0$ or $b = 0$ (or both $= 0$). | If a product of two factors is zero, then one or both of the factors are zero. |

Subtraction and division are defined as follows.

> **Subtraction:** $a - b = a + (-b)$.
> **Division:** $a \div b = \dfrac{a}{b} = a \cdot b^{-1} = a \cdot \dfrac{1}{b}$.

For the Praxis MS Math test, be prepared to identify properties of the real numbers used in a calculation. Here is an example.

> Which property of the real numbers is used first in the following calculation: $8(215) = 1{,}720$?

Since $8(215) = 8(200 + 10 + 5) = 8 \cdot 200 + 8 \cdot 10 + 8 \cdot 5 = 1{,}600 + 80 + 40 = 1{,}720$, the distributive property is used first in the calculation.

On the Praxis MS Math test, you might be asked whether a defined binary operation has given field properties. Symbols commonly used for defined operations are $\oplus$, $\otimes$, *, $\circ$, and #.

**Tip: A binary operation is one that is performed on only two elements of a set at a time.**

Here is an example.

> Consider the operation $\oplus$ defined by $a \oplus b = 2a + 3b$, where the operations on the right side of the equal sign denote the standard arithmetic operations. Is the operation $\oplus$ commutative over the set of real numbers?

To determine whether $\oplus$ is commutative over the set of real numbers, you should ask the question, "Does $a \oplus b$ equal $b \oplus a$ for all real numbers $a$ and $b$?" In other words, you need to determine whether $2a + 3b = 2b + 3a$ for all real numbers $a$ and $b$. Clearly, the answer is no. For example, when $a = 2$ and $b = 5$, $2 \cdot 2 + 3 \cdot 5 = 19$, which is not equal to $2 \cdot 5 + 3 \cdot 2 = 16$. Therefore, the operation $\oplus$ is not commutative over the set of real numbers.

**Tip: Even though commutativity (associativity and so on) might hold for some numbers from a given set, if it does not hold for *all* numbers from the set, the operation under consideration is not commutative (associative and so on) over the given set of numbers.**

# Scientific Notation

**Scientific notation** is a way to write very large or very small numbers in a shortened form. Scientific notation helps keep track of the decimal places and makes performing computations with these numbers easier.

A number written in scientific notation is written as a product of two factors. The first factor is a number that is greater than or equal to 1, but less than 10. The second factor is a power of 10. The idea is to make a product that will equal the given number. Any decimal number can be written in scientific notation. Here are examples of numbers written in scientific notation.

Written in scientific notation, 34,000 is $3.4 \times 10^4$.

Written in scientific notation, 6.5 is $6.5 \times 10^0$.

Written in scientific notation, 0.00047 is $4.7 \times 10^{-4}$.

Follow these steps to write a number in scientific notation:

*Step 1.* Move the decimal point to the immediate right of the first *nonzero* digit of the number.

*Step 2.* Indicate multiplication by the proper power of 10. The exponent for the power of 10 is the number of places you moved the decimal point in Step 1.

- If you moved the decimal point to the *left,* make the exponent positive.
- If you moved the decimal point to the *right,* make the exponent negative.

As long as you make sure your first factor is greater than or equal to 1 and less than 10, you can always check to see whether you did it right by multiplying out your answer to see whether you get your original number back. Look at these examples.

$254,000 = 2.54 \times 10^5$ (in scientific notation) $= 2.54 \times 10,000 = 254,000$

**Tip: A shortcut for multiplying by $10^n$ is to move the decimal point *n* places to the right, inserting zeros as needed.**

$0.00015 = 1.5 \times 10^{-4}$ (in scientific notation) $= \dfrac{1.5}{10,000} = 0.00015$

**Tip: A shortcut for multiplying by $10^{-n}$ is to move the decimal point *n* places to the left, inserting zeros as needed.**

# Complex Numbers

The main concepts about complex numbers are the following:

- Complex numbers have the form $a + bi$, where $a$ and $b$ are real numbers and $i$ represents the **imaginary unit** $\sqrt{-1}$.
- The square of the imaginary unit is $-1$; that is, $i^2 = -1$.
- The coefficients $a$ and $b$ of a complex number are the **real part** and **imaginary part,** respectively, of the number.
- The real numbers are a subset of the complex numbers, and result when the imaginary part ($b$) is zero.

Because the coefficients of complex numbers are real numbers, computations with complex numbers rely on the rules for computations with real numbers (see "Operations with Real Numbers," earlier in this chapter, for the rules).

Here are examples.

$(5 + 8i) + (7 - 2i) = 12 + 6i$

Add the real parts. Add the imaginary parts.

$(2 + 3i)(4 + i) = 8 + 14i + 3i^2 = 8 + 14i + 3(-1) = 8 + 14i - 3 = 5 + 14i$

Do the multiplication using F.O.I.L. (First terms, Outer terms, Inner terms, and Last terms), while keeping in mind that $i^2 = -1$. (See "Performing Operations with Polynomials" in Chapter 2 for a review of F.O.I.L.)

$(2 + 3i)(2 - 3i) = 4 - 9i^2 = 4 - 9(-1) = 4 + 9 = 13$

The complex numbers $2 + 3i$ and $2 - 3i$ are **complex conjugates.** The product of a complex number and its conjugate is a real number.

$i^2 = -1$ because

$i = \sqrt{-1}$

$\sqrt{-1} \cdot \sqrt{-1} = -1$

# Ratios, Rates, and Proportions

For this topic, you will use the concepts of ratio and rate to describe relationships between quantities or measures and recognize and represent proportional relationships.

## Ratios

A **ratio** is the result of a multiplicative comparison of two or more quantities or measures. When you find the ratio of two or more quantities, you must make sure they have the same units. When you write the ratio, the units will divide out. For example, the ratio of 2 pints to 5 quarts is *not* $\frac{2}{5}$ because these quantities are not expressed in the same units. From the measurement units and conversions table in Appendix D, 1 quart (qt) = 2 pints (pt).

Therefore, the ratio of 2 pt to 5 qt equals the ratio of 1 qt to 5 qt. This ratio is $\frac{1 \text{ qt}}{5 \text{ qt}} = \frac{1 \cancel{\text{ qt}}}{5 \cancel{\text{ qt}}} = \frac{1}{5}$ or 1 to 5, or 1:5.

If you have a problem in which two quantities are in the ratio $m$ to $n$ and their sum is $s$, first solve $mx + nx = s$ and then compute $mx$ or $nx$, as needed. Here is an example.

> The ratio of children to adults at a park is 5 to 3. If the total number of people at the park is 200, how many children are at the park?

Solve $5x + 3x = 200$ to obtain $8x = 200$, which implies $x = 25$. Thus, there are $5(25) = 125$ children at the park.

## Rates

A **rate** is a multiplicative comparison of two quantities that have different measurement units. Suppose a car travels 300 miles in 5 hours. The **rate** is $\frac{300 \text{ miles}}{5 \text{ hours}}$. *Miles* and *hours* are different measurement units. They do not cancel out. The **unit rate** per 1 hour is $\frac{(300 \div 5) \text{ miles}}{(5 \div 5) \text{ hours}} = \frac{60 \text{ miles}}{1 \text{ hour}}$. This rate tells you the number of miles traveled in 1 hour. The numerical factor of this quantity is $\frac{60}{1}$. In a unit rate, the second term (the denominator) of the numerical part is always 1. The unit rate tells the number of units of the first quantity for each 1 unit of the second quantity. In this example, there are 60 miles of distance for each 1 hour of time. The measurement unit for the unit rate is $\frac{\text{miles}}{\text{hour}}$. The rate $\frac{60 \text{ miles}}{1 \text{ hour}}$ is $60 \frac{\text{miles}}{\text{hour}}$ or 60 miles per hour.

## Proportions

A **proportion** is a mathematical statement that the values of two ratios are equal. The **terms** of the proportion are the four numbers that make up the two ratios. For example, the proportion $\frac{3}{4} = \frac{9}{12}$ has terms 3, 4, 9, and 12. The **fundamental property of proportions** is $\frac{a}{b} = \frac{c}{d}$ if and only if $ad = bc$. In other words, cross products of a proportion are equal. **Cross products** are the product of the numerator of the first ratio times the denominator of the second ratio and the product of the denominator of the first ratio times the numerator of the second ratio.

Here is an illustration of obtaining the cross products for $\frac{3}{4} = \frac{9}{12}$.

$$\frac{3}{4} \diagdown \diagup \frac{9}{12} \longrightarrow 3 \times 12 = 4 \times 9 \longrightarrow 36 = 36$$

When you know the values of three of the terms of a proportion, determine the fourth term by using the fundamental property of proportions as follows: Find and compute a cross product that results in a numerical value, and then divide by the numerical term that you did not use.

Here is an example.

> Suppose the ratio of red to green marbles in a box is 2 to 5. There are 36 red marbles in the box. How many marbles are in the box? (Assume the box contains only red and green marbles.)

Let $x$ = the number of green marbles in the box. The ratios 2 to 5 and 36 to $x$ are equivalent. Write a proportion and solve for $x$.

$$\frac{2}{5} = \frac{36}{x}$$
$$x = \frac{(5)(36)}{2}$$
$$x = 90$$

There are 90 green marbles in the box. There are 126 marbles in the box: $36 + 90 = 126$ marbles.

# Sample Questions

**Directions:** Read the directions for each question carefully. This set of questions has several different question types. For each question, select a single answer choice unless written instructions preceding the question state otherwise.

**1.** A scientist wants to divide a field that measures 18 by 30 feet into equal square plots with no land left over. What is the greatest length for each side of the square plots?

   Ⓐ 2
   Ⓑ 3
   Ⓒ 6
   Ⓓ 90

**For the following question, enter your numeric answer in the box below the question.**

**2.** Simplify $7 + 3(4^2) - 8 \div 2$.

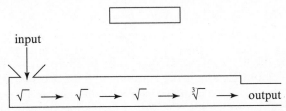

**3.** If $x^6$, $x > 0$, is used as the input for the sequence of root operations shown in the diagram above, which of the following is equivalent to the output?

   Ⓐ $x^{\frac{11}{6}}$

   Ⓑ $x^{\frac{1}{4}}$

   Ⓒ $x^7 \cdot x^{\frac{1}{6}}$

   Ⓓ $x^{11}$

**For the following question, select all that apply.**

$$23 + 39 + 77 + 11 = 23 + 77 + 39 + 11 = 100 + 50 = 150$$

**4.** Which of the following properties of the real numbers are illustrated by the preceding computation sequence?

   Ⓐ   commutativity

   Ⓑ   associativity

   Ⓒ   distributive property

   Ⓓ   additive inverse

**5.** What is the units digit of $2^{47}$?

   Ⓐ   2

   Ⓑ   4

   Ⓒ   6

   Ⓓ   8

# Answer Explanations

**1.** **C.** The greatest length for each side of the square plots is the greatest common factor of 18 and 30. Because $18 = 2 \cdot 3 \cdot 3$ and $30 = 2 \cdot 3 \cdot 5$, the gcf $(18, 30) = 2 \cdot 3 = 6$, choice C.

**2.** **51** Follow the order of operations.

$$
\begin{aligned}
7 + 3(4^2) - 8 \div 2 &= 7 + 3(16) - 8 \div 2 \qquad \text{First, do the exponentiation inside the parentheses.} \\
&= 7 + 48 - 4 \qquad \text{Next, multiply and divide from left to right.} \\
&= 51 \qquad \text{Finally, add and subtract from left to right.}
\end{aligned}
$$

**3.** **B.** Given that the answer choices are exponential expressions, work this problem by performing on $x^6$ the sequence of root operations shown in the diagram, using the exponential form for the radicals.

$$\left(\left(\left(\left(x^6\right)^{\frac{1}{2}}\right)^{\frac{1}{2}}\right)^{\frac{1}{2}}\right)^{\frac{1}{3}} = x^{(6)\left(\frac{1}{2}\right)\left(\frac{1}{2}\right)\left(\frac{1}{2}\right)\left(\frac{1}{3}\right)} = x^{\frac{6}{24}} = x^{\frac{1}{4}}, \text{ choice B.}$$

**4.** **A, B.** Looking at the properties in the answer choices, you can immediately eliminate choice C because there are no parentheses in the computation sequence, meaning that the distributive property did not come into play. Eliminate choice D because all the numbers have the same sign, so no additive inverses were involved. Commutativity (choice A) was used because the order of the numbers was changed. Associativity (choice B) was used because grouping of the numbers for purposes of computation was used.

**5.** **D.** Work this problem by identifying a pattern in the units digits of $2^n$, where $n$ is a positive integer.

$2^1 = 2, 2^2 = 4, 2^3 = 8, 2^4 = 16, 2^5 = 32, 2^6 = 64, 2^7 = 128, 2^8 = 256$, and so on. The units digits have a 4-digit repeating pattern of 2, 4, 8, 6, 2, 4, 8, 6, and so on. Let $k$ be a whole number. If $n$ has the form $4k + 1$, the units digit of $2^n$ is 2. If $n$ has the form $4k + 2$, the units digit of $2^n$ is 4. If $n$ has the form $4k + 3$, the units digit of $2^n$ is 8. If $n$ has the form $4k$, the units digit of $2^n$ is 6. In this question, $n = 47$, which has the form $4(11) + 3$. Thus, the units digit of $2^{47}$ is 8, choice D.

# Chapter 2

# Algebra

This chapter provides a review of the ideas and formulas of algebra that are important for you to know for the Praxis MS Math test. Sample questions, comparable to what might be presented on the Praxis MS Math test, are given at the end of the chapter. The answer explanations for the sample questions are provided immediately following.

## Basic Algebraic Terminology

A **variable** is a placeholder for a number (or numbers, in some cases) whose value may vary. Symbols (often lower- or uppercase letters such as $x$, $y$, $z$, $A$, $B$, or $C$) represent variables. The symbol that represents a variable is its name.

A **constant** is a numerical quantity whose value does not change. For example, all the real and complex numbers are constants. Each has a fixed, definite value. Thus, when a letter is used to name a constant, the letter has one fixed value. For example, the Greek letter $\pi$ stands for the number that equals the ratio of the circumference of a circle to its diameter, which is approximately 3.14159.

A **numerical expression** is any constant or combination of two or more constants joined by explicit or implied operational symbols. For example, 100, 3.5, $\frac{3 \cdot 25}{4 \cdot 5}$, $0.75(2,000) + 2,500$, and $\pi(6)^2$ are numerical expressions.

An **algebraic expression** is a symbol or combination of symbols that represents a number. Algebraic expressions consist of one or more variables joined by one or more operations with or without constants (explicitly) included. **Juxtaposition** is commonly used to indicate multiplication. That is, when constants and variables or two or more variables (with or without constants) are written side by side, they are products. For example, the quantity $7x$ is the result of multiplying 7 and $x$. Thus, $7 \cdot x = x \cdot 7 = (7)(x) = (7)x = x(7) = 7x$. Similarly, $axy$ means $a$ times $x$ times $y$. The expressions $7x$, $axy$, $uv$, $-t$, $6x + 3$, $5x^4 + 3x^3 - 12x^2 + 15$, $(a + 5)^2 - 3$, $7abc$, $y(2x + 3)$, $\frac{8xy}{4(y+2z)}$, and $\frac{3}{a+3} + \frac{10}{t-25}$ are algebraic expressions.

A **term** is a constant, variable, or product of constants or variables. For example, $x$, $8ab$, $-9z$, $10xyz$, $x(-6x)$, and 11 are terms. In algebraic expressions, terms are separated by either + or – symbols. For example, $6x^4 + 3x^3 - 12x^2 + 15$ has four terms: $6x^4$, $3x^3$, $12x^2$, and 15. Quantities enclosed within grouping symbols are considered single terms, even though they may contain + or – symbols. Thus, the algebraic expression $(a + 5)^2 - 3$ has two terms.

In a term that is a product of two or more factors, the **coefficient** of a factor is the product of the other factors in that term. For example, in the term $4y(2x + 3)$, $4y$ is the coefficient of $(2x + 3)$ and $4(2x + 3)$ is the coefficient of $y$. The numerical factor, or the product of the numerical factors, of a term is its **numerical coefficient.** For example, the coefficient of $(2)(5)xy$ is 10, which is $(2)(5)$. If no numerical coefficient is explicitly written, then the numerical coefficient is understood to be 1.

A **monomial** is an algebraic expression of one term, such as $6x^4y$, consisting of the product of a numerical coefficient and one or more variables each raised to a nonnegative integer power. The **degree of a monomial** is the sum of the exponents of its variables. For example, the degree of the monomial $6x^4y$ is 5. The degree of a non-zero constant $c$ is zero because $c = cx^0$ for any constant $c$. The degree of the monomial 0 is undefined. **Like terms** are monomial terms that differ only in their numerical coefficients. For example, $6x^4y$ and $-4x^4y$ are like terms; however, $6x^4y$ and $-4xy^4$ are **unlike terms**. All constants are like terms.

A **polynomial** is an algebraic expression composed of one or more monomials. Thus, a **monomial** is a polynomial of exactly one term. A **binomial** is a polynomial of exactly two terms, such as $x + 3$. A **trinomial** is a polynomial of exactly three terms, such as $9x^4 - 24x^2 + 16$. Beyond three terms, polynomials are general polynomials.

# Polynomials

For this topic, you must know how to perform operations on polynomials and manipulate polynomial expressions.

## Performing Operations with Polynomials

The following table summarizes rules for addition and subtraction of polynomials.

**Addition and Subtraction of Polynomials**

| Operation | Rule | Example |
|-----------|------|---------|
| Addition | Combine *like* monomial terms by adding their numerical coefficients; use the result as the coefficient of the common variable factor or factors. Indicate the sum/difference of *unlike* terms. | $(5x^2 + 10x - 6) + (3x^2 - 2x + 4) = 5x^2 + 10x - 6 + 3x^2 - 2x + 4 = 8x^2 + 8x - 2$ |
| Subtraction | *Mentally* change the subtraction symbol to addition, *change the sign of every term* in the second polynomial, and proceed as in addition. Indicate the sum/difference of unlike terms. | $(5x^2 + 10x - 6) - (3x^2 - 2x + 4) = 5x^2 + 10x - 6 - 3x^2 + 2x - 4 = 2x^2 + 12x - 10$ |

**Tip: When simple parentheses (or brackets or braces) are immediately preceded by a + symbol, they can be removed without changing the signs of the terms within, but if the parentheses are immediately preceded by a – symbol, the sign of *every* term within the grouping must be changed when the parentheses are removed. In the second case, you *mentally* change the – symbol that precedes the parentheses to a + symbol and do not explicitly write the change because + · + = + and + · – = –.**

The following table summarizes rules for multiplication of polynomials.

**Multiplication of Polynomials**

| Type of Multiplication | Rule | Example |
|------------------------|------|---------|
| Monomial by Monomial | Multiply both the numerical coefficients and the variable factors. | $(-5x^2y)(10xy) = -50x^3y^2$ |
| Polynomial by Monomial | Use the distributive property to multiply *each* term of the polynomial by the monomial. | $2x^2(3x^2 - 5x + 1) = 6x^4 - 10x^3 + 2x^2$ |
| Polynomial by Polynomial | Use the distributive property to multiply each term in the second polynomial by each term of the first polynomial, and then combine like terms. | $(x + 2)(x^2 - 2x + 4) = x^3 - 2x^2 + 4x + 2x^2 - 4x + 8 = x^3 + 8$ |
| Binomial by Binomial | Use the distributive property to multiply each term in the second binomial by each term of the first binomial, and then combine like terms. (See "Using F.O.I.L" on the next page for an efficient way to multiply two binomials.) | $(2x - 3)(x + 4) = 2x^2 + 8x - 3x - 12 = 2x^2 + 5x - 12$ |

# Using F.O.I.L.

Use F.O.I.L. (First terms, Outer terms, Inner terms, and Last terms) to multiply two binomials. Here is an e...

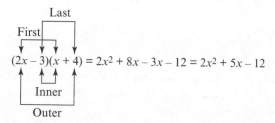

$$(2x - 3)(x + 4) = 2x^2 + 8x - 3x - 12 = 2x^2 + 5x - 12$$

**Tip: Remember that when you multiply variable factors, you *add* (not multiply) the exponents of like bases.**

**Tip: When multiplying polynomials, if possible, arrange the terms of the polynomials in descending or ascending powers of a common variable.**

## Special Products

Some special products to know for the Praxis MS Math test are given in the following table.

### Special Products

| Special Name | Special Product | Example(s) |
|---|---|---|
| Perfect Trinomial Square | $(x + y)^2 = (x + y)(x + y) = x^2 + 2xy + y^2$ <br> $(x - y)^2 = (x - y)(x - y) = x^2 - 2xy + y^2$ | $(x + 3)^2 = x^2 + 6x + 9$ <br> $(2x - 5)^2 = 4x^2 - 20x + 25$ |
| Difference of Two Squares | $(x + y)(x - y) = x^2 - y^2$ | $(x + 3)(x - 3) = x^2 - 9$ |
| Sum of Two Cubes | $(x + y)(x^2 - xy + y^2) = x^3 + y^3$ | $(x + 2)(x^2 - 2x + 4) = x^3 + 8$ |
| Difference of Two Cubes | $(x - y)(x^2 + xy + y^2) = x^3 - y^3$ | $(x - 2)(x^2 + 2x + 4) = x^3 - 8$ |
| Perfect Cube | $(x + y)^3 = x^3 + 3x^2y + 3xy^2 + y^3$ <br> $(x - y)^3 = x^3 - 3x^2y + 3xy^2 - y^3$ | $(x + 2)^3 = x^3 + 6x^2 + 12x + 8$ <br> $(x - 2)^3 = x^3 - 6x^2 + 12x - 8$ |

**Tip: It is a common mistake to omit the middle terms when squaring or cubing binomials. The square of a binomial has three terms (a trinomial), and the cube of a binomial has four terms. Just remember that the number of terms is *one more* than the exponent used.**

## Simplifying Polynomials

A polynomial is **simplified** when all indicated operations have been performed and it contains no uncombined like terms. The **degree of a polynomial** is the same as the greatest of the degrees of its monomial terms after the polynomial has been simplified.

To simplify a polynomial expression, use the following steps:

**Steps for Simplifying a Polynomial**

1. When grouping symbols are present, perform all operations within grouping symbols, starting with the innermost grouping symbol and working outward.
2. Perform all indicated multiplication, starting with exponentiation, being sure to enclose the product in parentheses if it is to be multiplied by an additional factor.
3. Remove all remaining parentheses and combine like terms using addition or subtraction as indicated.

Here are examples.

$$2 + 4(x + 3y - 10) = 2 + 4x + 12y - 40 = 4x + 12y - 38$$

For the example above, don't make the mistake of writing $2 + 4(x + 3y - 10)$ as $6(x + 3y - 10)$. Remember, multiplication must be performed before addition (or subtraction) unless grouping symbols indicate otherwise.

$$2(x + 3)(x - 3) - (x + 3)^2 = 2(x^2 - 9) - (x^2 + 6x + 9) = 2x^2 - 18 - x^2 - 6x - 9 = x^2 - 6x - 27$$

*Tip:* Enclosing products in parentheses helps prevent careless errors.

# Dividing Polynomials

The following table summarizes rules for division of polynomials by monomials.

**Rules for Division by a Monomial**

| Type of Division | Rule | Example |
|---|---|---|
| Monomial by Monomial | Divide the numerical coefficients. Divide the variable factors that have a common base. Leave other variable factors alone. Use the quotient of the numerical coefficients as the coefficient for the answer. | $\dfrac{-50x^3y^2z}{-5x^2y} = 10xyz$ |
| Polynomial by Monomial | Divide each term of the polynomial by the monomial. | $\dfrac{25x^5y^3 + 35x^3y^2 - 10x^2y}{-5x^2y} = -5x^3y^2 - 7xy + 2$ |

Do **long division of polynomials** in a manner analogous to long division in arithmetic. The result is usually written as a mixed expression: $\text{quotient} + \dfrac{\text{remainder}}{\text{divisor}}$. **Synthetic division** is a shortcut method commonly used to divide a polynomial by a binomial of the form $x - r$. See Appendix B for an example of long division and a discussion of synthetic division.

# Factoring Polynomials Completely

**Factoring a polynomial completely** means writing it as a product of prime polynomial factors. A **prime polynomial** is one whose only factors are itself and 1. Before you can say a polynomial is a prime factor, you must specify the set of numbers that are available as coefficients when you are factoring. For example, over the rationals, the polynomial $x^2 - 3$ is prime; but over the irrationals, $x^2 - 3$ is $(x + \sqrt{3})(x - \sqrt{3})$. Similarly, over the real numbers, $x^2 + 4$ is prime; but over the complex numbers, $x^2 + 4$ is $(x + 2i)(x - 2i)$. As a general rule, you can safely limit the coefficients of variable terms in polynomials to real numbers. However, when you have polynomial equations, the roots of the equations can be real or complex numbers. A polynomial that cannot be written as a product of two or more polynomial factors is said to be **prime**. To factor a polynomial that is not prime, you must find two or more polynomials whose product is the original polynomial. For example, $(2x - 3)(x + 4)$ is a **factorization** of

$2x^2 + 5x - 12$ because $(2x - 3)(x + 4) = 2x^2 + 5x - 12$. The polynomials $(2x - 3)$ and $(x + 4)$ cannot be factored further, so they are **prime polynomial factors** of $2x^2 + 5x - 12$.

When factoring polynomials, proceed systematically as follows.

1. Check for a greatest common monomial factor.
2. If a factor is a binomial, check for

    difference of two squares: $x^2 - y^2 = (x + y)(x - y)$.

    sum of two cubes: $x^3 + y^3 = (x + y)(x^2 - xy + y^2)$.

    difference of two cubes: $x^3 - y^3 = (x - y)(x^2 + xy + y^2)$.

3. If a factor is a trinomial, check for

    general factorable quadratic: $\quad x^2 + (a+b)x + ab = (x+a)(x+b)$

    $\qquad\qquad\qquad\qquad\qquad acx^2 + (ad+bc)x + bd = (ax+b)(cx+d)$

    perfect trinomial square: $\qquad a^2x^2 + 2abxy + b^2y^2 = (ax+by)^2$

    $\qquad\qquad\qquad\qquad\qquad a^2x^2 - 2abxy + b^2y^2 = (ax-by)^2$

4. If a factor has four terms, try grouping some of the terms together and factoring the groups separately first, and then factoring the entire expression.
5. Write the original polynomial as the product of all the factors obtained.

> **Tip: After making sure all factors are prime polynomials, check by multiplying the factors to obtain the original polynomial.**

Here are examples.

$x^2 - 3x - 4 = (x - 4)(x + 1)$

$16a^2b^2 - 4a^2 = 4a^2(4b^2 - 1) = 4a^2(2b + 1)(2b - 1)$

$18x^2 + 24xy + 8y^2 = 2(9x^2 + 12xy + 4y^2) = 2(3x + 2y)^2$

$80x^3y - 270y^4 = 10y(8x^3 - 27y^3) = 10y(2x - 3y)(4x^2 + 6xy + 9y^2)$

$3x^4y + 3x^3y - 27x^2y - 27xy = 3xy(x^3 + x^2 - 9x - 9) = 3xy[(x^3 + x^2) - (9x + 9)] = 3xy[x^2(x + 1) - 9(x + 1)] =$
$\quad 3xy[(x + 1)(x^2 - 9)] = 3xy[(x + 1)(x + 3)(x - 3)] = 3xy(x + 1)(x + 3)(x - 3)$

# Rational Expressions

A **rational expression** is an algebraic fraction in which both the numerator and denominator are polynomials.

Values for which the denominator evaluates to zero are excluded. For example, $\dfrac{2x}{5}$ (no excluded value), $\dfrac{5}{2x}(x \neq 0)$,

$\dfrac{10x}{x-1}(x \neq 1)$, $\dfrac{x^2 - 4}{x^2 - 3x - 4} = \dfrac{(x+2)(x-2)}{(x-4)(x+1)}$ $(x \neq 4,\ x \neq -1)$, $x^4 y^{-3} = \dfrac{x^4}{y^3}$ $(y \neq 0)$, and all polynomials (no excluded

values) are rational expressions. Hereafter, whenever a rational expression is written, it will be understood that any values for which the expression is undefined are excluded.

To perform computations with algebraic fractions, often you will need to factor the polynomials used in the algebraic fractions. For example, factoring is frequently necessary when reducing algebraic fractions to lowest terms and when finding a common denominator for algebraic fractions. The following table summarizes the process.

### Reducing Algebraic Fractions to Lowest Terms

| Type of Algebraic Fraction | Rule | Example(s) |
|---|---|---|
| $\dfrac{\text{monomial}}{\text{monomial}}$ | Divide numerator and denominator by the greatest common factor of the two monomials. | $\dfrac{9x^5y^2z}{12x^2y^3} = \dfrac{3x^2y^2 \cdot 3x^3z}{3x^2y^2 \cdot 4y} = \dfrac{3x^3z}{4y}$ |
| $\dfrac{\text{monomial}}{\text{polynomial}}$ or $\dfrac{\text{polynomial}}{\text{monomial}}$ | Factor out the greatest monomial factor, if any, from the polynomial, and then divide numerator and denominator by the greatest common factor. | $\dfrac{-9x^2y}{12x^3y - 36x^2y - 48xy} = \dfrac{-9x^2y}{12xy(x^2 - 3x - 4)} = \dfrac{3xy(-3x)}{3xy(4)(x^2 - 3x - 4)}$ $= \dfrac{3xy(-3x)}{3xy(4)(x^2 - 3x - 4)} = \dfrac{-3x}{4(x^2 - 3x - 4)} = -\dfrac{3x}{4(x-4)(x+1)};$ $\dfrac{12x^3y - 36x^2y - 48xy}{9x^2y} = \dfrac{12xy(x^2 - 3x - 4)}{3xy(3x)} = \dfrac{4(3xy)(x^2 - 3x - 4)}{3xy(3x)}$ $= \dfrac{4(x^2 - 3x - 4)}{3x} = \dfrac{4(x-4)(x+1)}{3x}$ |
| $\dfrac{\text{polynomial}}{\text{polynomial}}$ | Factor the polynomials completely, and then divide numerator and denominator by the greatest common factor. | $\dfrac{9x^2y - 9y}{12x^3y - 36x^2y - 48xy} = \dfrac{9y(x^2 - 1)}{12xy(x^2 - 3x - 4)} = \dfrac{3y(3)(x+1)(x-1)}{3y(4x)(x+1)(x-4)}$ $= \dfrac{3y(3)(x+1)(x-1)}{3y(4x)(x+1)(x-4)} = \dfrac{3(x-1)}{4x(x-4)}$ |

> **Tip:** When reducing algebraic fractions, make sure that you divide by factors only. For example, $\dfrac{x+2}{4}$ cannot be reduced further. Even though 2 is a factor of the denominator, it is not a factor of the numerator—it is a term of the numerator. Remember, divide by factors, *not* terms.

The following table summarizes computations with algebraic fractions.

### Rules for Computations with Algebraic Fractions

| Operation | Rule | Example(s) |
|---|---|---|
| Addition/Subtraction—Like Denominators | Add/subtract the numerators to find the numerator of the answer, which is placed over the common denominator. Simplify and reduce to lowest terms, if needed. | $\dfrac{x+2}{x-3} + \dfrac{2x-11}{x-3} = \dfrac{3x-9}{x-3} = \dfrac{3(x-3)}{(x-3)} = \dfrac{3}{1} = 3;$ $\dfrac{5x^2}{3(x+1)} - \dfrac{4x^2+1}{3(x+1)} = \dfrac{5x^2 - 4x^2 - 1}{3(x+1)} =$ $\dfrac{x^2-1}{3(x+1)} = \dfrac{(x+1)(x-1)}{3(x+1)} = \dfrac{x-1}{3}$ **Tip:** When subtracting, you must change the sign of *every* term of the numerator of the second fraction. |

*(Continued)*

## Rules for Computations with Algebraic Fractions

| Operation | Rule | Example(s) |
|---|---|---|
| Addition/Subtraction—Unlike Denominators | Factor each denominator completely. Find the common denominator, which is the product of each prime factor the *highest* number of times it is a factor in any one denominator. Write each algebraic fraction as an equivalent fraction having the common denominator as the denominator. Add/subtract the numerators to find the numerator of the answer, which is placed over the common denominator. Simplify and reduce to lowest terms, if needed. | $\dfrac{1}{x^2-3x-4}+\dfrac{2}{x^2-1}=$<br><br>$\dfrac{1}{(x+1)(x-4)}+\dfrac{2}{(x+1)(x-1)}=$<br><br>$\dfrac{1(x-1)}{(x+1)(x-4)(x-1)}+\dfrac{2(x-4)}{(x+1)(x-1)(x-4)}=$<br><br>$\dfrac{x-1}{(x+1)(x-1)(x-4)}+\dfrac{2x-8}{(x+1)(x-1)(x-4)}=$<br><br>$\dfrac{3x-9}{(x+1)(x-1)(x-4)}=\dfrac{3(x-3)}{(x+1)(x-1)(x-4)}$ |
| Multiplication | Factor all numerators and denominators completely and then divide numerators and denominators by their common factors (as in reducing). The product of the remaining numerator factors is the numerator of the answer and the product of the remaining denominator factors is the denominator of the answer. | $\dfrac{a^2+4a+4}{a^2+a-2}\cdot\dfrac{a^2-2a+1}{a^2-4}=$<br><br>$\dfrac{\cancel{(a+2)}\,\cancel{(a+2)}}{\cancel{(a+2)}\,\cancel{(a-1)}}\cdot\dfrac{\cancel{(a-1)}(a-1)}{\cancel{(a+2)}(a-2)}=\dfrac{a-1}{a-2}$ |
| Division | Multiply the first algebraic fraction by the reciprocal of the second algebraic fraction. | $\dfrac{a^2+4a+4}{a^2+a-2}\div\dfrac{a^2-4}{a^2-2a+1}=$<br><br>$\dfrac{a^2+4a+4}{a^2+a-2}\cdot\dfrac{a^2-2a+1}{a^2-4}=$<br><br>$\dfrac{\cancel{(a+2)}\,\cancel{(a+2)}}{\cancel{(a+2)}\,\cancel{(a-1)}}\cdot\dfrac{\cancel{(a-1)}(a-1)}{\cancel{(a+2)}(a-2)}=\dfrac{a-1}{a-2}$ |

# Complex Fractions

A **complex fraction** is a fraction that has fractions in its numerator, denominator, or both. One way to simplify a complex fraction is to interpret the fraction bar of the complex fraction as meaning division. For example,

$$\frac{\dfrac{1}{x}+\dfrac{1}{y}}{\dfrac{1}{x}-\dfrac{1}{y}}=\frac{\dfrac{y}{xy}+\dfrac{x}{xy}}{\dfrac{y}{xy}-\dfrac{x}{xy}}=\frac{\dfrac{y+x}{xy}}{\dfrac{y-x}{xy}}=\frac{y+x}{xy}\div\frac{y-x}{xy}=\frac{y+x}{xy}\cdot\frac{xy}{y-x}=\frac{y+x}{y-x}$$

Another way to simplify a complex fraction is to multiply its numerator and denominator by the least common denominator of all the fractions used in its numerator and denominator. For example,

$$\frac{\dfrac{1}{x}+\dfrac{1}{y}}{\dfrac{1}{x}-\dfrac{1}{y}}=\frac{xy\left(\dfrac{1}{x}+\dfrac{1}{y}\right)}{xy\left(\dfrac{1}{x}-\dfrac{1}{y}\right)}=\frac{xy\cdot\dfrac{1}{x}+xy\cdot\dfrac{1}{y}}{xy\cdot\dfrac{1}{x}-xy\cdot\dfrac{1}{y}}=\frac{y+x}{y-x}$$

# One-Variable Linear Equations

An **equation** is a statement that two mathematical expressions are equal. An equation has two sides. Whatever is on the left side of the equal sign is the left side (LS) of the equation, and whatever is on the right side of the equal sign is the right side (RS) of the equation. Equations containing only numerical expressions are either true or false. An equation is true when the LS has the same value as the RS. For example, $1 + 2 = 3$ is true, but $1 + 2 = 5$ is false. An equation containing one or more variables is an **open sentence.** For example, $x + 2 = 3$ and $x + 2y = 8$ are open sentences. Generally, you can determine whether an open sentence is true or false after numerical quantities are substituted for the variables in the sentence.

A **one-variable linear equation** has only one variable. The variable has an exponent of 1 (commonly not written, but understood), and no products of variables or variable divisors occur in the equation. A **solution,** or **root,** of a one-variable equation is a number that when substituted for the variable makes the equation true. To determine whether a number is a solution of a one-variable equation, replace the variable with the number and perform all operations indicated on each side of the equation. If the resulting statement is true, the number is a solution of the equation. This process is called **checking** a solution.

The **solution set** of an equation is the set consisting of all the solutions of the equation. **Equivalent equations** are equations that have the same solution set. If the solution set is the set of all possible values of the variable, the equation is an **identity.** For example, $x + 7 = x + 5 + 2$ is an identity because any number substituted for $x$ will make the equation true. Thus, an identity has an infinite number of solutions. If the solution set is empty, the equation has **no solution.** For example, $x + 7 = x + 5$ has no solution because there is no number that will make the equation true. To **solve an equation** means to find its solution set.

A one-variable linear equation can be written in the form $ax + b = 0$, where $a \neq 0$ and $b$ is a constant in the discussion. For example, $2x + 6 = 0$, $12x + 1 = 5(x - 4)$, $\dfrac{2y}{3} - 45 = y$, and $0.05x = 200 + 0.06(1,500 - x)$ are one-variable linear equations. Unless the equation is an identity or has no solution, the solution set of a one-variable linear equation consists of one number.

When you are solving an equation, the two main actions that will result in equivalent equations are the following:

1. Addition or subtraction of the same quantity on both sides of the equation.

2. Multiplication or division by the same *nonzero* quantity on both sides of the equation.

**Tip: It is important to remember that when you are solving an equation, you must never multiply or divide both sides by 0.**

To solve a one-variable linear equation, use the following procedure:

---

**Steps for Solving a One-Variable Linear Equation**

1. Remove grouping symbols, if any, by applying the distributive property and then simplify.

2. If the variable appears on both sides of the equation, eliminate the variable from one side of the equation. Undo indicated addition or subtraction to get all terms containing the variable on one side and all other terms on the other side. Then simplify.

3. If a number is added to the variable term, subtract that number from both sides of the equation. If a number is subtracted from the variable term, add that number to both sides of the equation. Then simplify.

4. If necessary, factor the side containing the variable so that one of the factors is the variable.

5. Divide both sides of the equation by the coefficient of the variable. If the coefficient is a fraction, divide by multiplying both sides of the equation by the fraction's reciprocal.

---

**Tip: You should check the solution in the original equation.**

Here is an example.

> Solve $\dfrac{2}{3}x - 45 = -\dfrac{1}{2}(x+48)$.

$$\frac{2}{3}x - 45 = -\frac{1}{2}(x+48)$$

$$\frac{2}{3}x - 45 = -\frac{1}{2}x - 24$$

$$\frac{2}{3}x - 45 + \frac{1}{2}x = -\frac{1}{2}x - 24 + \frac{1}{2}x$$

$$\frac{7}{6}x - 45 = -24$$

$$\frac{7}{6}x - 45 + 45 = -24 + 45$$

$$\frac{7}{6}x = 21$$

$$\frac{\cancel{6}}{\cancel{7}} \cdot \frac{\cancel{7}}{\cancel{6}}x = \frac{6}{\cancel{7}} \cdot \cancel{21}^{3}$$

$$x = 18$$

Of course, as long as you keep the equation in balance, you can modify the equation-solving process based on the particular equation you are trying to solve. For example, if an equation contains fractions, you first might multiply both sides of the equation by the lcm of all the denominators to eliminate fractions from both sides of the equation. You also might do some of the steps mentally to save time. Just always make sure that you are doing the same operation to both sides of the equation, whether or not you show all your work!

**Tip: Go to http://www.infinitysw.com/exams/tutorials to view a tutorial on using the ETS graphing calculator's Solver tool or the Solve command to find numerical solutions to equations. Be careful to key in equations correctly.**

# One-Variable Inequalities

If you replace the equal sign in a one-variable linear equation with < (less than), > (greater than), ≤ (less than or equal to), or ≥ (greater than or equal to), the result is a **one-variable linear inequality.** The solution sets of one-variable linear inequalities are subsets of the real numbers. (See "Set Terminology" in Chapter 6 for a discussion of the term *subset*.). You can graph the solution set of the inequality on a number line.

You solve an inequality just as you would an equation *except* for one important difference: If you multiply or divide both sides of the inequality by a *negative* number, you must *reverse* the direction of the inequality.

Here are examples.

> Solve $12x + 1 < 5(x - 4)$.

$$12x + 1 < 5(x - 4)$$

$$12x + 1 < 5x - 20$$

$$12x + 1 - 5x < 5x - 20 - 5x$$

$$7x + 1 < -20$$

$$7x + 1 - 1 < -20 - 1$$

$$7x < -21$$

$$\frac{\cancel{7}x}{\cancel{7}} < \frac{\cancel{-21}^{-3}}{\cancel{7}}$$

$$x < -3$$

Using **set-builder notation,** the solution set is $\{x \mid x < -3\}$, which is read "The set of all real numbers $x$ such that $x$ is less than $-3$." (See "Basic Set Operations and Venn Diagrams" in Chapter 6 for an additional discussion of set-builder notation.) To graph this solution set on a number line, shade the numbers to the left of $-3$. To indicate that the number 3 does *not* belong in the solution set, put a small *open* circle at the point $-3$.

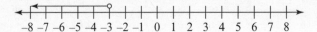

Solve $3x + 5 \geq 5x - 7$.

$$3x + 5 \geq 5x - 7$$
$$3x + 5 - 5x \geq 5x - 7 - 5x$$
$$-2x + 5 \geq -7$$
$$-2x + 5 - 5 \geq -7 - 5$$
$$-2x \geq -12$$
$$\frac{\cancel{-2}x}{\cancel{-2}} \leq \frac{\cancel{-12}^{\,6}}{\cancel{-2}} \quad \text{(Reverse the direction of the inequality because you divided by a negative number.)}$$
$$x \leq 6$$

Thus, the solution set is $\{x \mid x \leq 6\}$. To graph the solution set, shade the numbers to the left of 6. To indicate that the number 6 also belongs in the solution set, put a small *shaded* circle at the point 6.

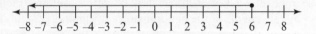

# Formulas and Two-Variable Equations

An equation that expresses the relationship between two or more variables is a **formula.** The procedure for solving one-variable linear equations can be used to solve a formula for a specific variable when the value(s) of the other variable(s) are known. The procedure also can be used to solve a formula or literal equation (an equation with no numbers, only letters) for a specific variable in terms of the other variable(s). What you must keep in mind when using the procedure for these purposes is that, when the word *variable* is used, it is referring only to the variable *for which you are solving.* In general, isolate the specific variable of interest and treat all other variable(s) as constants. This is called changing the subject of the formula or literal equation. Here is an example.

Solve $C = \frac{5}{9}(F - 32)$ for $F$.

$$C = \frac{5}{9}(F - 32)$$
$$C = \frac{5}{9}F - \frac{5}{9} \cdot 32$$
$$C = \frac{5}{9}F - \frac{160}{9}$$
$$C + \frac{160}{9} = \frac{5}{9}F$$
$$\frac{9}{5}\left(C + \frac{160}{9}\right) = \frac{\cancel{9}}{\cancel{5}} \cdot \frac{\cancel{5}}{\cancel{9}}F$$
$$\frac{9}{5}C + 32 = F$$
$$F = \frac{9}{5}C + 32$$

Use the procedure for solving one-variable linear equations to solve two-variable equations for one variable in terms of the other variable. For example, use the procedure to transform equations of lines into the form $y = mx + b$, where $m$ and $b$ are constants. (See "The Equation of a Line" later in this chapter for a discussion of this topic.) Here is an example.

> Write $-2x + 3y = 1$ in the form $y = mx + b$.

$$-2x + 3y = 1$$
$$-2x + 3y + 2x = 1 + 2x$$
$$3y = 2x + 1$$
$$y = \frac{2}{3}x + \frac{1}{3}$$

# One-Variable Absolute Value Equations and Inequalities

**You can solve one-variable absolute value equations** using the procedure for solving one-variable linear equations. To transform one-variable absolute value equations into linear equations, use the following statements:

$|ax + b| = 0$ if and only if $ax + b = 0$.

If $c$ is any positive number, $|ax + b| = c$ if and only if either $ax + b = c$ or $ax + b = -c$.

> **Tip: Notice that for equations like $|ax + b| = c$, you must solve *two* linear equations. Don't forget the second equation!**

Here are examples.

> Solve $|2x + 6| = 0$.

$$|2x + 6| = 0 \text{ implies}$$
$$2x + 6 = 0$$
$$2x + 6 - 6 = 0 - 6$$
$$2x = -6$$
$$\frac{\cancel{2}x}{\cancel{2}} = \frac{\cancel{-6}^{-3}}{\cancel{2}}$$
$$x = -3$$

> Solve $|2x + 6| = 10$.

$$|2x + 6| = 10 \text{ implies}$$
$$2x + 6 = 10 \text{ or } 2x + 6 = -10$$
$$2x = 4 \text{ or } 2x = -16$$
$$x = 2 \text{ or } x = -8$$

**You can solve one-variable absolute value inequalities** using the procedure for solving one-variable linear inequalities. To transform one-variable absolute value inequalities into linear inequalities, use the following statements:

If $c > 0$, $|ax + b| < c$ if and only if $-c < ax + b < c$.

If $c > 0$, $|ax + b| > c$ if and only if either $ax + b < -c$ or $ax + b > c$.

The expression $-c < ax + b < c$ is called a **double inequality** because it is a concise way to express the two inequalities: $-c < ax + b$ and $ax + b < c$.

*Note:* You can replace < with ≤ and > with ≥ everywhere in the given inequalities, and the statements will still hold.

> **Tip: Notice that for absolute value inequalities, you must set up and solve *two* linear inequalities. Don't forget the second inequality! If the inequality symbol is < (or ≤), the connecting word between the two inequalities is "and" (double inequality). If the inequality symbols is > (or ≥), the connecting word is "or."**

Here are examples.

> Solve $|2x + 6| < 10$.

$|2x + 6| < 10$ if and only if $-10 < 2x + 6 < 10$.

Solve this double inequality by applying the techniques for solving inequalities to the two inequalities simultaneously. Focus on isolating the variable in the middle variable expression. Whatever you do to the middle expression, you must do to each of the two expressions on either side, as shown here.

$$-10 < 2x + 6 < 10$$
$$-10 - 6 < 2x + 6 - 6 < 10 - 6$$
$$-16 < 2x < 4$$
$$\frac{\overset{-8}{\cancel{-16}}}{\cancel{2}} < \frac{\cancel{2}x}{\cancel{2}} < \frac{\overset{2}{\cancel{4}}}{\cancel{2}}$$
$$-8 < x < 2$$

The solution set for $|2x + 6| < 10$ is $\{x \mid -8 < x < 2\}$.

> Solve $|2x + 6| > 10$.

$|2x + 6| > 10$ if and only if either $2x + 6 < -10$ or $2x + 6 > 10$. Solve each of these two linear inequalities as shown here.

$$
\begin{array}{ll}
2x + 6 < -10 & \qquad 2x + 6 > 10 \\
2x + 6 - 6 < -10 - 6 & \qquad 2x + 6 - 6 > 10 - 6 \\
2x < -16 & \qquad 2x > 4 \\
\dfrac{\cancel{2}x}{\cancel{2}} < \dfrac{\overset{-8}{\cancel{-16}}}{\cancel{2}} & \qquad \dfrac{\cancel{2}x}{\cancel{2}} > \dfrac{\overset{2}{\cancel{4}}}{\cancel{2}} \\
x < -8 & \qquad x > 2
\end{array}
$$

The solution set for $|2x + 6| > 10$ is $\{x \mid x < -8 \text{ or } x > 2\}$.

# Quadratic Equations

A **one-variable quadratic equation** is an equation that can be written in the **standard form** $ax^2 + bx + c = 0$, where $a \neq 0$ and $a$, $b$, and $c$ are real-valued constants in the discussion. Specifically, $a$ is the numerical coefficient of $x^2$, $b$ is the numerical coefficient of $x$, and $c$ is the constant coefficient, or simply the constant term. The solutions of a quadratic equation are its **roots.** A quadratic equation may have exactly *one* real root, exactly *two* real unequal roots, or *no* real roots.

*Note:* Quadratic equations in which $a$, $b$, or $c$ is not an element of the real numbers are not covered on the Praxis MS Math test.

# Solving Quadratic Equations of the Form $x^2 = C$

Quadratic equations that can be written in the form $x^2 = C$ have the solution $x = \pm\sqrt{C}$. If the quantity $C$ is 0, there is *one* real root that has the value 0; if *positive,* there are *two* unequal real roots; and if *negative,* there are *no* real roots.

Here are examples.

> Solve $3x^2 = 48$.

$$3x^2 = 48$$
$$x^2 = 16$$
$$x = \pm\sqrt{16}$$
$$x = \pm 4$$

> Solve $2x^2 - 5 = 25$.

$$2x^2 - 5 = 25$$
$$2x^2 = 30$$
$$x^2 = 15$$
$$x = \pm\sqrt{15}$$

> Solve $4x^2 - 9 = 0$.

$$4x^2 - 9 = 0$$
$$4x^2 = 9$$
$$x^2 = \frac{9}{4}$$
$$x = \pm\sqrt{\frac{9}{4}}$$
$$x = \pm\frac{3}{2}$$

This process can be extended to quadratic equations when they are rewritten in the form $(x + k)^2 = C$, where $C$ is a constant. For such equations, it is evident that $x + k$ must be one of the square roots of $C$. Thus, $(x + k) = \pm\sqrt{C}$.

Here is an example.

> Solve $(x + 3)^2 = 49$.

$$(x + 3)^2 = 49$$
$$(x + 3) = \pm\sqrt{49}$$
$$x + 3 = \pm 7$$
$$x + 3 = -7 \text{ or } x + 3 = 7$$
$$x = -10 \text{ or } x = 4$$

# Solving Quadratic Equations by Factoring

The procedure for solving a quadratic equation by factoring is based on the **property of zero products** for numbers: If the product of two quantities is zero, at least one of the quantities is zero.

To solve a quadratic equation by factoring, use the following procedure:

> **Steps for Solving a Quadratic Equation by Factoring**
>
> 1. Express the equation in standard form: $ax^2 + bx + c = 0$.
> 2. Factor the left side of the equation completely.
> 3. Set each factor containing the variable equal to zero.
> 4. Solve each of the resulting linear equations.

**Tip: You should check each root by substituting its value into the original equation.**

Here is an example.

> Solve $x(x + 8) = 20$ by factoring.

$$x(x+8) = 20$$
$$x^2 + 8x - 20 = 0$$
$$(x+10)(x-2) = 0$$
$$x = -10 \text{ or } x = 2$$

**Tip: Some beginners start solving $x(x + 8) = 20$ by setting each factor on the left equal to 20. This is incorrect. The property of zero products can only be applied when the product is *zero*, not 20 or any other nonzero number.**

# Solving Quadratic Equations by Completing the Square

To solve a quadratic equation by completing the square, use the following procedure:

> **Steps for Solving a Quadratic Equation by Completing the Square**
>
> 1. Express the equation in the form $ax^2 + bx =$ numerical expression.
> 2. If the coefficient $a$ is not 1, divide each term by $a$ to obtain an equation of the form $x^2 + \dfrac{b}{a}x =$ numerical expression.
> 3. Add the square of half the coefficient of $x$ to both sides of the equation and then simplify to obtain an equation of the form $x^2 + \dfrac{b}{a}x + \left(\dfrac{b}{2a}\right)^2 = C$, where $C$ is a constant.
> 4. Factor the perfect trinomial square on the left side of the equation as the square of a binomial so that you have an equation of the form $\left(x + \dfrac{b}{2a}\right)^2 = C$.
> 5. Recognizing that $x + \dfrac{b}{2a}$ must be one of the square roots of $C$, write $\left(x + \dfrac{b}{2a}\right) = \pm\sqrt{C}$, being sure to prefix a $\pm$ symbol to the square root of the right side of the equation.
> 6. Solve each of the resulting two linear equations.

**Tip: You should check each root by substituting its value into the original equation.**

Here is an example.

Solve $x(x + 8) = 20$ by completing the square.

$$x(x+8)=20$$
$$x^2+8x=20$$
$$x^2+8x+4^2=20+4^2$$
$$x^2+8x+16=36$$
$$(x+4)^2=36$$
$$(x+4)=\pm\sqrt{36}$$
$$x+4=\pm6$$
$$x+4=-6 \text{ or } x+4=6$$
$$x=-10 \text{ or } x=2$$

*Note:* In most instances, this method would not be an efficient way to solve a quadratic equation on the Praxis MS Math test. Use factoring or the quadratic formula instead.

## Solving Quadratic Equations by Using the Quadratic Formula

To solve a quadratic equation by using the quadratic formula, use the following procedure:

**Steps for Solving a Quadratic Equation by Using the Quadratic Formula**

1. Express the equation in standard form: $ax^2 + bx + c = 0$.
2. Determine the values of $a$, $b$, and $c$.
3. Substitute into the quadratic formula: $x = \dfrac{-b \pm \sqrt{b^2 + 4ac}}{2a}$.
4. Evaluate and simplify each of the two resulting expressions on the right side of the equation.

**Tip: You should check each root by substituting its value into the original equation.**

Here is an example.

Solve $x(x + 8) = 20$ by using the quadratic formula.

$$x(x+8)=20$$
$$x^2+8x-20=0$$

$a = 1$, $b = 8$, $c = -20$ (include the $-$ sign).

$$x=\frac{-8\pm\sqrt{8^2-4(1)(-20)}}{2(1)}$$
$$x=\frac{-8\pm\sqrt{64+80}}{2}$$
$$x=\frac{-8\pm\sqrt{144}}{2}$$
$$x=\frac{-8\pm12}{2}$$
$$x=\frac{-8-12}{2} \text{ or } x=\frac{-8+12}{2}$$
$$x=-10 \text{ or } x=2$$

> **Tip:** When solving quadratic equations, *never* divide both sides of the equation by the variable or by an expression containing the variable.

The quantity $b^2 - 4ac$ is the **discriminant** of the quadratic equation $ax^2 + bx + c = 0$. The equation has exactly *one* real root if $b^2 - 4ac = 0$, *two* real unequal roots if $b^2 - 4ac > 0$, and *no* real roots if $b^2 - 4ac < 0$.

You also can solve quadratic (and linear) equations that have real zeros by using features of the ETS graphing calculator. For example, the Solver function (and the Solve command) will find numerical solutions to equations, one at a time, after you make smart guesses. You can graph the equation as $y = ax^2 + bx + c$, and then use the **Trace/Evaluate** or **Zero** mode under the **Analysis** menu to find the roots. Check the calculator manual for instructions (http://infinitysw.s3.amazonaws.com/ets/ets_calculator_manual.pdf).

Equations that are not quadratic equations but that can be written in the form of a quadratic equation can be solved using the methods for solving quadratic equations. It naturally follows that equations that can be written so one side is a factorable higher degree polynomial and the other side contains only 0 can be solved by factoring completely, setting each factor equal to 0, and then solving the resulting equations.

Here is an example.

> Solve $x^4 - 13x^2 + 36 = 0$.

$$x^4 - 13x^2 + 36 = 0$$
$$\left(x^2 - 4\right)\left(x^2 - 9\right) = 0$$
$$(x+2)(x-2)(x+3)(x-3) = 0$$
$$x+2 = 0, \ x-2 = 0, \ x+3 = 0, \ \text{or } x-3 = 0$$
$$x = -2, 2, -3, \text{ or } 3$$

## Solving One-Variable Quadratic Inequalities

Quadratic inequalities have the standard forms $ax^2 + bx + c < 0$, $ax^2 + bx + c > 0$, $ax^2 + bx + c \le 0$, and $ax^2 + bx + c \ge 0$. The solution sets for quadratic inequalities in standard form are based on the rules for multiplying signed numbers: If two factors have the same sign, their product is positive; if they have opposite signs, their product is negative. To solve a quadratic inequality, put it in standard form with $a > 0$ and apply the following.

If $ax^2 + bx + c = 0$ has no real roots, $ax^2 + bx + c$ is always positive (and $-ax^2 - bx - c$ is always negative).

If $ax^2 + bx + c = 0$ has exactly one real root, $ax^2 + bx + c$ is 0 at that root and positive everywhere else.

If $ax^2 + bx + c = 0$ has two real roots, $ax^2 + bx + c$ is negative between them, positive to the left of the leftmost root, positive to the right of the rightmost root, and 0 only at its roots.

For example, $x^2 + 2x - 24 = (x + 6)(x - 4) = 0$ has two real roots, −6 and 4. So $x^2 + 2x - 24$ is negative in the interval (−6, 4) and positive in the intervals (−∞, −6) and (4, ∞).

*Note:* If you have a quadratic inequality in which $a < 0$, to put the inequality in standard form with $a > 0$, multiply both sides of the inequality by −1 and reverse the direction of the inequality.

## Other Common One-Variable Equations

In this section, you will solve fractional equations, radical equations, and simple exponential equations.

## Solving Fractional Equations

A **fractional equation** is one in which a variable appears in the denominator of one or more terms. For example, $\frac{1}{2} + \frac{1}{x} = \frac{5}{6}$ and $\frac{x-2}{x} = \frac{4}{x(x-2)}$ are fractional equations. Linear equations that have fractional coefficients, such as

$\frac{1}{2}x - 6 = 4$, are not fractional equations. Many fractional equations can be transformed into linear or quadratic equations by multiplying both sides of the equation by the lcm of the equation's fractions. However, this action does not necessarily result in an equivalent equation. Check your result against the excluded values for the equation's variable. A result that is an excluded value is rejected. It cannot be in the solution set.

Here are examples.

Solve $\frac{1}{2} + \frac{1}{x} = \frac{5}{6}$.

$$\frac{1}{2} + \frac{1}{x} = \frac{5}{6}$$

$$6x\left(\frac{1}{2} + \frac{1}{x}\right) = 6x\left(\frac{5}{6}\right)$$

$$3x + 6 = 5x$$

$$6 = 2x$$

$$3 = x$$

Check: The equation $\frac{1}{2} + \frac{1}{x} = \frac{5}{6}$ has one excluded value; $x$ cannot be 0. Thus, $\frac{1}{2} + \frac{1}{x} = \frac{5}{6}$ has solution $x = 3$.

Solve $\frac{x-2}{x} = \frac{4}{x(x-2)}$.

$$\frac{x-2}{x} = \frac{4}{x(x-2)}$$

$$\cancel{x}(x-2)\left(\frac{x-2}{\cancel{x}}\right) = \cancel{x}\,(\cancel{x-2})\left(\frac{4}{\cancel{x}\,(\cancel{x-2})}\right)$$

$$(x-2)(x-2) = 4$$

$$x^2 - 4x + 4 = 4$$

$$x^2 - 4x = 0$$

$$x(x-4) = 0$$

$$x = 0 \text{ or } x = 4$$

Check: The equation $\frac{x-2}{x} = \frac{4}{x(x-2)}$ has two excluded values; $x$ cannot be 0 or 2. Thus, 0 is rejected, meaning $x = 4$ is the only solution of $\frac{x-2}{x} = \frac{4}{x(x-2)}$.

# Solving Radical Equations

A **radical equation** is one in which the variable appears in a radical. For example, $\sqrt{2x-4}+1=7$ and $x+3=\sqrt{x+5}+4$ are radical equations. To solve a radical equation that contains only one radical, use the following procedure:

| **Steps for Solving a One-Radical Equation** |
| --- |
| 1. Get the radical on one side of the equation and all other terms on the other side. |
| 2. Eliminate the radical by raising both sides of the equation to an appropriate power. For square root radicals, square both sides. For cube root radicals, cube both sides, and so forth. |
| 3. Solve the resulting equation. |
| 4. Check for extraneous roots by substituting your obtained value(s) in the original radical equation. Do not skip this step. |

**Tip: Squaring both sides of an equation (or raising to any even power) can introduce "solutions," called extraneous roots, that did not exist previously. Extraneous roots are not true solutions of the original radical equation and should be rejected as answers.**

Here are examples.

| Solve $\sqrt{2x-4}+1=7$. |
| --- |

$$\sqrt{2x-4}+1=7 \qquad \text{Check:} \qquad \sqrt{2x-4}+1=7$$
$$\sqrt{2x-4}=6 \qquad\qquad \sqrt{2\cdot 20-4}+1\overset{?}{=}7$$
$$(\sqrt{2x-4})^2=6^2 \qquad\qquad \sqrt{40-4}+1\overset{?}{=}7$$
$$2x-4=36 \qquad\qquad \sqrt{36}+1\overset{?}{=}7$$
$$2x=40 \qquad\qquad 6+1\overset{?}{=}7$$
$$x=20 \qquad\qquad 7\overset{\checkmark}{=}7$$

The solution of $\sqrt{2x-4}+1=7$ is $x=20$.

| Solve $x+3=\sqrt{x+5}+4$. |
| --- |

$$x+3=\sqrt{x+5}+4$$
$$x-1=\sqrt{x+5}$$
$$(x-1)^2=(\sqrt{x+5})^2$$
$$x^2-2x+1=x+5$$
$$x^2-3x-4=0$$
$$(x+1)(x-4)=0$$
$$x=-1 \text{ or } x=4$$

$$\text{Check } x = -1: \quad x + 3 = \sqrt{x+5} + 4$$
$$(-1) + 3 \overset{?}{=} \sqrt{(-1)+5} + 4$$
$$2 \overset{?}{=} \sqrt{4} + 4$$
$$2 \overset{?}{=} 2 + 4$$
$$2 \neq 6 \text{ (Reject } x = -1)$$

$$\text{Check } x = 4: \quad x + 3 = \sqrt{x+5} + 4$$
$$(4) + 3 \overset{?}{=} \sqrt{(4)+5} + 4$$
$$7 \overset{?}{=} \sqrt{9} + 4$$
$$7 \overset{?}{=} 3 + 4$$
$$7 \overset{\checkmark}{=} 7$$

The solution of $x + 3 = \sqrt{x+5} + 4$ is $x = 4$.

## Solving Exponential Equations

An **exponential equation** is one in which the variable appears in an exponent. For example, $5^{2x-1} = 125$ and $2^x = 64$ are exponential equations. Some exponential equations can be easily solved by equating exponents of like bases. Here are examples.

Solve $5^{2x-1} = 125$.

$$5^{2x-1} = 125$$
$$5^{2x-1} = 5^3, \text{ which implies}$$
$$2x - 1 = 3$$
$$2x = 4$$
$$x = 2$$

Solve $2^x = 64$.

$$2^x = 64$$
$$2^x = 2^6, \text{ which implies}$$
$$x = 6$$

# Systems of Equations and Inequalities

For this topic, you solve and graph systems of equations and inequalities.

## Basic Concepts of Systems of Equations

A set of equations, each with the same set of variables, is called a **system** when the equations in the set are considered simultaneously. The system possesses a **solution** when the equations in the system are all satisfied by at least one set of values of the variables. A system that has a solution is **consistent.** A system that has no solution is **inconsistent.**

A **system of two linear equations in two variables** consists of a pair of linear equations in the same two variables. To **solve a system** of linear equations in two variables means to find all pairs of values for the two variables that make *both* equations true simultaneously. A pair of values—for example, an $x$ value paired with a corresponding $y$ value—is called an **ordered pair** and is written as $(x, y)$. An ordered pair that makes an equation true is said to **satisfy** the equation. When an ordered pair makes both equations in a system true, the ordered pair **satisfies** the system. The **solution set** is the collection of all solutions. There are three possibilities: The system has exactly *one solution, no solution,* or *infinitely many solutions.*

Geometrically, the two equations of a system of linear equations in two variables can be represented as lines in the coordinate plane. For the two lines, there are three possibilities that can occur, corresponding to the three possibilities for the solution set. If the system is consistent and has exactly one solution, then the two lines intersect in a unique point in the plane. The ordered pair that corresponds to the point of intersection is the solution to the system. If the system is consistent and has infinitely many solutions, then the two lines are coincident (that is, have all points in common). If the system is inconsistent and has no solutions, then the two lines are parallel in the plane. Here are examples.

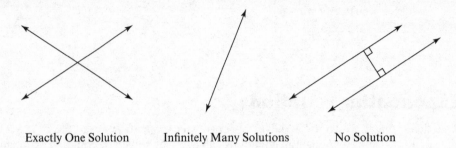

Exactly One Solution    Infinitely Many Solutions    No Solution

*Note:* See "Basic Function Concepts" in Chapter 3 for a discussion of the coordinate plane.

A quick way to decide whether a system of two linear equations has exactly one solution, infinitely many solutions, or no solution is to look at ratios of the coefficients of the two equations, where $A_1$, $B_1$, and $C_1$ are the coefficients in the first equation and $A_2$, $B_2$, and $C_2$ are the corresponding coefficients in the second equation.

If $\dfrac{A_1}{A_2} \neq \dfrac{B_1}{B_2}$, the system has exactly one solution; if $\dfrac{A_1}{A_2} = \dfrac{B_1}{B_2} = \dfrac{C_1}{C_2}$, the system has infinitely many solutions; and if $\dfrac{A_1}{A_2} = \dfrac{B_1}{B_2} \neq \dfrac{C_1}{C_2}$, the system has no solution.

## Solving a System of Two Linear Equations by Substitution

To solve a system of linear equations by **substitution,** use the following procedure:

| Steps for Solving a System of Linear Equations by Substitution |
| --- |
| 1. Select the simpler equation and solve it for one of the variables in terms of the other. You can solve for either variable. Use your judgment to decide. |
| 2. Using the other given equation, replace the variable solved for in Step 1 with the expression obtained, simplify, and solve for the second variable. |
| 3. Using the simpler equation, substitute the value obtained in Step 2 for the second variable, simplify, and solve for the first variable. |

**Tip: You should check the solution in the original equations.**

Here is an example (for convenience, the equations are numbered).

Solve the system $\begin{array}{ll} (1) & x+y=1{,}950 \\ (2) & 9x+6y=13{,}950 \end{array}$ by the method of substitution.

Quick check: The system has exactly one solution because $\dfrac{1}{9} \neq \dfrac{1}{6}$.

Solve equation (1) for $x$ to obtain $x = 1{,}950 - y$. Substitute this result into equation (2) and solve for $y$.

$$9x + 6y = 13{,}950$$
$$9(1{,}950 - y) + 6y = 13{,}950$$
$$17{,}550 - 9y + 6y = 13{,}950$$
$$17{,}550 - 3y = 13{,}950$$
$$-3y = -3{,}600$$
$$y = 1{,}200$$

Using equation (1), $x = 1{,}950 - y = 1{,}950 - 1{,}200 = 750$.

The solution is $x = 750$, $y = 1{,}200$.

# Solving a System of Two Linear Equations by Elimination

To solve a system of linear equations by **elimination,** use the following procedure:

---

**Steps for Solving a System of Linear Equations by Elimination**

1. Write both equations in standard form: $Ax + By = C$.
2. Eliminate one of the variables. If necessary, multiply one or both of the equations by a nonzero constant or constants to make the coefficients of one of the variables sum to zero. You can eliminate either variable. Use your judgment to decide.
3. Add the transformed equations and then solve for the variable that was not eliminated.
4. Substitute the value obtained in Step 3 into one of the original equations, simplify, and solve for the other variable.

---

**Tip: You should check the solution in the original equations.**

Here is an example (for convenience, the equations are numbered).

---

Solve the system $\begin{array}{l}(1)\ 3y = 2x + 1 \\ (2)\ 3x - 7y = 6\end{array}$ by the method of elimination.

---

Write both equations in standard form: $\begin{array}{l}(1)\ -2x + 3y = 1 \\ (2)\ \ \ 3x - 7y = 6\end{array}$

Quick check: The system has exactly one solution because $\dfrac{-2}{3} \neq \dfrac{3}{-7}$.

To eliminate $x$, multiply equation (1) by 3 and equation (2) by 2.

$$\begin{array}{l} -2x + 3y = 1 \\ 3x - 7y = 6 \end{array} \text{ implies } \begin{array}{l} 3(-2x + 3y) = 3(1) \\ 2(3x - 7y) = 2(6) \end{array} \text{ implies } \begin{array}{l} -6x + 9y = 3 \\ 6x - 14y = 12 \end{array}$$

Add the transformed equations and solve for $y$.

$$-6x + 9y = 3$$
$$\underline{6x - 14y = 12}$$
$$0 - 5y = 15$$
$$y = -3$$

Substitute $y = -3$ into (1) and solve for $x$.

$$-2x + 3y = 1$$
$$-2x + 3(-3) = 1$$
$$-2x - 9 = 1$$
$$-2x = 10$$
$$x = -5$$

The solution is $x = -5$, $y = -3$.

> **Tip: Another way to solve a system of two linear equations in two variables is to use the Intersection feature under the Analysis menu of the ETS graphing calculator. See the tutorial at http://www.infinitysw.com /exams/tutorials for a demonstration of this feature.**

You can use the methods in this section to solve systems of equations in two variables when one of the equations is nonlinear.

Here is an example.

Solve the system $\begin{array}{l} 5x - y = 12 \\ 2x^2 + y = 0 \end{array}$.

Observe that the coefficients of $y$ sum to zero. Add the two equations.

$$5x - y = 12$$
$$2x^2 \quad + \quad y = 0$$
$$\overline{2x^2 + 5x + 0 = 12}$$

Solve the resulting quadratic equation.

$$2x^2 + 5x = 12$$
$$2x^2 + 5x - 12 = 0$$
$$(2x - 3)(x + 4) = 0$$
$$2x - 3 = 0 \text{ or } x + 4 = 0$$
$$2x = 3 \text{ or } x = -4$$
$$x = 1.5 \text{ or } x = -4$$

Do not make the mistake of stopping at this point and writing (1.5, –4) as the solution. You have obtained two distinct values for $x$ and now must obtain the corresponding $y$ value for each.

Substitute $x = 1.5$ and $x = -4$ into $5x - y = 12$ to find the corresponding $y$ value for each.

$$5(1.5) - y = 12 \quad \text{ or } \quad 5(-4) - y = 12$$
$$-y = 4.5 \quad \text{ or } \quad -y = 12$$
$$y = -4.5 \quad \text{ or } \quad y = -32$$

Thus, two ordered pairs, (1.5, –4.5) and (–4, –32), satisfy the system $\begin{array}{l} 5x - y = 12 \\ 2x^2 + y = 0 \end{array}$.

You can extend the procedures for solving a system of two linear equations to systems of three equations or more. Proceed systematically, taking two equations at a time.

# Formulas Used in a Two-Dimensional (

To find the **slope $m$ of the line** that connects the points $(x_1, y_1)$ and $(x_2, y_2)$ in a formula:

$$\text{Slope of line} = m = \frac{y_2 - y_1}{x_2 - x_1}, \ (x_1 \neq x_2)$$

When a line slopes *upward* to the right, its slope is *positive,* and when a line slop is *negative.* All horizontal lines have slope 0. Vertical lines have no slope (it's un their slopes are equal. If two lines are perpendicular, their slopes are negative re

*Note:* See "Features of Common Functions" in Chapter 3 for an additional disc

To find the **distance $d$ between two points** $(x_1, y_1)$ and $(x_2, y_2)$ in a coordinate plane, use the following formula:

$$\text{Distance between two points} = d = \sqrt{(x_2 - x_1)^2 + (y_2 - y_1)^2}$$

The distance $d$ between two points $(x_1, y_1)$ and $(x_2, y_2)$ in a coordinate plane can be interpreted geometrically as the length of the hypotenuse of a right triangle having legs of length $x_2 - x_1$ and $y_2 - y_1$ as illustrated here.

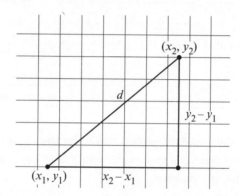

To find the **midpoint between two points** $(x_1, y_1)$ and $(x_2, y_2)$ in a coordinate plane, use the following formula:

$$\text{Midpoint between two points} = \left( \frac{x_1 + x_2}{2}, \frac{y_1 + y_2}{2} \right)$$

**Tip: Notice that you add, not subtract, the coordinates in the numerator.**

To find the distance $d$ from point $(x_1, y_1)$ to line $Ax + By + C = 0$, use the following formula:

$$d = \frac{|Ax_1 + By_1 + C|}{\sqrt{A^2 + B^2}}$$

**Tip: When substituting values into formulas, enclose in parentheses any negative substituted value to avoid making a sign error.**

# The Equation of a Line

The equation of a nonvertical line can be determined using one of the following:

- The **slope-intercept form:** $y = mx + b$, where the line determined by the equation has slope $= m$ and $y$-intercept $= b$
- The **standard form:** $Ax + By = C$, where the line determined by the equation has slope $= -\dfrac{A}{B}$ and $y$-intercept $= \dfrac{C}{B}$, $(B \neq 0)$
- The **point-slope form:** $y - y_1 = m(x - x_1)$, where $m$ is the slope of the line and $(x_1, y_1)$ is a point on the line

slope-intercept form of the equation of the line that passes through the points (–3, 4) and (–5, 2).

ope of the line is $m = \dfrac{y_2 - y_1}{x_2 - x_1} = \dfrac{2-4}{(-5)-(-3)} = \dfrac{2-4}{-5+3} = \dfrac{-2}{-2} = 1$. Selecting (–3, 4) from the two points and

substituting into $y - y_1 = m(x - x_1)$ gives $y - 4 = 1(x - (-3))$ or, equivalently, $y - 4 = x + 3$, which yields the equation $y = x + 7$.

> **Note:** See the previous section, "Formulas Used in a Two-Dimensional Coordinate Plane," for the formula for finding the slope of a line given two points on the line.

Two special cases of linear equations are the equations for horizontal and vertical lines. Horizontal lines have equations of the form $y = k$ ($m = 0$). Vertical lines have equations of the form $x = h$ (undefined slope).

Here is a summary of equations of lines.

**Equations of Lines**

| | |
|---|---|
| Slope-intercept form (functional form) | $y = mx + b$ |
| Point-slope form | $y - y_1 = m(x - x_1)$ |
| Standard form | $Ax + By = C$ ($A$ and $B$ not both zero) |
| Horizontal line | $y = k$ for any constant $k$ |
| Vertical line (not a function) | $x = h$ for any constant $h$ |

> **Note:** Not all authorities agree on the standard form. Some write the standard form as $Ax + By + C = 0$; others designate $y = mx + b$ as the standard form. We do not anticipate that your correct responses on the Praxis MS Math test will be jeopardized by this inconsistency.

# Systems of Two-Variable Linear Inequalities

For this topic, you will graph two-variable linear inequalities and find the maximum (or minimum) value of an equation that is subject to inequality constraints.

## Graphing Two-Variable Linear Inequalities

The graph of a two-variable linear inequality, such as $3x + y \le 5$, $3x - y \ge 1$, and $x - y < 0$, is a half-plane.

To graph a two-variable inequality, use the following procedure:

---

**Steps for Graphing a Two-Variable Linear Inequality**

1. Rewrite the inequality in an equivalent form with only $y$ on the left side of the inequality symbol.
2. Graph the linear equation that results when the inequality symbol is replaced with an equal sign. Use a dashed line for < or > inequalities and a solid line for ≤ or ≥ inequalities. This is the boundary line.
3. If the inequality contains < or ≤, shade the portion of the plane beneath the line. If the inequality contains > or ≥, shade the portion of the plane above the line.

---

Here is an example.

> Graph the inequality $3x + y \leq 5$.

Rewrite the inequality as $y \leq -3x + 5$. Graph $y = -3x + 5$. Make the line a solid line and shade the portion of the plane beneath the line as shown here.

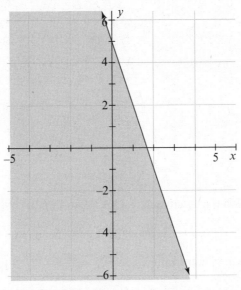

Graph of $y \leq -3x + 5$

# Find the Maximum Value of an Equation Subject to Inequality Constraints

Suppose you want to find the maximum value of the equation $z = 2x + 5y$ subject to the following constraints:

$$3x + y \leq 5$$
$$3x - y \geq 1$$
$$x - y \leq 0$$

The general process to find the maximum value of the given equation (called the "optimization" equation) is to graph the set of constraint inequalities to produce a region in the plane that represents their intersections. The maximum value of the equation will occur at one of the corners of the region. To algebraically determine the corner points, find the points of intersection of the boundary lines of the region. In other words, pair the following equations and solve for the intersection of each pair (for convenience, the equations are numbered):

(1) $3x + y = 5$ or, equivalently, $y = -3x + 5$

(2) $3x - y = 1$ or, equivalently, $y = 3x - 1$

(3) $x - y = 0$ or, equivalently, $y = x$

Solve (1) and (2) to obtain the corner point (1, 2). Solve (1) and (3) to obtain the corner point (1.25, 1.25). Solve (2) and (3) to obtain the corner point (0.5, 0.5). Here is the graph. The shading is the intersection of the half-planes described by the original inequalities.

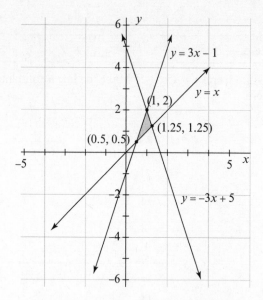

Substitute the corner point values into the equation, $z = 2x + 5y$, to find the maximum.

At $(1, 2)$, $z = 2(1) + 5(2) = 12$; at $(1.25, 1.25)$, $z = 2(1.25) + 5(1.25) = 8.75$; and at $(0.5, 0.5)$, $z = 2(0.5) + 5(0.5) = 3.5$.

Subject to the given constraints, the maximum value for $z = 2x + 5y$ is 12.

*Tip:* As this problem demonstrates, you can find the maximum (or minimum) of an equation that is subject to inequality constraints by determining the corner points of the intersection region of the set of constraint inequalities.

# Algebraic Problem Solving

You can expect to encounter application problems on the Praxis MS Math test. This section presents some helpful ideas for algebraically dealing with application problems.

## General Problem-Solving Guidelines

Here are some general problem-solving guidelines for solving application problems using algebraic techniques.

---

**Problem-Solving Guidelines**

1. **Analyze the problem.** Ask yourself: What is the question's primary focus? Is the problem a familiar type (for example, an age problem)? Determine what you need to find. Look for words like *find, determine, what is, how many, how far, how much, what time,* and the like.

   Decide how many unknowns are in the problem. If there is one unknown, let the variable represent this unknown quantity. (Be precise in specifying a variable. State its units, if any.) Sometimes you will have two or more unknowns in a problem. In this case, you can assign the unknowns different variable names. Using the first letter of the name of an unknown as a variable name can be helpful. As another option, you might assign a variable name to one unknown and express the other unknowns in terms of that variable. For example, if a first unknown is described in terms of a second unknown, assign the variable name to the *second* unknown. No matter whether you use one variable or two or more variables, the process will culminate in a one-variable linear equation (or its equivalent).

---

(*Continued*)

2. **Write one or more equations that represent the facts in the problem.** Identify the information in the problem. Is there a formula that you should know? If measurement units are given, determine what units the answer should have. Decide whether making a table or sketching a diagram would be helpful. Try to relate the current problem to problems you have worked in the past. Keep in mind that you will need as many equations as you have variables in order to obtain numerical values for the variables. Make sure your solution answers the question.

3. **Solve the equation(s).** Carefully work out your solution. Make sure you copy all information accurately. Write neatly so that you can check over your work. If the answer should have units, check whether your calculations will result in the proper units for the answer. When solving an equation, you might find it convenient to omit the units, given that you have already checked that the answer will have the proper units.

4. **Check back.** Did you answer the question that was asked? Check your solution in the context of the problem. Does it make sense? Is it reasonable? Are the units correct?

## Translating Verbal Relationships

The following table summarizes commonly used algebraic symbolism for verbal relationships. The letter $x$ is used in the table to represent an unknown number.

| Signal Words or Phrases | Example | Algebraic Symbolism |
|---|---|---|
| add, plus, sum of, increased by, added to, more than, exceeds | a number that exceeds $x$ by 10 | $x + 10$ |
| minus, subtracted from, difference between, less than, decreased by, reduced by, diminished by | 10 less than $x$ | $x - 10$ |
| times, multiplied by, product of, twice, double, triple, quadruple, fraction of, percent of | twice $x$ | $2x, 2 \cdot x, 2(x), (2)(x),$ or $(2)x$ |
| divided by, quotient of, ratio of, for each, $x$ for every, per | ratio of $x$ and 5 | $\dfrac{x}{5}$ |
| equals, is, was, are, were, will be, gives, yields, results in | 50% of $x$ is 20 more than the quotient of $x$ and 4. | $50\%x = \dfrac{x}{4} + 20$ |

## Geometry Problems

> The length of a rectangular garden is 3 meters more than its width. The garden's perimeter is 54 meters. Find the garden's area.

The garden is rectangular. You do not know its length or width. You will need the values of both to find the garden's area, so this problem has two unknowns. Let $l$ = the garden's length and $w$ = the garden's width. Its perimeter is 54 meters. The formula for the perimeter of a rectangle is $P = 2l + 2w = 2(l + w)$ and the formula for the area of a rectangle is $A = lw$, where $l$ is the rectangle's length and $w$ is its width. (See "Perimeter, Area, and Volume" in Chapter 5 for common geometric formulas.)

Make a sketch.

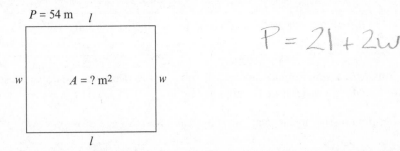

*Tip:* For geometry problems, making a sketch helps you visualize the problem.

**Method 1.** Use one variable.

The garden's length is described in terms of its width. Let $w$ = the garden's width in meters. Then $l = w + 3$ meters = the garden's length in meters. Write an equation that represents the facts given in the question.

$$2[(w + 3 \text{ meters}) + w] = 54 \text{ meters}$$

Solve the equation, omitting the units for convenience.

$$2[(w+3) + w] = 54$$
$$2[w+3 + w] = 54$$
$$2[2w+3] = 54$$
$$4w+6 = 54$$
$$4w = 48$$
$$w = 12$$
$$w+3 = 15$$

The area of the garden is $(12 \text{ m})(15 \text{ m}) = 180 \text{ m}^2$.

**Method 2.** Use two variables.

Let $w$ = the garden's width in meters and $l$ = the garden's length in meters. Write two equations that represent the facts given in the question.

(1) $l = w + 3$ meters
(2) $2(l + w) = 54$ meters

Simultaneously solve the two equations, omitting the units for convenience.

(1) $l = w + 3$
(2) $2(l + w) = 54$

Using the substitution method, substitute $l = w + 3$ from equation (1) into equation (2) to obtain

$$2[(w + 3) + w] = 54$$

Complete the solution as shown in Method 1.

Make sure you answer the question that was asked. In this question, after you obtain the garden's length and width, you must calculate the garden's area to answer the question.

*Note:* Hereafter, only one solution method will be shown.

# Age Problems

> Reima is twice as old as Dustin. In 5 years, Reima's age will be 55 years minus Dustin's age. What is Reima's age now?

You don't know Reima's age or Dustin's age now. Reima's age now is described as "twice as old as Dustin," so designate the variable as Dustin's age now.

Let $d$ = Dustin's age in years now, and $2d$ = Reima's age in years now.

Make a table to organize the information in the question.

| When? | Dustin's Age | Reima's Age |
|-------|--------------|-------------|
| Now | $d$ | $2d$ |
| 5 years from now | $d + 5$ years | $2d + 5$ years |

From the question, you know that Reima's age 5 years from now is 55 years minus Dustin's age 5 years from now. Use the information in the table to set up an equation to match the facts in the question.

$$(2d + 5\,\text{years}) = 55\,\text{years} - (d + 5\,\text{years})$$

Solve the equation, omitting the units for convenience.

$$(2d+5) = 55 - (d+5)$$
$$2d + 5 = 55 - d - 5$$
$$2d + 5 = 50 - d$$
$$3d + 5 = 50$$
$$3d = 45$$
$$d = 15$$
$$2d = 30$$

Reima's age now is 30 years.

Make sure you answer the question asked. In this question, after you obtain Dustin's age now, calculate Reima's age now.

## Coin Problems

A collection of 250 U.S. quarters and dimes has a total value of $40.00. How many quarters are in the collection?

*Note:* In coin problems, you must assume there are no rare coins in a collection.

You don't know the number of quarters or the number of dimes, so use two variables. Let $q$ = the number of quarters and $d$ = the number of dimes. Make a table to organize the information given.

| Denomination | Quarters | Dimes | Total |
|--------------|----------|-------|-------|
| Face Value per Coin | $0.25 | $0.10 | N/A |
| Number of Coins | $q$ | $d$ | 250 |
| Value of Coins | $0.25q | $0.10d | $40.00 |

Use the table to write two equations to represent the facts given. *Remember:* You need two equations when you have two variables.

$$q + d = 250$$
$$\$0.25q + \$0.10d = \$40.00$$

Solve the system, omitting the units for convenience.

(1) $q + d = 250$

(2) $0.25q + 0.10d = 40.00$

Solve equation (1) for $d$ and substitute the result into equation (2). Then solve for $q$.

(1) $d = 250 - q$

(2) $0.25q + 0.10(250 - q) = 40.00$

$$0.25q + 0.10(250 - q) = 40$$
$$0.25q + 25 - 0.10q = 40$$
$$0.15q + 25 = 40$$
$$0.15q = 15$$
$$q = 100$$

There are 100 quarters in the collection.

# Mixture Problems

A chemist has a 36% alcohol solution and a 90% alcohol solution. How many milliliters of each should be used to make 1,200 milliliters of a 72% alcohol solution?

You have two unknowns. Let $x$ = the number of milliliters of the 36% alcohol solution to be used, and let $y$ = the number of milliliters of the 90% alcohol solution to be used.

Make a table to organize the mixture information.

| When? | Percent Alcohol Strength | Number of Milliliters | Amount of Alcohol |
|---|---|---|---|
| Before mixing | 36% | $x$ | 36%$x$ |
| | 90% | $y$ | 90%$y$ |
| After mixing | 72% | 1,200 | 72%(1,200) |

Use the table to write two equations to represent the facts given.

$$x + y = 1,200$$
$$36\%x + 90\%y = 72\%(1,200)$$

The amount of alcohol before mixing equals the amount of alcohol after mixing.

Solve the system, changing percents to decimals before proceeding.

(1) $x + y = 1,200$

(2) $0.36x + 0.90y = 0.72(1,200)$

Solve equation (1) for $y$ and substitute the result into equation (2). Then solve for $x$.

(1) $y = 1,200 - x$

(2) $0.36x + 0.90(1,200 - x) = 0.72(1,200)$

$$0.36x + 0.90(1,200 - x) = 0.72(1,200)$$
$$0.36x + 1,080 - 0.90x = 864$$
$$-0.54x + 1,080 = 864$$
$$-0.54x = -216$$
$$x = 400$$
$$y = 1,200 - x = 1,200 - 400 = 800$$

Therefore, 400 milliliters of the 36% alcohol solution and 800 milliliters of the 90% alcohol solution should be used to make 1,200 milliliters of a 72% alcohol solution.

*Tip:* In mixture problems, the "before mixing" amount (or value) of a substance equals the "after mixing" amount (or value) of that substance.

# Distance-Rate-Time Problems

> A car and a truck leave the same location at the same time. The car travels due east at 70 miles per hour. The truck travels due west at 65 miles per hour. If the two vehicles continue to travel at their respective rates, in how many hours will the two vehicles be 405 miles apart?

The distance, $d$, a vehicle travels at a uniform rate of speed, $r$, for a given length of time, $t$, is $d = rt$.

There is one unknown. Let $t$ = the time in hours the two vehicles will be 405 miles apart. Make a table to organize the vehicle information. You might find a rough sketch helpful as well.

| Vehicle | Rate (in mph) | Time (in hours) | Distance (in miles) |
|---------|---------------|-----------------|---------------------|
| Car | 70 mph | $t$ | $70t$ |
| Truck | 65 mph | $t$ | $65t$ |
| Total | N/A | N/A | 405 miles |

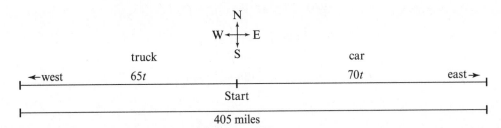

Write an equation that represents the facts given.

$$70t + 65t = 405 \text{ miles}$$

Solve the equation, omitting the units for convenience.

$$70t + 65t = 405$$
$$135t = 405$$
$$t = 3$$

In 3 hours the two vehicles will be 405 miles apart.

# Work Problems (Quick Solution Method for Two Workers)

> Working alone, machine A can make 500 units of a product in 4 hours. Working alone, machine B can make 500 units of the product in 3 hours. How long will it take both machines, working together, to make 500 units of the product?

In this problem, you have two machines that will work together to produce 500 units of a product. When you have two "workers" (in this case, the two machines) that can do the same job, a quick way to determine the time it will take them to do it together is to *multiply* their individual times, then divide this product by the *sum* of their individual times. *Tip:* Think "product over sum."

In the problem given, machine A's time working alone is 4 hours, and machine B's time working alone is 3 hours. Omitting units, their time working together is $\frac{(3)(4)}{3+4} = \frac{12}{7} = 1\frac{5}{7}$.

Working together, it will take the two machines $1\frac{5}{7}$ hours (or about 1 hour and 43 minutes) to make 500 units of the product.

*Tip:* Their time working together will be less than either of their times working alone.

## Consecutive Integer Problems

> The greatest of four consecutive integers is $-\frac{1}{3}$ times the sum of the other three integers. What is the value of the greatest integer?

*Tip:* For consecutive integer problems, let $n$ = the least integer, $n + 1$ = the next integer, and so on.

Let $n$ = the first integer (the least one), $n + 1$ = the second integer, $n + 2$ = the third integer, and $n + 3$ = the fourth integer (the greatest one).

Write and solve an equation that represents the facts given.

$$-\frac{1}{3}\left[(n)+(n+1)+(n+2)\right] = (n+3)$$

$$-\frac{1}{3}\left[n+n+1+n+2\right] = n+3$$

$$-\frac{1}{3}\left[3n+3\right] = n+3$$

$$-n-1 = n+3$$

$$-2n = 4$$

$$n = -2$$

$$n+3 = 1$$

The greatest of the four integers is 1.

For consecutive even or odd integers, let $n$ = the first integer, $n + 2$ = the second integer, $n + 4$ = the third integer, and so on.

*Tip:* If you know the sum of three consecutive integers, the middle integer is the sum divided by 3. For example, if the sum of three consecutive even integers is 102, the middle integer is $\frac{102}{3} = 34$, and the other two even integers are 32 and 36.

## Percentage Problems

Percentage problems use the formula $P = RB$ (or, equivalently, $RB = P$), where $P$ is the **percentage** (the portion of the whole), $R$ is the **rate** (the quantity with a % sign or the word *percent* attached), and $B$ is the **base** (the whole amount).

Here are examples.

> Sylvia works at a computer store that pays a commission rate of 3% to employees for all sales. Last week, Sylvia's sales totaled $4,500. What is Sylvia's commission for last week?

In this problem, Sylvia's commission is $P$, which is unknown, $R$ is 3%, and $B$ is \$4,500. Write and solve an equation that represents the facts, omitting the units for convenience.

$$P = RB$$
$$P = 3\%(4,500)$$
$$P = 0.03(4,500)$$
$$P = 135$$

Sylvia's commission for last week is \$135.

**Tip: Change percents to equivalent decimals or fractions to perform calculations. Or, if you prefer, you can use the $\boxed{x\%}$ key on the ETS graphing calculator.**

An online clothing store offers a 20% discount on orders during a one-day sale. Elyes gets \$24.80 off the price of a jacket during the sale. What is the original price of the jacket?

In this problem, the original price of the jacket is $B$, which is unknown, $R$ is 20%, and $P$ is \$24.80. Write and solve an equation that represents the facts, omitting the units for convenience.

$$RB = P$$
$$20\%(B) = 24.80$$
$$0.20B = 24.80$$
$$B = 124$$

The jacket's original price is \$124.

Moana pays a sales tax of \$7.60 at a restaurant on a meal that costs \$95.00. What is the sales tax rate for the purchase?

In this problem, the sales tax rate is $R$, which is unknown, $P$ is \$7.60, and $B$ is \$95.00. Write and solve an equation that represents the facts, omitting the units for convenience.

$$RB = P$$
$$R(95.00) = 7.60$$
$$95R = 7.60$$
$$R = 0.08$$
$$R = 8\%$$

The sales tax rate is 8%.

*Tip:* For convenience, when $P$ is unknown, write the formula as $P = RB$, but when $B$ or $R$ is unknown, write the formula as $RB = P$.

# A Note About Using the ETS Graphing Calculator to Solve Equations

This chapter presented algebraic methods for solving equations. You can solve equations that have real numerical zeros by using the Solver feature of the ETS graphing calculator. View a tutorial on using the Solver at http://www.infinitysw.com/exams/tutorials. The calculator's manual (available at http://infinitysw.s3.amazonaws.com/ets/ets_calculator_manual.pdf) has detailed information about the Solver. The manual explains that the Solver uses an iterative method that could take a significant amount of time to complete and might return inexact results. If an equation has multiple solutions (for example, a quadratic equation can have two solutions), the Solver will return only one of the solutions, the one that is closest to your guess and within the limits that you set. You also instead could use the Solve command that lets you input a variable equation that you want to solve.

Like Solver, the Solve command returns only one solution at a time, regardless of the number of solutions in the solution set. You should spend time practicing with Solver and the Solve command so that you can determine all solutions for equations you want to solve.

Another way to use the ETS graphing calculator to solve a one-variable equation is to put the equation in the form $y =$ expression and graph it. Then use modes from the Analysis menu (such as Trace/Evaluate, Zero, and Table) to determine $x$ values that correspond to $y$ values of zero. You can view a tutorial on analyzing a graph at http://www.infinitysw.com/exams/tutorials. Also, see the calculator manual for instructions.

> **Tip:** The ETS graphing calculator is a useful tool, but you need to make sure you can use its features correctly when you take the Praxis MS Math test. You should practice using them while you are working through this book.

# Sample Questions

**Directions:** Read the directions for each question carefully. This set of questions has several different question types. For each question, select a single answer choice unless written instructions preceding the question state otherwise.

**1.** $(3xy^3)(-2x^2y^4) =$

   Ⓐ   $-6x^2y^{12}$
   Ⓑ   $-6x^3y^7$
   Ⓒ   $x^3y^7$
   Ⓓ   $6x^3y^7$

**2.** Simplify $\dfrac{18x^2 + 54}{3x^2 + 6}$.

   Ⓐ   $15$
   Ⓑ   $6x + 9$
   Ⓒ   $\dfrac{6x^2 + 9}{x^2 + 1}$
   Ⓓ   $\dfrac{6x^2 + 18}{x^2 + 2}$

**For the following question, select <u>all</u> that apply.**

**3.** Which of the following is a factor of $2x^2 + x - 6$?

   Ⓐ   $x - 2$
   Ⓑ   $x + 2$
   Ⓒ   $2x - 3$
   Ⓓ   $2x + 3$

**4.** If $\dfrac{1}{2}x - 5 = 14$, what is the value of $3x - 1$?

   Ⓐ   $19$
   Ⓑ   $38$
   Ⓒ   $113$
   Ⓓ   $114$

**5.** What is the sum of the roots of $x^2 + x - 20 = 0$?

   Ⓐ   $-9$
   Ⓑ   $-1$
   Ⓒ   $1$
   Ⓓ   $9$

**For the following question, enter your numeric answer in the box below the question.**

**6.** What is the $y$ value of the ordered pair that is a solution to the system $\begin{array}{l} 2x-3y=12 \\ 4x+5y=2 \end{array}$ ?

$-2$

**For the following question, enter your fractional answer in the boxes below the question.**

**7.** What is the slope of the line that has equation $5x + 3y = 9$?

$\dfrac{-5}{3}$

**For the following question, enter your numeric answer in the box below the question.**

**8.** A candy store owner wants to mix candy that sells for $10 per pound with candy that sells for $5 per pound to make a 2-pound mixture to sell for $8 per pound. What percent of the mixture should come from the $10-per-pound candy so that the mixture is offered at a fair price?

[    ] %

# Answer Explanations

**1. B.** Follow the rule for multiplying two monomials.

$(3xy^3)(-2x^2y^4) = (3)(-2)(xy^3)(x^2y^4) = -6x^{1+2}y^{3+4} = -6x^3y^7$, choice B.

*Remember:* When you multiply variable factors, you *add* (not multiply) the exponents of like bases.

**2. D.** Follow the procedure for simplifying polynomials.

$\dfrac{18x^2+54}{3x^2+6} = \dfrac{18(x^2+3)}{3(x^2+2)} = \dfrac{6(x^2+3)}{(x^2+2)} = \dfrac{6x^2+18}{x^2+2}$, choice D.

**3. B, C.** Factor $2x^2 + x - 6$ into the product of two binomials by using F.O.I.L. in reverse.

$2x^2 + x - 6 = (x + 2)(2x - 3)$, choices B and C.

*Tip:* After factoring, mentally multiply the two factors to check your work.

**4. C.** First, use the procedure for solving linear equations to solve $\dfrac{1}{2}x - 5 = 14$.

$$\frac{1}{2}x - 5 = 14$$

$$\frac{1}{2}x - 5 + 5 = 14 + 5$$

$$\frac{1}{2}x = 19$$

$$\frac{\cancel{2}}{1} \cdot \frac{1}{\cancel{2}}x = 2 \cdot 19$$

$$x = 38$$

Next, substitute 38 for $x$ in $3x - 1$ and evaluate: $3(38) - 1 = 113$, choice C.

*Tip:* After you determine $x$, remember to calculate $3x - 1$.

**5. B.** First, solve the quadratic equation $x^2 + x - 20 = 0$ using a convenient method.

$$x + x - 20 = 0$$

$$(x + 5)(x - 4) = 0$$

$$(x + 5) = 0 \text{ or } (x - 4) = 0$$

$$x = -5 \text{ or } x = 4$$

Next, sum the two roots: $-5 + 4 = -1$, choice B.

**6.** **−2** Solve the system $\begin{aligned} (1) \ \ & 2x - 3y = 12 \\ (2) \ \ & 4x + 5y = 2 \end{aligned}$ using a convenient method. Be clever! Given you want to determine the $y$ value, solve by eliminating the $x$ variable.

Multiply equation (1) by −2 and add the resulting equation to equation (2). Then solve for $y$.

$$
\begin{aligned}
(1) \quad & -4x + 6y = -24 \\
(2) \quad & \underline{4x + 5y = 2} \\
& 0 + 11y = -22 \\
& 11y = -22 \\
& y = -2
\end{aligned}
$$

**7.** $-\dfrac{5}{3}$ The slope of $Ax + By = C$ is $-\dfrac{A}{B}$. Thus, the slope of $5x + 3y = 9$ is $-\dfrac{5}{3}$.

**8.** **60** This question is a mixture problem. First, determine the amount of $10-per-pound candy in the mixture. Next, determine the percent of the mixture that should come from the $10-per-pound candy. Let $x$ = the amount (in pounds) of $10-per-pound candy in the mixture and $y$ = the amount (in pounds) of $5-per-pound candy in the mixture.

Make a table to organize the mixture information.

| When? | Price per Pound | Amount in Pounds | Value |
|---|---|---|---|
| Before mixing | $10 | $x$ | $10x$ |
| | $5 | $y$ | $5y$ |
| After mixing | $8 | 2 pounds | $8(2) |

Use the table to write two equations to represent the facts given.

$$x + y = 2 \text{ pounds}$$
$$\$10x + \$5y = \$8(2)$$

*Tip:* The value of the candy before mixing equals the value after mixing.

Solve the system, omitting the units for convenience.

$$
\begin{aligned}
(1) \ \ & x + y = 2 \\
(2) \ \ & 10x + 5y = 8(2)
\end{aligned}
$$

Solve equation (1) for $y$ and substitute the result into equation (2). Then solve for $x$.

$$
\begin{aligned}
(1) \ \ & y = 2 - x \\
(2) \ \ & 10x + 5(2 - x) = 8(2)
\end{aligned}
$$

$$
\begin{aligned}
10x + 5(2 - x) &= 8(2) \\
10x + 10 - 5x &= 16 \\
5x + 10 &= 16 \\
5x &= 6 \\
x &= 1.2
\end{aligned}
$$

The amount of $10-per-pound candy in the mixture is 1.2 pounds (lb). This amount represents $\dfrac{1.2 \ \cancel{\text{lb}}}{2 \ \cancel{\text{lb}}} = 0.6 = 60\%$ of the total mixture.

# Chapter 3

# Functions and The

This chapter provides a review of key ideas and d
you to know for the Praxis MS Math test. Sample
Praxis MS Math test, are given at the end of the
provided immediately following.

## Basic Function Concept

For this topic, you must demonstrate an ability t

### Ordered Pairs and Relation

An **ordered pair** of numbers, denoted $(x, y)$, is a
is written first in the ordered pair, and the other
**component** (or $x$-coordinate), and $y$ is the **second**
only if they have *exactly* the same coordinates in the same order, that is, $(a, b)$
$d$. The set consisting of all possible ordered pairs of real numbers is denoted $R \times R$, or simply $R^2$. A **relation** $\Re$ in
$R^2$ is any subset of $R^2$. The set consisting of all the first components in the ordered pairs contained in $\Re$ is the
**domain** of $\Re$, and the set of all second components is the **range** of $\Re$.

### xy-Coordinate Plane

Graphically, $R^2$ is represented by the **xy-coordinate plane.** Here is an illustration.

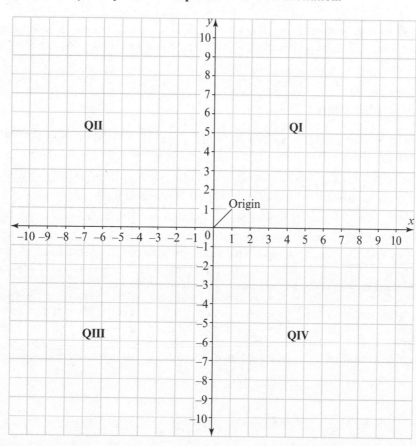

Two intersecting real number lines form the a
tion to the right is commonly designated th
commonly designated the *y*-axis. Their
into four **quadrants.** The Roman num
the upper right quadrant and proc

Every ordered pair, $(x, y)$, of r
nate plane has a location d
**coordinates** of the point

## Definitio

A **function** i
compon
but di
Th

**xes** of the coordinate plane. The **horizontal axis** with positive direc-
...e **x-axis,** and the **vertical axis** with positive direction upward is
...point of intersection is the **origin.** The axes divide the coordinate plane
...erals I, II, III, and IV name the quadrants. The numbering process starts in
...eeds counterclockwise.

...eal numbers defines a point in the coordinate plane, and every point in the coordi-
...fined by an ordered pair, $(x, y)$, of real numbers. The numbers $x$ and $y$ are the

## ...n and Representations of a Function

...s a set of ordered pairs for which each first component is paired with *one and only one* second
...ent. In other words, a function is a relation in which no two ordered pairs have the same first component
...fferent second components; that is, if $(a, b)$ and $(a, d)$ are ordered pairs in the same function, then $b = d$.
...us, the ordered pairs $(1, 2)$ and $(2, 3)$ can both be elements of the same function, but the ordered pairs $(1, 2)$
...nd $(1, 3)$ cannot.

Single letters, such as $f$ and $g$, are commonly used as names for functions. For the function $f$, the ordered pairs are
written $(x, f(x))$ or $(x, y)$, where $y = f(x)$. You read the function notation $f(x)$ as "$f$ of $x$."

Functions are represented in various ways. If a function consists of a *finite* number of ordered pairs, you can
define the function by listing or showing its ordered pairs in a set, in a table, as an arrow diagram, or as a graph
in a coordinate plane. You also might define the function by giving a rule or an equation. When the number of
ordered pairs is *infinite,* more often than not the function is defined by either an equation or a graph. *Note:* In
this book, equations that define functions will use only real numbers as coefficients or constants.

In the function defined by $y = f(x)$, $x$ is the **independent variable** and $y$ is the **dependent variable.** The variable $y$ is
"dependent" on $x$ in the sense that you substitute a value of $x$, called an **argument** of $f$, into $y = f(x)$ to find $y$, the
value of $f$ at $x$ (also called the **image** of $x$ under $f$).

Two functions $f$ and $g$ are equal, written $f = g$, if and only if their domains are equal and $f(x) = g(x)$ for all $x$ in
their common domain. (See "Domain and Range of Functions" on the next page for a discussion of the domain
of a function.)

## Evaluating Functions

Think of a function as a process $f$ that takes an input number $x$ and produces from it the output number $y = f(x)$.
That is, $f(\text{input}) = \text{output}$. Here are examples.

For every input, $x$, the function defined by $y = 2x + 1$ produces exactly one output, $y$. When $x = -5$, $y =$
$2(-5) + 1 = -10 + 1 = -9$; when $x = 3$, $y = 2(3) + 1 = 6 + 1 = 7$; and so forth.

For every input, $x$, the function defined by $f(x) = x^2$ produces exactly one output, $f(x)$. When $x = -2$, $f(-2)$
$= (-2)^2 = 4$; when $x = 2$, $f(2) = (2)^2 = 4$; and so forth. Notice in this example that the output for the input
$-2$ is the same as the output for the input 2. That is, the ordered pairs $(-2, 4)$ and $(2, 4)$ are both in the
function defined by $f(x) = x^2$. This situation is permissible in a function. It's okay that the outputs of
distinct ordered pairs are the same, as long as their inputs are different.

*Note:* Although, by definition, a function $f$ is a set of ordered pairs, it is commonplace to refer to the equation
that defines a function as the function; that is, to speak of "the function $y = 2x + 1$" or "the function "$f(x) = x^2$.""

**Evaluating a function** means finding the corresponding output for a given input. Here are examples.

When $f(x) = 8x - 13$, $f\left(\dfrac{3}{4}\right) = 8\left(\dfrac{3}{4}\right) - 13 = 6 - 13 = -7$.

When $g(x) = \dfrac{2x+3}{x-1}$, $x \neq 1$, $g(5a+1) = \dfrac{2(5a+1)+3}{(5a+1)-1} = \dfrac{10a+2+3}{5a+1-1} = \dfrac{10a+5}{5a} = \dfrac{2a+1}{a}$, $a \neq 0$.

# Domain and Range of Functions

The set of possible $x$ values for a function $f$ is the **domain** of $f$, denoted $D_f$, and the set of possible $y$ values is the **range** of $f$, denoted $R_f$. In a real-valued function, the range consists of real numbers.

*Note:* The functions on the Praxis MS Math test are real-valued functions. Hereafter in this book, all functions are real-valued functions.

When a function $f$ is defined by an equation $y = f(x)$ and no domain is specified, the domain of $f$ is the largest possible subset of the real numbers for which each $x$ value gives a corresponding $y$ value that is a *real* number. To determine the domain, start with the set of real numbers and exclude all values for $x$, if any, that would make the equation undefined over the real numbers. If $y = f(x)$ contains a rational expression, to avoid division by zero, exclude values for $x$, if any, that would make a denominator zero. If $y = f(x)$ contains a radical with an *even* index, to avoid even roots of negative numbers, exclude all values for $x$, if any, that would cause the expression under the radical to be negative.

> **Tip: Division by zero and even roots of negative numbers are the two types of domain problems that you are most likely to encounter on the Praxis MS Math test.**

You can determine the range of $f$ in a manner similar to that used to find the domain of $f$ if you can first solve the equation $y = f(x)$ explicitly for $x$. Otherwise, analyze $y = f(x)$ for insight into the possible values of $y$.

Here are examples of finding the domain and range of a function.

> Determine the domain, $D_f$, and the range, $R_f$, for the function $f$ defined by $y = \dfrac{1}{x-3}$.

When $x = 3$, the rational expression $\dfrac{1}{x-3}$ is $\dfrac{1}{0}$, which is undefined. Therefore, the number 3 is excluded from $D_f$.

For every real number $x$, except 3, the quantity $\dfrac{1}{x-3}$ is a real number. Thus, the domain of $f$ consists of all real numbers except 3, written $D_f = \{x \mid x \neq 3\}$.

To determine the range of $f$, solve $y = \dfrac{1}{x-3}$ explicitly for $x$ to obtain $x = \dfrac{1+3y}{y}$. For every real number $y$, except 0, the quantity $\dfrac{1+3y}{y}$ is a real number. So, the range of $f$ consists of all real numbers except 0, written $R_f = \{y \mid y \neq 0\}$.

> **Tip: The ETS graphing calculator can be helpful if you need to determine a function's domain and/or range while taking the Praxis MS Math test. A tutorial for graphing functions using the on-screen graphing calculator is available at http://www.infinitysw.com/exams/tutorials. When using the graphing calculator to explore a function, use trial and error and the Zoom feature to find a good viewing window of its graph; otherwise, you might be misled by the graph displayed.**

Here is the graph of $y = \dfrac{1}{x-3}$. For your reference, a dashed vertical line has been constructed at $x = 3$. Observe that the graph is composed of a portion to the left of $x = 3$ and a portion to the right of $x = 3$. The graph never crosses the dashed vertical line at $x = 3$, meaning that 3 is excluded from $D_f$. Also, the graph never crosses the $x$-axis, meaning that $y$ is never zero. These observations affirm that $D_f = \{x \mid x \neq 3\}$ and $R_f = \{y \mid y \neq 0\}$.

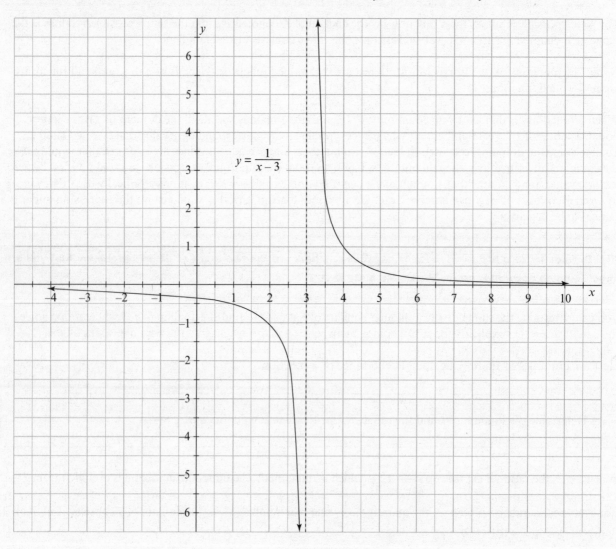

$$y = \frac{1}{x-3}$$

Determine the domain and range of the function $g$ defined by $g(x) = \sqrt{x-5} + 2$.

When $x - 5 < 0$, the expression $\sqrt{x-5}$ is the square root of a negative number, so it is not defined over the real numbers. However, for every real number $x$ for which $x - 5 \geq 0$, the quantity $\sqrt{x-5}$ is a real number. Therefore, the domain of $g$ is all real numbers such that $x - 5 \geq 0$; therefore, $D_g = \{x \mid x \geq 5\}$. For all real numbers $x$, the quantity $\sqrt{x-5}$ is nonnegative. So, $y = g(x) = \sqrt{x-5} + 2 \geq 2$. Therefore, $R_g = \{y \mid y \geq 2\}$.

Here is the graph of $g(x) = \sqrt{x-5} + 2$. For your reference, a dashed horizontal line has been constructed at $y = 2$. Observe that the graph starts at $x = 5$, meaning that $x$ is always greater than or equal to 5, and that it remains at or above the horizontal line $y = 2$, meaning that $y$ is always greater than or equal to 2. These observations affirm that $D_g = \{x \mid x \geq 5\}$ and $R_g = \{y \mid y \geq 2\}$.

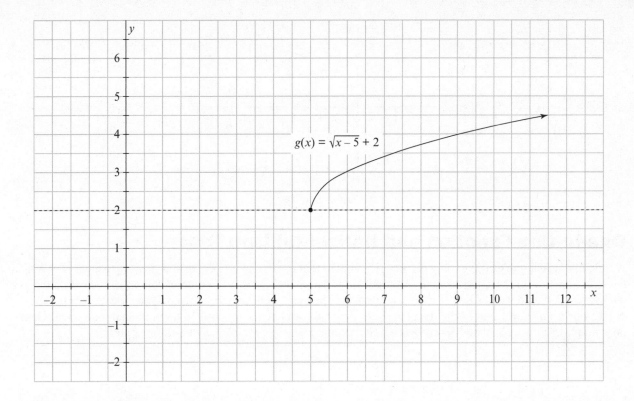

# Graphs of Functions

Because a function is a set of ordered pairs, its graph can be plotted in a coordinate plane. Each ordered pair is represented by a point in the plane. The **graph** of a function $f$ is the set of all ordered pairs $(x, y)$ for which $x$ is in the domain of $f$ and $y = f(x)$. The graph of a function is a visual representation of its solutions, the set of ordered pairs that make the statement $y = f(x)$ true.

> **Tip:** A graphing calculator is an indispensable tool when you are exploring graphs of functions. Most graphing calculators require that you enter the equation of the graph in the form $y = f(x)$. This form excludes graphs of relations that are not functions (such as graphs of circles, ellipses, and so on). For such relations, break the equation into two parts, so that each part defines a function, and then graph the two parts on the same coordinate grid.

# Vertical Line Test

**Vertical line test:** A relation is a function if any vertical line in the plane intersects the graph of the relation in no more than one point. By definition, each element in the domain of a function is paired with exactly one element in the range. Thus, if a vertical line can be drawn so that it cuts the graph of a relation in more than one point, the relation is not a function. Here is an example of a relation that does *not* pass the vertical line test, so it is *not* a function. There are two points on the graph that correspond to $x = 2$, namely $(2, 1.7)$ and $(2, -1.7)$.

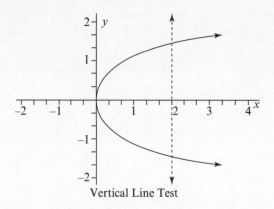

Vertical Line Test

# One-to-One Function and Horizontal Line Test

A function $f$ is **one-to-one** if and only if $f(a) = f(b)$ implies that $a = b$; that is, if $(a, c)$ and $(b, c)$ are elements of $f$, then $a = b$. In a one-to-one function, each first component is paired with *exactly one* second component *and* each second component is paired with *exactly one* first component. Therefore, you have the **horizontal line test:** A function is one-to-one if any horizontal line in the plane intersects the graph of the function in no more than one point. Here is an example of a function that does *not* pass the horizontal line test, so it is *not* a one-to-one function.

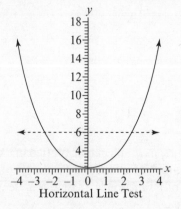

Horizontal Line Test

# Increasing-Decreasing-Constant Behavior

Suppose a function $f$ is defined over an interval. Then the following are true:

- $f$ is increasing on the interval if, for every pair of numbers $x_1$ and $x_2$ in the interval, $f(x_1) < f(x_2)$ whenever $x_1 < x_2$.
- $f$ is decreasing on the interval if, for every pair of numbers $x_1$ and $x_2$ in the interval, $f(x_1) > f(x_2)$ whenever $x_1 < x_2$.
- $f$ is constant on the interval if $f(x_1) = f(x_2)$ for every pair of numbers $x_1$ and $x_2$ in the interval.

Thus, a function is increasing on an interval if its graph moves upward from left to right as the independent variable assumes values from left to right in the interval. A function is decreasing on an interval if its graph moves downward from left to right as the independent variable assumes values from left to right in the interval. A function is constant on an interval if the function value stays the same as the independent variable assumes values from left to right in the interval.

# Monotonic Function

A function is **monotonic** if, on its entire domain, the function is either only increasing or only decreasing. A monotonic increasing or decreasing function is **one-to-one.** Here is an example.

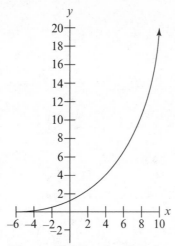

Monotonic Increasing Function

# Positive and Negative Behavior

A function $f$ is positive on an interval if its graph lies above the $x$-axis for all $x$ values in the interval; similarly, a function $f$ is negative on an interval if its graph lies below the $x$-axis for all $x$ values in the interval. Here is an example.

Describe the positive and negative behavior of the function $f$ shown that crosses the $x$-axis at $(-1, 0)$, $(0, 0)$, $(2, 0)$, and $(3, 0)$.

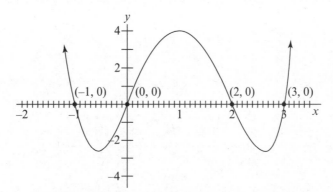

Positive and Negative Behavior of the Function $f$

The function $f$ is positive in the intervals $(-\infty, -1)$, $(0, 2)$, and $(3, \infty)$, and negative in the intervals $(-1, 0)$ and $(2, 3)$.

**Tip: Do not misread open interval notation as representing ordered pairs. The context of the notation should serve to remove the ambiguity. See "Intervals and Interval Notation" in Chapter 1 for a review of this topic.**

# Even and Odd Functions

A function is even if for every $x$ in $D_f$, $-x$ is in $D_f$ and $f(-x) = f(x)$. A function is odd if for every $x$ in $D_f$, $-x$ is in $D_f$ and $f(-x) = -f(x)$. The graphs of even functions are symmetric about the $y$-axis. The graphs of odd functions are symmetric about the origin. Here are examples.

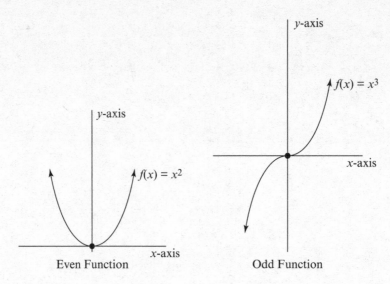

Even Function  Odd Function

*Note:* Many functions are neither even nor odd. Their graphs show no symmetry with respect to either the *y*-axis or the origin.

# Zeros and Intercepts

A **zero** of a function $f$ is a solution to the equation $f(x) = 0$. It is an input value that produces a zero output value. The zeros are determined by finding all values $x$ for which $f(x) = 0$. For example, 2 and $-2$ are zeros of the function $f$ defined by $f(x) = x^2 - 4$ because $f(2) = (2)^2 - 4 = 4 - 4 = 0$ and $f(-2) = (-2)^2 - 4 = 4 - 4 = 0$.

An ***x*-intercept** of the graph of a function is the *x*-coordinate of a point at which the graph intersects the *x*-axis, and the ***y*-intercept** is the *y*-coordinate of the point at which the graph intersects the *y*-axis. See the following figure.

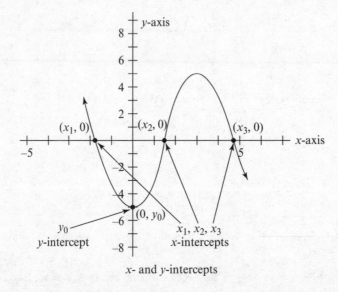

*x*- and *y*-intercepts

The graph of a function has at most *one y*-intercept. A function $f$ cannot have more than one *y*-intercept because, by definition, each *x* value in the domain of $f$ is paired with *exactly one y* value in the range. If 0 is in the domain of $f$, then $f(0)$ is the *y*-intercept of the graph of $f$. To determine the *y*-intercept, if any, of a function $f$, let $x = 0$, provided that 0 is in the domain of $f$, and then solve $f(0) = y$ for $y$.

A graph can have many *x*-intercepts, or it might not have any. To determine the *x*-intercept(s), if any, for a function $f$, set $f(x) = 0$ and then solve for $x$. The *x*-intercepts, if any, are the real zeros of $f$. You can describe a **real zero** of a function as one of the following: an *x*-intercept for the graph of $y = f(x)$, a real number $x$ for which $f(x) = 0$, or a real root of the equation $f(x) = 0$. See "Polynomial Functions" later in this chapter for an illustration of the zeros of a function.

# Composition and Inverses of Fun

For this topic, you must be able to determine the composition of two fun
function in simple cases, and understand that only one-to-one functions ha

## Composition of Functions

The **composition**, denoted $f \circ g$ (read "$f$ of $g$"), of two functions $f$ and $g$ is the function defined by
$(f \circ g)(x) = f(g(x))$ where the range of $g$, $R_g$, is a subset of the domain of $f$, $D_f$.

Here are examples.

> If $f = \{(-3, -5), (-2, -4), (0, -5), (1, 3), (2, 0), (4, 7)\}$ and $g = \{(-4, 8), (-3, -8), (-2, -3), (0, 1), (1, 4)\}$, find
> **(a)** $f \circ g$ and **(b)** $g \circ f$ and, if possible, evaluate **(c)** $(f \circ g)(1)$, **(d)** $(g \circ f)(-3)$, **(e)** $(f \circ g)(-4)$, and
> **(f)** $(g \circ f)(2)$.

**(a)** $f \circ g = \{(-2, -5), (0, 3), (1, 7)\}$

**(b)** $g \circ f = \{(-2, 8), (2, 1)\}$

**(c)** $(f \circ g)(1) = f(g(1)) = f(4) = 7$

**(d)** $(g \circ f)(-3) = g(f(-3)) = g(-5) = $ undefined because $-5$ is not in the domain of $g$.

**(e)** $(f \circ g)(-4) = f(g(-4)) = f(8) = $ undefined because $8$ is not in the domain of $f$.

**(f)** $(g \circ f)(2) = g(f(2)) = g(0) = 1$

> Given $f(x) = 3x$ and $g(x) = x^2$, find **(a)** $(f \circ g)(x)$ and **(b)** $(g \circ f)(x)$.

**(a)** $(f \circ g)(x) = f(g(x)) = 3(g(x)) = 3x^2$

**(b)** $(g \circ f)(x) = g(f(x)) = (f(x))^2 = (3x)^2 = 9x^2$

## Inverses of Functions

If the function $f$ is a one-to-one function, its **inverse**, denoted $f^{-1}$ (read "$f$ inverse"), is the function such that
$(f^{-1} \circ f)(x) = x$ for all $x$ in the domain of $f$ and $(f \circ f^{-1})(x) = x$ for all $x$ in the domain of $f^{-1}$, and $R_{f^{-1}} = D_f$ and
$R_f = D_{f^{-1}}$. Graphically, $f^{-1}$ is a reflection of $f$ over the line $y = x$.

y a set of ordered pairs is one-to-one, then $f^{-1}$ may be found by interchanging $x$ and $y$ in airs of $f$. For example, if $f = \{(-1, 2), (3, 5), (6, -1)\}$, then $f^{-1} = \{(2, -1), (5, 3), (-1, 6)\}$.

e function $f$ is defined by an equation, two ways you can find the equation of $f^{-1}$ are as follows:

ve $\left(f \circ f^{-1}\right)(x) = x$ for $f^{-1}(x)$. Here is an example.

ven $y = f(x) = 3x$, find $f^{-1}(x)$.

lve $\left(f \circ f^{-1}\right)(x) = x$ for $f^{-1}(x)$.

$$(f \circ f^{-1})(x) = x$$
$$f\left(f^{-1}(x)\right) = x$$
$$3f^{-1}(x) = x$$
$$f^{-1}(x) = \frac{x}{3}$$

**Method 2.** First, in $y = f(x)$, replace $x$ with $y$ and $y$ with $x$, and then solve $x = f(y)$ for $y$. Here is an example.

Given $y = f(x) = 3x$, find $f^{-1}(x)$.

First, interchanging $x$ and $y$ gives $x = 3y$. Next, solving for $y$ gives $\frac{x}{3} = y$ or $y = \frac{x}{3}$.

Only one-to-one functions have inverses that are functions. Therefore, when a function $f$ is not one-to-one, it might be possible to restrict its domain so that $f$ is one-to-one in the **restricted domain.** Then, $f$ will have an inverse function in the restricted domain.

# Features of Common Functions

This section presents features of common functions including their defining equations, domains and ranges, zeros, and intercepts.

## Linear Functions

**Linear functions** are defined by equations of the form $y = mx + b$. The domain for all linear functions is $R$, the set of real numbers. When $m \neq 0$, the range is $R$. When $m = 0$, the range is the set $\{b\}$, containing the single value $b$.

The graph of a linear function $f$ defined by $y = mx + b$ is always a nonvertical line with slope $m$ and $y$-intercept $b$. When $m \neq 0$, the graph has exactly one $y$-intercept, which is $b$, and exactly one $x$-intercept, which is $-\frac{b}{m}$. Thus, the points $(0, b)$ and $\left(-\frac{b}{m}, 0\right)$ are contained in the graph. The only zero is the real number $-\frac{b}{m}$; thus, the graph crosses the $x$-axis at the point $\left(-\frac{b}{m}, 0\right)$. If $m > 0$, $f$ is increasing; if $m < 0$, $f$ is decreasing. The following figure shows the graph of the linear function $y = -\frac{1}{2}x + 6$ that has slope of $-\frac{1}{2}$, $y$-intercept of 6, and $x$-intercept of 12.

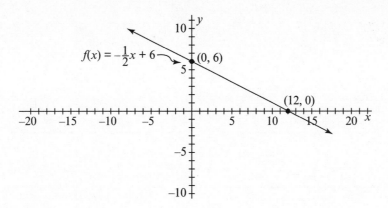

*Note:* The equation $y = mx + b$ is the **slope-intercept** form of the equation of a line. Every linear equation $Ax + By = C$ ($B \neq 0$) determines a linear function. (See the section "The Equation of a Line" in Chapter 2 for an additional discussion of linear equations.)

The **identity function** is the linear function defined by the equation $y = x$. It is called the identity function because it matches each $x$ value with an identical $y$ value. The domain and range are both $R$, the set of real numbers. The graph has slope of 1. The graph passes through the origin, so both the $x$- and $y$-intercepts are zero. The only zero is $x = 0$.

**Constant functions** are linear functions defined by equations of the form $y = b$, where $b \in R$. The domain is the set $R$ of real numbers, and the range is the set $\{b\}$ containing the single element $b$. The slope is zero. Constant functions either have no zeros or infinitely many zeros according to the following guideline: If $b \neq 0$, they have no zeros; if $b = 0$, every real number $x$ is a zero. The graph of a constant function is a horizontal line that is $|b|$ units above or below the $x$-axis when $b \neq 0$ and coincident with the real axis when $b = 0$.

**Directly proportional functions** are linear functions defined by equations of the form $y = kx$, where $k$ is the non-zero **constant of proportionality.** A function is a directly proportional function when the output is equal to the input multiplied by a constant. The domain and range are both $R$, the set of real numbers. The graph has slope $k$. The graph passes through the origin, so both the $x$- and $y$-intercepts are zero. The only zero is $x = 0$.

Here are examples of linear functions.

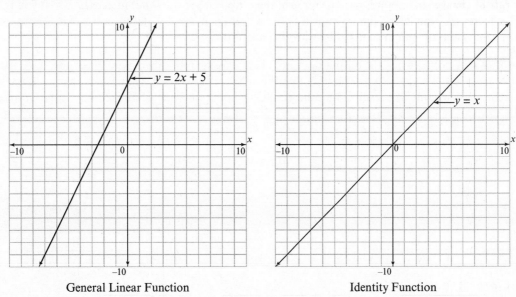

General Linear Function                    Identity Function

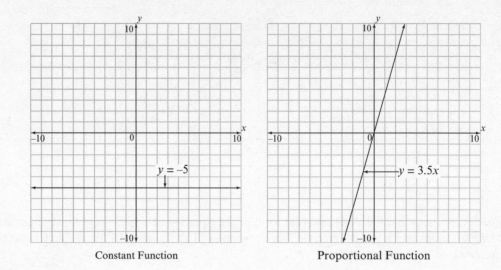

Constant Function                    Proportional Function

# Rate of Change

The slope $m$ of a linear function's graph is the function's **rate of change.** Because the slope of a line is constant, a linear function's rate of change is constant over the entire graph. The rate of change describes how the output changes in relation to the input. For every 1-unit change in the input, there are $m$ units of change in the output. If the input changes by $k$ units, the output changes by $km$ units.

For example, for the function $y = 2x + 5$, for every 1-unit change in $x$, there is a 2-unit change in $y$.

In general, if $(x_1, y_1)$ and $(x_2, y_2)$ are any two distinct ordered pairs in a linear function's graph, the function's rate of change is $m = \dfrac{\text{change in } y}{\text{change in } x} = \dfrac{y_2 - y_1}{x_2 - x_1}$. Rates of change can be positive, negative, or zero.

A **positive rate of change** corresponds to an increase in the output when the input increases. When you trace the input, $x$, as it increases from left to right, you will observe that the output, $y$, increases from lower to higher values. The result is that the graph slants upward from left to right.

A **negative rate of change** corresponds to a decrease in the output when the input increases. When you trace the input, $x$, as it increases from left to right, you will observe that the output, $y$, decreases from higher to lower values. The result is that the graph slants downward from left to right.

A **zero rate of change** occurs when the output does not change as the input increases. When you trace the input, $x$, as it increases from left to right, you will observe that the value of the output, $y$, does not change. That is, the output's value remains constant. The result is that the graph is a horizontal line. Here are graphical examples.

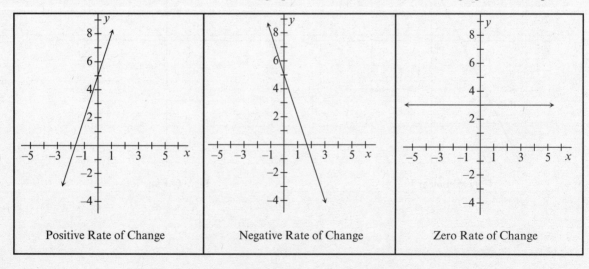

Positive Rate of Change          Negative Rate of Change          Zero Rate of Change

Therefore, linear functions are either increasing, decreasing, or remaining constant, from left to right, at a steady rate. Their graphs do not change direction.

# Quadratic Functions

**Quadratic functions** are defined by equations of the form $y = ax^2 + bx + c$, $(a \neq 0)$. The domain is the set $R$ of real numbers, and the range is a subset of $R$. The zeros are the roots of the quadratic equation $ax^2 + bx + c = 0$. The quantity $b^2 - 4ac$ is the **discriminant** of the quadratic equation. It determines three cases for the zeros of the quadratic function:

- If $b^2 - 4ac > 0$, the quadratic function has two real *unequal* zeros.
- If $b^2 - 4ac = 0$, the quadratic function has one real zero (double root).
- If $b^2 - 4ac < 0$, the quadratic function has no real zeros.

The graph of $f(x) = ax^2 + bx + c$ is a parabola. The vertex is $\left( -\dfrac{b}{2a}, f\left( -\dfrac{b}{2a} \right) \right)$. When $a > 0$, the parabola opens upward and the $y$-coordinate of the vertex is an absolute minimum of $f$. When $a < 0$, the parabola opens downward and the $y$-coordinate of the vertex is an absolute maximum of $f$. The parabola is symmetric about its axis of symmetry, a vertical line, with the equation $x = -\dfrac{b}{2a}$, through its vertex that is parallel to the $y$-axis.

Depending on the solution set of $ax^2 + bx + c = 0$, the graph of a quadratic function might or might not intersect the $x$-axis. Three cases occur:

- If there are *two* real *unequal* roots, the parabola will intersect the $x$-axis at those *two* points.
- If there is exactly *one* real root, the parabola will intersect the $x$-axis at only that *one* point.
- If there are no real roots, the parabola will *not* intersect the $x$-axis.

Here are examples of quadratic functions defined by $y = ax^2 + bx + c$ with $a > 0$.

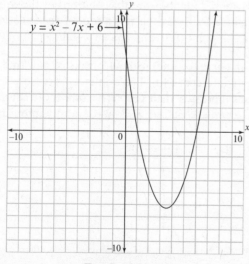

Two Real Zeros

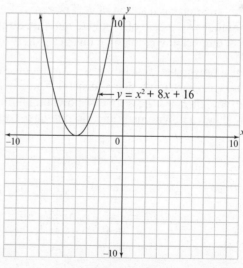

One Real Zero

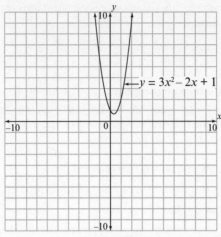

No Real Zeros

The **standard form** for the equation of a parabola that opens upward or downward is $y = a(x - h)^2 + k$ $(a \neq 0)$ with vertex $(h, k)$. Any quadratic function can be put in standard form by using the process of **completing the square.** (See the section "Solving Quadratic Equations by Completing the Square" in Chapter 2 for a discussion on completing the square.)

# Polynomial Functions

**Polynomial functions** are defined by equations of the form $y = P(x) = a_n x^n + a_{n-1} x^{n-1} + a_{n-2} x^{n-2} + \ldots + a_1 x^1 + a_0$, with **leading coefficient** $a_n \neq 0$. The degree of the polynomial is $n$, a nonnegative integer. Linear and quadratic functions are polynomial functions of degree one and two, respectively. A constant polynomial function, defined by $P(x) = c$ (a nonzero constant), has degree zero. The degree of the zero polynomial function, defined as $P(x) = 0$, is undefined.

The domain of a polynomial function is the set $R$ of real numbers. If $n$ is odd, the polynomial function has range $R$. If $n$ is even, the range is a subset of $R$. The zeros of a polynomial function are the solutions of the equation $P(x) = 0$. A number $r$ is a zero of a polynomial function $P$ defined by $y = P(x)$ if it is a root of the equation $P(x) = 0$. If $r$ is a real number, the graph of $P$ intersects the $x$-axis at the point $(r, 0)$ and has an $x$-intercept at $r$.

The graph of a polynomial function $P$ is a continuous smooth curve (or line) with no breaks of any kind; moreover, it has no cusps (meaning sharp corners). The graph has $y$-intercept $P(0)$. The $x$-intercepts correspond to the real zeros (if any) of $P$. As the degree of polynomial functions increases, their graphs become more complex. The graph below shows a polynomial function that has zeros (and $x$-intercepts) $-1$, $0$, $2$, and $3$, and $y$-intercept $0$.

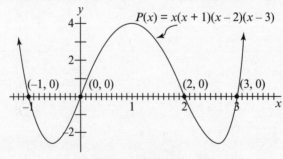

Graph of $P(x) = x(x + 1)(x - 2)(x - 3)$

Useful theorems to know about polynomial functions are the following:

- **Intermediate Value Theorem for Polynomials:** If $a$ and $b$ are real numbers such that $P(a)$ and $P(b)$ have opposite signs, then $P$ has at least one zero between $a$ and $b$.
- **Factor Theorem:** $P(r) = 0$ if and only if $x - r$ is a factor of the polynomial $P(x)$. Thus, you can factor $P(x)$ by determining the zeros of $P$; conversely, you can determine the zeros of $P$ by factoring $P(x)$. For example, for

the cubic equation $P(x) = x^3 - 2x^2 - x + 2$, you have $P(-1) = (-1)^3 - 2(-1)^2 - (-1) + 2 = -1 - 2 + 1 + 2 = 0$, $P(1) = (1)^3 - 2(1)^2 - (1) + 2 = 1 - 2 - 1 + 2 = 0$, and $P(2) = (2)^3 - 2(2)^2 - (2) + 2 = 8 - 8 - 2 + 2 = 0$. Thus, by the factor theorem, you know that $x - (-1) = x + 1$, $x - 1$, and $x - 2$ are factors of $P(x) = x^3 - 2x^2 - x + 2$.

- **Remainder Theorem:** If a polynomial $P(x)$ is divided by $x - a$, the remainder is $P(a)$. For example, you can use synthetic division to show that when $5x^3 - 2x + 3$ is divided by $x - 2$, the remainder is 39 (see Appendix B for an explanation of synthetic division). Thus, by the remainder theorem, $P(2) = 39$.

- **Complex Conjugate Rule:** If $P(x)$ has real coefficients, and $a + bi$, $(b \neq 0)$, is a complex zero of $P(x)$, then its complex conjugate $a - bi$ is also a zero of $P(x)$. Thus, if $(x - 2i)$ is a zero of $x^3 + x^2 + 4x + 4$, then $(x + 2i)$ is also a zero.

- **Descartes' Rule of Signs:** If $P(x)$ has real coefficients and is written in descending (or ascending) powers of $x$, then the number of positive real roots of $P(x) = 0$ is either the number of sign changes, from left to right, occurring in the coefficients of $P(x)$, or it is less than this number by an even number. Similarly, the number of negative real roots of $P(x) = 0$ is either the number of sign changes, from left to right, occurring in the coefficients of $P(-x)$, or it is less than this number by an even number. *Note:* When using this rule, ignore missing powers of $x$. For example, $P(x) = x^3 - 2x^2 - x + 2$ has two sign changes and $P(-x) = -x^3 - 2x^2 + x + 2$ has one sign change. Therefore, $P(x) = x^3 - 2x^2 - x + 2$ has 2 or 0 positive real roots and 1 negative real root.

- **Fundamental Theorem of Algebra:** Over the complex numbers, every polynomial of degree $n \geq 1$ has at least one root. It follows that, if you allow complex roots and count a root again each time it occurs more than once, every polynomial of degree $n$ has exactly $n$ roots. Thus, every linear function (except for constant functions) has exactly one root, every quadratic function has exactly two roots, and so on. This theorem guarantees that for every polynomial function $P$ of degree $n \geq 1$, there exist complex zeros $r_1, r_2, \ldots,$ and $r_n$, so that you can factor $P(x)$ completely as $P(x) = a_n(x - r_1)(x - r_2) \ldots (x - r_n)$, where $a_n$ is the leading coefficient of $P(x)$. In general, a zero $r$ of a polynomial function $P$ has **multiplicity $k$,** meaning it occurs as a zero exactly $k$ times, if $(x - r)^k$ is a factor of $P(x)$ and $(x - r)^{k+1}$ is not a factor of $P(x)$. Hence, the $n$ zeros of a polynomial function $P$ are not necessarily all different from each other. For example, 3 is a zero of multiplicity 2 for the second degree polynomial function $P$ defined by $P(x) = x^2 - 6x + 9 = (x - 3)(x - 3)$.

> **Tip:** Go to http://www.infinitysw.com/exams/tutorials to view a tutorial on using the ETS graphing calculator's Solver tool or the Solve command to solve equations. You can use the Solver tool or the Solve command to find real zeros of a function by solving $P(x) = 0$. Be careful. The Solver tool and the Solve command return only one value at a time for the solution set. For $P(x) = 0$, each determines the real zero closest to a guess you input or within an interval specified by you. Neither will return complex zeros. Use your knowledge of the concepts discussed in this section to make sure you determine the correct number of zeros and their values.

# Square Root Functions

**Square root functions** are defined by equations of the form $y = \sqrt{ax + b}$. The domain is the set $\{x \mid x$ is a real number for which $ax + b \geq 0\}$. The range is the set $\{y \mid y$ is a real number, $y \geq 0\}$. There is one zero at $x = -\dfrac{b}{a}$. The graph is nonnegative. Here is an example of a square root function.

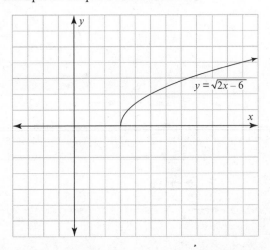

$y = \sqrt{2x - 6}$

# Absolute Value Functions

**Absolute value functions** are defined by equations of the form $y = |ax + b|$. The domain is the set $R$ of real numbers, and the range is the set $\{y \mid y \text{ is a real number, } y \geq 0\}$. There is one zero at $x = -\dfrac{b}{a}$, and the $y$-intercept is at $|b|$.

Technically, the absolute value function is a **piecewise function** because you can write it as $y = \begin{cases} ax + b & \text{if } x \geq -\dfrac{b}{a} \\ -(ax + b) & \text{if } x < -\dfrac{b}{a} \end{cases}$.

Here is an example of an absolute value function.

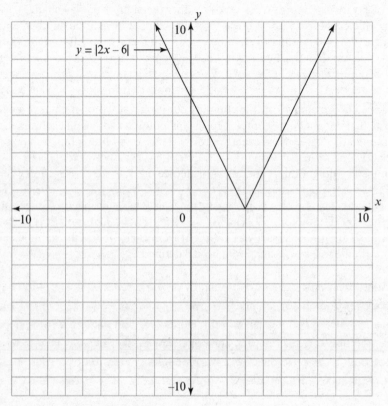

# Greatest Integer Functions

The **greatest integer function** is defined by $y = f(x) = [\![x]\!]$, where the brackets denote to find the greatest integer less than or equal to $x$. The domain is the set $R$ of real numbers, and the range is the set of integers. The zeros lie in the interval $[0, 1)$.

Here is an example.

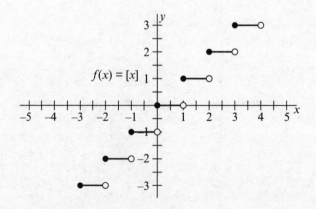

# Exponential Functions

**Exponential functions** are defined by equations of the form $y = b^x$ ($b \neq 1$, $b > 0$), where $b$ is the **base** of the exponential function. The domain is the set $R$ of real numbers, and the range is the set $\{y \mid y > 0\}$, which is to say $b^x > 0$ for every real number $x$. The graph of the function does not cross the $x$-axis, so there are no zeros. The graph of $y = b^x$ passes through the points $(0, 1)$ and $(1, b)$ and is located in the first and second quadrants only. It never crosses the $x$-axis.

The following figure shows the graph of the exponential function $f(x) = 2^x$.

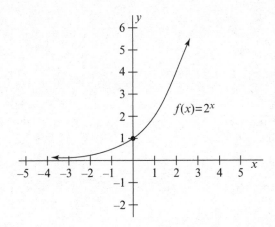

Two important exponential functions are $y = 10^x$, with base 10, and $y = e^x$, the **natural exponential function,** with base $e$, the irrational number whose rational decimal approximation is 2.718281828 (to nine digits).

# Transformations

Adding or subtracting a positive constant $k$ to $f(x)$ is a **vertical shift.** Adding or subtracting a positive constant $h$ to $x$ is a **horizontal shift.** Vertical and horizontal shifts are summarized in the following table:

**Vertical and Horizontal Shifts**

| Type of Change | Effect on $y = f(x)$ |
|---|---|
| ($h, k$ both positive) | |
| $y = f(x) + k$ | Vertical shift: $k$ units up |
| $y = f(x) - k$ | Vertical shift: $k$ units down |
| $y = f(x + h)$ | Horizontal shift: $h$ units to left |
| $y = f(x - h)$ | Horizontal shift: $h$ units to right |

Multiplying $f(x)$ by $k > 1$ enlarges or **stretches** the graph of $f$. Multiplying $f(x)$ by $0 < k < 1$ reduces or **shrinks** the graph of $f$. The graph of $y = -f(x)$ is a **reflection** of $y = f(x)$ over the $x$-axis. Here are illustrations using the quadratic function $y = x^2$.

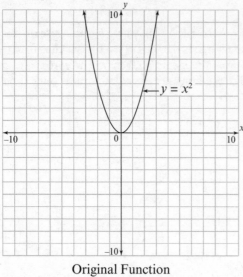

Original Function

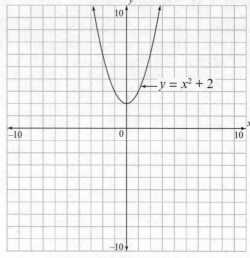

Vertical Shift 2 Units Up

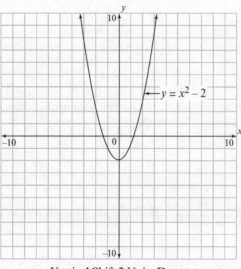

Vertical Shift 2 Units Down

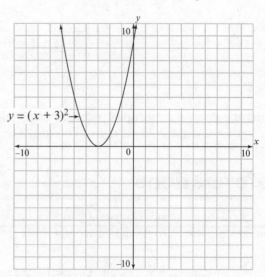

Horizontal Shift 3 Units Left

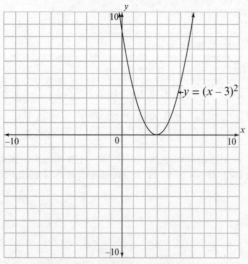

Horizontal Shift 3 Units Right

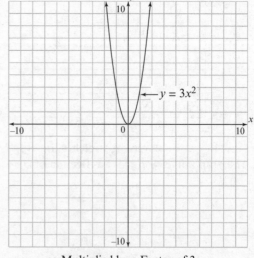

Multiplied by a Factor of 3

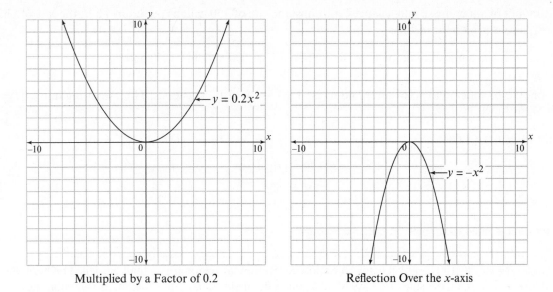

Multiplied by a Factor of 0.2          Reflection Over the x-axis

*Note:* For a general discussion of geometric transformations, see "Geometric Transformations" in Chapter 4.

# Functions as Mathematical Models

Families of functions (for example, the families of linear functions, quadratic functions, step functions, exponential functions, and so on) are used to model phenomena in the real world.

Linear functions model processes in which the rate of change is constant. For example, in science a linear function can be used to model the distance a moving object travels at a constant rate of speed as a function of time or to model the volume occupied by a sample of gas at a constant pressure as a function of its absolute temperature.

Quadratic functions model processes that involve a maximum or a minimum value. For example, in business a quadratic function can be used to model the profit or revenue of a company as a function of the number of units sold.

Step functions model processes that increase or decrease in increments but remain constant over fixed intervals. For example, a step function can be used to model the cost of postage for a letter or package as a function of the weight of the letter or package.

Exponential functions model processes that grow or decline rapidly. For example, they are used to model physical phenomena such as population growth and population decay as a function of time. This family of functions is also used in business for determining the growth of money as a function of time when interest is compounded at a fixed rate.

Here are examples.

---

A water tank that holds 1,000 gallons of water is one-fourth full. Suppose water is added to the tank at a constant rate of 150 gallons per hour. Let $f(t)$ be the amount of water (in gallons) in the tank after $t$ hours.

**(a)** What is the rate of change of the function $f$?

**(b)** What is the amount of water in the tank at time $t = 0$?

**(c)** Write a formula for $f(t)$.

**(d)** At what time $t$ will the water tank be filled to capacity?

---

**(a)** The amount of water in the tank changes at a constant rate of 150 gallons per hour. Thus, the rate of change of *f* is 150 gallons per 1 hour of time.

**(b)** At time $t = 0$, the initial amount of water in the tank is $\frac{1}{4}(1{,}000 \text{ gallons}) = 250$ gallons.

**(c)** The amount of water in the tank after *t* hours is $\left(150\dfrac{\text{gallons}}{\text{hour}}\right)t + 250$ gallons. Thus, omitting units, $f(t) = 150t + 250$, a linear function.

**(d)** Find *t* when $f(t) = 1{,}000$.

$$1{,}000 = 150t + 250$$
$$750 = 150t$$
$$5 = t$$

The water tank is filled to capacity at time $t = 5$ hours.

---

A homeowner has 100 feet of fencing to enclose a rectangular region for a small garden. The homeowner will use a portion of the side of a large shed as one side of the rectangular region, as shown in the following figure.

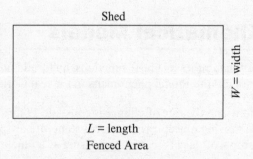

Shed

$W$ = width

$L$ = length

Fenced Area

Let $f(W)$ be the area of the rectangular region expressed in terms of its width, $W$.

**(a)** Write a formula for $f(W)$.

**(b)** Find the dimensions of the rectangular region that give the maximum area for the garden.

---

**(a)** Let $W$ = the width (in feet) and $L$ = the length (in feet) of the rectangular region. The fence does not go along the shed, so (omitting units) $100 = 2W + L$, which implies that $L = 100 - 2W$. The area of the rectangular region equals length times width. Thus, $f(W) = (100 - 2W)W = 100W - 2W^2 = -2W^2 + 100W$, a quadratic function.

**(b)** The graph of $f(W)$ is a parabola opening downward. The vertex formula is $\left(-\dfrac{b}{2a}, f\left(-\dfrac{b}{2a}\right)\right)$, so the maximum value for $f(W)$ occurs when $W = -\dfrac{b}{2a} = -\dfrac{100}{2(-2)} = 25$. The corresponding value of $L = 100 - 2W = 100 - 2 \cdot 25 = 100 - 50 = 50$. The dimensions that maximize the area are 50 feet by 25 feet.

# Sample Questions

**Directions:** Read the directions for each question carefully. This set of questions has several different question types. For each question, select a single answer choice unless written instructions preceding the question state otherwise.

**For the following question, select __all__ that apply.**

1. Which of the following sets of ordered pairs represents a function?

   - Ⓐ $\{(4, 5), (2, 1), (2, 10), (-2, 0)\}$
   - Ⓑ $\{(4, 5), (4, 5^2), (4, 5^3), (4, 5^4)\}$
   - Ⓒ $\{(2, 3), (4, 3), (8, 3), (16, 3)\}$
   - Ⓓ $\{(-2, 4), (-4, 16), (2, 4), (4, 16)\}$

2. Which of the following sets is the domain of the function defined by $y = \dfrac{x-5}{x^2-6x+9}$?

   - Ⓐ $\{x \mid x \text{ is a real number, } x \neq 5\}$
   - Ⓑ $\{x \mid x \text{ is a real number, } x \neq -3\}$
   - Ⓒ $\{x \mid x \text{ is a real number, } x \neq 3\}$
   - Ⓓ $\{x \mid x \text{ is a real number}\}$

3. Given the cubic function $f(x) = x^3$, which of the following best describes the function $g(x) = (x-3)^3 + 8$?

   - Ⓐ the same as the graph of $f(x) = x^3$ shifted right by 3 units and up by 8 units
   - Ⓑ the same as the graph of $f(x) = x^3$ shifted left by 3 units and up by 8 units
   - Ⓒ the same as the graph of $f(x) = x^3$ shifted right by 3 units and down by 8 units
   - Ⓓ the same as the graph of $f(x) = x^3$ shifted left by 3 units and down by 8 units

**For the following question, enter your numeric answer in the box below the question.**

4. If $f(x) = 16x^3 - 4x^2 + 6x - 15$, then what is the value of $f\left(-\dfrac{1}{2}\right)$?

$\boxed{-21}$

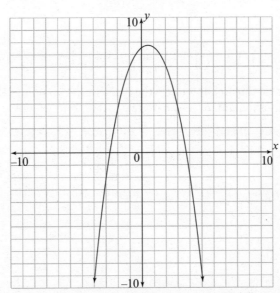

5. A quadratic function $f(x) = ax^2 + bx + c$ has the graph shown. Which of the statements about the discriminant of $f(x) = 0$ is true?

   - Ⓐ $b^2 - 4ac < 0$
   - Ⓑ $b^2 - 4ac = 0$
   - Ⓒ $b^2 - 4ac > 0$
   - Ⓓ $b^2 - 4ac$ is undefined

$= a(0)^2 + b(0) + c \qquad \dfrac{\pm\sqrt{b^2 - 4ac}}{2a}$

$= 0 + 0 + c$

**For the following question, enter your numeric answer in the box below the question.**

6. What is the $x$-intercept of the graph of $5x - 3y = 45$?

$$\boxed{\phantom{xxxxxxxxxxxx}}$$

# Answer Explanations

1. **C, D.** In a function, each first component is paired with *one and only one* second component. Only the ordered pairs in choices C and D satisfy this requirement. In choice A, the first component 2 is paired with two different second components, 1 and 10. In choice B, the first component 4 is paired with four different second components.

2. **C.** The domain of the function defined by $y = \dfrac{x-5}{x^2 - 6x + 9}$ excludes any value of $x$ that makes the denominator equal zero. Set $x^2 - 6x + 9 = 0$ and solve for $x$.

$$x^2 - 6x + 9 = 0$$
$$(x - 3)^2 = 0$$
$$x = 3$$

Thus, the domain is the set $R$ of real numbers excluding $x = 3$, choice C.

3. **A.** Subtracting 3 from $x$ will result in a horizontal shift of 3 units to the right. Adding 8 to $f(x)$ will result in a vertical shift of 8 units up. Thus, the graph of $g(x) = (x - 3)^3 + 8$ is the same as the graph of $f(x) = x^3$ shifted right by 3 units and up by 8 units, choice A.

   *Tip:* If you are unsure whether the shift is to the right or left or up or down, graph the two functions on the ETS graphing calculator to check.

4. **−21**

$$f\left(-\frac{1}{2}\right) = 16\left(-\frac{1}{2}\right)^3 - 4\left(-\frac{1}{2}\right)^2 + 6\left(-\frac{1}{2}\right) - 15 = 16\left(-\frac{1}{8}\right) - 4\left(\frac{1}{4}\right) + 6\left(-\frac{1}{2}\right) - 15 = -2 - 1 - 3 - 15 = -21$$

5. **C.** The graph of the quadratic function intersects the real axis at two points, indicating the function has two real zeros. Therefore, the discriminant, $b^2 - 4ac$, is greater than zero, choice C.

6. **9** To find the $x$-intercept, set $y = 0$ and solve for $x$.

$$5x - 3(0) = 45$$
$$5x = 45$$
$$x = 9$$

This chapter provides a review of key ideas and formulas of geometry that are important for you to know for the Praxis MS Math test. Sample questions, comparable to what might be presented on the Praxis MS Math test, are given at the end of the chapter. The answer explanations for the sample questions are provided immediately following.

## Congruence, Similarity, and Symmetry

**Congruent** (symbolized by ≅) geometric figures have exactly the same size and same shape. They are superimposable, meaning that they will fit exactly on top of each other. Corresponding parts of congruent figures are congruent, and thereby, have the same measure. Here are examples of congruent figures.

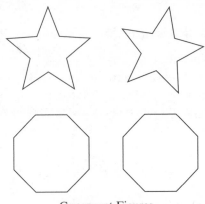

Congruent Figures

Hash marks (as shown in the following figure) can be used to draw attention to corresponding congruent parts. *Tip:* Congruent parts have the same number of strokes.

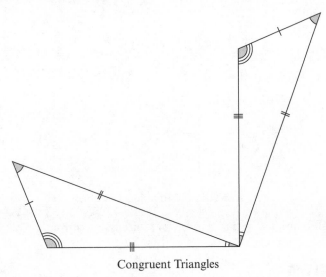

Congruent Triangles

*Note:* See "Geometric Transformations" in this chapter for an additional discussion of *congruence*.

**Similar** (symbolized by ~) geometric figures have the same shape, but not necessarily the same size. Corresponding angles of similar shapes are congruent, and corresponding lengths of similar shapes are proportional. Here are examples of similar figures. Notice that congruent figures are also similar figures, but similar figures are not necessarily congruent.

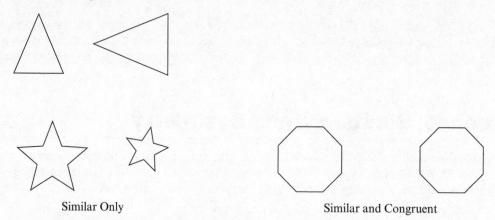

Similar Only                              Similar and Congruent

*Note:* See "Geometric Transformations" in this chapter for an additional discussion of *similarity*.

**Symmetry** describes a characteristic of the shape of a figure or object. A figure has **reflective** (or **bilateral**) **symmetry** if it can be folded exactly in half and the resulting two parts are congruent. The line along the fold is the **line of symmetry.** A figure has **rotational symmetry** if it can be rotated onto an exact copy of itself before it comes back to its original position. The center of rotation is called the **center of symmetry.** Here are examples.

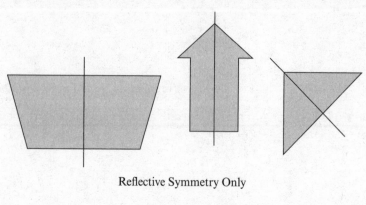

Reflective Symmetry Only

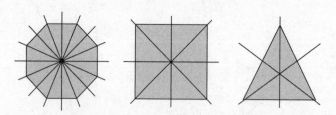

Both Reflective and Rotational Symmetry

*Note:* See "Geometric Transformations" in this chapter for a discussion of *rotation* of geometric figures.

# Angles and Lines

In geometry, the terms *point, line,* and *plane* are undefined. Think of a point as a location in space. Think of a line as a set of points that extends infinitely in both directions. Think of a plane as a set of points that form a flat infinite surface. For discussions in this chapter, unless specifically stated otherwise, all figures and objects are considered to lie in the same plane.

# Angles

A **ray** is a portion of a line extending infinitely in one direction from a point. $\overrightarrow{AB}$ is the ray that starts at $A$, goes through $B$, and continues on.

When two rays meet at a common point, they form an **angle.** The point where the rays meet is the angle's **vertex** (the plural of *vertex* is *vertices*) and the rays are its **sides.** The symbol for angle is $\angle$.

You measure an angle with reference to a circle with its center as the vertex of the angle. The amount of rotation required to form the angle can be expressed as a number of **degrees.** The symbol for degrees is °. A full rotation around the circle is 360°. An angle that turns $\frac{1}{360}$ of a complete rotation around the circle measures 1°. A counterclockwise rotation results in a positive measure. A clockwise rotation results in a negative measure.

The number of degrees in an angle is its **measure.** If there are $k$ degrees in angle $A$, then you write $m\angle A = k°$. An **acute angle** measures between 0° and 90°; that is, if angle $A$ is acute, $0° < m\angle A < 90°$. An **obtuse angle** measures between 90° and 180°; that is, if angle $B$ is obtuse, $90° < m\angle B < 180°$. A **right angle** measures exactly 90°; that is, if angle $C$ is a right angle, $m\angle C = 90°$. A **straight angle** measures exactly 180°; that is, if angle $D$ is a straight angle, $m\angle D = 180°$. Here are examples.

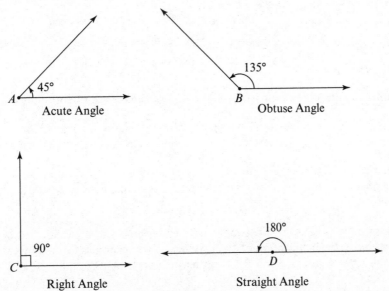

Acute Angle    Obtuse Angle

Right Angle    Straight Angle

**Tip: The box in the corner of $\angle C$ denotes a right angle.**

Two angles whose measures sum to 90° are **complementary angles.** Each angle is the other angle's **complement.** Two angles whose measures sum to 180° are **supplementary angles.** Each angle is the other angle's **supplement.** **Adjacent angles** are angles that have a common vertex and a common side. Here are examples.

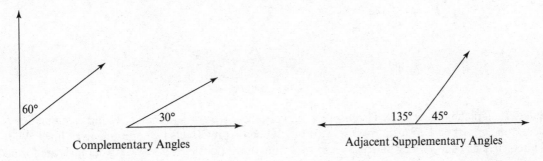

Complementary Angles    Adjacent Supplementary Angles

A **bisector of an angle** is a line or ray that passes through the vertex of the angle and divides it into two congruent angles. Here is an example.

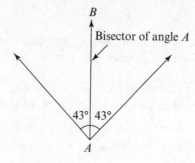

Following are theorems about angles that are useful to know.

- Two angles that are complementary are both acute.
- Two angles that are both congruent and supplementary are both right angles.
- Complements of congruent angles are congruent.
- Supplements of congruent angles are congruent.

# Lines

The notation $\overleftrightarrow{PQ}$ denotes the line containing the points $P$ and $Q$ and extending infinitely in both directions.

A **line segment** $\overline{PQ}$ is a part of a line that connects the points $P$ and $Q$ and includes $P$ and $Q$. The points $P$ and $Q$ are the segment's **endpoints.** Its length is denoted $PQ$. Congruent segments have equal lengths.

Two lines in a plane can be the *same line, parallel lines,* or *intersecting lines*. Two lines are the **same** if they have all points in common. **Parallel** lines have no points in common. **Intersecting** lines cross at exactly one point in the plane.

Two intersecting lines form four angles. **Vertical angles** are two *nonadjacent* angles formed by the two intersecting lines with a common vertex at the intersection of the two lines. Vertical angles formed by two intersecting lines are congruent. In the following figure, $\angle 1$ and $\angle 3$ are congruent vertical angles and $\angle 2$ and $\angle 4$ are congruent vertical angles.

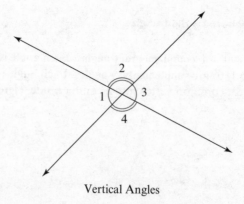

Vertical Angles

**Parallel lines** (in a plane) never meet. The distance between them is always the same. To indicate that line $l$ is parallel to line $m$, write $l \parallel m$. A **transversal** is a straight line that intersects two or more given lines. When two parallel lines, such as $l$ and $m$ shown here, are cut by a transversal (labeled $n$ below), eight angles are formed.

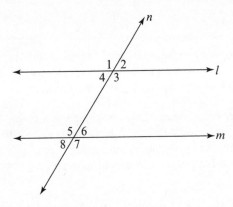

The **interior angles** are ∠3, ∠4, ∠5, and ∠6. The **exterior angles** are ∠1, ∠2, ∠7, and ∠8. The **corresponding angles** are the pair of angles ∠1 and ∠5, the pair of angles ∠2 and ∠6, the pair of angles ∠4 and ∠8, and the pair of angles ∠3 and ∠7. The **alternate exterior angles** are the pair of angles ∠1 and ∠7 and the pair of angles ∠2 and ∠8. The **alternate interior angles** are the pair of angles ∠4 and ∠6 and the pair of angles ∠3 and ∠5.

**Perpendicular lines** intersect at right angles. To indicate that line *l* is perpendicular to line *m*, write $l \perp m$. The **perpendicular bisector** of a line segment is the set of all points in the plane of the line segment that are equidistant from the endpoints of the line segment. In the figure shown, line *m* is the perpendicular bisector of line segment $\overline{AB}$.

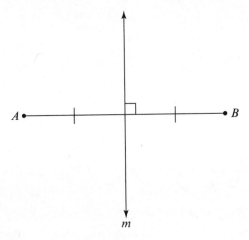

Following are theorems about lines that are useful to know.

- **Euclid's Parallel Postulate:** Given a line and a point in the same plane but not on the line, there is one and only one line through the given point that is parallel to the given line.
- If two parallel lines are cut by a transversal, then any pair of corresponding angles, alternate exterior angles, or alternate interior angles are congruent.
- Two lines that are cut by a transversal are parallel if any pair of corresponding angles, alternate exterior angles, or alternate interior angles are congruent.
- Two lines that are cut by a transversal are parallel if a pair of interior angles on the same side of the transversal are supplementary.
- Two distinct lines (in a plane) that are perpendicular to the same line are parallel.
- A line in a plane that is perpendicular to one of two parallel lines is perpendicular to the other parallel line.
- A line in a plane that intersects one of two parallel lines in exactly one point intersects the other parallel line.
- The shortest distance from a point to a line is the length of the perpendicular line segment from the point to the line.
- If one angle of two intersecting lines is a right angle, then all four of the angles formed by the two lines are right angles.

# Polygons

A **polygon** is a simple, closed, plane figure composed of line segments, fitted end to end. The segments meet only at their endpoints, and no two segments with a common endpoint are collinear. The segments are the polygon's **sides.** The point at which the two sides of a polygon intersect is a **vertex.**

Polygons are classified by the number of sides they have. A **triangle** is a three-sided polygon. A **quadrilateral** is a four-sided polygon. A **pentagon** is a five-sided polygon. A **hexagon** is a six-sided polygon. A **heptagon** is a seven-sided polygon. An **octagon** is an eight-sided polygon. A **nonagon** is a nine-sided polygon. A **decagon** is a ten-sided polygon. In general, an **n-gon** is an $n$-sided polygon. A **regular polygon** is a polygon for which all sides and angles are congruent.

An $n$-sided polygon has $n$ interior angles and $n$ exterior angles. An **interior angle** of a polygon is formed at a vertex by two adjacent sides and lies within the polygon. The sum of the measures of the interior angles of an $n$-sided polygon equals $(n-2)180°$. An **exterior angle** of a polygon is formed at a vertex by one side of the polygon and the extension of the adjacent side. The sum of the measures of a polygon's exterior angles equals $360°$, no matter how many sides the polygon has. *Note:* It is possible to draw two congruent exterior angles at each vertex of a polygon, but only one is considered when speaking of the exterior angle at a particular vertex. Here is an illustration of an interior and exterior angle of a pentagon.

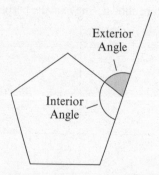

A line segment that connects two nonconsecutive vertices of a polygon is called a **diagonal.** The number of diagonals of an $n$-sided polygon is $\dfrac{n(n-3)}{2}$. Here are examples of regular polygons with the number of diagonals indicated below the figure.

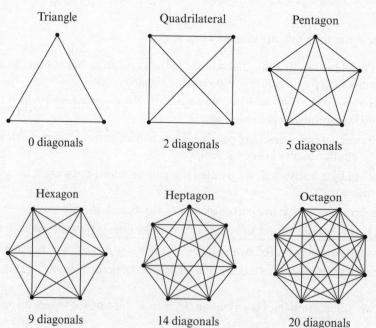

If all the diagonals of a polygon lie within the interior of the polygon, the polygon is **convex;** otherwise, the polygon is **concave.** Here are examples.

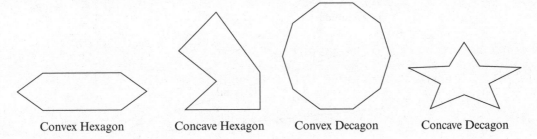

Convex Hexagon    Concave Hexagon    Convex Decagon    Concave Decagon

# Triangles

A **triangle** is a three-sided polygon. For this topic, you must demonstrate an understanding of properties of triangles.

## Classifying Triangles

You can classify triangles according to their sides as scalene, isosceles, or equilateral. A **scalene** triangle has no two sides congruent. An **isosceles** triangle has at least two congruent sides, and the angles opposite the congruent sides are called the **base angles.** An **equilateral** triangle has three congruent sides. Here are examples.

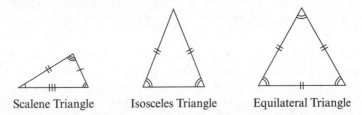

Scalene Triangle    Isosceles Triangle    Equilateral Triangle

You can classify triangles according to the measures of their interior angles. The sum of the measures of the interior angles of a triangle is 180°. An **acute** triangle has three acute interior angles. A **right** triangle has exactly one right interior angle. An **obtuse** triangle has exactly one obtuse interior angle. Here are examples.

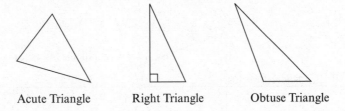

Acute Triangle    Right Triangle    Obtuse Triangle

## Altitudes, Medians, Perpendicular Bisectors, and Angle Bisectors

An **altitude** of a triangle is a perpendicular line segment from a vertex to a line containing the opposite side, called the **base.** The **height** of a triangle is the length of the altitude. *Note:* The term *altitude* is sometimes used to mean the *height* of the triangle, rather than the line segment that determines the height. On the Praxis MS Math test, you will be able to tell from the context of the problem what meaning is intended for the term *altitude.* Every triangle has three altitudes, one from each vertex. The lines containing the altitudes of a triangle are **concurrent,** meaning they intersect in a point. Here is an illustration.

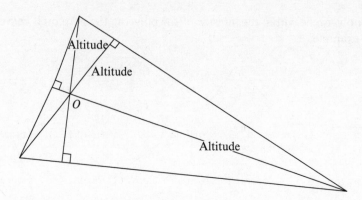

A **median** of a triangle is a line segment connecting a vertex of the triangle to the midpoint of the side opposite that vertex. The lines containing the medians of a triangle are concurrent, and their point of concurrency is two-thirds of the way along each median, from the vertex to the opposite side. Here is an illustration.

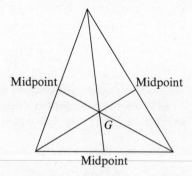

A **perpendicular bisector** of the side of a triangle is a line perpendicular to that side at its midpoint. The perpendicular bisectors of the sides of a triangle are concurrent, and their point of concurrency is equidistant from the vertices of the triangle. Therefore, if a circle is circumscribed about the triangle, the point where the perpendicular bisectors meet is the center of the circumscribed circle. A circle that is **circumscribed** about a triangle passes through the triangle's three vertices and contains the entire triangle in its interior. Here is an illustration.

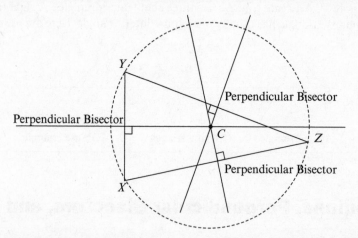

The **angle bisectors** of the interior angles of a triangle are concurrent, and their point of concurrency is equidistant from the three sides. Thus, if a circle is inscribed in a triangle, the point where the angle bisectors meet is the center of the inscribed circle. A circle that is **inscribed** in a triangle touches each side of the triangle in only one point and is the largest circle contained entirely within the triangle's interior. Here is an illustration.

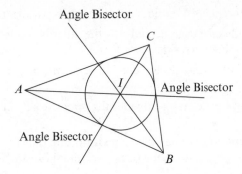

# Congruent Triangles

**Congruent triangles** are triangles for which corresponding sides and corresponding angles are congruent. You can use the following theorems to prove two triangles are congruent.

- If three sides of one triangle are congruent, correspondingly, to three sides of another triangle, then the two triangles are congruent (**SSS**).
- If two sides and the included angle of one triangle are congruent, correspondingly, to two sides and the included angle of another triangle, then the two triangles are congruent (**SAS**).
- If two angles and the included side of one triangle are congruent, correspondingly, to two angles and the included side of another triangle, then the two triangles are congruent (**ASA**).
- If two angles and the nonincluded side of one triangle are congruent, correspondingly, to two angles and the nonincluded side of another triangle, then the two triangles are congruent (**AAS**).

**Tip: Two methods that do NOT work for proving congruence are AAA (three corresponding angles congruent) and SSA (two corresponding sides and the *nonincluded* angle congruent).**

(See "Geometric Transformations" in this chapter for an additional discussion of *congruence*.)

# Similar Triangles

**Similar triangles** are triangles for which corresponding sides are proportional and corresponding angles are congruent. You can use the following theorems to prove two triangles are similar.

- If corresponding angles of two triangles are congruent, the two triangles are similar.
- If corresponding sides of two triangles are proportional, the two triangles are similar.
- If two angles of one triangle are congruent to two corresponding angles of another triangle, then the two triangles are similar.
- If two sides of one triangle are proportional to two corresponding sides of another triangle, and the included angles are congruent, then the two triangles are similar.

# Other Theorems About Triangles

Here are other theorems about triangles that are useful to know.

- **Triangle inequality:** The sum of the measures of any two sides of a triangle must be greater than the measure of the third side. Essentially, for a triangle to exist, the length of the longest side must be shorter than the sum of the lengths of the other two sides.
- The measure of an exterior angle of a triangle equals the sum of the measures of the nonadjacent (remote) interior angles.

- The segment between the midpoints of two sides of a triangle is parallel to the third side and half as long.
- A line that is parallel to one side of a triangle and cuts the other two sides in distinct points cuts off segments that are proportional to these two sides.
- A line that intersects two sides of a triangle and cuts off segments proportional to these two sides is parallel to the third side.
- The bisector of an interior angle of a triangle divides the opposite side in the ratio of the sides that form the angle bisected.
- If two sides of a triangle are congruent, then the angles opposite those sides are congruent. Conversely, if two angles of a triangle are congruent, then the sides opposite those angles are congruent.
- The ratio of the perimeters of two similar triangles is the same as the ratio of any two corresponding sides.
- The ratio of the areas of two similar triangles is the square of the ratio of any two corresponding sides.

# Right Triangles

In a right triangle the side opposite the right angle is the **hypotenuse** of the right triangle. The hypotenuse is *always* the longest side of the right triangle. The other two sides are called the **legs** of the right triangle. Commonly, the letter $c$ is used to represent the hypotenuse of a right triangle and the letters $a$ and $b$ to represent the legs. Here is an illustration.

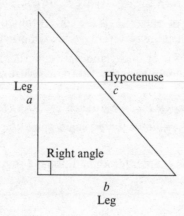

# The Pythagorean Theorem

A special relationship, named after the famous Greek mathematician Pythagoras, exists between the sides of a right triangle. This special relationship is the **Pythagorean theorem,** which states that $c^2 = a^2 + b^2$. The Pythagorean theorem applies only to right triangles. If you know any two sides of a right triangle, you can find the third side by using the formula $c^2 = a^2 + b^2$. Here is an example.

> Find the hypotenuse of a right triangle that has legs 8 centimeters and 15 centimeters.

Substitute into the formula, omitting the units for convenience, and solve for $c$.

$$c^2 = a^2 + b^2$$
$$c^2 = 8^2 + 15^2$$
$$c^2 = 64 + 225$$
$$c^2 = 289$$
$$c = \sqrt{289}$$
$$c = 17$$

Thus, $c = 17$ centimeters.

*Tip:* The number 289 has two square roots, 17 and –17. The negative value is discarded because the length of the hypotenuse (or any side of a triangle) cannot be negative.

The converse of the Pythagorean theorem also is true. If the measures of the three sides of a triangle satisfy the Pythagorean theorem, the triangle is a right triangle. To be precise: If the square of the length of the longest side of a triangle equals the sum of the squares of the lengths of the other two sides, the triangle is a right triangle.

For example, a triangle with sides of lengths 3, 4, and 5 is a right triangle because $3^2 + 4^2 = 9 + 16 = 25 = 5^2$. The numbers (3, 4, 5) are a **Pythagorean triple,** so called because they are natural numbers that satisfy the relation $a^2 + b^2 = c^2$. Other well-known Pythagorean triples are (5, 12, 13) and (8, 15, 17).

After you identify a Pythagorean triple, any multiple of the three numbers is also a Pythagorean triple. That is, if each number of a Pythagorean triple is multiplied by a positive number $k$, the resulting triple also satisfies $a^2 + b^2 = c^2$. Thus, $(3k, 4k, 5k)$, $(5k, 12k, 13k)$, and $(8k, 15k, 17k)$ are Pythagorean triples. For example, let $k = 2$, then $(3k, 4k, 5k)$ equals (6, 8, 10). A triangle with sides of lengths 6, 8, and 10 is a right triangle because $6^2 + 8^2 = 36 + 64 = 100 = 10^2$.

## Additional Theorems About Right Triangles

Here are additional theorems about right triangles that are useful to know.

- The length of the median to the hypotenuse of a right triangle is one-half the length of the hypotenuse.
- The altitude to the hypotenuse of a right triangle divides the triangle into two right triangles that are similar to each other and to the original right triangle. Furthermore, the length of the altitude is the geometric mean of the lengths of the two segments into which it separates the hypotenuse. In the figure shown, $\triangle ACB \sim \triangle AHC \sim \triangle CHB$ and $\dfrac{AH}{h} = \dfrac{h}{HB}$.

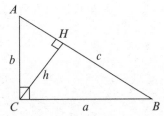

- The lengths of the sides of a 45°-45°-90° right triangle are in the ratio $\dfrac{1}{\sqrt{2}} : \dfrac{1}{\sqrt{2}} : 1$ or, equivalently, $1 : 1 : \sqrt{2}$.
- The lengths of the sides of a 30°-60°-90° right triangle are in the ratio $\dfrac{1}{2} : \dfrac{\sqrt{3}}{2} : 1$, or equivalently, $1 : \sqrt{3} : 2$, where the shortest side is opposite the 30° angle.
- Given two right triangles, if the hypotenuse and one leg of one triangle are congruent to the hypotenuse and the corresponding leg of the other triangle, then the two right triangles are congruent.

# Quadrilaterals

For this topic, you must demonstrate an understanding of properties of quadrilaterals.

# Classifying Quadrilaterals

A **quadrilateral** is a four-sided polygon. Quadrilaterals are commonly subclassified as trapezoids or parallelograms.

A **trapezoid** has two definitions, both of which are widely accepted. One definition is that a trapezoid is a quadrilateral that has *exactly* one pair of opposite sides that are parallel. This definition would exclude parallelograms as a special case. The other definition is that a trapezoid is a quadrilateral that has *at least* one pair of parallel sides. This definition would allow any parallelogram to be considered a special kind of trapezoid. This situation is one of the few times that mathematicians do not agree on the definition of a term. For purposes of this CliffsNotes book, you will have to assume that answers to problems involving trapezoids on the Praxis MS Math test will not hinge on the definition for trapezoid you choose to use during the test.

A **parallelogram** is a quadrilateral that has two pairs of opposite sides that are parallel. Some useful properties of parallelograms are the following:

- Opposite sides are congruent.
- Opposite interior angles are congruent.
- The sum of the four interior angles is 360°.
- Consecutive interior angles are supplementary.
- The diagonals bisect each other.
- Each diagonal divides the parallelogram into two congruent triangles.

Some parallelograms have special names because of their special properties. A **rhombus** is a parallelogram that has four congruent sides. A **rectangle** is a parallelogram that has four right angles. A **square** is a parallelogram that has four right angles and four congruent sides. These three figures have all the general properties of parallelograms. In addition, in rectangles and squares, the diagonals are congruent. In rhombuses and squares, the diagonals intersect at right angles.

Here are examples of quadrilaterals.

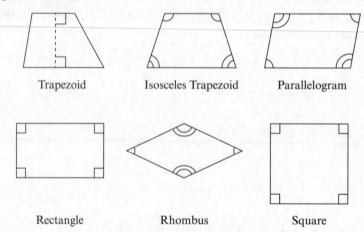

| Trapezoid | Isosceles Trapezoid | Parallelogram |
| Rectangle | Rhombus | Square |

# Useful Theorems About Quadrilaterals

Following are theorems about quadrilaterals that are useful to know.

- The sum of the interior angles of a quadrilateral is 360°.
- If the diagonals of a quadrilateral bisect each other, the quadrilateral is a parallelogram.
- If both pairs of opposite sides of a quadrilateral are congruent, the quadrilateral is a parallelogram.
- If two sides of a quadrilateral are parallel and congruent, the quadrilateral is a parallelogram.
- If the diagonals of a quadrilateral are perpendicular bisectors of each other, the quadrilateral is a rhombus.
- If a parallelogram has one right angle, it has four right angles and is a rectangle.
- If a rhombus has one right angle, it has four right angles and is a square.

# Circles

A **circle** is a closed plane figure for which all points are the same distance from a point within, called the **center.** A **radius** of a circle is a line segment joining the center of the circle to any point on the circle (the plural of radius is **radii**). A **chord** of a circle is a line segment with both endpoints on the circle. A **diameter** is a chord that passes through the center of the circle. The diameter of a circle is twice the radius. Conversely, the radius of a circle is half the diameter. Here is an illustration.

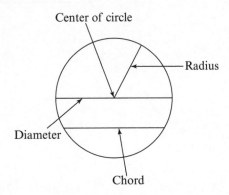

In a circle, a radius that is perpendicular to a chord bisects the chord. Consequently, the perpendicular bisector of a chord passes through the center of the circle. Here is an illustration.

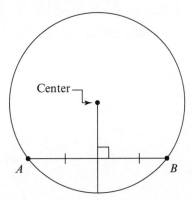

An **arc** is part of a circle; it is the set of points between and including two points on the circle. The two points determine two arcs on the circle. Arcs are measured in degrees. If the two arcs are of unequal measure, the arc with the smaller measure is the **minor arc** and the arc with the greater measure is the **major arc.** A **semicircle** is an arc whose endpoints are the endpoints of a diameter of the circle. The degree measure of a semicircle is 180°.

A **central angle** of a circle is an angle that has its vertex at the center of the circle. A central angle determines two arcs on the circle. The arc with the smaller measure is the central angle's **intercepted arc.** A central angle and its **intercepted arc** have the same degree measure. In the circle shown, the intercepted arc of the central angle shown is minor arc $\overset{\frown}{AB}$. Its measure is 80°.

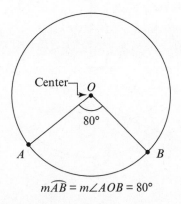

$$m\overset{\frown}{AB} = m\angle AOB = 80°$$

**109**

An **inscribed angle** is an angle whose vertex is on a circle and whose sides are chords of the circle. The arc of the circle that is in the interior of the inscribed angle and whose endpoints are on the sides of the angle is its **intercepted arc.** The measure of an inscribed angle is half the measure of its intercepted arc. An angle inscribed in a semicircle is a right angle. Look at these examples.

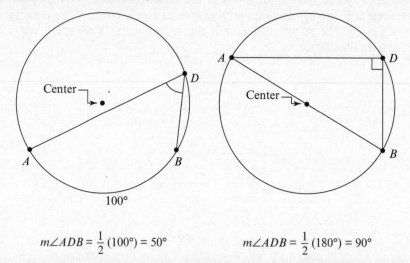

$$m\angle ADB = \frac{1}{2}(100°) = 50°  \qquad  m\angle ADB = \frac{1}{2}(180°) = 90°$$

If two chords intersect within a circle, each of the angles formed equals one-half the sum of the intercepted arcs. Furthermore, the product of the lengths of the segments formed for one chord equals the product of the lengths of the segments formed for the other chord. In the circle shown, $\angle RVU = \angle SVT = \frac{1}{2}(50° + 70°) = \frac{1}{2}(120°) = 60°$ and $(RV)(VS) = (UV)(VT)$.

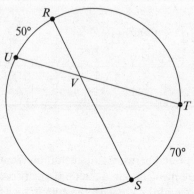

A **secant** to a circle is a line that contains a chord. A **tangent** to a circle is a line in the plane of the circle that intersects the circle in only one point. The point of contact is called the **point of tangency.** If a line is tangent to a circle, then the radius drawn to the point of tangency is perpendicular to the tangent. Here is an illustration.

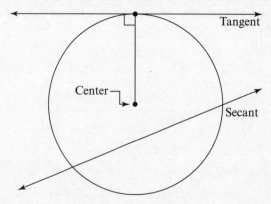

The **length,** $L$, of an arc that has measure $a°$ is $L = \dfrac{a°}{360°} \cdot 2\pi r = \dfrac{a}{180} \cdot \pi r$. For example, in a circle that has radius 18 cm, the length of an arc of 60° is $\dfrac{60}{180} \cdot \pi(18\text{ cm}) = 6\pi$ cm.

A **sector** of a circle is a region bounded by two radii and an arc of the circle. The **area,** $A$, of a sector with radius $r$ and arc measure of $a°$ is $A = \dfrac{a}{360} \cdot \pi r^2$. For example, in a circle that has radius 18 cm, the area of a sector whose arc has measure of 60° is $\dfrac{60}{360} \cdot \pi(18\text{ cm})^2 = \dfrac{1}{6} \cdot \pi(324\text{ cm}^2) = 54\pi$ cm$^2$.

Additional useful properties of circles are the following.

- The measure of an angle formed outside a circle by the intersection of two secants, two tangents, or a tangent and a secant equals one-half the difference of the measures of the intercepted arcs.
- The measure of an angle with its vertex on a circle formed by a secant and a tangent equals one-half the measure of the intercepted arc.
- The ratio of the length of the arc intercepted by a central angle to the circumference of the circle equals the ratio of the degree measure of the central angle to 360°.
- Two tangent segments to a circle from an exterior point are congruent. *Note:* If a line through a point $E$ that is exterior to a circle is tangent to the circle at point $T$, then $\overline{ET}$ is a **tangent segment** from $E$ to the circle.
- If two arcs have congruent radii, then the lengths of the arcs are proportional to their measures.
- **Concentric circles** are circles that have the same center.
- A polygon is **inscribed** in a circle if each of its vertices lies on the circle.
- A polygon is **circumscribed** about a circle if each of its sides is tangent to the circle.
- Opposite pairs of interior angles of a quadrilateral inscribed in a circle are supplementary.

# Geometric Transformations

A **geometric transformation** is a one-to-one mapping between the points of the plane and themselves. A transformation maps a **preimage** point, $P$, onto a unique **image** point, $P'$. Each point is associated with itself or with some other point in the plane. In symbols, this mapping is represented as $P \rightarrow P'$ and is read as "the image of $P$ is $P$ prime." In this section, you will learn about four common transformations in the plane: reflections, translations, rotations, and dilations.

## Reflections

A **reflection over a line** is a geometric transformation in which every point $P$ is mapped to a new point $P'$ that is the same distance from a fixed line, but on the opposite side of the line. The fixed line is the **line of reflection.** This line is the perpendicular bisector of the segment joining any point to its image. *Note:* Any line in the plane can serve as a line of reflection.

A **reflection over the $x$-axis** is a transformation in which $P(x, y) \rightarrow P'(x, -y)$. Corresponding points are equidistant from the $x$-axis as shown below.

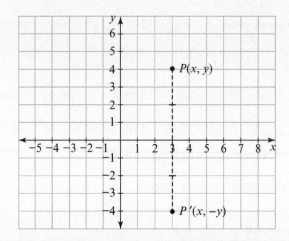

Tip: Under a reflection over the *x*-axis, every *x*-coordinate stays the same and every *y*-coordinate is changed to its opposite.

Here is an illustration.

In the diagram below, triangle $A'B'C'$ is the image of triangle $ABC$ under a reflection over the *x*-axis. Observe that $A(-4, 3) \rightarrow A'(-4, -3)$, $B(-4, 1) \rightarrow B'(-4, -1)$, and $C(2, 1) \rightarrow C'(2, -1)$.

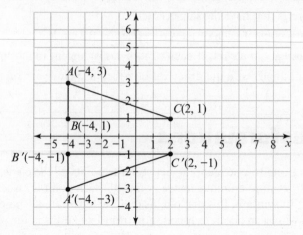

A **reflection over the *y*-axis** is a transformation in which $P(x, y) \rightarrow P'(-x, y)$. Corresponding points are equidistant from the *y*-axis as shown below.

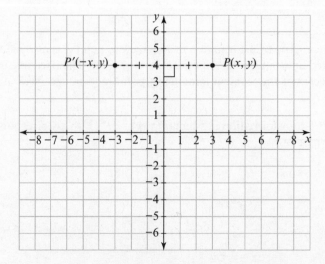

**Tip: Under a reflection over the *y*-axis, every *y*-coordinate stays the same and every *x*-coordinate is changed to its opposite.**

Here is an illustration.

In the diagram below, segment $\overline{A'B'}$ is the image of segment $\overline{AB}$ under a reflection over the *y*-axis. Observe that $A(2, 4) \rightarrow A'(-2, 4)$ and $B(5, 1) \rightarrow B'(-5, 1)$.

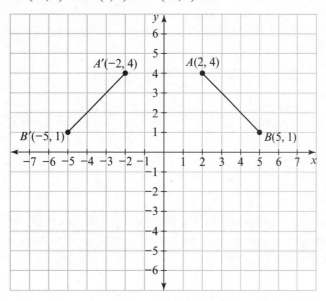

A **reflection in a point** is a geometric transformation about a fixed **point of reflection** for which every point $P$ is mapped to a new point $P'$ directly opposite it on the other side of the point of reflection, so that the point of reflection is the midpoint of the segment joining the original point with its image. *Note:* Any point in the plane can serve as a point of reflection.

A **reflection in the origin** is a transformation in which $P(x, y) \rightarrow P'(-x, -y)$. The origin is the midpoint of segment $\overline{PP'}$ joining corresponding points as shown below.

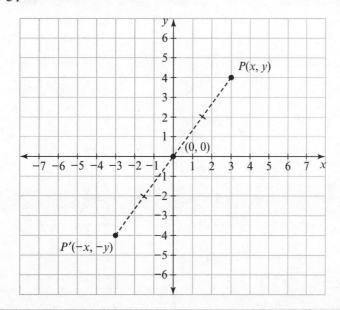

**Tip: Under a reflection in the origin, every *x*-coordinate and every *y*-coordinate is changed to its opposite.**

Here is an illustration.

In the diagram below, rectangle $A'B'C'D'$ is the image of rectangle $ABCD$ under a reflection in the origin. Observe that $A(2, -3) \rightarrow A'(-2, 3)$, $B(2, -5) \rightarrow B'(-2, 5)$, $C(5, -5) \rightarrow C'(-5, 5)$, and $D(5, -3) \rightarrow D'(-5, 3)$.

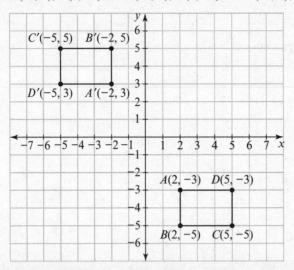

**Tip:** As the illustrations in this discussion of reflections show, you can think of reflections as "flips." The image is the result of flipping the preimage over the line of reflection so that the new figure is a mirror image of the original.

# Translations

A **translation** is a geometric transformation in which every point $P$ is mapped a fixed distance in the same direction along a straight line to a new point $P'$. A **translation of $h$ units in the horizontal direction and $k$ units in the vertical direction** is a transformation in which $P(x, y) \rightarrow P'(x + h, y + k)$. A translation moves every point $h$ units horizontally and $k$ units vertically.

**Tip:** In a translation, you merely add $h$ to each $x$-coordinate and $k$ to each $y$-coordinate.

Here is an illustration.

In the diagram below, segment $\overline{A'B'}$ is the image of segment $\overline{AB}$ under a translation of 3 units horizontally and –2 units vertically. Observe that $A(2, 4) \rightarrow A'(5, 2)$ and $B(3, 1) \rightarrow B'(6, -1)$.

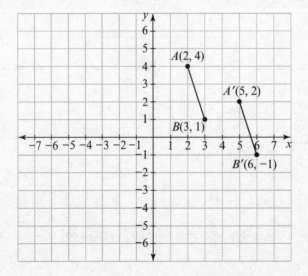

Tip: You can think of translations as "slides," which is shown in the previous illustration. You slide the preimage right or left or up or down, or a combination of these moves. The result is the image.

# Rotations

A **rotation** is a geometric transformation in which every point $P$ is "rotated" through an angle around a fixed point, called the **center of rotation**. A figure has **rotational symmetry** if there is a rotation of less than 360° in which the image and its preimage coincide under the rotation.

The following discussion presents coordinate rules for three types of rotations about the origin $O$: a counterclockwise rotation of 90° about $O$, a counterclockwise rotation of 180° about $O$, and a counterclockwise rotation of 270° about $O$.

Tip: Think of rotations as "turns" around a point.

A **counterclockwise rotation of 90° about the origin** $O$ is a transformation in which $P(x, y) \rightarrow P'(-y, x)$. The angle $POP'$ is a right angle as shown below.

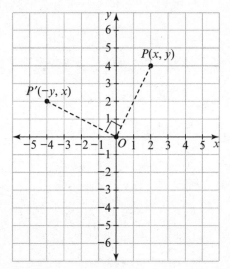

Here is an illustration.

In the diagram below, rectangle $A'B'C'D'$ is the image of rectangle $ABCD$ under a rotation of 90° about the origin. Observe that $A(2, -3) \rightarrow A'(3, 2)$, $B(2, -5) \rightarrow B'(5, 2)$, $C(5, -5) \rightarrow C'(5, 5)$, and $D(5, -3) \rightarrow D'(3, 5)$.

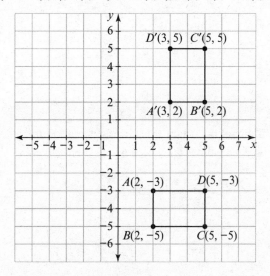

A **counterclockwise rotation of 180° about the origin** $O$ is a transformation in which $P(x, y) \rightarrow P'(-x, -y)$. The measure of angle $POP'$ is 180° as shown below.

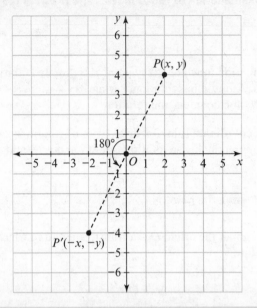

**Tip: A counterclockwise rotation of 180° about the origin O is equivalent to a reflection in the origin.**

Here is an illustration.

In the diagram below, segment $\overline{A'B'}$ is the image of segment $\overline{AB}$ under a rotation of 180° about the origin. Observe that $A(2, 4) \rightarrow A'(-2, -4)$ and $B(5, 1) \rightarrow B'(-5, -1)$.

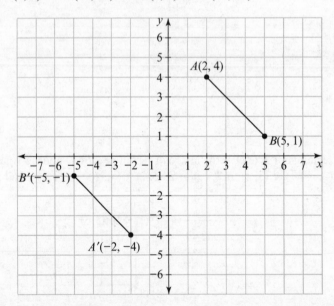

A **counterclockwise rotation of 270° about the origin** $O$ is a transformation in which $P(x, y) \rightarrow P'(y, -x)$. The measure of angle $POP'$ is 270° as shown below. The angle is measured *counterclockwise* from $\overline{OP}$ to $\overline{OP'}$.

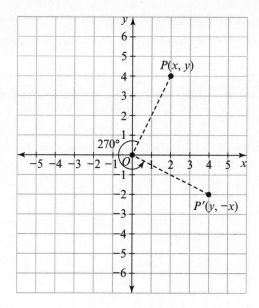

Here is an illustration.

In the diagram below, triangle $A'B'C'$ is the image of triangle $ABC$ under a rotation of 270° about the origin. Observe that $A(3, -2) \rightarrow A'(-2, -3)$, $B(2, -5) \rightarrow B'(-5, -2)$, and $C(5, -5) \rightarrow C'(-5, -5)$.

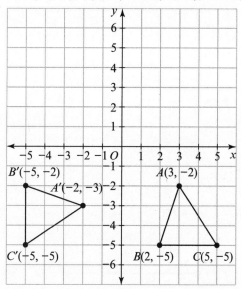

# Dilations

A **dilation** is a geometric transformation in which every point $P$ is mapped to a new point $P'$, where the point $P'$ lies on a ray through a fixed point $O$ and the point $P$, so that the $OP' = |k|OP$, where $k$ is a nonzero real number, called the **scale factor.** Informally, a dilation is an expanding ($|k| > 1$) or contracting ($|k| < 1$) of a geometric shape using a scale factor, while its shape, location, and orientation remain the same. In the case that $|k| = 1$, the dilated image is congruent to the original geometric shape, and the dilation is a rigid motion.

*Note:* Some sources insist that a dilation must change a figure's size. This requirement would exclude the scale factor $k$, where $|k| = 1$. However, to be consistent with the *2008 National Mathematics Advisory Panel Report of the Task Group on Learning Processes* (www.ed.gov/about/bdscomm/list/mathpanel/index.html), which suggests the use of dilation in defining similarity, the case that results in congruency between the image and preimage must be included (given that similar figures can be congruent).

A **dilation of scale factor $r$ where the center of dilation is the origin $O$** is a transformation in which $P(x, y) \rightarrow P'(rx, ry)$, where $r > 0$. Under a dilation, the ratio of $OP'$ to $OP$ equals the dilation's scale factor $r$. That is, $\dfrac{OP'}{OP} = r$.

**Note: Any point can be chosen as the center of dilation. Also, scale factors can be negative. In this book, dilations are limited to those where the origin is the center of dilation and scale factors are positive.**

Under a dilation, if the scale factor $r$ is greater than 1, the image is an **enlargement** of the preimage and has the same shape. If the scale factor is between 0 and 1, the image is a **reduction** of the preimage and has the same shape. If the scale factor equals 1, the preimage and image are the same size and shape.

Here are illustrations.

In the diagram below, segment $\overline{A'B'}$ is the image of segment $\overline{AB}$ under a dilation of 2. Observe that $A(2, 1) \rightarrow A'(4, 2)$ and $B(3, -2) \rightarrow B'(6, -4)$.

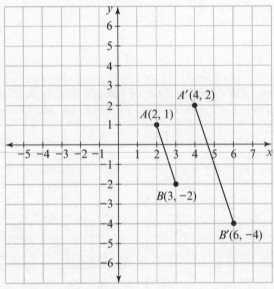

In the diagram below, rectangle $A'B'C'D'$ is the image of rectangle $ABCD$ under a dilation of $\dfrac{1}{2}$. Observe that $A(-4, 5) \rightarrow A'(-2, 2.5)$, $B(-4, -5) \rightarrow B'(-2, -2.5)$, $C(4, -5) \rightarrow C'(2, -2.5)$, and $D(4, 5) \rightarrow D'(2, 2.5)$.

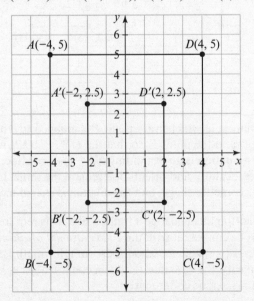

# Summary of Coordinate Rules for Geometric Transformations

The following is a summary of the coordinate rules for the common transformation types presented in this chapter.

| Transformation | Coordinate Rule |
|---|---|
| Reflection over the $x$-axis | $P(x, y) \rightarrow P'(x, -y)$ |
| Reflection over the $y$-axis | $P(x, y) \rightarrow P'(-x, y)$ |
| Reflection in the origin | $P(x, y) \rightarrow P'(-x, -y)$ |
| Counterclockwise rotation of 90° about the origin | $P(x, y) \rightarrow P'(-y, x)$ |
| Counterclockwise rotation of 180° about the origin | $P(x, y) \rightarrow P'(-x, -y)$ |
| Counterclockwise rotation of 270° about the origin | $P(x, y) \rightarrow P'(y, -x)$ |
| Translation of $h$ units in the horizontal direction and $k$ units in the vertical direction | $P(x, y) \rightarrow P'(x + h, y + k)$ |
| Dilation of scale factor $r$ where center of dilation is the origin | $P(x, y) \rightarrow P'(rx, ry), r > 0$ |

# Properties Preserved Under Reflections, Translations, Rotations, and Dilations

The following five properties are preserved under *reflections, translations,* and *rotations:*

- Distance—Lengths in the image equal their corresponding lengths in the preimage.
- Angle measure—Angles in the image have the same measure as their corresponding angles in the preimage.
- Parallelism—The images of two parallel lines are also parallel lines.
- Collinearity—The images of three or more points that lie on a straight line (that is, the points are collinear) will also lie on a straight line in the same order.
- Midpoint—The image of the midpoint of a line segment is the midpoint of the line segment's image.

The properties preserved under *dilations* include only four of the five properties preserved under reflections, translations, and rotations. These properties are angle measure, parallelism, collinearity, and midpoint. Dilations do not preserve distance (except when the scale factor is 1). Lengths in the image figure are equal to their corresponding lengths in the preimage figure multiplied by the scale factor $r$.

> Tip: A dilation maps a line not containing the center of dilation to a parallel line.

# Congruence and Similarity in the Context of Geometric Transformations

Reflections, translations, and rotations are **rigid motions.** These transformations are rigid motions because they move a figure to a different location in the plane without altering its shape or size. They take lines to lines. They take line segments to line segments of the same length. They take angles to angles of the same measure. They take parallel lines to parallel lines. And they take points to their same relative locations.

Under reflections, translations, and rotations, figures (preimages) and their corresponding images are congruent. Therefore, **congruence** of two plane geometric figures is defined as follows: A two-dimensional figure is congruent to another if the first can be transformed into the second by a sequence of rotations, reflections, and translations.

> Tip: The sequence of transformations that results in two congruent figures is not necessarily unique.

Here is an illustration.

In the diagram, trapezoids I and II are congruent. One possible sequence of transformations whereby Trapezoid I can be transformed into Trapezoid II is a reflection across the $y$-axis, followed by a translation

**119**

of 1 unit right and 8 units down. Specifically, $(-5, 5) \rightarrow (5, 5) \rightarrow (6, -3)$; $(-5, 3) \rightarrow (5, 3) \rightarrow (6, -5)$; $(-2, 3) \rightarrow (2, 3) \rightarrow (3, -5)$; $(-3, 5) \rightarrow (3, 5) \rightarrow (4, -3)$.

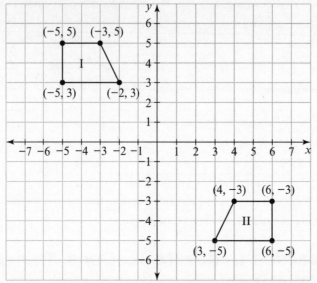

Dilations are *not* rigid motions. However, dilations *do* take angles to angles of the same measure. They take parallel lines to parallel lines. And they take points to their same relative locations. Under dilations, figures (preimages) and their images are similar. Therefore, **similarity** of two plane geometric figures is defined as follows: A two-dimensional figure is similar to another if the first can be transformed into the second by a sequence of rotations, reflections, translations, and dilations.

> **Tip:** The sequence of transformations that results in two similar figures is not necessarily unique.

Here is an illustration.

In the diagram, triangles I and II are similar. A possible sequence of transformations that transforms Triangle I into Triangle II is a counterclockwise rotation of 90°, followed by a dilation of 1.5. Specifically, $(2, 5) \rightarrow (-5, 2) \rightarrow (-7.5, 3)$; $(3, 2) \rightarrow (-2, 3) \rightarrow (-3, 4.5)$; $(6, 4) \rightarrow (-4, 6) \rightarrow (-6, 9)$.

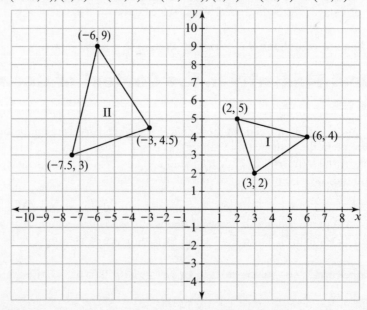

*Note:* See "Congruence, Similarity, and Symmetry" and "Triangles" earlier in this chapter for additional discussions of congruence and similarity.

# Sample Questions

**Directions:** Read the directions for each question carefully. This set of questions has several different question types. For each question, select a single answer choice unless written instructions preceding the question state otherwise.

1. The center of a circle that is inscribed in a triangle coincides with which of the following points associated with the triangle?

   Ⓐ the point where the triangle's medians intersect
   Ⓑ the point where the perpendicular bisectors of the triangle's sides intersect
   Ⓒ the point where the bisectors of the triangle's interior angles intersect
   Ⓓ the point where the triangle's altitudes intersect

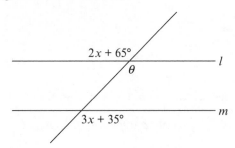

2. In the preceding figure, lines *l* and *m* are parallel. What is the measure of angle *θ*?

   Ⓐ 125°
   Ⓑ 97°
   Ⓒ 30°
   Ⓓ 16°

   $2x + 65 + 3x + 35 = 180$
   $5x + 100 = 180$
   $5x = 80$
   $x = 16$

3. A length of cable is attached to the top of a 12-foot pole. The cable is anchored 9 feet from the base of the pole. What is the length of the cable?

   Ⓐ $3\sqrt{7}$ feet
   Ⓑ 13 feet
   Ⓒ 15 feet
   Ⓓ 21 feet

      $12^2 + 9^2 = c^2$   $\sqrt{225}$
   $144 + 81 = c^2$

**For the following question, enter your numeric answer in the box below the question.**

4. What is the sum of the measures, in degrees, of the interior angles of an octagon?

   ┌─────────┐
   │ 1080 │ °
   └─────────┘

   $(n-2)180$

**5.** In the figure shown, $\triangle ABC \sim \triangle EGF$, line segment $\overline{AB}$ has length of 4 cm, line segment $\overline{EG}$ has length of 7 cm, and line segment $\overline{AC}$ has length of 2 cm. Find the length of line segment $\overline{EF}$.

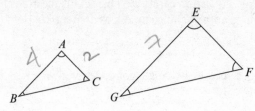

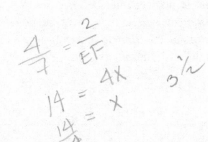

Ⓐ $\dfrac{2}{7}$ cm

Ⓑ $\dfrac{6}{7}$ cm

Ⓒ $3\dfrac{1}{2}$ cm

Ⓓ 14 cm

**For the following question, enter your numeric answer in the box below the question.**

**6.** What is the measure, in degrees, of an inscribed angle whose intercepted arc is 100°?

**For the following question, select all that apply.**

**7.** Which of the following properties is preserved under the geometric transformation of rotation?

Ⓐ distance
Ⓑ angle measure
Ⓒ parallelism
Ⓓ collinearity

**8.** In a coordinate plane, triangle $ABC$ has vertices $A(2, 1)$, $B(2, 5)$, and $C(5, 2)$. Triangle $A'B'C'$ is the image of triangle $ABC$ after a reflection over the $y$-axis followed by a translation of 4 units to the right and 2 units down. What are the coordinates of $B'$?

Ⓐ $(-4, 9)$
Ⓑ $(0, -1)$
Ⓒ $(6, -7)$
Ⓓ $(2, 3)$

# Answer Explanations

**1. C.** The angle bisectors of a triangle intersect in a point, and their point of intersection is equidistant from the three sides. Thus, if a circle is inscribed in a triangle, the point where the bisectors of the triangle's interior angles intersect is the center of the inscribed circle, choice C.

**2. A.** From the figure, you can see that the angle whose measure is $2x + 65°$ and angle $\theta$ are vertical angles, so they are congruent. Angle $\theta$ and the angle whose measure is $3x + 35°$ are corresponding angles of parallel lines, so they are congruent. Thus, the angles whose measures are $2x + 65°$ and $3x + 35°$ are congruent and have the same measure. To find the measure of $\theta$, do two steps. First, set the expressions $2x + 65°$ and $3x + 35°$ equal to each other and then solve the resulting equation for $x$. Next, substitute the value obtained for $x$

into one of the expressions, $2x + 65°$ or $3x + 35°$, to find the measure of angle $\theta$.

*Step 1.* Solve for $x$.

$2x + 65° = 3x + 35°$ implies $30° = x$.

*Step 2.* Substitute the value obtained for $x$ into $2x + 65°$.

$\theta = 2x + 65° = 2(30°) + 65° = 125°$, choice A.

*Tip:* Be sure to answer the question! Choice C results if you fail to do Step 2 above.

**3. C.** Make a sketch.

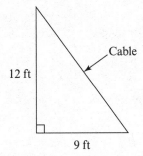

The pole, the cable, and the ground form a right triangle. From the sketch, you can see that the cable is the hypotenuse of a right triangle that has legs of 12 feet and 9 feet. Use the Pythagorean theorem to find the length of the hypotenuse, denoted by $c$.

Substitute into the formula, omitting the units for convenience, and solve for $c$.

$$c^2 = a^2 + b^2$$
$$c^2 = 12^2 + 9^2$$
$$c^2 = 144 + 81$$
$$c^2 = 225$$
$$c = \sqrt{225}$$
$$c = 15$$

Thus, $c = 15$ feet, choice C.

*Tip:* Sketching a figure for problems dealing with geometric figures is a smart test-taking strategy.

**4. 1,080** The sum of the measures of the interior angles of an $n$-sided polygon equals $(n - 2)180°$. An octagon has eight sides, so the sum of the measures of its interior angles is $(8 - 2)180° = (6)180° = 1,080°$.

**5. C.** The two triangles are similar. Therefore, corresponding sides are proportional. Set up a proportion.

$$\frac{EF}{AC} = \frac{EG}{AB}$$
$$\frac{EF}{2 \text{ cm}} = \frac{7 \text{ cm}}{4 \text{ cm}}$$

Solve for $EF$, omitting the units for convenience.

$$\frac{EF}{2} = \frac{7}{4}$$
$$EF = \frac{(2)(7)}{4}$$
$$EF = \frac{7}{2} = 3\frac{1}{2}$$

$\overline{EF}$ has length of $3\frac{1}{2}$ cm, choice C.

*Tip:* When you're going to solve a proportion for a missing element, write the proportion so that the missing element is in the numerator of the first ratio.

6. **50** The measure of an inscribed angle is half the measure of its intercepted arc. Thus, the measure of the inscribed angle is $\frac{1}{2}(100°) = 50°$.

7. **A, B, C, D.** Reflections, translations, and rotations are rigid motions. These transformations are rigid motions because they move a figure to a different location in the plane without altering its shape or size. They preserve distance (choice A), angle measure (choice B), parallelism (choice C), collinearity (choice D), and midpoint.

8. **D.** Under a reflection over the *y*-axis, $(2, 5) \rightarrow (-2, 5)$. Under a translation of 4 units right and 2 units down, $(-2, 5) \rightarrow (-2 + 4, 5 - 2) = (2, 3)$. The coordinates of $B'$ are $(2, 3)$, choice D.

# Chapter 5

# Measurement

This chapter provides a review of key ideas and formulas of measurement that are important for you to know for the Praxis MS Math test. Sample questions, comparable to what might be presented on the Praxis MS Math test, are given at the end of the chapter. The answer explanations for the sample questions are provided immediately following.

## Dimensional Analysis

On the Praxis MS Math test, you have to demonstrate your knowledge of measurement using the U.S. customary system and the metric system. See Appendix D, "Measurement Units and Conversions," for some common conversion facts you should know.

Convert from one measurement unit to another by using an appropriate "conversion fraction." You make conversion fractions by using a conversion fact, such as 1 gallon = 4 quarts. For each conversion fact, you can write *two* conversion fractions. For example, for the conversion fact given, you have $\dfrac{1 \text{ gal}}{4 \text{ qt}}$ and $\dfrac{4 \text{ qt}}{1 \text{ gal}}$ as your two conversion fractions.

Every conversion fraction is equivalent to the number 1 because the numerator and denominator are different names for measures of the same quantity. Therefore, if you multiply a quantity by a conversion fraction, you will not change the value of the quantity.

To change one measurement unit to another unit, multiply by the conversion fraction whose *denominator has the same units as those of the quantity to be converted.* This strategy falls under **dimensional analysis,** a powerful tool used by scientists (including mathematicians) and engineers to analyze units and to guide or check equations and calculations. When you do the multiplication, the units you started out with will "cancel" (divide) out, and you will be left with the desired new units. If this doesn't happen, then you used the wrong conversion fraction. Do it over again with the other conversion fraction.

Additionally, for some conversions you might need to make a "chain" of conversion fractions to obtain your desired units.

Here is an example.

> Convert 3 gallons to cups.

You know that 1 pint = 2 cups, 1 quart = 2 pints, and 1 gallon = 4 quarts. These facts yield six conversion fractions, respectively: $\dfrac{1 \text{ pt}}{2 \text{ c}}$ and $\dfrac{2 \text{ c}}{1 \text{ pt}}$, $\dfrac{1 \text{ qt}}{2 \text{ pt}}$ and $\dfrac{2 \text{ pt}}{1 \text{ qt}}$, $\dfrac{1 \text{ gal}}{4 \text{ qt}}$ and $\dfrac{4 \text{ qt}}{1 \text{ gal}}$.

Start with the quantity to be converted and keep multiplying by conversion fractions until, after canceling like units, you obtain the desired units.

$$\frac{3 \text{ gal}}{1} \cdot \frac{4 \text{ qt}}{1 \text{ gal}} \cdot \frac{2 \text{ pt}}{1 \text{ qt}} \cdot \frac{2 \text{ c}}{1 \text{ pt}} = \frac{3 \, \cancel{\text{gal}}}{1} \cdot \frac{4 \, \cancel{\text{qt}}}{1 \, \cancel{\text{gal}}} \cdot \frac{2 \, \cancel{\text{pt}}}{1 \, \cancel{\text{qt}}} \cdot \frac{2 \text{ c}}{1 \, \cancel{\text{pt}}} = 48 \text{ c}$$

Thus, 3 gallons equals 48 cups.

It is a good idea to assess your final answer to see if it makes sense. When you convert from a larger unit to a smaller unit, you should expect that it will take more of the smaller units to equal the same amount. When you convert from a smaller unit to a larger unit, you should expect that it will take less of the larger units to equal the same amount.

Here is an example of converting from a larger unit to a smaller unit.

> Convert 5 yards to feet.

$$5 \text{ yards} = \frac{5 \text{ yd}}{1} \times \frac{3 \text{ ft}}{1 \text{ yd}} = \frac{5 \text{ yd}}{1} \times \frac{3 \text{ ft}}{1 \text{ yd}} = 15 \text{ feet}$$

Feet are smaller than yards, so it should take more of them to equal the same length as 5 yards.

Here is an example of converting from a smaller unit to a larger unit.

> Convert 250 centimeters to meters.

$$250 \text{ centimeters} = \frac{250 \text{ cm}}{1} \times \frac{1 \text{ m}}{100 \text{ cm}} = \frac{250 \text{ cm}}{1} \times \frac{1 \text{ m}}{100 \text{ cm}} = \frac{250 \text{ m}}{100} = 2.5 \text{ meters}$$

Meters are larger than centimeters, so it should take fewer of them to equal the same length as 250 centimeters.

As seen in conversion of units, in calculations involving measured quantities that have units, the units are part of the completed defined measure and must undergo the same mathematical operations. You can add or subtract like units, but not unlike units. You can multiply or divide whether you have like or unlike units, provided the product or quotient has meaning.

# Perimeter, Area, and Volume

For the Praxis MS Math test, you are expected to know how to compute perimeter and area of triangles, quadrilaterals, circles, and regions that are combinations of these figures; and how to compute the surface area and volume of right prisms, cones, cylinders, spheres, and solids that are combinations of these figures. For particular questions on the test, applicable formulas might be provided. To be on the safe side, you should commit to memory formulas that are commonly used. Here are important formulas for perimeter, area, surface area, and volume that you should know for the Praxis MS Math test.

**Triangle:** height $h$, base $b$

area $= \dfrac{1}{2}bh$

sides $a$, $b$, and $c$

perimeter $= a + b + c$

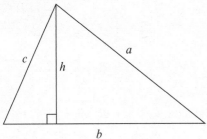

**Square:** side $s$

area $= s^2$

perimeter $= 4s$

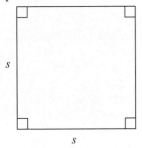

**Rectangle:** length $l$, width $w$

area $= lw$

perimeter $= 2l + 2w = 2(l + w)$

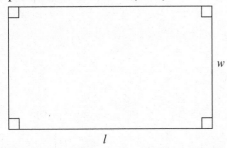

**Parallelogram:** height $h$, base $b$, width $a$

area $= bh$

perimeter $= 2a + 2b = 2(a + b)$

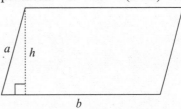

**Circle:** radius $r$, diameter $d$

area $= \pi r^2$

circumference $= 2\pi r = \pi d$

diameter $d = 2r$

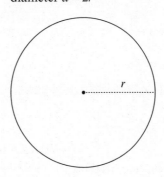

**Trapezoid:** height $h$, bases $a$, $b$

area $= \dfrac{1}{2}h(a + b)$

perimeter $= a + b + c + d$

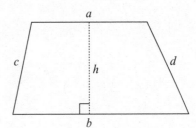

**Sphere:** radius $r$

volume $= \dfrac{4}{3}\pi r^3$

lateral surface area $= 4\pi r^2$

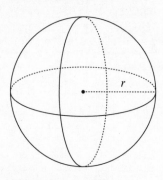

**Right prism:** height $h$, area of base $B$
volume $= Bh$
total surface area $= 2B +$ sum of areas of rectangular sides.

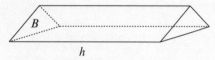

**Rectangular prism:** length $l$, width $w$, height $h$
volume $= lwh$
total surface area $= 2hl + 2hw + 2lw$

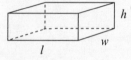

**Cube:** edge $s$
volume $= s^3$
total surface area $= 6s^2$

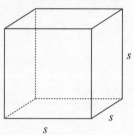

**Right circular cylinder:** height $h$, radius of base $r$
volume $= \pi r^2 h$
lateral surface area $= 2\pi rh$
total surface area $= (2\pi r)h + 2(\pi r^2)$

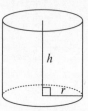

**Right pyramid:** height $h$, area of base $B$

volume $= \dfrac{1}{3}Bh$

total surface area $= B +$ sum of areas of triangular lateral faces

**Right circular cone:** height $h$, radius of base $r$

volume $= \dfrac{1}{3}\pi r^2 h$

lateral surface area $= \pi r\sqrt{r^2 + h^2} = \pi rs$, where $s$ is the slant height $= \sqrt{r^2 + h^2}$

total surface area $= \pi r\sqrt{r^2 + h^2} + \pi r^2 = \pi rs + \pi r^2$

Here are additional formulas that could be helpful to know.

**Triangle:** sides $a$, $b$, and $c$

area $= \sqrt{s(s-a)(s-b)(s-c)}$

where $s = \dfrac{a+b+c}{2}$

perimeter $= a + b + c$

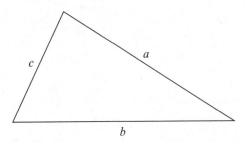

**Equilateral triangle:** side $a$

area $= \dfrac{\sqrt{3}}{4}a^2$

Perimeter $= 3a$

**Isosceles triangle:** sides $a$, $a$, and $b$

area $= \dfrac{1}{2}b\sqrt{a^2 - \dfrac{b^2}{4}}$

Perimeter $= 2a + b$

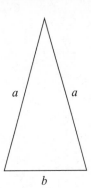

**Sector of circle:** radius $r$, $\theta$ measure of subtended central angle in radians

area $= \dfrac{\theta r^2}{2}$

arc length $= s = r\theta$

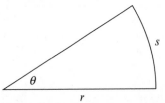

*Tip:* In the radian system of angular measurement, $360° = 2\pi$ radians. Thus, $1° = \dfrac{\pi}{180}$ radians and $1 \text{ radian} = \left(\dfrac{180}{\pi}\right)°$.

# Perimeter and Circumference

The **perimeter** of a figure is the distance around it. You measure perimeter in units of length, such as inches (in), feet (ft), yards (yd), miles (mi), kilometers (km), meters (m), centimeters (cm), and millimeters (mm). To find the perimeter of a closed figure that is made up of line segments, add up the lengths of the line segments.

Here is an example.

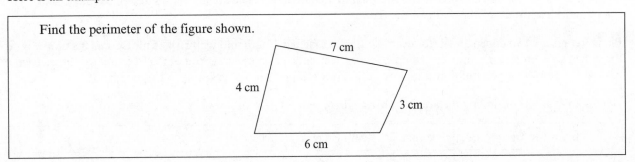

Find the perimeter of the figure shown.

To find the perimeter, add the lengths of the four sides. Perimeter = 6 cm + 3 cm + 7 cm + 4 cm = 20 cm.

The perimeter of a circle is called its **circumference.** The formula for the circumference of a circle is $C = \pi d = 2\pi r$, where $d$ and $r$ are the diameter and radius of the circle, respectively.

Here is an example of finding the circumference of a circle.

---

Find the circumference of the circle in the figure shown. Round your answer to the nearest inch.

20 in

radius

---

From the figure, the radius is 20 in. Substitute into the formula: $C = 2\pi r = 2\pi(20 \text{ in}) \approx 126$ inches.

**Tip: Use the $\pi$ key when doing calculations involving $\pi$ unless you have instructions to use an approximation for $\pi$.**

Here is an example of finding the perimeter of a figure that is a combination of figures.

---

The figure shown consists of a semicircle of radius $r$ and a rectangle whose longer side is $2r$ and whose shorter side is $r$. What is the perimeter of the figure in terms of $r$?

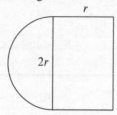

$r$

$2r$

---

The perimeter = the circumference of the semicircle + 2 times the length of the shorter side of the rectangle + the length of the longer side of the rectangle $= \dfrac{1}{2}(2\pi r) + 2 \cdot r + 2r = \pi r + 4r$.

# Area

The **area** of a plane figure is the amount of surface enclosed by the boundary of the figure. You measure area in square units, such as square inches (in$^2$), square feet (ft$^2$), square miles (mi$^2$), square meters (m$^2$), square kilometers (km$^2$), square centimeters (cm$^2$), and square millimeters (mm$^2$). The area is always described in terms of square units, regardless of the shape of the figure.

Plane figures are two dimensional (for example, a rectangle has length and width). The measurements units for the dimensions are linear units (for example, inches, feet, miles, and meters). You obtain the square units needed to describe area when you multiply a unit by itself. For example, 1 in × 1 in = 1 in$^2$ = 1 square inch.

Here is an example of finding the area of a rectangle.

---

What is the area of a rectangle that is 8.5 cm by 6 cm?

---

Sketch a diagram and label it.

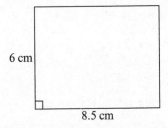

The formula for the area of a rectangle is $A = lw$, where $l$ is the **length** and $w$ is the **width.** Substitute into the formula.

$A = lw = (8.5 \text{ cm})(6 \text{ cm}) = 51 \text{ cm}^2$. The rectangle has an area of $51 \text{ cm}^2$.

Here is an example of finding the area of a triangle.

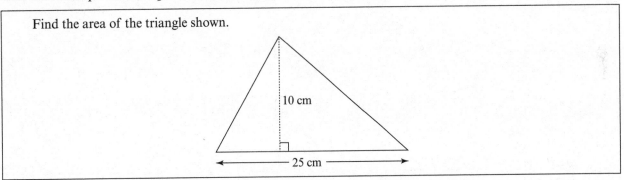

To find the area of a triangle, you must know the measure of the triangle's **base** and **height.** The base can be any of the three sides of the triangle. The height for a particular base is the length of the perpendicular line segment drawn from the opposite vertex to the line containing that base. The formula for the area of a triangle is $A = \frac{1}{2}bh$, where $b$ is the length of a base of the triangle and $h$ is the height for that base. When you are finding the area of a triangle, you can pick any convenient side of the triangle to serve as the base in the formula.

From the figure, you can see that $b = 25$ cm and $h = 10$ cm. Substitute into the formula.

$$A = \frac{1}{2}bh = A = \frac{1}{2}(25 \text{ cm})(10 \text{ cm}) = \frac{(25 \text{ cm})(10 \text{ cm})}{2} = 125 \text{ cm}^2$$

The triangle has an area of $125 \text{ cm}^2$.

Here is an example of finding the area of a circle.

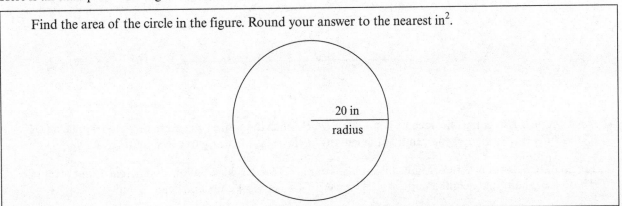

The formula for the area of a circle is $A = \pi r^2$, where $r$ is the radius of the circle.

From the figure, the radius is 20 in. Substitute into the formula.

$$A = \pi r^2 = \pi(20 \text{ in})^2 = \pi(400 \text{ in}^2) \approx 1{,}257 \text{ in}^2$$

The circle's area is approximately $1{,}257 \text{ in}^2$.

Here is an example of finding the area of a triangle in the coordinate plane.

The vertices of the triangle shown are $A(-3, 3)$, $B(1, 5)$, and $C(4, 2)$. Determine the area of $\triangle ABC$.

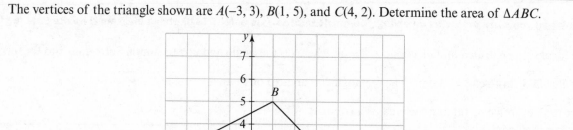

The figure has no horizontal or vertical sides, so you cannot easily find the lengths of the sides or altitudes. To determine the area, enclose the triangle in a rectangle as shown below. Make the rectangle's top side parallel to the $x$-axis and passing through vertex $B$ of the triangle. Make the rectangle's bottom side parallel to the $x$-axis and passing through vertex $C$ of the triangle. Make the left side of the rectangle perpendicular to its top and bottom sides and passing through vertex $A$. Make the right side of the rectangle perpendicular to its top and bottom sides and passing through vertex $C$. To help keep track of your work, label the coordinates of the vertices in the figure.

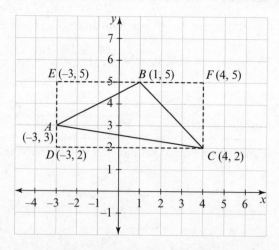

The area, $A$, of $\triangle ABC$ equals the area of rectangle $EDCF$ minus the sum of the areas of right triangles $ADC$, $CFB$, and $BEA$. In this figure, you can find the lengths of the sides of the figures by counting.

Rectangle $EDCF$ has dimensions 7 units by 3 units. Triangle $ADC$ has base 7 units and height 1 unit. Triangle $CFB$ has base 3 units and height 3 units. And triangle $BEA$ has base 4 units and height 2 units.

$$A = (7 \text{ units})(3 \text{ units}) - \frac{1}{2}(7 \text{ units})(1 \text{ unit}) - \frac{1}{2}(3 \text{ units})(3 \text{ units}) - \frac{1}{2}(4 \text{ units})(2 \text{ units})$$

$$= 21 \text{ units}^2 - 3.5 \text{ units}^2 - 4.5 \text{ units}^2 - 4 \text{ units}^2$$

$$= 9 \text{ units}^2$$

$\triangle ABC$ has area of $9 \text{ units}^2$.

# Surface Area

When you have a solid figure such as a rectangular prism (a box), a cylinder, or a pyramid, you can find the area of every face (surface) and add the areas together. The sum is the **surface area** (*S.A.*) of the solid figure.

Here is an example of finding the surface area of a rectangular box.

What is the surface area of the box shown?

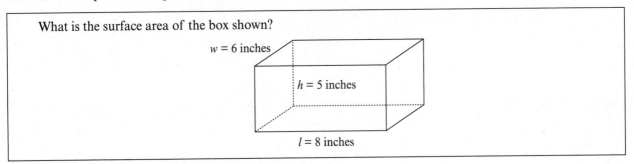

$w = 6$ inches

$h = 5$ inches

$l = 8$ inches

The box is composed of six **faces,** all of which are rectangles. Use the length and height to find the areas of the front and back faces. Use the length and width to find the areas of the top and bottom faces. Use the width and height to find the areas of the two side faces.

$S.A. = 2(8 \text{ in})(5 \text{ in}) + 2(8 \text{ in})(6 \text{ in}) + 2(6 \text{ in})(5 \text{ in}) = 80 \text{ in}^2 + 96 \text{ in}^2 + 60 \text{ in}^2 = 236 \text{ in}^2$. The box has surface area of $236 \text{ in}^2$.

Nets are helpful when you want to find the surface area of a solid figure. **A net** is a two-dimensional shape that can be folded to make a three-dimensional solid figure in which each face is a flat surface. Here are six three-dimensional solids and a corresponding net for each. *Tip:* Nets are not unique. A solid can have more than one net configuration.

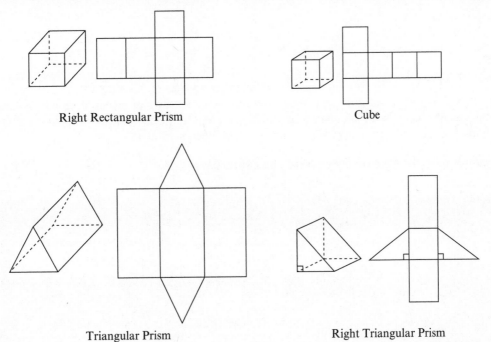

Right Rectangular Prism

Cube

Triangular Prism

Right Triangular Prism

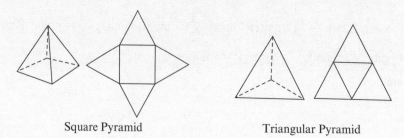

Square Pyramid                     Triangular Pyramid

Here is an example of using a net to find surface area.

> The grid shows the net for a square pyramid. Find the surface area of the pyramid. Assume each grid box represents a 1-inch by 1-inch square.
>
>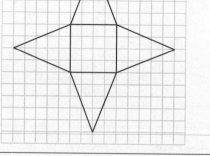

The surface area of the pyramid is the sum of the area of its square base and the areas of its four triangular faces. The square base measures 4 inches by 4 inches. Each triangle has base 4 inches and height 5 inches.

$$S.A. = (4 \text{ in})(4 \text{ in}) + 4\left(\frac{1}{2}\right)(4 \text{ in})(5 \text{ in}) = 16 \text{ in}^2 + 40 \text{ in}^2 = 56 \text{ in}^2$$

The pyramid has surface area of 56 in$^2$.

# Volume

The **volume** of a solid figure is the amount of space inside the solid. Solid figures have three dimensions (for example, length, width, and height of a box). When you use the dimensions of a solid to find its volume, the units for the volume are cubic units, such as cubic inches (in$^3$), cubic feet (ft$^3$), cubic miles (mi$^3$), cubic meters (m$^3$), cubic kilometers (km$^3$), cubic centimeters (cm$^3$), and cubic millimeters (mm$^3$).

Here is an example of finding the volume of a rectangular prism.

> What is the volume of the box shown?
>
>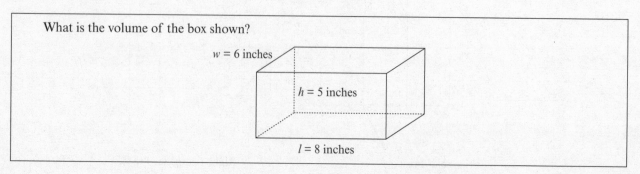

The box is in the shape of a right prism. A **right prism** is a prism whose bases are perpendicular to its sides. The formula for the volume of a right prism is $V = Bh$, where $B$ = the area of the **Base** of the prism. For a rectangular prism, $B = lw$. Thus, the formula for the volume of a rectangular prism is $V = lwh$, where $l$ is the **length,** $w$ is the **width,** and $h$ is the **height.**

Determine the dimensions from the figure and substitute into the formula.

$$V = Bh = lwh = (8 \text{ in})(6 \text{ in})(5 \text{ in}) = 240 \text{ in}^3$$

The box has volume of 240 in$^3$.

> **Tip:** Notice that the units for the volume of the box are in$^3$ = cubic inches. Cubic units are obtained when a unit is used as a factor in a product three times, as in the following: (in)(in)(in) = in$^3$.

# Precision, Accuracy, and Approximate Error

In the physical world, measurement of continuous quantities is always approximate. The precision and accuracy of the measurement relate to the worthiness of the approximation.

**Precision** refers to the degree to which a measurement is repeatable and reliable; that is, consistently getting the same data each time the measurement is taken. The precision of a measurement depends on the magnitude of the smallest measuring unit used to obtain the measurement (for example, to the nearest meter, to the nearest centimeter, or to the nearest millimeter). In theory, the smaller the measurement unit used, the more precise the measurement.

**Accuracy** refers to the degree to which a measurement is true or correct. A measurement can be precise without being accurate. This can occur, for example, when a measuring instrument needs adjustment, so that the measurements obtained, no matter how precisely measured, are inaccurate.

The amount of error involved in a physical measurement is the **approximate error** of the measurement. The **maximum possible error** of a measurement is half the magnitude of the smallest measurement unit used to obtain the measurement. For example, if the smallest measurement unit is 1 inch, the maximum possible error is 0.5 inch. The most accurate way of expressing a measurement is as a **tolerance interval.** For example, a measurement of 10 inches, to the nearest inch, should be reported as 10 inches ± 0.5 inches. In other words, the true measurement lies between 9.5 inches and 10.5 inches. Closer approximations can be obtained by refining the measurement to a higher degree of precision (for example, by measuring to the nearest half-inch).

When you do calculations with measurements that are reported as tolerance intervals, you need to consider the amount of error that will ensue. The results of such calculations should be reported as tolerance intervals that indicate the potential minimum and maximum error. To determine these tolerance intervals for the different arithmetic operations, use the guidelines in the following table. *Note:* The symbol "⇨" is used in the table to mean "implies."

### Determining Total Minimum or Maximum Error

| Operation | Guideline | Example |
|---|---|---|
| **Addition** | Add the minimum/maximum values of the measurement, respectively. | $(12 \text{ in} \pm 0.2 \text{ in}) + (10 \text{ in} \pm 0.5 \text{ in}) \Rightarrow (12 \text{ in} - 0.2 \text{ in}) + (10 \text{ in} - 0.5 \text{ in}) \leq \text{sum} \leq (12 \text{ in} + 0.2 \text{ in}) + (10 \text{ in} + 0.5 \text{ in}) = 11.8 \text{ in} + 9.5 \text{ in} \leq \text{sum} \leq 12.2 \text{ in} + 10.5 \text{ in} = 21.3 \text{ in} \leq \text{sum} \leq 22.7 \text{ in}.$ |
| **Subtraction** | The minimum error is the difference between the *least* possible first number and the *greatest* possible second number, and the maximum error is the difference between the *greatest* possible first number and the *least* possible second number. | $(12 \text{ in} \pm 0.2 \text{ in}) - (10 \text{ in} \pm 0.5 \text{ in}) \Rightarrow (12 \text{ in} - 0.2 \text{ in}) - (10 \text{ in} + 0.5 \text{ in}) \leq \text{difference} \leq (12 \text{ in} + 0.2 \text{ in}) - (10 \text{ in} - 0.5 \text{ in}) = 11.8 \text{ in} - 10.5 \text{ in} \leq \text{difference} \leq 12.2 \text{ in} - 9.5 \text{ in} = 1.3 \text{ in} \leq \text{difference} \leq 2.7 \text{ in}.$ |
| **Multiplication** | Multiply the minimum/maximum values of the measurement, respectively. | $(12 \text{ in} \pm 0.2 \text{ in})(10 \text{ in} \pm 0.5 \text{ in}) \Rightarrow (12 \text{ in} - 0.2 \text{ in})(10 \text{ in} - 0.5 \text{ in}) \leq \text{product} \leq (12 \text{ in} + 0.2 \text{ in})(10 \text{ in} + 0.5 \text{ in}) = (11.8 \text{ in})(9.5 \text{ in}) \leq \text{product} \leq (12.2 \text{ in})(10.5 \text{ in}) = 112.1 \text{ in}^2 \leq \text{product} \leq 128.1 \text{ in}^2.$ |
| **Division** | The minimum error is the quotient of the *least* possible first number and the *greatest* possible second number, and the maximum error is the quotient of the *greatest* possible first number and the *least* possible second number. | $(12 \text{ in} \pm 0.2 \text{ in}) \div (10 \text{ in} \pm 0.5 \text{ in}) \Rightarrow (12 \text{ in} - 0.2 \text{ in}) \div (10 \text{ in} + 0.5 \text{ in}) \leq \text{quotient} \leq (12 \text{ in} + 0.2 \text{ in}) \div (10 \text{ in} - 0.5 \text{ in}) = 11.8 \text{ in} \div 10.5 \text{ in} \leq \text{quotient} \leq 12.2 \text{ in} \div 9.5 \text{ in} = 1.1 \text{ in} \leq \text{quotient} \leq 1.3 \text{ in}$ (rounded to nearest tenth). |

Here is an example.

> The length of a rectangular field is 100 ft ± 1 ft and the width is 50 ft ± 1 ft. Determine a tolerance interval for the area of the field.

Since the area of the field equals length times width, the tolerance interval for the area is $(100 \text{ ft} \pm 1 \text{ ft})(50 \text{ ft} \pm 1 \text{ ft}) \Rightarrow (99 \text{ ft})(49 \text{ ft}) \leq \text{area} \leq (101 \text{ ft})(51 \text{ ft}) = 4{,}851 \text{ ft}^2 \leq \text{area} \leq 5{,}151 \text{ ft}^2.$

Two ways of conveying the magnitude of error in a measurement are absolute error and relative error (which can be expressed as a decimal or a percent). The **absolute error** of the measurement is the amount of physical error in the measurement, and the **relative error** of the measurement is the ratio of the absolute error to the correct value, or, if the correct value is unknown, to the measurement taken. The formula for relative error is given by $\dfrac{\text{absolute error}}{\text{correct value}}$ or $\dfrac{\text{absolute error}}{\text{measured value}}$ (if the correct value is unknown). When relative error is expressed as a percent, it is called **percent error**.

Here are examples.

> If a protractor is used to measure the sum of the measures of the interior angles of a triangle yielding a measurement of 178.2°, what are the absolute error, relative error, and percent error of the measurement?

The absolute error is the difference between the correct value 180° and the measured value 178.2°. That is, the absolute error = $180° - 178.2° = 1.8°$. The relative error is $\dfrac{1.8°}{180°} = 0.01$, and the percent error is 1%.

Find the percent error of the measurement 25 ft ± 0.5 ft.

Since the correct value is unknown, the absolute error is 0.5 ft and the percent error is $\dfrac{0.5 \ \cancel{ft}}{25 \ \cancel{ft}} = 0.02 = 2\%$.

**Tip: Notice that the absolute error has the same units as the units of the measurement, while the relative error and percent error have no units.**

Results of calculations with approximate measurements should not be reported with a degree of precision that would be misleading, that is, suggesting a degree of accuracy greater than the actual accuracy that could be obtained using the approximate measurements. Generally, such calculations should be rounded, *after* all calculations have been made, to have the same precision as the measurement with least precision in the calculation. *Caution:* Rounding before final calculations can compound error.

# Sample Questions

**Directions:** Read the directions for each question carefully. This set of questions has several different question types. For each question, select a single answer choice unless written instructions preceding the question state otherwise.

1. For disaster relief in a hurricane-damaged area, $2.5 billion is needed. This amount of money is equivalent to spending one dollar per second for approximately how many years?

   Ⓐ   10 years
   Ⓑ   40 years
   Ⓒ   80 years
   Ⓓ   1,000 years

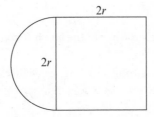

2. The figure shown above consists of a semicircle of radius $r$ and a square whose side is $2r$. What is the perimeter of the figure in terms of $r$?

   Ⓐ   $\pi r + 4r$
   Ⓑ   $\pi r + 8r$
   Ⓒ   $2\pi r + 6r$
   Ⓓ   $\pi r + 6r$

**For the following question, enter your numeric answer in the box below the question.**

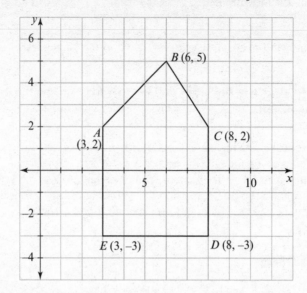

**3.** Find the area of the figure shown.

☐ units$^2$

**4.** The exterior of a spherical tank with radius 12 feet is to be painted with one coat of paint. The paint sells for $22.40 per gallon and can be purchased in 1-gallon cans only. If a can of paint will cover approximately 400 square feet, what is the cost of the paint needed to paint the exterior of the tank?

Ⓐ    $22.40

Ⓑ    $44.80

Ⓒ    $101.36

Ⓓ    $112.00

**For the following question, enter your numeric answer in the box below the question.**

**5.** A ball with a radius of 6 centimeters is inflated to capacity with air. How many cubic centimeters of air are in the ball? (Round your answer to the nearest whole number.)

☐ cm$^3$

**6.** A pharmacist measures the mass of a medical substance and uses the appropriate number of significant figures to record the mass as 7 grams, to the nearest gram. Which of the following ways most accurately expresses the range of possible values of the mass of the substance?

Ⓐ    7 grams ± 1.0 grams

Ⓑ    7 grams ± 0.5 grams

Ⓒ    7 grams ± 0.1 grams

Ⓓ    7 grams ± 0.0 grams

**7.** Using a protractor, a student determines the sum of the measures of the interior angles of a triangle to be 174.6°. What is the percent error of this measurement?

Ⓐ    0.03%

Ⓑ    3%

Ⓒ    3.1%

Ⓓ    5.4%

# Answer Explanations

1.  **C.** You need to determine approximately how many years it would take to spend $2.5 billion per second at a rate of $1 per second $\left(\dfrac{\$1}{1\text{ s}}\right)$. Convert $2.5 billion into seconds by multiplying by $\dfrac{1\text{ s}}{\$1}$, and then convert the results into years.

    Write $2.5 billion as a fraction with denominator 1 and let dimensional analysis tell you which conversion fractions to multiply by, keeping in mind that you want years as your final answer.

    $$\frac{\$2{,}500{,}000{,}000}{1}\cdot\frac{1\text{ s}}{\$1}\cdot\frac{1\text{ min}}{60\text{ s}}\cdot\frac{1\text{ h}}{60\text{ min}}\cdot\frac{1\text{ d}}{24\text{ h}}\cdot\frac{1\text{ yr}}{365\text{ d}}\approx 80\text{ years, choice C.}$$

2.  **D.** The perimeter = the circumference of the semicircle + 3 times the length of the side of the square = $\dfrac{1}{2}(2\pi r)+3\cdot 2r=\pi r+6r$, choice D.

3.  **32.5** Cut the figure into a triangle and a square as shown below. Construct the altitude of the triangle and label its endpoint and coordinates.

    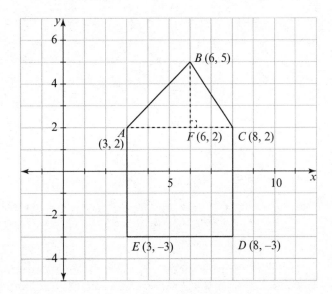

    The area of the figure is the sum of the area of $\triangle ABC$ and the area of square $AEDC$. In this figure, find dimensions by counting. Triangle $ABC$ has base 5 units and height 3 units. Square $AEDC$ has dimensions 5 units by 5 units.

    $$\begin{aligned}\text{Total area } &=\frac{1}{2}(5\text{ units})(3\text{ units})+(5\text{ units})(5\text{ units})\\ &=7.5\text{ units}^2+25\text{ units}^2\\ &=32.5\text{ units}^2\end{aligned}$$

4. **D.** You want to find the cost of the paint needed to cover the surface area of the sphere. To determine the cost of the paint, do three steps. First, find the surface area of the sphere. Next, find the number of gallons of paint needed. Then find the cost of the paint.

*Step 1.* Find the surface area (*S.A.*) of the sphere with $r = 12$ ft.

$S.A. = 4\pi r^2 = 4\pi(12\ \text{ft})^2 = 4\pi(144\ \text{ft}^2) = 1{,}809.557...\ \text{ft}^2$ (***Tip:*** Don't round this answer.)

*Step 2.* Find the number of gallons needed.

$1{,}809.557\ ...\ \cancel{\text{ft}^2} \times \dfrac{1\ \text{gal}}{400\ \cancel{\text{ft}^2}} \approx 4.52$ gallons, so 5 gallons will need to be purchased (because the paint is sold in gallon containers only).

*Step 3.* Find the cost of 5 gallons of paint.

$5\ \cancel{\text{gal}} \times \dfrac{\$22.40}{1\ \cancel{\text{gal}}} = \$112.00$, choice D.

5. **905** Find the volume of a sphere of radius 6 centimeters.

Sketch a figure.

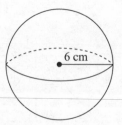

The formula for a sphere's volume is $V = \dfrac{4}{3}\pi r^3$.

Substitute into the formula and round the answer to the nearest whole number.

$$V = \frac{4}{3}(\pi)(6\ \text{cm})^3 = \frac{4}{3}(\pi)\left(216\ \text{cm}^3\right) \approx 905\ \text{cm}^3$$

6. **B.** The maximum possible error of a measurement is half the magnitude of the smallest measurement unit used to obtain the measurement. The most accurate way of expressing the measurement is as a tolerance interval. Thus, a measurement of 7 grams, to the nearest gram, should be reported as 7 grams $\pm\, 0.5$ grams, choice B.

7. **B.** The sum of the measures of the interior angles of a triangle is 180°. The absolute error is $180° - 174.6° = 5.4°$. The percent error $= \dfrac{5.4°}{180°} = 0.03 = 3\%$, choice B.

# Chapter 6

# Discrete Mathematics

This chapter provides a review of key ideas and formulas for discrete mathematics that are important for you to know for the Praxis MS Math test. Sample questions, comparable to what might be presented on the Praxis MS Math test, are given at the end of the chapter. The answer explanations for the sample questions are provided immediately following.

## Sets

This topic presents basic ideas about sets (for example, terminology, unions, intersections, and Venn diagrams).

### Set Terminology

A **set** is a collection of objects or things. Commonly, uppercase letters, such as $A$ and $B$, are used to name sets. The objects in a set $A$ are its **elements** or **members.** To show that $x$ is an element of $A$, write $x \in A$ (read as "$x$ is an element of set $A$"). If $y$ is *not* an element of $A$, write $y \notin A$. (Note that a diagonal slash through a symbol negates the original meaning of the symbol.) A set is defined by means of braces in which you describe the members of the set by roster (that is, a list of the elements separated by commas), a verbal description, or mathematical symbolism. For example, the set $D$ of digits used in the base-ten place value system can be defined in the following ways: $D = \{0, 1, 2, 3, 4, 5, 6, 7, 8, 9\}$, $D = \{$digits used in the base-ten place value system$\}$, or $D = \{x \in$ Integers $\mid 0 \le x < 10\}$. The third way is read "The set of all $x$ that are integers such that $x$ is greater than or equal to 0 and less than 10." The vertical line, $\mid$, is read "such that." This latter way of describing a set is **set-builder notation.** The set that contains no items is called the **empty set** and is designated by the symbol $\varnothing$ or $\{\ \}$.

> **Tip:** The symbol for the empty set is $\varnothing$, not $\{\varnothing\}$. The set $\{\varnothing\}$ is not an empty set; it has one element, namely $\varnothing$.

Sets need to be **well-defined.** This term means that if you are given a set, you can tell which objects belong in the set and which objects do not belong in the set. For example, the set $I = \{$important people$\}$ is *not* well-defined because you are not given enough information to know who qualifies as an "important person." However, the set $P = \{$Presidents of the United States who were elected before 2016$\}$ is well-defined because you can decide whether a given individual does or does not belong in $P$.

Two sets $A$ and $B$ are **equal,** written $A = B$, if and only if they contain *exactly* the same elements, without regard to the order in which the elements are listed in the two sets or whether elements are repeated. For example, $\{1, 4, 8\} = \{1, 8, 4\} = \{4, 1, 8\} = \{4, 8, 1\} = \{8, 1, 4\} = \{8, 4, 1\}$ and $\{1, 4, 8\} = \{1, 1, 4, 4, 8, 8\}$.

A set $A$ is a **subset** of set $B$, denoted $A \subseteq B$, if every element of $A$ is an element of $B$. For example, $\{1, 4\} \subseteq \{1, 4, 8\}$. Additionally, if $B$ contains at least one element that is not in $A$, then $A$ is a **proper subset** of $B$, denoted $A \subset B$. Thus, $\{1, 4\} \subset \{1, 4, 8\}$. You can show two sets $A$ and $B$ are equal by showing that $A \subseteq B$ and $B \subseteq A$. In a discussion, all the sets under consideration are subsets of a universal set (commonly denoted $U$), and the empty set is a subset of every set.

> **Tip:** Do not confuse the relationship "is an element of" with the relationship "is a subset of." For example, $4 \in \{1, 4, 8\}$, but $\{4\} \notin \{1, 4, 8\}$; on the other hand, $\{4\} \subseteq \{1, 4, 8\}$, but $4 \not\subset \{1, 4, 8\}$.

The **cardinality** (or **cardinal number**) of a set $A$ is the number of distinct elements in $A$. The cardinality of a set can be **finite,** meaning the set has a definite number of elements that can be counted, or **infinite,** meaning the set has an unlimited number of elements. Throughout this book, the cardinality of a finite set $A$ will be denoted $|A|$. For example, if $A = \{1, 4, 8\}$, $|A| = 3$. Note that you do not include duplications when counting the elements in a set. Other notations for the cardinality of a set $A$ are $n(A)$ or $\#A$.

# Basic Set Operations and Venn Diagrams

If in a discussion all the sets under consideration are subsets of a given set $U$, then $U$ is the **universal set of discourse,** or simply, **the universal set.** In this section, assume that all sets under consideration are subsets of a given universal set $U$.

The three basic operations for sets are union, intersection, and complement.

The **union** of two sets $A$ and $B$, denoted, $A \cup B$, is the set of all elements that are in $A$ or in $B$ or in both. In set-builder notation, $A \cup B = \{x \mid x \in A \text{ or } x \in B\}$. For example, if $A = \{2, 4, 6, 8\}$ and $B = \{1, 2, 4, 5, 6\}$, then $A \cup B = \{1, 2, 4, 5, 6, 8\}$. When you form the union of two sets, do not list an element more than once because it is unnecessary to do so. Note that the word *or* is used in the *inclusive* sense; that is, *or* means "one or the other, or possibly both at the same time."

The **intersection** of two sets $A$ and $B$, denoted $A \cap B$, is the set of all elements that are in both $A$ and $B$. That is, the intersection of two sets is the set of elements that are common to both sets. In set-builder notation, $A \cap B = \{x \mid x \in A \text{ and } x \in B\}$. For example, if $A = \{2, 4, 6, 8\}$ and $B = \{1, 2, 4, 5, 6\}$, then $A \cap B = \{2, 4, 6\}$. When two sets have no elements in common, their intersection is the empty set, and the sets are said to be **disjoint.** For example, for $A = \{2, 4, 6, 8\}$ and $C = \{1, 3, 5\}$, $A \cap C = \varnothing$, and $A$ and $C$ are disjoint.

The **complement** of a set $A$, denoted $A^C$, is the set of all elements in the universal set $U$ that are *not* in $A$. In set-builder notation, $A^C = \{x \mid x \in U, x \notin A\}$. For example, If $U = \{x \in \text{Integers} \mid 0 \le x < 10\}$ and $A = \{2, 4, 6, 8\}$, then $A^C = \{0, 1, 3, 5, 7, 9\}$.

A **Venn diagram** is a visual depiction of a set operation or relationship. In a Venn diagram, the universal set is usually represented by a rectangular region, which encloses everything else in the diagram. The sets in $U$ are represented by circles. Shading depicts relationships or the results of a set operation. Here are examples of Venn diagrams.

| Verbal Description | Symbolism | Venn Diagram |
|---|---|---|
| $x$ is an element of $A$ | $x \in A$ | 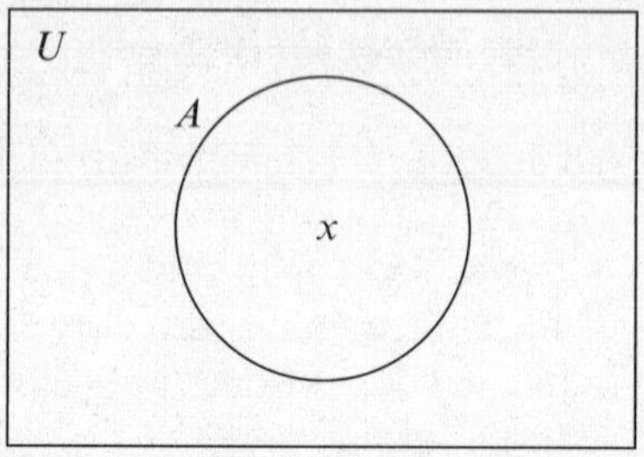 |
| $C$ is a proper subset of $A$ | $C \subset A$ | 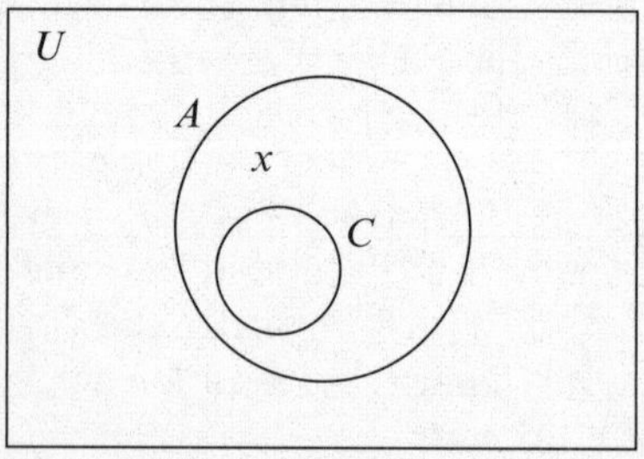 |
| $A$ and $B$ are disjoint | $A \cap B = \varnothing$ | 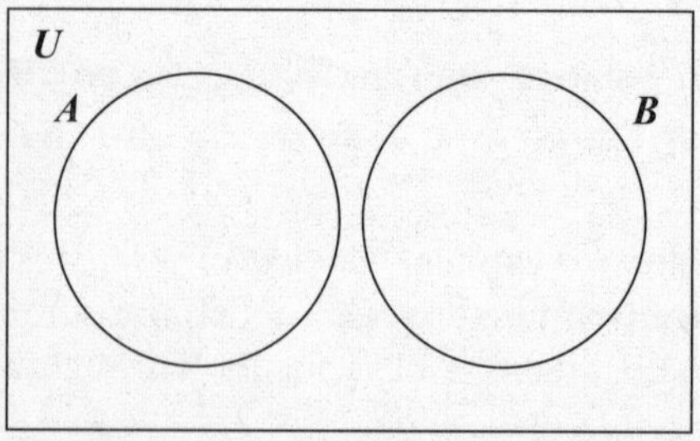 |

*(Continued)*

| Verbal Description | Symbolism | Venn Diagram |
|---|---|---|
| The union of $A$ and $B$ | $A \cup B$ | |
| The intersection of $A$ and $B$ | $A \cap B$ | |
| The complement of $A$ | $A^C$ | |

*Note:* An $x$ in a diagram means the region in which it is located is not empty.

# Counting Techniques

For this topic, you must be able to solve basic problems that involve counting techniques, including the fundamental counting principle, and permutations and combinations (for example, the number of arrangements of a set of objects or the number of ways to choose a committee from a club's membership).

# Fundamental Counting Principle

**Fundamental Counting Principle (FCP):** If one of two tasks can be done in any one of $m$ different ways, and, for each of these ways, a subsequent second task can be done in any one of $n$ different ways, then the first task *and* the second task can both be done, in the order given, in $m \cdot n$ ways.

You can extend the FCP to any number of tasks. Thus, in general, for a sequence of $k$ tasks, if a first task can be done in any one of $n_1$ different ways, and, for each of these ways, a subsequent second task can be done in any one of $n_2$ different ways, and, for each of these ways, a subsequent third task can be done in any one of $n_3$ different ways, and so on to the $k$th task, which can be done in any one of $n_k$ different ways, then the total number of different ways the sequence of $k$ tasks can be done, in the order given, is $n_1 \cdot n_2 \cdot n_3 \ldots \cdot n_k$. *Note:* This counting technique produces results in which *order determines different outcomes.* Here are examples.

> How many different 10-digit telephone numbers can begin with area code 210 and prefix 569?

Four additional digits are needed to complete telephone numbers that begin (210) 569-. Therefore, in this problem, there are four tasks to do: Namely, determine each of the additional four digits. Think of each of the positions of the four digits as a slot to fill. In this example, you make your selection for each slot from the same set: the 10 digits 0 to 9. Since digits in a telephone number can repeat, you say that "repetitions are allowed." There are 10 ways to fill the first slot, and for each of these ways, 10 ways to fill the second slot, and for each of these, 10 ways to fill the third slot, and for each of these, 10 ways to fill the fourth slot. Thus, the total number of different telephone numbers that can begin (210) 569- is $10 \cdot 10 \cdot 10 \cdot 10 = 10,000$.

> In how many possible ways can a president, vice-president, secretary, and membership chairperson be selected from 25 members of a club if all members are eligible for each position and no member can hold more than one office?

In this problem, there are four tasks: Namely, to select each of the four officers. Think of each of the officer positions as a slot to fill. Because the officers must all be different people, repetitions are not allowed in the selection process. There are 25 ways to fill the president's slot; after that, there are 24 ways remaining to fill the vice-president's slot; after that, there are 23 ways remaining to fill the secretary's slot; and, finally, there are 22 ways remaining to fill the membership chairperson's slot. Thus, there are $25 \cdot 24 \cdot 23 \cdot 22 = 303,600$ possible ways to select a president, vice-president, secretary, and membership chairperson from the 25 members of the club.

## Addition Principle

**Addition Principle:** If one task can be done in any one of $m$ ways and a second task can be done in any one of $n$ ways and if the two tasks *cannot* be done at the same time, then the number of different ways to do the first *or* the second task is $m + n$ ways. This principle can be extended to more than one task. Here is an example.

> A student must select 1 elective from a list of 3 art classes, 10 kinesiology classes, and 2 music classes. How many possible classes are there from which to choose?

The student can choose an elective from the art classes in 3 ways, from the kinesiology classes in 10 ways, and from the music classes in 2 ways. The student can choose only one elective. Therefore, there are $3 + 10 + 2 = 15$ classes from which to choose.

You can modify the addition principle for situations in which two tasks overlap; that is, when the two tasks can be done at the same time. If one task can be done in any one of $m$ ways and a second task can be done in any one of $n$ ways and if the two tasks *can* be done at the same time in $k$ different ways, then the number of ways to do the first or the second task is $m + n - k$. Here is an example.

> In drawing one card from the deck at random (that is, without looking or making a special selection), how many different ways can a king or a diamond be selected?

In a random drawing of a card from a well-shuffled deck of standard playing cards, there are 52 possible outcomes: ace, 2, 3, 4, 5, 6, 7, 8, 9, 10, jack, queen, and king of clubs (♣); ace, 2, 3, 4, 5, 6, 7, 8, 9, 10, jack, queen, and king of spades (♠); ace, 2, 3, 4, 5, 6, 7, 8, 9, 10, jack, queen, and king of hearts (♥); and ace, 2, 3, 4, 5, 6, 7, 8, 9, 10, jack, queen, and king of diamonds (♦). Clubs and spades have black coloration, and hearts and diamonds have red coloration. Jacks, queens, and kings are face cards. Here is a black-and-white illustration of a standard deck of playing cards.

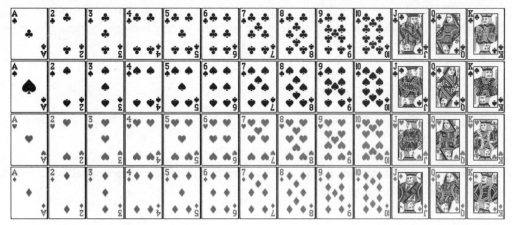

Source: *www.jfitz.com/cards/*

There are 4 ways to select a king, 13 ways to select a diamond, and 1 way to select a king and a diamond at the same time (the king of diamonds). Therefore, there are 4 + 13 – 1 = 16 ways to select a king or a diamond.

# Permutations

A **permutation** is an ordered arrangement of a set of distinctly different objects. For permutations, different orderings of the same objects are counted as different permutations. For example, two different permutations of the numbers 1 through 4 are 1234 and 4213. Thus, when the order of the objects in an arrangement is a differentiating factor in a problem, you are working with permutations.

Through a direct application of the FCP, the number of permutations of $n$ distinct objects is $n! = n(n-1)(n-2) \cdots (2)(1)$.

*Note:* The notation $n!$ is read "$n$ factorial." A factorial is the product of all positive integers less than or equal to a given positive integer. By definition, $0! = 1$.

Here is an example of a permutation problem.

> In how many different ways can five people be seated in a row of five identical seats?

You can work this problem using the FCP, or you can recognize that the seating arrangement is the permutation of five distinct objects (persons). Thus, there are $5! = 5 \cdot 4 \cdot 3 \cdot 2 \cdot 1 = 120$ different ways for the five people to be seated.

**Tip: On the ETS graphing calculator, fact(value) returns the factorial of a value (for example, fact(5) returns 120).**

The number of permutations of $r$ objects selected from $n$ distinct objects is $_nP_r = \dfrac{n!}{(n-r)!}$. When you apply this formula, it is important that you make sure the following conditions are met: The $n$ objects must be $n$ *distinct* objects, the $r$ objects must be selected *without repetition* from the same set, and you must count different orderings of the same objects as *different* outcomes. Here is an example.

> In how many possible ways can a president, vice-president, secretary, and membership chairperson be selected from 25 members of a club if all members are eligible for each position and no member can hold more than one office?

This problem was previously worked using the FCP, but now you can recognize that this problem satisfies the conditions for a permutation; that is, the 25 members of the club are distinct individuals, the 4 officers are selected without repetition from the same set of 25 members (no member can hold more than one office), and different orderings of the same people are counted as a different slate of officers. Thus, the number of permutations of 4 people selected from 25 people is $_{25}P_4 = \dfrac{25!}{(25-4)!} = \dfrac{25!}{(21)!} = \dfrac{25 \cdot 24 \cdot 23 \cdot 22 \cdot 21!}{21!} = 25 \cdot 24 \cdot 23 \cdot 22 = 303,600.$

There are 303,600 possible ways to select a president, vice-president, secretary, and membership chairperson from the 25 members of the club.

**Tip: On the ETS graphing calculator, the function nPr(n;r) returns the number of permutations of n taken r at a time (for example, nPr(25;4) returns 303600).**

The number of permutations of $n$ objects for which $n_1$ of the $n$ objects are identical, $n_2$ of the $n$ objects are identical, ..., $n_k$ of the $n$ objects are identical is $\dfrac{n!}{n_1! n_2! ... n_k!}$. Here is an example.

How many different "words" can you make using the 11 letters in the word *MISSISSIPPI* if you use all 11 letters each time?

Because the order in which different letters appear results in different words, this is a permutation problem. The word *MISSISSIPPI* consists of 11 letters: one *M*, four *I*'s, four *S*'s, and two *P*'s. Since the 11 objects (that is, the letters) to be arranged are not all mutually different objects, the number of different words is $\dfrac{n!}{n_1! n_2! \cdots n_k!} = \dfrac{11!}{4!4!2!} = 34,650.$

# Combinations

A **combination** is an arrangement of a set of distinct objects in which different orderings of the same objects are considered to be identical arrangements. For example, the set of three coins quarter, dime, and nickel is the same as the set nickel, dime, and quarter. That is, in a combination problem, different orderings of the same objects are *not* counted as separate results. When the order in which objects are arranged does *not* determine different outcomes, you are working with combinations.

The number of combinations of $r$ objects selected from $n$ distinct objects is $_nC_r = \dfrac{n!}{r!(n-r)!}.$

**Note: The notation $_nC_r$ is also written as $\begin{pmatrix} n \\ r \end{pmatrix}$.**

When you apply this formula, it is important that you make sure the following conditions are met: The $n$ objects must be $n$ *distinct* objects; the $r$ objects must be selected *without repetition* from the same set; and you must consider different orderings of the same objects to be *indistinguishable*. Here is an example.

How many ways can a 4-member committee be formed from the 25 members of a club?

Since the order in which committee members are arranged does not change the makeup of the committee, you would *not* try to work this problem using the FCP because it produces results in which order determines different outcomes. This example satisfies the conditions for a combination. That is, the 25 members of the club are distinct individuals, the 4 committee members are selected without repetition from the same set of 25 members, and different orderings of the same people are counted as the same committee. The number of combinations of 4 people selected from 25 people is $_{25}C_4 = \dfrac{25!}{4!(25-4)!} = \dfrac{25!}{4!(21)!} = \dfrac{25\cdot24\cdot23\cdot22\cdot21!}{4!21!} = \dfrac{25\cdot24\cdot23\cdot22}{4\cdot3\cdot2\cdot1} = 12{,}650$. There are 12,650 possible ways to form a 4-member committee from the 25 members of the club.

> **Tip: On the ETS graphing calculator, the function nCr(n;r) returns the number of combinations of n taken r at a time (for example, nCr(25;4) returns 12650).**

## Situations Indicating Permutations or Combinations

The one important way that combinations and permutations differ is that different orderings of the same objects are counted as separate results for permutation problems, but not for combination problems. The following table categorizes some situations as (most likely) indicating either a permutation or combination problem.

| Permutations | Combinations |
|---|---|
| creating passwords, license plates, words, or codes | forming a committee |
| assigning roles | making a collection of things (coins, books, and so on) |
| filling positions | counting subsets of a set |
| making ordered arrangements of things (people, books, colors, and so on) | dealing hands from a deck of cards |
| | listing the combinations from a set of objects |
| selecting first, second, third place, and such | selecting pizza toppings |
| distributing objects among several people or things | selecting questions from a test |
| | selecting students for groups |

For the Praxis MS Math test, you should be able to work most, if not all, of the permutation problems you might encounter by using the FCP rather than the formula $_nP_r$. For the situations similar to those given for combinations in the table, you should use $_nC_r$ (unless you can easily list the possibilities).

You can use the combination formula in conjunction with the FCP to determine the number of possible outcomes in certain situations. Here is an example.

> A party planner chooses 3 toy trucks, 7 toy cars, and 10 action figures from collections of 8 different toy trucks, 10 different toy cars, and 12 different action figures. How many possible ways can the party planner make the combined selections?

Thinking in terms of the FCP, the party planner has three tasks to do: Select 3 of the 8 toy trucks, select 7 of the 10 toy cars, and select 10 of the 12 action figures. Since the arrangement of the toy items in the individual selections of trucks, cars, and action figures is not a differentiating factor in the problem, you can determine the number of ways to select each of the toy items using the combination formula. Then, following those calculations, you can use the FCP to determine the total number of possible ways the party planner can make the combined selections. Thus, the number of possible ways the party planner can make the combined selections is

(number of ways to select 3 of 8 toy trucks) × (number of ways to select 7 of 10 toy cars) × (number of ways to select 10 of 12 action figures) =

$$_8C_3 \cdot {}_{10}C_7 \cdot {}_{12}C_{10} = \frac{8!}{3!(8-3)!} \cdot \frac{10!}{7!(10-7)!} \cdot \frac{12!}{10!(12-10)!} = \frac{8!}{3!5!} \cdot \frac{10!}{7!3!} \cdot \frac{12!}{10!2!} = 56\cdot120\cdot66 = 443{,}520$$

> **Tip:** The ETS graphing calculator is designed to numerically evaluate both $_nP_r$ and $_nC_r$. Make a point to practice using this time-saving feature of the calculator before you take the Praxis MS Math test.

# The Binomial Theorem and Pascal's Triangle

This section presents the binomial theorem and Pascal's triangle.

## The Binomial Theorem

The binomial theorem is used to expand a binomial to a power using the following formula:

$$(x+y)^n = \sum_{k=0}^{n} \binom{n}{k} x^{n-k} y^k$$

The values $\binom{n}{k}$ are the **binomial coefficients.**

> **Tip:** In each term, the sum of the exponents on x and y is n, and the exponent on x decreases from n to 0, while the exponent on y increases from 0 to n.

Here is an example.

---

Expand $(x+y)^3$.

---

$$(x+y)^3 = \sum_{k=0}^{3} \binom{3}{k} x^{3-k} y^k = \binom{3}{0} x^3 y^0 + \binom{3}{1} x^2 y^1 + \binom{3}{2} x^1 y^2 + \binom{3}{3} x^0 y^3 = x^3 + 3x^2 y + 3xy^2 + y^3$$

**Tip:** Notice that $\binom{3}{0} = \binom{3}{3}$ and $\binom{3}{1} = \binom{3}{2}$. In general, $\binom{n}{r} = \binom{n}{n-r}$.

You can use the binomial theorem to show that, counting the empty set, the number of subsets of a set consisting of $n$ elements is $2^n$. For example, when $n = 3$, the number of subsets of size 0 is $\binom{3}{0}$, of size 1 is $\binom{3}{1}$, of size 2 is $\binom{3}{2}$, and of size 3 is $\binom{3}{3}$ for a total of $= \binom{3}{0} + \binom{3}{1} + \binom{3}{2} + \binom{3}{3} = \sum_{k=0}^{3} \binom{3}{k} 1^{3-k} 1^k = (1+1)^3 = 2^3$ (which is 8).

## Pascal's Triangle

**Pascal's triangle** is a triangular array of numbers that can be derived from the formula $\binom{n}{r}$. Row 0, the top row, of the triangle has one element; Row 1, the next row, has two elements; Row 2 has three elements; Row 3 has four elements; and so on. Each row begins and ends with a 1 and is symmetric from left to right, including Row 0, whose one element is 1. An element, other than a 1, in a row is the sum of the two elements most directly above it. Here is an example of Pascal's triangle showing Row 0 through Row 8.

```
0:                          1
1:                       1     1
2:                    1     2     1
3:                 1     3     3     1
4:              1     4     6     4     1
5:           1     5    10    10     5     1
6:        1     6    15    20    15     6     1
7:     1     7    21    35    35    21     7     1
8:  1     8    28    56    70    56    28     8     1
        ⋮     ⋮     ⋮     ⋮     ⋮     ⋮     ⋮     ⋮
```

For any row $n$ in Pascal's triangle, the elements are the numbers $\binom{n}{r}$ for $r = 0, \ldots, n$, in this order. These numbers also are the **binomial coefficients** in the expansion of $(x + y)^n$. For example, the elements in Row 3 of Pascal's triangle are $\binom{3}{0} = 1$, $\binom{3}{1} = 3$, $\binom{3}{2} = 3$, and $\binom{3}{3} = 1$. When you expand $(x + y)^3$, you obtain $x^3 + 3x^2y + 3xy^2 + y^3$, which has coefficients 1, 3, 3, 1, the same numbers that are in Row 3 of Pascal's triangle.

If you find it convenient, you can use Pascal's triangle to find values of $\binom{n}{r}$, rather than working out the formula $_nC_r$ or using the ETS graphing calculator. For example, to determine $\binom{6}{2}$, locate the third term in Row 6 of Pascal's triangle, which is 15.

**Tip:** Keep in mind that for each row in Pascal's triangle, $\binom{n}{r}$ starts at $r = 0$, not 1.

# Sequences

A **sequence** is a function whose domain is a subset of the integers, usually the natural numbers $N = \{1, 2, 3, \ldots\}$ or the whole numbers $W = \{0, 1, 2, \ldots\}$. (For this section, sequences are restricted, without loss of generality, to domains equal to $N$.) The notation $a_n$ denotes the image of the integer $n$; that is, $a_n$ is the **$n$th term** (or **element**) of the sequence. The **initial term** (or first term) of the sequence is denoted $a_1$. When $a_n$ can be expressed as a formula that you can use to generate any term of the sequence, it is conventional to call $a_n$ the **general term** of the sequence. Even though a sequence is a function (a set of ordered pairs), it is customary to describe a sequence by listing the terms in the order in which they correspond to the natural numbers. For example, the list of terms of the sequence with initial term $a_1$ is $a_1, a_2, a_3, a_4, \ldots, a_n, \ldots$.

*Note:* The three dots (…) indicate that the sequence continues in the same manner.

## Arithmetic Sequences

In an **arithmetic sequence,** the same number, called the **common difference,** is added (algebraically) to each term to obtain the subsequent term in the sequence. An arithmetic sequence (also called arithmetic progression) has the form $a_1, a_1 + d, a_1 + 2d, \ldots, a_1 + (n-1)d, \ldots$, where $a_1$ is the initial term, $d$ is the common difference between terms, and $a_n = a_1 + (n-1)d$ is the general term. Here are examples.

> What is the next term in the sequence 4, 9, 14, 19, 24, …?

The number 5 is added to a term to obtain the term that follows it, so the next term in the sequence is $24 + 5 = 29$.

> What is the next term in the sequence 10, 6, 2, –2, –6, …?

The number –4 is added to a term to obtain the term that follows it, so the next term in the sequence is $-6 + -4 = -10$.

> What is the 50th term in the sequence –2, 2, 6, 10, 14, …?

The first term $a_1$ is –2. The common difference is 4. The general term is $a_n = a_1 + (n-1)d = -2 + (n-1)(4)$. Thus, the 50th term is $a_{50} = -2 + (50-1)(4) = -2 + (49)(4) = -2 + 196 = 194$.

## Geometric Sequences

In a **geometric sequence,** each term is multiplied by the same number, called the **common ratio,** to obtain the subsequent term in the sequence. A geometric sequence (also called geometric progression) has the form $a_1, a_1r, a_1r^2, …, a_1r^{n-1}, …$, where $a_1$ is the initial term, $r$ is the common ratio between terms, and $a_n = a_1r^{n-1}$ is the general term. Here are examples.

> What is the next term in the sequence 4, 8, 16, 32, 64, …?

Each term is multiplied by 2 to obtain the term that follows it, so the next term in the sequence is $64 \cdot 2 = 128$.

> What is the next term in the sequence 25, 5, 1, $\frac{1}{5}$, $\frac{1}{25}$, …?

Each term is multiplied by $\frac{1}{5}$ to obtain the term that follows it, so the next term in the sequence is $\frac{1}{25} \cdot \frac{1}{5} = \frac{1}{125}$.

> What is the 9th term in the sequence –1, –2, –4, –8, –16, …?

The first term $a_1$ is –1. The common ratio is 2. The general term is $a_n = a_1r^{n-1} = (-1)2^{n-1}$. Thus, the 9th term is $a_9 = (-1)2^{9-1} = (-1)2^8 = (-1)(256) = -256$.

Of course, you could have worked this problem by continuing to multiply by 2 until you reached the 9th term as shown here.

$$-1, \quad -2, \quad -4, \quad -8, \quad -16, \quad -32, \quad -64, \quad -128, \quad -256$$
$$\text{1st} \quad \text{2nd} \quad \text{3rd} \quad \text{4th} \quad \text{5th} \quad \text{6th} \quad \text{7th} \quad \text{8th} \quad \text{9th}$$

*Tip:* If you use this latter approach, count the terms to be sure you have the correct term.

## Figurate-Number Sequences

Some sequences consist of numbers called **figurate numbers,** so called because they can be displayed as geometric shapes. Here is an example of a sequence of **triangular numbers** with their corresponding geometric shapes. The $n$th term is $\frac{n(n+1)}{2}$.

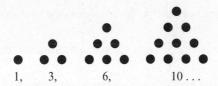

1,     3,     6,     10 . . .

Here is an example of a sequence of **square numbers** with their corresponding geometric shapes. The $n$th term is $n^2$.

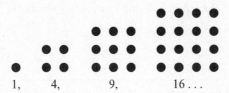

1,     4,     9,     16 . . .

# Recursive Sequences

A **recursive sequence** is one whose terms are obtained by means of a recursive definition. A **recursive definition** for a sequence is a definition that includes the value of one or more initial terms of the sequence and a formula that tells you how to find each term from previous terms. Here is an example.

List the first four terms of the sequence defined as follows: $f(1) = 1$, $f(n) = 3f(n - 1) + 1$ for $n \geq 2$.

For the recursive formula given in the problem, you will need to find the previous term before you can find the next term. You proceed as shown here.

$f(1) = 1$
$f(2) = 3f(1) + 1 = 3(1) + 1 = 3 + 1 = 4$
$f(3) = 3f(2) + 1 = 3(4) + 1 = 12 + 1 = 13$
$f(4) = 3f(3) + 1 = 3(13) + 1 = 39 + 1 = 40$

Thus, the first four terms are 1, 4, 13, and 40.

A **Fibonacci sequence** is defined by the recursive definition: $a_1 = 1$, $a_2 = 1$, and $a_n = a_{n-1} + a_{n-2}$, $n \geq 3$. A list showing the first seven terms is 1, 1, 2, 3, 5, 8, 13, ….

# Identifying Patterns for Sequences

For the Praxis MS Math test, you might be asked to determine the general term or the next term of a sequence when a few terms of the sequence are given. Even though, in reality, the initial terms do not necessarily determine a unique sequence, you will have to assume there is a pattern that continues in the same manner, and then you can make an educated guess about the general term or the next term. Look for an identifiable pattern such as:

**Arithmetic:** $a_1 + (n - 1)d$ (Is there a common difference?)

**Geometric:** $a_1 r^{n-1}$ (Is there a common ratio?)

**Figurate:** $\dfrac{n(n+1)}{2}$ or $n^2$ (Are the terms triangular numbers or perfect squares?)

**Quadratic:** $n^2 \pm c$ or $kn^2 \pm c$ (Are the terms perfect squares or a multiple of perfect squares plus or minus a constant?)

**Cubic:** $n^3 \pm c$ or $kn^3 \pm c$ (Are the terms perfect cubes or a multiple of perfect cubes plus or minus a constant?)

**Exponential:** $2^n \pm c$, $3^n \pm c$, $k2^n \pm c$, or $k3^n \pm c$ (Are the terms powers of 2 or 3 or a multiple of powers of 2 or 3 plus or minus a constant?)

**Factorial:** $n!$ (Are the terms obtained by multiplying the previous terms in some way?)

**Recursive:** $a_n = a_{n-1} \pm a_{n-2}$ (Are the terms obtained by adding or subtracting the previous terms in some way?)

Here are examples.

> Find the 20th term in the sequence 2, 5, 8, 11, 14, ….

The terms shown have a common difference of 3 with initial term $a_1 = 2$. If this pattern continues in the same manner, the general term is $a_1 + (n-1)d = 2 + (n-1)(3)$. Thus, the 20th term is $2 + (20-1)(3) = 2 + (19)(3) = 59$.

> Find the 10th term in the sequence 2, 6, 18, 54, 162, ….

The terms shown have a common ratio of 3 with initial term $a_1 = 2$. If this pattern continues in the same manner, the general term is $a_1 r^{n-1} = 2 \cdot 3^{n-1}$. Thus, the 10th term is $2 \cdot 3^{10-1} = 2 \cdot 3^9 = 39{,}366$.

> Find the 8th term in the sequence 2, 5, 10, 17, 26, ….

The terms shown can be rewritten as $1^2 + 1$, $2^2 + 1$, $3^2 + 1$, $4^2 + 1$, $5^2 + 1$, …. If this pattern continues in the same manner, the general term is $n^2 + 1$. Thus, the 8th term is $8^2 + 1 = 64 + 1 = 65$.

> **Tip:** Sometimes it is convenient to begin an arithmetic or geometric sequence at $n = 0$ instead of $n = 1$, so be sure to check for the starting value of $n$ when you work problems involving sequences on the Praxis MS Math test.

# Algorithms and Flowcharts

Algorithms and flowcharts are tools that standardize processes. Each provides an outline of the steps in a process. The amount of detail you include in an algorithm or flowchart depends on how you want to use it and the level of sophistication of the intended audience concerning the topic. All necessary steps should be listed in a logical order. The algorithm or flowchart should be clear and easy to follow.

# Algorithms

An **algorithm** is a step-by-step procedure for performing a task or solving a problem. The steps are numbered to indicate the sequence of steps.

Here is an example of using an algorithm to solve a problem.

---

Petra makes an online purchase from Store X. She selects three items: a blouse for $34.50, a pajama set for $29.95, and a set of soup spoons for $15.75. Use the following algorithm to determine the standard shipping charge for Petra's online purchase at Store X.

**Algorithm for Determining the Standard Shipping Charge for an Online Purchase at Store X**

1. Record the price for each item.
2. Find the sum of the prices listed in step 1.
3. Use the shipping charges table (shown below) to determine the shipping charge that applies to the sum in step 2.

### Store X Standard Shipping Charges per Address

| | |
|---|---|
| up to $9.99 | $3.95 |
| $10.00–$24.99 | $5.95 |
| $25.00–$39.99 | $7.95 |
| $40.00–$54.99 | $10.95 |
| $55.00–$79.99 | $13.95 |
| $80.00–$99.99 | $16.95 |
| $100 or over | $18.95 |

---

Proceed step-by-step through the algorithm's instructions.

1. Record the price for each item.

$$\$34.50, \$29.95, \$15.75$$

2. Find the sum of the prices listed in step 1.

$$\$34.50 + \$29.95 + \$15.75 = \$80.20$$

3. Use the shipping charge table (shown above) to determine the shipping charge that applies to the sum in step 2.

Petra's total of $80.20 falls between $80.00 and $99.99. Therefore, according to the table, the shipping charge for Petra's online purchase is $16.95.

# Flowcharts

A **flowchart** is a visual depiction of the steps in a process. The following table shows some standard symbols that are usually included in a flowchart.

| Symbol | Explanation |
|--------|-------------|
| Start/End (oval) | **Start** and **End** steps are enclosed in ovals. |
| Action (rectangle) | **Action** steps are enclosed in rectangles. |
| Decision (diamond) | **Decision** steps are enclosed in diamonds. Each diamond should have at least two exits. For example, one path if the decision is yes; another path if the decision is no. |
| Sequence (flowline) | The **sequence** of steps is indicated by **flowlines** with **arrows** indicating the next step. |

Here is an example of using a flowchart to solve a problem.

Tyrell makes an online purchase from Store Y. He selects two items: an apple corer for $8.95 and a pair of socks for $15.75. Use the following flowchart to determine the standard shipping charge for Tyrell's online purchase at Store Y.

**Flowchart for Determining the Standard Shipping Charges for an Online Purchase at Store Y**

List the prices of the items selected.

Compute, $S$, the sum of the prices of the items selected.

$S < \$25.00$ — Yes → Shipping Charge = $4.00

No

$\$25.00 \leq S \leq \$49.99$ — Yes → Shipping Charge = $6.00

No

$S > \$49.99$ — Yes → Shipping Charge = $0.00

Follow the arrows step-by-step through the flowchart.

The sum of the prices of Tyrell's items is $8.95 + $15.75, which is $24.70. This amount is less than $25.00. Therefore, according to the flowchart, Tyrell's shipping charge is $4.00.

# Sample Questions

**Directions:** Read the directions for each question carefully. This set of questions has several different question types. For each question, select a single answer choice unless written instructions preceding the question state otherwise.

1. Let the universal set $U$ = {whole numbers ≤ 10}, $A$ = {$x \in U \mid x$ is odd}, and $B$ = {$x \in U \mid x$ is prime}. Find $A \cap B$.

   Ⓐ  {3, 5, 7}
   Ⓑ  {2, 3, 5, 7}
   Ⓒ  {1, 2, 3, 5, 7}
   Ⓓ  {1, 2, 3, 5, 7, 9}

2. Ximena's password for a certain online account consists of four letters of the English alphabet followed by two digits. The account login is not case sensitive and repetitions are allowed. Which of the following computations could be used to calculate the number of different passwords for Ximena's online account?

   Ⓐ  $(4)(2)$
   Ⓑ  $(_{26}C_4)(_{10}C_2)$
   Ⓒ  $(26^4)(10^2)$
   Ⓓ  $36^6$

**For the following question, enter your numeric answer in the box below the question.**

3. A civic club has 150 members. A committee of 3 members is to be selected to attend a national conference. How many different committees could be formed?

   ☐

**For the following question, select <u>all</u> that apply.**

4. Given the recursive sequence defined by $f(1) = 1$ and $f(n) = 2f(n-1) + 1$ for $n \geq 2$, which of the following numbers are terms of the sequence?

   Ⓐ  1
   Ⓑ  5
   Ⓒ  7
   Ⓓ  15

**For the following question, enter your numeric answer in the box below the question.**

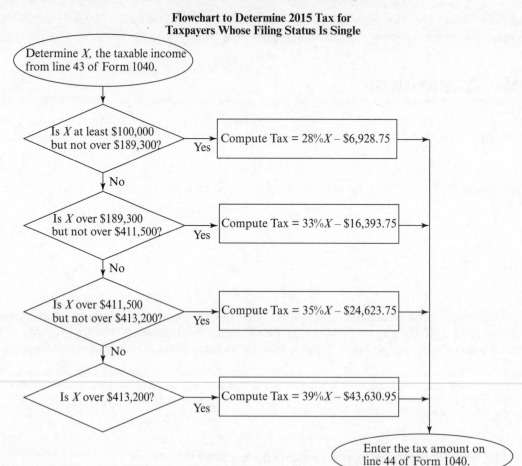

**Flowchart to Determine 2015 Tax for
Taxpayers Whose Filing Status Is Single**

Determine $X$, the taxable income from line 43 of Form 1040.

Is $X$ at least \$100,000 but not over \$189,300? — Yes → Compute Tax = 28%$X$ – \$6,928.75

No

Is $X$ over \$189,300 but not over \$411,500? — Yes → Compute Tax = 33%$X$ – \$16,393.75

No

Is $X$ over \$411,500 but not over \$413,200? — Yes → Compute Tax = 35%$X$ – \$24,623.75

No

Is $X$ over \$413,200? — Yes → Compute Tax = 39%$X$ – \$43,630.95

Enter the tax amount on line 44 of Form 1040.

5.  In 2015, a taxpayer's taxable income on line 43 of Form 1040 was \$195,400. This taxpayer's filing status was "Single" in 2015. Use the flowchart shown to determine the 2015 tax amount to be entered on line 44 of Form 1040 for this individual.

$ [_____]

# Answer Explanations

**1.  A.** The set $U$ = {0, 1, 2, 3, ..., 10}, the set $A$ = {1, 3, 5, 7, 9}, and the set $B$ = {2, 3, 5, 7}. The intersection of $A$ and $B$ is the set of elements common to both. Thus, $A \cap B$ = {3, 5, 7}, choice A.

**2.  C.** Use the FCP. There are six slots to fill for a password. There are 26 possibilities for each of the four letters and 10 possible values for each of the two digits. Thus, the total number of possible passwords is $26 \cdot 26 \cdot 26 \cdot 26 \cdot 10 \cdot 10 = (26^4)(10^2)$, choice C.

**3.  551,300** Because the order in which committee members are arranged does not make a difference in the composition of the committee, the number of different 3-member committees that can be selected from the 150 members is $_{150}C_3$ = 551,300. *Tip:* Use the ETS graphing calculator to compute nCr(150; 3).

**4.  A, C, D.** For the recursive sequence given, $f(1) = 1$ (choice A); $f(2) = 2f(1) + 1 = 2(1) + 1 = 2 + 1 = 3$; $f(3) = 2f(2) + 1 = 2(3) + 1 = 6 + 1 = 7$ (choice C); and $f(4) = 2f(3) + 1 = 2(7) + 1 = 14 + 1 = 15$ (choice D).

**5.  \$48,088.25** The taxpayer's taxable income of \$195,400 is over \$189,300, but not over \$411,500. According to the flowchart, the 2015 tax amount for this individual with taxable income, $X$, of \$195,400 is 33%$X$ – \$16,393.75 = 0.33(\$195,400) – \$16,393.75 = \$64,482.00 – \$16,393.75 = \$48,088.25.

# Chapter 7

# Probability

This chapter provides a review of key ideas and formulas of probability that are important for you to know for the Praxis MS Math test. Sample questions, comparable to what might be presented on the Praxis MS Math test, are given at the end of the chapter. The answer explanations for the sample questions are provided immediately following.

## Random Experiments, Sample Spaces, and Probability Measures

This topic presents the concepts of random experiments and their corresponding sample spaces and introduces you to probability measures associated with sample spaces.

### Random Experiments and Sample Spaces

A **chance process** gives results that cannot be determined beforehand. A **random experiment** is a chance process such that, on any single repetition of the experiment, exactly one outcome occurs. It is assumed that all the possible outcomes are known before the random experiment is performed, but which of the possibilities will in fact occur is uncertain. Here are examples. (*Note:* To facilitate the discussion that follows, the experiments are numbered; when no confusion might occur, experiment means "random experiment.")

---

**Experiment 1:** Flip a U.S. coin one time and observe the coin's up face.

**Experiment 2:** Perform one toss of a number cube, whose six faces are numbered 1 through 6, and observe the up face.

**Experiment 3:** Draw one card without looking from a well-shuffled standard deck of 52 playing cards and observe which card was drawn. (*Note:* When you draw "without looking," you are making a **random** selection.)

**Experiment 4:** Draw one tile (without looking) from a box containing five wooden, 1-inch-square tiles numbered 1 through 5, and observe the up face.

**Experiment 5:** Spin the pointer of a circular spinner one time. In one spin, the pointer will turn a random number of times and stop. The spinner has three sectors. The color of each sector and the percentage of the spinner that color occupies are blue (50%), green (25%), and yellow (25%).

---

For each of these random experiments, you get a single outcome that occurs by chance. You cannot determine with certainty the outcome beforehand. That is, you cannot say for certain what the exact outcome will be. However, for each experiment you can produce its set of *possible* outcomes. The set, $S$, of possible outcomes of a random experiment is its **sample space.** Each element of $S$ is an **outcome** (or simple event, sample point, or elementary outcome). Here are the sample spaces of the five experiments listed above.

**Experiment 1:** $S = \{H, T\}$, where "H" represents the outcome "Heads appears on the up face" and "T" represents the outcome "Tails appears on the up face." *Note:* U.S. coins have an image of a historical figure (person) on one side, which is referred to as "Heads." The image on the opposite side is referred to as "Tails."

**Experiment 2:** $S = \{1, 2, 3, 4, 5, 6\}$, where "1" represents "1 appears on the up face," "2" represents "2 appears on the up face," and so on to "6" represents "6 appears on the up face."

**Experiment 3:** $S = \{♣A, ♣2, ♣3, ♣4, ♣5, ♣6, ♣7, ♣8, ♣9, ♣10, ♣J, ♣Q, ♣K, ♠A, ♠2, ♠3, ♠4, ♠5, ♠6, ♠7, ♠8, ♠9, ♠10, ♠J, ♠Q, ♠K, ♥A, ♥2, ♥3, ♥4, ♥5, ♥6, ♥7, ♥8, ♥9, ♥10, ♥J, ♥Q, ♥K, ♦A, ♦2, ♦3, ♦4, ♦5, ♦6, ♦7, ♦8, ♦9, ♦10, ♦J, ♦Q, ♦K\}$, where ♣A represents the ace of clubs, ♣2 represents the 2 of clubs, ... ♣J represents the jack of clubs, ♣Q represents the queen of clubs, ♣K represents the king of clubs, and so on to ♦A represents the ace of diamonds, ♦2 represents the 2 of diamonds, ... ♦J represents the jack of diamonds, ♦Q represents the queen of diamonds, and ♦K represents the king of diamonds. *Note:* A standard deck of 52 playing cards consists of four suits: clubs (♣), spades (♠), hearts (♥), and diamonds (♦). Clubs and spades are black-colored suits; hearts and diamonds are red-colored suits. Each suit has 13 cards consisting of three face cards (king, queen, and jack) and number cards from 1 (ace) to 10 as shown in the following black-and-white illustration.

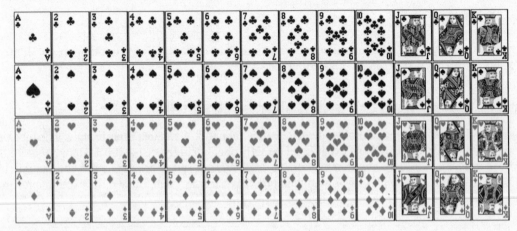

Source: *www.jfitz.com/cards/*

**Experiment 4:** $S = \{1, 2, 3, 4, 5\}$, where "1" represents the outcome "the tile drawn shows a 1," "2" represents the outcome "the tile drawn shows a 2," and so on to "5" represents the outcome "the tile drawn shows a 5."

**Experiment 5:** $S = \{B, G, Y\}$, where "B" represents the outcome "the pointer stops on blue," "G" represents the outcome "the pointer stops on green," and "Y" represents the outcome "the pointer stops on yellow."

**Note: A sample space can be finite or infinite. For the Praxis MS Math test, only finite sample spaces are considered.**

Random experiments can have several stages. For example, consider the experiment of flipping two coins and observing the up faces. Think of the experiment as having two stages. First, flip the first coin and observe the up face. Next, flip the second coin and observe the up face. Three common methods for generating the possible outcomes for such an experiment are organized lists, tables, and tree diagrams.

Here is an example of using an **organized list** to generate the possible outcomes.

Proceed systematically. First, list H twice on the first coin with each of the possibilities (H, T) for the second coin. Next, list T twice on the first coin with each of the possibilities (H, T) for the second coin.

| First Coin | Second Coin |
|------------|-------------|
| H | H |
| H | T |
| T | H |
| T | T |

**Tip: When you use an organized list to count possibilities, be careful to proceed in a systematic manner, as illustrated in this example. Otherwise, you might overlook a possibility or count one more than once.**

Here is an example of using a **table** to generate the possible outcomes.

|  | First Coin | |
| --- | --- | --- |
| **Second Coin** | **H** | **T** |
| H | HH | HT |
| T | TH | TT |

Here is an example of using a **tree diagram** to generate the possible outcomes.

First, draw a branch for each possibility for the first stage (in this case, the first coin). Next, attach branches for each possibility for the second stage (in this case, the second coin) to each of the possibilities for the first stage. Then, list the possible outcomes by tracing along the branches.

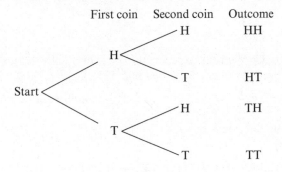

Each of the three methods results in the same four outcomes. The possible outcomes when two coins are flipped are HH (representing heads on the first coin and heads on the second coin), HT (representing heads on the first coin and tails on the second coin), TH (representing tails on the first coin and heads on the second coin), and TT (representing tails on the first coin and tails on the second coin). Therefore, $S = \{HH, HT, TH, TT\}$ is the sample space for flipping two coins.

Notice that HT and TH are NOT the same outcome. HT is the outcome of heads on the first coin and tails on the second coin, but TH is the outcome of tails on the first coin and heads on the second coin.

You can extend organized lists and tree diagrams to three or more stages. Here is a tree diagram for flipping three coins.

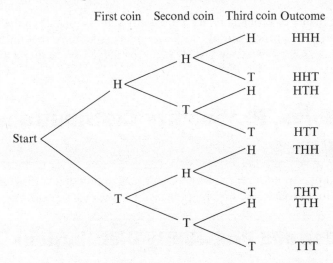

$S = \{HHH, HHT, HTH, HTT, THH, THT, TTH, TTT\}$ is the sample space for flipping three coins. The number of possible outcomes is 8.

Determining the outcomes in a sample space is a critical step in solving a probability problem. For simple experiments, organized lists, tables, and tree diagrams are useful ways to generate a list of the outcomes. More sophisticated counting techniques, which include the fundamental counting principle, permutations, and combinations, are needed for problems that are less straightforward. See the topic "Counting Techniques" in Chapter 6 for a discussion of these methods.

## Probability Measures

A **probability measure** on a sample space, $S$, is a function that assigns to each outcome in $S$ a real number between 0 and 1, inclusive, so that the values assigned to the outcomes in $S$ sum to 1 (see Chapter 3 for a general discussion of functions). The value assigned to an outcome in $S$ is the **probability value** of that outcome.

Consider the sample space $S = \{1, 2, 3, 4, 5\}$ from Experiment 4 of drawing one tile (without looking) from a box containing five wooden, 1-inch-square tiles numbered 1 through 5. Given that the tiles are physically identical and the drawing is performed without looking (that is, randomly), each tile has a 1 in 5 chance of being drawn. Thus, a logical probability value for each of the five outcomes in $S$ is $\frac{1}{5}$. The sum of the probability values of the five outcomes in $S$ is $\frac{1}{5}+\frac{1}{5}+\frac{1}{5}+\frac{1}{5}+\frac{1}{5}=\frac{5}{5}=1$.

Consider the sample space $S = \{B, G, Y\}$ from Experiment 5 of spinning the pointer of a circular spinner one time, where the spinner has three sectors that are colored blue (50%), green (25%), and yellow (25%). A logical probability value for the outcome B is $\frac{1}{2}$, for the outcome G is $\frac{1}{4}$, and for the outcome Y is $\frac{1}{4}$. The sum of the probability values of the three outcomes in $S$ is $\frac{1}{2}+\frac{1}{4}+\frac{1}{4}=\frac{4}{4}=1$.

Consider the sample space $S = \{HHH, HHT, HTH, HTT, THH, THT, TTH, TTT\}$ from the experiment of flipping three coins. A logical probability value for each of the eight outcomes in $S$ is $\frac{1}{8}$. The sum of the probability values of the eight outcomes in $S$ is $\frac{1}{8}+\frac{1}{8}+\frac{1}{8}+\frac{1}{8}+\frac{1}{8}+\frac{1}{8}+\frac{1}{8}+\frac{1}{8}=\frac{8}{8}=1$.

> **Tip:** For a sample space resulting from a real-world chance experiment, usually there is only one probability measure that is considered appropriate. In particular, objects such as coins and number cubes are considered to be fair; that is, such objects do not favor one outcome over another.

According to the frequency theory of probability, the probability values assigned to the outcomes of a sample space are the limiting values of the proportions of times over many repetitions that the experiment will result in the different possible outcomes (see "Frequency Theory of Probability" later in this chapter for a discussion of this topic).

# Random Variables, Probability Distributions, and Expected Value

This topic presents the concept of random variables and their related probability distributions. You will calculate the expected value of a random variable and interpret the result as the mean of the probability distribution.

## Random Variables and Probability Distributions

A **random variable** is a function $X$ that assigns a real number $x$, determined by chance, to each and every outcome in a sample space $S$. The number $x$ is the **value** of the random variable. It is determined by the outcome of a random experiment.

*Note:* Random variables are usually denoted by uppercase letters, often $X$, $Y$, or $Z$.

Like probability measures, a random variable is a function over a sample space; however (unlike probability measures), there are no restrictions on the values assigned to the outcomes of $S$, nor to their sum.

**Note: Random variables can be discrete or continuous. This chapter deals only with discrete random variables. A discrete random variable is one in which its values can be counted or listed.**

The **probability distribution** of a discrete random variable gives the probability for each value of the random variable in a graph, table, or by means of a formula.

Consider the sample space $S = \{1, 2, 3, 4, 5\}$ from Experiment 4 (given previously) of drawing one tile (without looking) from a box containing five wooden, 1-inch-square tiles numbered 1 through 5. Define the random variable $X$ as the function that assigns the value 1 to the outcomes that show an even number on the drawn tile and the value 6 to the outcomes that show an odd number on the drawn tile. The possible values for the random variable $X$ are 1 and 6. Specifically, the values of the random variable $X$ for each of the outcomes in $S$ are $X(1) = 6$, $X(2) = 1$, $X(3) = 6$, $X(4) = 1$, and $X(5) = 6$. Notice that a random variable can assign the same value to more than one outcome in the sample space. The following table represents the probability distribution for the random variable $X$, where $x$ is the value of the random variable $X$ and $P(X = x)$ is the probability that the random variable $X$ assumes the value $x$.

| $x$ | $P(X = x)$ |
|---|---|
| 1 | $\dfrac{2}{5}$ |
| 6 | $\dfrac{3}{5}$ |

The entries in the $P(X = x)$ column sum to 1 (that is, $\dfrac{2}{5} + \dfrac{3}{5} = \dfrac{5}{5} = 1$) because $X$ assigns every outcome in $S$ one and only one of the values 1 or 6.

Consider the sample space $S = \{$HHH, HHT, HTH, HTT, THH, THT, TTH, TTT$\}$ from the experiment (given previously) of flipping three coins. Define the random variable $Y$ as the number of heads observed in an outcome. The possible values for the random variable $Y$ are 0, 1, 2, and 3. Specifically, the values of the random variable $Y$ for each of the outcomes in $S$ are $Y(\text{HHH}) = 3$, $Y(\text{HHT}) = 2$, $Y(\text{HTH}) = 2$, $Y(\text{HTT}) = 1$, $Y(\text{THH}) = 2$, $Y(\text{THT}) = 1$, $Y(\text{TTH}) = 1$, and $Y(\text{TTT}) = 0$. The following graph represents the probability distribution for $Y$.

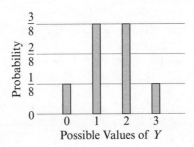

The probabilities for the possible values of $Y$ sum to 1 (that is, $\dfrac{1}{8} + \dfrac{3}{8} + \dfrac{3}{8} + \dfrac{1}{8} = \dfrac{8}{8} = 1$) because $Y$ assigns every outcome in $S$ one and only one of the values 0, 1, 2, or 3.

# Expected Value

If $X$ is a discrete random variable that takes on values $x_1$, $x_2$, ..., $x_n$, with respective probabilities $P(x_1)$, $P(x_2)$, ..., $P(x_n)$, then the **expected value,** denoted $E(X)$, is the **theoretical mean** $\mu$ of $X$ and is given by

$$\mu = E(X) = x_1 P(x_1) + x_2 P(x_2) + ... + x_n P(x_n)$$

Suppose $X$ is the random variable that has the probability distribution shown.

| $x$ | $P(X = x)$ |
|---|---|
| 1 | $\dfrac{2}{5}$ |
| 6 | $\dfrac{3}{5}$ |

The expected value of $X$ is

$$\mu = E(X) = x_1 P(x_1) + x_2 P(x_2) = 1\left(\frac{2}{5}\right) + 6\left(\frac{3}{5}\right) = \frac{20}{5} = 4$$

You can use your understanding of probability distributions and expected value to decide whether a game is fair. For example, suppose you pay 5 chips to play a game with the numbered tiles. You receive 6 chips if the tile drawn shows an odd number and 1 chip if the tile drawn shows an even number. Your expected value for the game is 4 chips. Because you are paying a 5-chip fee to play the game, on average, you lose 1 chip per play. The game is not fair, because you, the player, can expect to lose.

# Events

For this topic, you will learn basic concepts related to events and use the classical method for computing probabilities of simple events.

# Basic Concepts of Events

An **event,** $E$, is a collection of outcomes from a sample space $S$; that is, an event $E$ is a subset of $S$. (See "Sets" in Chapter 6 for a discussion of sets and subsets.) $E$ can consist of no outcomes (the null set) or from a single outcome up to all the outcomes in $S$. By convention, capital letters are used to designate events, with the word *event* being omitted in cases where the meaning is clear.

An event $E$ is said to **occur** if a member of $E$ occurs when the experiment is performed. For example, if the sample space is the set of outcomes from Experiment 4 (given previously) of drawing one tile (without looking) from a box containing five wooden, 1-inch-square tiles numbered 1 through 5, and $E$ is the event that the tile drawn shows an odd number, then $S = \{1, 2, 3, 4, 5\}$ and $E = \{1, 3, 5\}$.

The **probability of an event $E$,** denoted $P(E)$, is the sum of the probability values assigned to the individual outcomes in $E$. It is a numerical value between 0 and 1, inclusive, that quantifies the chance or likelihood that $E$ will occur.

For example, given the sample space $S = \{1, 2, 3, 4, 5\}$, the set of outcomes from the tile-drawing experiment (Experiment 4), let $E = \{1, 3, 5\}$, the event that the tile drawn shows an odd number. Then,

$P(E) = P(1) + P(3) + P(5) = \dfrac{1}{5} + \dfrac{1}{5} + \dfrac{1}{5} = \dfrac{3}{5}$.

An **impossible event** is one that cannot occur. The probability of an impossible event is 0. A **certain event** is one that is guaranteed to occur. The probability of a certain event is 1. A probability near zero indicates an unlikely event; a probability around $\frac{1}{2}$ is neither likely nor unlikely; and a probability near 1 indicates a likely event. Thus, the lowest probability you can have is 0, and the highest probability you can have is 1. All other probabilities fall between 0 and 1. Symbolically, $0 \le P(E) \le 1$, for any event $E$.

> **Tip: If you determine a probability and your answer is greater than 1 or your answer is negative, you've made a mistake! Go back and check your work.**

Here are examples of events and their corresponding probabilities for the sample space $S = \{1, 2, 3, 4, 5\}$, the set of outcomes from Experiment 4, the tile-drawing experiment.

If $E_1 = \{1\}$, then $P(E_1) = P(\{1\}) = \frac{1}{5}$. *Note:* Hereafter, probability of single outcomes, such as $P(\{1\})$, will be written as $P(1)$.

If $E_2 = \{2, 4\}$, the event that the tile drawn shows an even number, then $P(E_2) = P(2) + P(4) = \frac{1}{5} + \frac{1}{5} = \frac{2}{5}$.

If $E_3 = \{4, 5\}$, the event that the tile drawn shows a number greater than 3, then
$P(E_3) = P(4) + P(5) = \frac{1}{5} + \frac{1}{5} = \frac{2}{5}$.

If $E_4$ is the event that the tile drawn shows a number greater than 5, then $E_4$ is an impossible event; thus, $P(E_4) = 0$.

If $E_5$ is the event that the tile drawn shows a whole number, then $E_5$ is a certain event; thus, $P(E_5) = 1$.

# Classical Method for Computing Probabilities

When each of the possible outcomes in a sample space has an equal chance of occurring, the sample space has **equally likely outcomes.** The probability distribution for a sample space with equally likely outcomes is a **uniform probability distribution.** The probability of each outcome is $\frac{1}{n}$, where $n$ is the number of possible outcomes.

If all outcomes in the sample space are equally likely, the **classical method** for computing the **probability of an event $E$** is given by $P(E) = \dfrac{\text{Number of outcomes in } E}{\text{Total number of outcomes in the sample space}}$.

For example, if the sample space is $S = \{1, 2, 3, 4, 5\}$, the set of outcomes from Experiment 4, the tile-drawing experiment, and $E$ is the event the tile drawn shows an odd number, then
$P(E) = \dfrac{\text{Number of outcomes in } E}{\text{Total number of outcomes in the sample space}} = \dfrac{3}{5}$.

> **Tip: In a probability problem involving equally likely outcomes, the number of total outcomes possible will always be greater than or equal to the number of outcomes in the event, so check to make sure that the denominator is *larger than* or *equal to* the numerator when you plug into the formula.**

Probabilities can be expressed as fractions, decimals, or percents. In the example given, the probability of drawing an odd-numbered tile can be expressed as $\frac{3}{5}$, 0.6, or 60 percent.

Keep in mind that the rule for the classical method of computing probability will *not* apply to sample spaces in which the events are not equally likely. For example, the sample space for spinning the pointer of the spinner shown (Experiment 5) is $S = \{\text{blue, green, yellow}\}$.

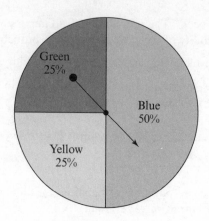

The probabilities for the different outcomes are the following: $P(\text{blue}) = \frac{1}{2}$, $P(\text{green}) = \frac{1}{4}$, and $P(\text{yellow}) = \frac{1}{4}$. The three outcomes are not equally likely because the blue section is twice as large as the other two sections.

**Tip: Always remember to check whether the outcomes are equally likely before using the rule for the classical method of computing probability.**

# Combinations of Events

For this topic, you must demonstrate an understanding of complements, unions, and intersections of events.

## Complement of an Event

The **complement of an event E,** denoted $E^c$, is the event that $E$ does not occur. The probability of the complement of an event $E$ is $P(E^C) = 1 - P(E)$. For example, if $P(E) = 0.06$, then $P(E^C) = 1 - P(E) = 1 - 0.06 = 0.94$.

Conversely, $P(E) = 1 - P(E^C)$. For example, if the probability of not guessing correctly on a multiple-choice test question is $\frac{3}{4}$, then the probability of guessing correctly on that question is $1 - \frac{3}{4} = \frac{1}{4}$.

## Compound Events

Suppose $A$ and $B$ are two events in a sample space $S$.

The event **A or B,** denoted $A \cup B$ (read "A union B"), is the event consisting of all outcomes in $S$ that are in at least one of the events $A$ or $B$. That is, the event $A \cup B$ includes all the outcomes that are in only one or the other of the two events as well as those that are common to both events.

The $P(A \cup B)$ is the probability that event $A$ occurs or event $B$ occurs or that both events occur simultaneously.

**Tip: You will find it helpful to know that P(A ∪ B) is the probability that at least one of the events A or B occurs.**

The event **A and B,** denoted $A \cap B$ (read "A intersection B"), is the event consisting of all outcomes in $S$ that are in both events $A$ and $B$. That is, the event $A \cap B$ includes all the outcomes that are common to both events.

The $P(A \cap B)$ is the probability that events $A$ and $B$ both occur simultaneously.

# The Addition Rule and Mutually Exclusive Events

For this topic, you will demonstrate an understanding of the addition rule and mutually exclusive events.

# Addition Rule

**Addition Rule:** $P(A \cup B) = P(A) + P(B) - P(A \cap B)$. For the addition rule, the events under consideration are associated with one task (getting a job offer, drawing one card, selecting one number, and so on).

Here is an example.

> Jere, a recent college graduate, applies for jobs at two different companies, Company $X$ and Company $Y$. Let $P(X)$ be the probability that Jere gets a job offer from Company $X$, $P(Y)$ be the probability Jere gets a job offer from Company $Y$, and $P(X \cap Y)$ be the probability Jere gets job offers from both companies. Suppose $P(X) = 0.8$, $P(Y) = 0.6$, and $P(X \cap Y) = 0.5$. What is the probability that Jere will get a job offer from at least one of the companies?

The probability that Jere will get a job offer from at least one of the companies is $P(X \cup Y) = P(X) + P(Y) - P(X \cap Y) = 0.8 + 0.6 - 0.5 = 0.9 = 90\%$.

In many situations, you must calculate the probabilities used in the addition rule. Here is an example.

> Suppose a card is drawn at random from a well-shuffled standard deck of 52 playing cards. What is the probability that the card drawn is a face card or a diamond? (See page 158 for an illustration of a standard deck of 52 playing cards.)

There are 12 face cards in the deck, so $P(\text{face card}) = \dfrac{12}{52}$. There are 13 diamonds in the deck, so $P(\text{diamond}) = \dfrac{13}{52}$. There are 3 diamond face cards, so $P(\text{face card} \cap \text{diamond}) = \dfrac{3}{52}$. Thus, $P(\text{face card or diamond}) = P(\text{face card} \cup \text{diamond}) = P(\text{face card}) + P(\text{diamond}) - P(\text{face card} \cap \text{diamond}) = \dfrac{12}{52} + \dfrac{13}{52} - \dfrac{3}{52} = \dfrac{22}{52} = \dfrac{11}{26}$.

In applying the addition rule, you can reduce fractions as you go along or wait until your final computation to reduce fractions. Waiting until the final computation to reduce fractions (as shown in this example) can save time. Given that the number of elements in $S$ is the same for $P(A)$, $P(B)$, and $P(A \cap B)$, the denominators for these probabilities in the computation will be the same number if you do not reduce fractions beforehand.

When you can determine the possible outcomes for the sample space, an efficient and straightforward way to find $P(A \cup B)$ is to sum the number of ways that event $A$ can occur and the number of ways that event $B$ can occur, *being sure to add in such a way that no outcome is counted twice*. Then divide by the total number of outcomes in the sample space.

Employing this strategy for the example given, you have the following: There are 12 face cards in the deck. There are 10 diamonds in the deck that are *not* face cards. Thus, there are $12 + 10 = 22$ distinct cards in the event "face card or diamond." Therefore, $P(\text{face card} \cup \text{diamond}) = \dfrac{12 + 10}{52} = \dfrac{22}{52} = \dfrac{11}{26}$.

# Mutually Exclusive Events and the Addition Rule

Two events $A$ and $B$ are **mutually exclusive** if they cannot occur at the same time; that is, they have no outcomes in common. Therefore, events $A$ and $B$ are mutually exclusive if and only if $P(A \cap B) = 0$. For example, suppose you draw one card from a well-shuffled standard deck of 52 playing cards; the event of drawing a king and the event of drawing an ace are mutually exclusive. Thus, $P(\text{king} \cap \text{ace}) = 0$.

When two events $A$ and $B$ are mutually exclusive, the addition rule is $P(A \cup B) = P(A) + P(B)$. Here is an example.

> One card is randomly drawn from a well-shuffled standard deck of 52 playing cards. Find the probability that the card drawn is a king or an ace. (See page 158 for an illustration of a standard deck of 52 playing cards.)

There are 4 kings in the deck, so $P(\text{king}) = \dfrac{4}{52}$. There are 4 aces in the deck, so $P(\text{ace}) = \dfrac{4}{52}$. The event of drawing a king and the event of drawing an ace are mutually exclusive (because you cannot draw both at the same time on one draw from the deck). Hence, $P(\text{king or ace}) = P(\text{king} \cup \text{ace}) = P(\text{king}) + P(\text{ace}) = \dfrac{4}{52} + \dfrac{4}{52} = \dfrac{1}{13} + \dfrac{1}{13} = \dfrac{2}{13}$.

# Conditional Probability

The probability of an event $E$, given that an event $A$ has occurred, is a **conditional probability,** denoted $P(E|A)$ (read as "the probability of $E$ given $A$").

One way to obtain the conditional probability, $P(E|A)$, is to compute the probability of event $E$ in a "reduced" sample space that you determine after taking into account that the event $A$ has already occurred. Here is an example.

> Suppose you draw one card at random from a well-shuffled standard deck of 52 playing cards. Find the probability that the card drawn is a 6, given that the card drawn is greater than 2 and less than 8. (See page 158 for an illustration of a standard deck of 52 playing cards.)

Let $E$ be the event "the card drawn is a 6" and $A$ be the event "the card drawn is greater than 2 and less than 8." There are 20 cards between 2 and 8 (four 3s, four 4s, four 5s, four 6s, and four 7s). Of these 20 cards, four are 6s. Hence, $P(E|A) = \dfrac{4}{20} = \dfrac{1}{5}$.

Here is an example using a summary table.

> The table shows the gender and type of residence of 2,000 senior students at a university.
>
> **Gender and Type of Residence of Senior Students ($n = 2,000$)**
>
> | | Female | Male | Row Total |
> |---|---|---|---|
> | Apartment | 229 | 180 | 409 |
> | Dorm | 203 | 118 | 321 |
> | House | 258 | 272 | 530 |
> | With Parent(s) | 200 | 201 | 401 |
> | Sorority/Fraternity House | 241 | 98 | 339 |
> | **Column Total** | 1,131 | 869 | 2,000 |
>
> **(a)** What is the probability that a senior selected at random lives in a dorm given that the senior is female? Give your answer as a decimal to the nearest hundredth.
>
> **(b)** What is the probability that a senior selected at random is a female given that the senior lives in a dorm? Give your answer as a decimal to the nearest hundredth.

**(a)** Let $D$ be the event "the senior selected lives in the dorm" and $F$ be the event "the senior selected is female." The total number of female seniors is 1,131. Of that total, 203 live in a dorm. Thus, $P(D|F) = \dfrac{203}{1{,}131} \approx 0.18$.

**(b)** Let $F$ be the event "the senior selected is female" and $D$ be the event "the senior selected lives in the dorm." The total number of seniors living in a dorm is 321. Of that total, 203 are female. Thus, $P(F|D) = \dfrac{203}{321} \approx 0.63$.

*Note:* Notice that in the above examples, the total number of outcomes under consideration is "reduced" to a lower number than the original problem began with.

Another way to obtain the conditional probability, $P(E|A)$, is to use the following formula:

$$P(E|A) = \frac{P(E \cap A)}{P(A)}, \text{ provided } P(A) > 0$$

Here is the formula applied to the previously shown examples.

> Suppose you draw one card at random from a well-shuffled standard deck of 52 playing cards. Find the probability that the card drawn is a 6, given that the card drawn is greater than 2 and less than 8. (See page 158 for an illustration of a standard deck of 52 playing cards.)

Let $E$ be the event "the card drawn is a 6" and $A$ be the event "the card drawn is greater than 2 and less than 8."

$P(E \cap A) = \dfrac{4}{52}$ and $P(A) = \dfrac{20}{52}$. Hence, $P(E|A) = \dfrac{P(E \cap A)}{P(A)} = \dfrac{\frac{4}{52}}{\frac{20}{52}} = \dfrac{4}{20} = \dfrac{1}{5}$.

> The table shows the gender and type of residence of 2,000 senior students at a university.
>
> **Gender and Type of Residence of Senior Students ($n = 2,000$)**
>
> | | Female | Male | Row Total |
> |---|---|---|---|
> | Apartment | 229 | 180 | 409 |
> | Dorm | 203 | 118 | 321 |
> | House | 258 | 272 | 530 |
> | With Parent(s) | 200 | 201 | 401 |
> | Sorority/Fraternity House | 241 | 98 | 339 |
> | **Column Total** | 1,131 | 869 | 2,000 |
>
> **(a)** What is the probability that a senior selected at random lives in a dorm given that the senior is female? Give your answer as a decimal to the nearest hundredth.
>
> **(b)** What is the probability that a senior selected at random is a female given that the senior lives in a dorm? Give your answer as a decimal to the nearest hundredth.

**(a)** Let $D$ be the event "the senior selected lives in the dorm" and $F$ be the event "the senior selected is female."

$P(D \cap F) = \dfrac{203}{2,000}$ and $P(F) = \dfrac{1,131}{2,000}$. Thus, $P(D|F) = \dfrac{P(D \cap F)}{P(F)} = \dfrac{\frac{203}{2,000}}{\frac{1,131}{2,000}} = \dfrac{203}{1,131} \approx 0.18$.

**(b)** Let $F$ be the event "the senior selected is female" and $D$ be the event "the senior selected lives in the dorm."

$P(F \cap D) = \dfrac{203}{2,000}$ and $P(D) = \dfrac{321}{2,000}$. Thus, $P(F|D) = \dfrac{P(F \cap D)}{P(D)} = \dfrac{\frac{203}{2,000}}{\frac{321}{2,000}} = \dfrac{203}{321} \approx 0.63$.

As you can see, for both examples, you get the same answers as previously obtained.

# Multiplication Rule and Independent and Dependent Events

For this topic, you must demonstrate an understanding of the multiplication rule and independent and dependent events.

# Multiplication Rule

**Multiplication Rule:** $P(A \cap B) = P(A)P(B|A)$. For the multiplication rule, the events under consideration are associated with two or more tasks (drawing two cards, flipping a coin followed by tossing a number cube, and so on).

Here are examples.

> Suppose you draw two cards at random, one after the other, from a well-shuffled standard deck of 52 playing cards. Let $J$ be the event "a jack is drawn on the first draw" and $K$ be the event "a king is drawn on the second draw." (See page 158 for an illustration of a standard deck of 52 playing cards.)
>
> **(a)** What is the probability of drawing a jack on the first draw, without replacement, and a king on the second draw? *Note:* "**Without replacement**" means the first item selected is *not* put back before the second selection takes place.
>
> **(b)** What is the probability of drawing a jack on the first draw, with replacement, and a king on the second draw? *Note:* "**With replacement**" means the first card is put back before the second drawing takes place.

**(a)** $P(J) = \dfrac{4}{52} = \dfrac{1}{13}$ (This is true because there are 4 jacks in the deck of 52 cards) and $P(K|J) = \dfrac{4}{51}$ (this is true because after the jack is drawn and not put back in the deck, there are 4 kings in the remaining deck of 51 cards).
Thus, $P(J \cap K) = \dfrac{1}{13} \cdot \dfrac{4}{51} = \dfrac{4}{663}$.

**(b)** $P(J) = \dfrac{4}{52} = \dfrac{1}{13}$ (this is true because there are 4 jacks in the deck of 52 cards) and $P(K|J) = \dfrac{4}{52} = \dfrac{1}{13}$ (this is true because after the jack is drawn and put back in the deck, there are 4 kings in the remaining deck of 52 cards).
Thus, $P(J \cap K) = \dfrac{1}{13} \cdot \dfrac{1}{13} = \dfrac{1}{169}$.

> **Tip: For the Praxis MS Math test, remember that to obtain the probability that event *A* occurs followed by event *B*, you multiply the probability of event *A* times the *conditional* probability of event *B*. This means you must take into account that event *A* has already occurred when determining the second factor.**

# Independent and Dependent Events and the Multiplication Rule

Two events $A$ and $B$ are **independent** if $P(A|B) = P(A)$ and $P(B|A) = P(B)$. This definition means events $A$ and $B$ are independent if the occurrence of one does not affect the probability of the occurrence of the other. It follows that if events $A$ and $B$ are independent, then the multiplication rule is $P(A \cap B) = P(A)P(B)$. Here are examples.

> Suppose you flip a coin, and then toss a number cube, whose faces are numbered 10, 20, 30, 40, 50, and 60. Find the probability that a head appears on the up face of the coin and the number 50 appears on the up face of the number cube.

Let $H$ be the event "a heads appears on the up face of the coin" and $F$ be the event "the number 50 appears on the up face of the number cube." $P(H|F) = P(H) = \dfrac{1}{2}$ (this is true because what happens with the coin is not affected by what happens with the number cube) and $P(F|H) = P(F) = \dfrac{1}{6}$ (this is true because what happens with the number cube is not affected by what happens with the coin). Thus, $P(H \cap F) = P(H)P(F) = \dfrac{1}{2} \cdot \dfrac{1}{6} = \dfrac{1}{12}$.

You can extend the multiplication rule for two independent events to any number of independent events. For example, suppose you flip a coin three times; the probability of obtaining three heads is

$$P(H) \cdot P(H) \cdot P(H) = \frac{1}{2} \cdot \frac{1}{2} \cdot \frac{1}{2} = \frac{1}{8}.$$

> Suppose you randomly draw two marbles, one after the other, from a box containing 6 red marbles and 4 blue marbles. Find the probability of drawing a red marble, with replacement, on the first draw and then drawing a blue marble on the second draw.

Let $R$ be the event "the first marble drawn is red" and $B$ be the event "the second marble drawn is blue." $P(R) = \frac{6}{10} = \frac{3}{5}$ (this is true because on the first draw there are 6 red marbles in the box of 10 marbles) and $P(B|R) = P(B) = \frac{4}{10} = \frac{2}{5}$ (this is true because after the red marble is drawn and replaced, the probability of drawing a blue marble has not changed given there are still 4 blue marbles and 6 red marbles in the box). Therefore, $P(R \cap B) = P(R)P(B) = \frac{3}{5} \cdot \frac{2}{5} = \frac{6}{25}.$

If events $A$ and $B$ are not independent, they are said to be **dependent.** Here is an example.

> Suppose you randomly draw two marbles, one after the other, from a box containing 6 red marbles and 4 blue marbles. Find the probability of drawing a red marble, without replacement, on the first draw and then drawing a blue marble on the second draw.

Let $R$ be the event "the first marble drawn is red" and $B$ be the event "the second marble drawn is blue." $P(R) = \frac{6}{10} = \frac{3}{5}$ (this is true because on the first draw there are 6 red marbles in the box of 10 marbles) and $P(B|R) = \frac{4}{9}$ (this is true because after the red marble is drawn without replacement, there are 4 blue marbles and

5 red marbles remaining in the box). Therefore, $P(R \cap B) = P(R)P(B|R) = \frac{3}{5} \cdot \frac{4}{9} = \frac{4}{15}.$

Notice that selecting "with replacement" results in independent events, while selecting "without replacement" results in dependent events.

# Complement Rule

For some problems, you might find it convenient to determine the probability that at least one of something of interest occurs by using the following **Complement Rule:** $P$(at least one) $= 1 - P$(none). Here is an example.

> A coin is flipped three times. Find the probability that at least one tails occurs.

The sample space is {HHH, HHT, HTH, HTT, THH, THT, TTH, TTT}. Thus, $P$(at least one tails) $= 1 - P$(no tails) $= 1 - P(\text{HHH}) = 1 - \frac{1}{8} = \frac{7}{8}$. By looking at the sample space, you can see that this answer is correct because there are seven outcomes in which tails occurs. In fact, you could have worked the problem directly as follows: $P$(at least one tails) $= \frac{7}{8}$. With larger sample spaces, rather than working out the probability directly, it is often more convenient to determine the probability of "at least one" by using $1 - P$(none).

# Odds

The **odds in favor** of an event $E$ occurring are given by $\dfrac{P(E)}{1-P(E)}$, usually expressed in the form $p: q$ (or $p$ to $q$),

where $p$ and $q$ are integers with no common factors and $\dfrac{P(E)}{1-P(E)}=\dfrac{p}{q}$. The **odds against** an event $E$ occurring are

given by $\dfrac{1-P(E)}{P(E)}$, usually expressed in the form $q: p$ (or $q$ to $p$), where $p$ and $q$ are integers with no common fac-

tors and $\dfrac{1-P(E)}{P(E)}=\dfrac{q}{p}$.

Here is an example.

> Suppose you perform one toss of a number cube, whose six faces are numbered 1 through 6, and observe the up face. What are the odds of observing a 2 on the up face?

The probability of observing a 2 on the up face is $P(2)=\dfrac{1}{6}$ (this is true because 2 has a 1 in 6 chance of showing

on the up face). Thus, the odds in favor of observing 2 on the up face are $\dfrac{\frac{1}{6}}{1-\frac{1}{6}}=\dfrac{\frac{1}{6}}{\frac{5}{6}}=\dfrac{1}{5}$, which is 1 to 5. The

odds against observing a 2 on the up face are 5 to 1.

# Frequency Theory of Probability

An empirical way to assign probability to a random experiment is to view probability as long-run relative frequency. The **frequency theory of probability** assumes that as the number of trials increases, the proportion of times that $E$ occurs approaches $E$'s true probability. In general, the **probability of an event $E$** is interpreted to mean the limiting value of the relative frequency of the occurrence of $E$ if the experiment were conducted an indefinitely large number of times. It is the proportion of times the event would occur in a large number of repetitions of the experiment. For example, as a coin is flipped repeatedly, the proportion of heads obtained gets closer and closer to $\dfrac{1}{2}$ as the number of repetitions increases. The value of $\dfrac{1}{2}$ is the limiting value of this process and, as a result, is called the probability of heads.

This way of assigning probability is the **relative frequency method.** The probability of an event $E$ is estimated by conducting the experiment a large number of times, called **trials,** and counting the number of times that event $E$ actually occurred. Based on these results, the probability of $E$ is estimated as $P(E)=\dfrac{\text{Number of times } E \text{ occurred}}{\text{Total number of trials}}$.
As the number of trials increases, the relative frequency probability approaches the true probability of the event.

Here is an example.

> Out of 100 light bulbs tested at Company $X$, two are defective. What is the estimated probability that a Company $X$ light bulb is defective?

$$P(\text{Company } X \text{ light bulb is defective}) \approx \frac{2}{100}=0.02=2\%$$

In many situations in the real world, the only feasible way to assign a probability to an event is to make a relative frequency interpretation of probability. For example, insurance companies set premiums based on relative frequency probabilities.

# Geometric Probability

**Geometric probability** involves determining probabilities associated with geometric objects. Here is an example.

The figure shown is a circle inscribed in a 10-inch square. A point is randomly selected within the square. What is the probability that the point will be inside the circle as well? Round your answer to three decimal places.

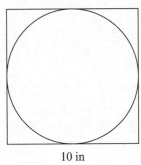

10 in

To calculate the probability that the point will be inside the circle, calculate the ratio of the area of the circle to the area of the square (see "Perimeter, Area, and Volume" in Chapter 5 for formulas for areas of geometric shapes).

$$P(\text{Point is inside circle}) = \frac{\text{area of circle}}{\text{area of square}} = \frac{\pi r^2}{s^2} = \frac{\pi (5 \text{ in})^2}{(10 \text{ in})^2} = \frac{25\pi}{100} \approx 0.785$$

# Sample Questions

**Directions:** Read the directions for each question carefully. This set of questions has several different question types. For each question, select a single answer choice unless written instructions preceding the question state otherwise.

1. A bag of 25 colored tiles contains 10 blue, 7 red, 5 green, and 3 yellow tiles, all identical except for color. If a person picks out a single tile from the bag without looking, what is the probability that it is a green tile?

   Ⓐ $\frac{3}{25}$

   Ⓑ $\frac{7}{25}$

   Ⓒ $\frac{1}{5}$

   Ⓓ $\frac{2}{5}$

**2.** One card is drawn at random from a well-shuffled standard deck of 52 playing cards. What is the probability that the card drawn is a 5 or a red card?

- Ⓐ $\dfrac{1}{26}$

- Ⓑ $\dfrac{1}{13}$

- Ⓒ $\dfrac{7}{13}$

- Ⓓ $\dfrac{15}{26}$

**For the following question, enter your fractional answer in the boxes below the question.**

**3.** Two cards are drawn at random without replacement from a well-shuffled standard deck of 52 playing cards. What is the probability of drawing a queen on the second draw, if the first card, drawn without replacement, is a jack? Give your answer as a fraction.

**4.** Two cards are drawn at random with replacement from a well-shuffled standard deck of 52 playing cards. What is the probability of drawing a jack on the first draw and a queen on the second draw?

- Ⓐ $\dfrac{1}{169}$

- Ⓑ $\dfrac{1}{221}$

- Ⓒ $\dfrac{4}{663}$

- Ⓓ $\dfrac{16}{2,601}$

**5.** A box contains red and yellow marbles, all the same size. There are three times as many red marbles as yellow marbles in the box. If one marble is drawn at random, what is the probability that it is yellow?

- Ⓐ $\dfrac{1}{4}$

- Ⓑ $\dfrac{1}{3}$

- Ⓒ $\dfrac{2}{3}$

- Ⓓ $\dfrac{3}{4}$

**6.** A sequence of integers begins with 10 and ends with 50. If one integer is randomly selected from the sequence, what is the probability that the integer is even?

- Ⓐ $\dfrac{20}{41}$

- Ⓑ $\dfrac{1}{2}$

- Ⓒ $\dfrac{21}{41}$

- Ⓓ $\dfrac{21}{40}$

**For the following question, enter your fractional answer in the boxes below the question.**

7. A bag contains 10 blue, 8 green, and 6 red marbles, all the same size. Another bag contains 8 blue, 2 green, and 2 red marbles, all the same size. If one marble is randomly drawn, one after the other, from each bag, what is the probability that both marbles will be the same color? Give your answer as a fraction.

**For the following question, enter your numeric answer in the box below the question.**

8. Each of the two triangles in the figure shown is a 3-4-5 right triangle. The shaded rectangular region in the middle of the figure measures 12 by 4 units. If a point is selected at random inside the figure, what is the probability that the point will NOT be in the shaded region? Give your answer as a percent.

%

# Answer Explanations

1. **C.** The tiles are identical except for color and the drawing is random, so each outcome of the drawing is equally likely. There are 5 green tiles out of a total of 25 tiles. The probability of drawing a green tile is

   $$P(\text{green}) = \frac{\text{number of green tiles}}{\text{total number of tiles}} = \frac{5}{25} = \frac{1}{5}, \text{ choice C.}$$

   *Tip:* Problems of this type might not state that the objects are physically identical as was given in this problem. Nevertheless, you will have to make that assumption to work the problem.

2. **C.** There are four 5 cards in the deck (♣5, ♠5, ♥5, and ♦5), so $P(5 \text{ card}) = \frac{4}{52}$. There are 26 red cards in the deck (13 hearts and 13 diamonds), so $P(\text{red card}) = \frac{26}{52}$. There are two red 5 cards (♥5 and ♦5), so

   $P(5 \text{ card} \cap \text{red card}) = \frac{2}{52}$. Thus, $P(5 \text{ card or red card}) = P(5 \text{ card} \cup \text{red card}) = P(5 \text{ card}) + P(\text{red card}) -$

   $P(5 \text{ card} \cap \text{red card}) = \frac{4}{52} + \frac{26}{52} - \frac{2}{52} = \frac{28}{52} = \frac{7}{13}$, choice C.

3. $\frac{4}{51}$ After the jack is drawn, there are 51 cards left, 4 of which are queens. Therefore, $P(\text{queen} \mid \text{jack drawn}$

   without replacement) $= \frac{4}{51}$.

4. **A.** There are 4 jacks in the deck of 52 cards, so the probability of a jack on the first draw is $\frac{4}{52}$. After the

   jack is drawn and replaced in the deck, there are 4 queens in the deck of 52 cards. Therefore, $P(\text{jack on first}$

   draw and queen on second draw) = $P(\text{jack on first draw}) \cdot P(\text{queen on second draw} \mid \text{jack on first draw}) =$

   $\frac{4}{52} \cdot \frac{4}{52} = \frac{1}{13 \cdot 13} = \frac{1}{169}$, choice A.

5. **A.** The marbles are identical except for color and the drawing is random, so each outcome is equally likely. Let

   $x$ = the number of yellow marbles in the box. Then $3x$ = the number of red marbles in the box. The probability

   of drawing a yellow marble is $P(\text{yellow}) = \frac{\text{number of yellow marbles}}{\text{total number of marbles}} = \frac{x}{x + 3x} = \frac{x}{4x} = \frac{1}{4}$, choice A.

**173**

**6. C.** There are $(50 - 10) + 1 = 41$ integers in the sequence. The sequence starts and ends with an even integer, so the number of even integers in the sequence is 1 more than the number of odd integers. Let $x =$ the number of odd integers in the sequence, and $x + 1 =$ the number of even integers. To determine the number of even integers in the sequence, solve the following equation for $x + 1$:

$$x + (x + 1) = 41$$
$$x + x + 1 = 41$$
$$2x = 40$$
$$x = 20$$
$$x + 1 = 21$$

There are 21 even integers out of a total of 41 integers. The probability that the integer selected is even is

$$P(\text{even}) = \frac{\text{number of even integers}}{\text{total number of integers}} = \frac{21}{41} \text{, choice C.}$$

**7.** $\dfrac{3}{8}$ The drawings from the bags are independent of each other; that is, the outcome from one bag does not influence the outcome of the other bag. Let B represent the outcome "the marble drawn is blue," G represent the outcome "the marble drawn is green," and R represent the outcome "the marble drawn is red." Bag 1 contains 24 marbles. For this bag, $P(B) = \dfrac{10}{24} = \dfrac{5}{12}$, $P(G) = \dfrac{8}{24} = \dfrac{1}{3}$, and $P(R) = \dfrac{6}{24} = \dfrac{1}{4}$. Bag 2 contains 12 marbles. For this bag, $P(B) = \dfrac{8}{12} = \dfrac{2}{3}$ and $P(G) = P(R) = \dfrac{2}{12} = \dfrac{1}{6}$. Sketch a tree diagram of the situation.

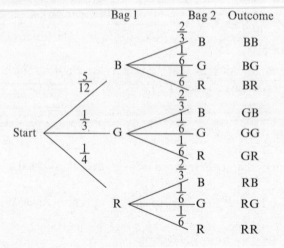

The diagram shows there are three (mutually exclusive) ways for both marbles to be the same color: BB, which has probability $\dfrac{5}{12} \cdot \dfrac{2}{3} = \dfrac{5}{18}$; GG, which has probability $\dfrac{1}{3} \cdot \dfrac{1}{6} = \dfrac{1}{18}$; and RR, which has probability $\dfrac{1}{4} \cdot \dfrac{1}{6} = \dfrac{1}{24}$. Thus, the probability both marbles are the same color is

$$P(\text{BB or GG or RR}) = P(\text{BB}) + P(\text{GG}) + P(\text{RR}) = \frac{5}{18} + \frac{1}{18} + \frac{1}{24} = \frac{3}{8}.$$

**8. 20** The total area of the figure equals the sum of the areas of the two triangles plus the area of the rectangle

$$= 2\left[\frac{1}{2}(3 \text{ units} \cdot 4 \text{ units})\right] + (12 \text{ units})(4 \text{ units}) = 12 \text{ unit}^2 + 48 \text{ unit}^2 = 60 \text{ unit}^2.$$

The probability that the point will NOT be in the shaded region is $1 - P(\text{point is in the shaded region}) =$

$$1 - P(\text{point is in the rectangle}) = 1 - \frac{\text{area of rectangle}}{\text{total area of figure}} = 1 - \frac{48}{60} = \frac{12}{60} = \frac{1}{5} = 20\%.$$

# Chapter 8

# Statistics

This chapter provides a review of key ideas of basic statistical concepts that are important for you to know for the Praxis MS Math test. Sample questions, comparable to what might be presented on the Praxis MS Math test, are given at the end of the chapter. The answer explanations for the sample questions are provided immediately following.

## Statistical Questions and Types of Data

When you have a statistical question, you need information, called **data,** to answer it. A **statistical question** is one that anticipates the data collected to answer it will vary. The question does not have a specific predetermined answer. For example, "What is the average salary of teachers in your state?" is a statistical question. You expect the salaries of teachers to vary from teacher to teacher. However, "What is the salary of a certain middle school band director at a particular school in your state?" is *not* a statistical question. The band director has a specific salary. There is no variability in the answer at the time of the question. Accounting for the **variability** in data is the main purpose of statistical analysis.

The salary of a randomly selected teacher in your state is a **variable.** In statistics, a **variable** is a characteristic (or attribute) that describes an object, person, or thing. The variable's value varies from entity to entity. When you collect data related to a variable, the data are qualitative data or quantitative data.

**Qualitative data** (also called **categorical data**) are non-numerical information such as names, labels, codes, colors, race, educational level, and other qualities that result from sorting objects, things, or people into categories.

**Quantitative data** are numerical data that represent a measurement (such as lengths, heights, weights, temperature, test scores, and other amounts) or from counts (such as family size, number of pets, and so forth). Quantitative data that results from taking a measurement is **measurement data.**

The **distribution** of a variable is a representation of a variable's data that shows what values the variable assumes and the frequency of those values.

## Graphical Representations of Data

For this topic, you should be able to read and interpret information about variables from tables, pictographs, circle graphs, bar graphs, line graphs, dot plots, stem-and-leaf plots, and histograms. These graphical representations of data show the distributions of the variables.

### Tables

A **table** organizes information as entries in rows and columns. Row and column labels explain the data recorded in the table. A **frequency table** is a tabular representation of data that shows the frequency of each value in the data set. A **relative frequency table** shows the frequency of each value as a proportion or percentage of the whole data set. The total of all relative frequencies should be 1.00 or 100 percent (but instead might be very close to 1.00 or 100 percent, due to round-off error). Here is an example.

**Grade Distribution of 25 Students for Test 1**

| Grade | Frequency | Relative Frequency |
|-------|-----------|--------------------|
| A | 5 | 0.20 |
| B | 8 | 0.32 |
| C | 9 | 0.36 |
| D | 2 | 0.08 |
| F | 1 | 0.04 |
| **Total** | **25** | **1.00** |

According to the information in the table, 0.20 + 0.32 + 0.36 = 0.88 or 88% of the students made a C or better on Test 1.

# Pictographs

A **pictograph** (or **picture graph**) uses symbols or pictures to represent data. Each symbol stands for a definite number of a specific item. This information should be stated on the graph. To read a pictograph, count the number of symbols shown and then multiply by the number it represents. Fractional portions of symbols are approximated and used accordingly. Here is an example.

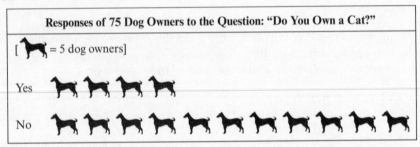

According to the graph, 4 × 5 = 20 of the 75 dog owners responded "Yes" to the survey question.

# Circle Graphs

A **circle graph** (or **pie chart**) is a graph in the shape of a circle. A circle graph visually displays the relative contribution of each category of data within a set of data belonging to a whole, which is represented by the circle. A circle graph can only compare parts of a whole. Circle graphs are also called "pie" charts because each looks like a pie cut into wedges. The wedges are labeled to show the categories for the graph. Usually the portion of the graph that corresponds to each category is shown as a percent. The total amount of percentage on the graph is 100 percent. The graph is made by dividing the 360 degrees of the circle into portions that are proportional to the percentages for each category. You read a circle graph by reading the percents displayed on the graph for the different categories. Here is an example.

**Grade Distribution of 25 Students for Test 1**

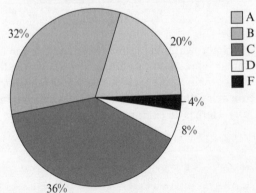

According to the graph, over half of the students (32% + 20% = 52%) received a grade of B or better on Test 1.

# Bar Graphs

A **bar graph** is a useful way to organize and represent categorical data. Bar graphs can display categories that are not parts of a whole as well as categories that are parts of a whole. A bar graph uses rectangular bars of the same width to show the frequency (or relative frequency) of the different categories in which the data are classified. Labels at the base of the bars specify the categories. The bars are equally spaced from each other and may be oriented vertically or horizontally. (*Note:* For ease of discussion, the following explanation is limited to bar graphs that are oriented vertically; the explanation for bar graphs that are oriented horizontally is similar.) The categories for the data are labeled on the horizontal axis. The horizontal axis is not a scale as such, meaning the ordering of the categories and their horizontal positions are not dictated by the data. A bar's height (or length) indicates the frequency (or relative frequency) for the category represented by that particular bar. A vertical scale, marked in whole numbers for determining the frequency counts (or marked as proportions/percentages for determining relative frequencies), is shown on the graph. To read a bar graph, examine the vertical scale to determine the count (or relative frequency) represented by each tick mark. Then determine where the bars' heights fall relative to the scale. Here is an example.

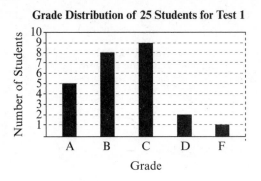

The graph shows that 5 + 8 + 9 = 22 students received a grade of C or better on Test 1.

Two or more sets of data can be displayed on the same graph to facilitate comparison of the data sets to each other. Here is an example.

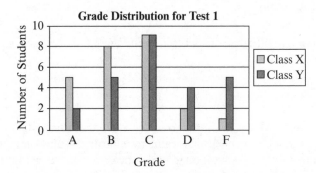

The graph shows that Class X had more As and Bs and fewer Ds and Fs than did Class Y; so, in general, Class X performed better on Test 1 than did Class Y.

# Line Graphs

A **line graph** displays measurement data that have been collected over equal consecutive time intervals. The data values are plotted as ordered pairs on a grid that has a horizontal time scale. The vertical scale corresponds to the measurement scale that was used to obtain the data. Consecutive points are connected by line segments to aid the eye in identifying changes over time. The slants of the line segments between points indicate which direction the data might be trending. Upward slants from left to right indicate increasing data values. Downward slants from left to right indicate decreasing data values. Line segments with no slant (horizontal line) indicate that the data values are remaining constant. **Trends** are patterns of (relatively) long-term upward or downward changes. Here is an example of a line graph.

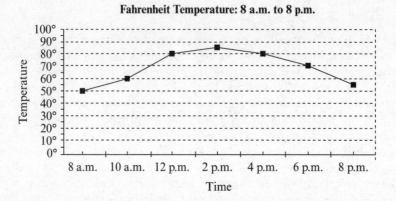

The graph shows that the temperature steadily increased between 8 a.m. and 2 p.m. (upward trend), and then steadily decreased between 2 p.m. and 8 p.m. (downward trend).

You can plot two or more sets of data on the same graph, a display that facilitates comparisons between the data sets. Here is an example.

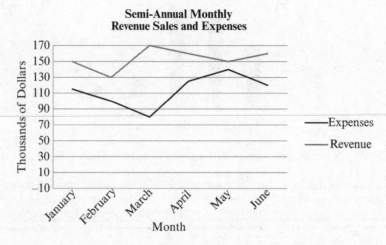

The graph shows that the maximum difference between revenue sales and expenses occurred in March, and the minimum difference occurred in May.

# Dot Plots

A **dot plot** (or **line plot**) is a graph in which the data's possible values are indicated along the horizontal axis, and dots (or other similar symbols) are placed above each value to indicate the number of times that particular value occurs in the data set. The horizontal axis corresponds to the measurement scale that was used to obtain the data. An important advantage of dot plots is that they show a symbol for every data value. You can easily determine the minimum (least) and the maximum (greatest) data values, and the frequency of occurrence of values. Features of the data's distribution including clusters, gaps, and outliers are visually apparent. A **cluster** is a group of data that are close together. A **gap** is an interval where no data are plotted. An **outlier** is a data value that is extremely high or extremely low in comparison to most of the other data values. Here is an example.

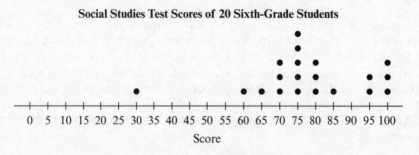

The dot plot provides visual information about the shape and spread of the data distribution. It shows a cluster of scores between 60 and 85 and a smaller cluster between 95 and 100. There is a large gap between 30 and 60 and a smaller one between 85 and 95. Because the gap between 30 and 60 is very large (indicating 30 is extremely low in comparison to the other data values), 30 is an outlier in the data set. The score that occurs most frequently is 75. The least score is 30 and the greatest score is 100.

**Tip: Dot plots are used mostly with small data sets (those with fewer than 50 data values).**

# Stem-and-Leaf Plots

A **stem-and-leaf plot** is a graphical display of data in which each data value is separated into two parts: a stem and a leaf. For a given data value, the **leaf** is the last digit, and the **stem,** the remaining digits. For example, for the data value 198, 19 is the stem and 8 is the leaf. A stem-and-leaf plot includes a legend that explains what the stem and leaf represent so the reader can interpret the information in the plot; for example, 19|8 = 198. Usually, the stems are listed vertically, from smallest to largest, in a column labeled "Stem." The leaves are listed horizontally, from smallest to largest, in the row of their corresponding stem under a column labeled "Leaves." Each leaf is listed to the right of its corresponding stem as many times as it occurs in the original data set. A feature of a stem-and-leaf plot is that the original data are retained and displayed in the plot. Reading information from a stem-and-leaf plot is a matter of interpreting the plot's stems and leaves. Here is an example.

### Ages of 40 Attendees at a Retirement Party

| Stem | Leaves |
|------|--------|
| 4 | 0 3 3 5 6 9 |
| 5 | 3 4 4 5 6 6 7 7 7 7 7 8 8 8 9 |
| 6 | 0 0 0 1 1 1 2 3 3 3 7 |
| 7 | 1 4 7 8 |
| 8 | 1 3 |
| 9 | 0 1 |
| Legend: 4|6 = 46 | |

According to the plot, 40 people attended the retirement party. Of the 40 attendees, 6 were in their 40s, 15 were in their 50s, 11 were in their 60s, 4 were in their 70s, 2 were in their 80s, and 2 were in their 90s.

# Histograms

A **histogram** summarizes measurement data that have been grouped by nonoverlapping **class intervals.** Histograms have two scales: a measurement scale, corresponding to the measurement scale used to obtain the data, and a frequency (or relative frequency) scale. The histogram displays the data's frequencies (or relative frequencies) within the successive class intervals that lie along the measurement scale. Class intervals are of equal width and cover from the lowest to the highest data value. The left and right endpoints for the class intervals are selected so that each data value clearly falls within one and only one class interval. The frequency or relative frequency of the data's occurrence within a class interval is represented by a rectangular bar whose width is the same as the width of the class interval. The height of the bar is proportional to the data's frequency (or relative frequency) within that interval. *Tip:* There are no horizontal spaces between the bars unless a bar's height is zero, meaning no data values fall in its class interval.

In a **frequency histogram,** the scale for measuring a bar's height is marked with actual frequencies (or counts). In a **relative frequency histogram,** the scale is marked with relative frequencies instead of actual frequencies. The total of the relative frequencies corresponding to the class intervals should be 1.00 or 100 percent (but might instead be very close to 1.00 or 100 percent due to round-off error). Here is an example of a frequency histogram.

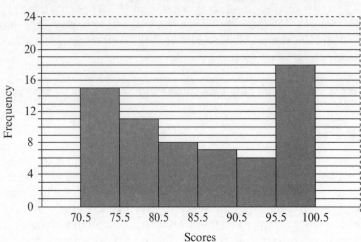

Scores of 65 Tenth Graders on a Basic Arithmetic Skills Assessment

The histogram shows that the data are clustered between 70.5 and 100.5 with no student scoring below 70. There are no gaps in the data and no noticeable outliers.

# Misleading Graphs

Drawing valid conclusions from graphical representations of data requires that you have read the graph accurately and analyzed the graphical information correctly. Sometimes a graphical representation will distort the data in some way, leading you to draw an invalid conclusion. Here is an example.

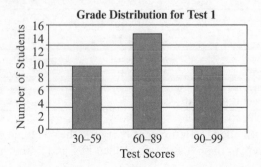

Grade Distribution for Test 1

At first glance, the data for this graph look evenly distributed. However, upon closer examination, you can see that each of the first two intervals covers a 29-point spread, but the last interval covers only a 9-point spread, making it difficult to draw conclusions from the graph.

# Guidelines for Interpreting Graphs

When you interpret graphical information, follow these suggestions:

- Make sure that you understand the title of the graph.
- Read the labels on the parts of the graph to understand what is being represented.
- Make sure you know what each symbol in a pictograph represents; check that the symbols are a uniform size.
- Examine carefully horizontal and vertical scales; make sure the numbers are equally spaced.
- Look for trends such as rising values (upward-slanting line segments), falling values (downward-slanting line segments), and periods of inactivity (horizontal line segments) in line graphs.
- Look for clusters, gaps, and outliers and note the general shape of dot plots, stem-and-leaf plots, and histograms.

- Be ready to do simple arithmetic computations.
- Make sure that the numbers add up correctly.
- Use only the information in the graph. Do not answer based on your personal knowledge or opinion.

Here is an example of using graphical information to determine a probability (see Chapter 7, "Probability," for a further discussion of this topic).

Shown below is the frequency histogram for the scores of 65 tenth graders. Assuming the scores on the assessment are recorded as whole numbers, find the probability that a student randomly selected from the 65 tenth graders scored above 90.5.

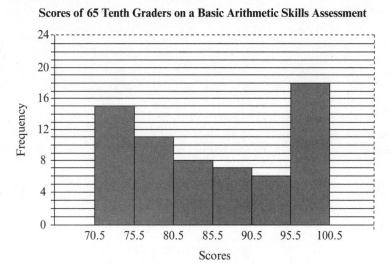

Scores of 65 Tenth Graders on a Basic Arithmetic Skills Assessment

According to the graph, 6 + 18 = 24 of the 65 students scored above 90.5. Thus, given that the student is randomly selected, $P(\text{score is above } 90.5) = \dfrac{\text{Number of outcomes in the event}}{\text{Total number of outcomes}} = \dfrac{24}{65}$.

# Measures of Central Tendency

A **measure of central tendency** is a numerical value that describes a data set by attempting to provide a "central" or "typical" value of the data set. It is a single number that summarizes all the values in the data set. Three common measures of central tendency are the mean, median, and mode. Each of these measures is a way to describe a central value of a set of data.

> **Tip: Measures of central tendency should have the same units as those of the data values from which they are determined. If no units are specified for the data values, no units are specified for the measures of central tendency.**

## Mean

The **mean** of a data set is the arithmetic average of the data values. Thus, $\text{mean} = \dfrac{\text{sum of the data values}}{\text{number of data values}}$. Here is an example.

Find the mean of the following data set: 21, 35, 34, 30, 32, 36, 24, 35, 28, 35.

$$\text{mean} = \frac{\text{sum of the data values}}{\text{number of data values}} = \frac{21+24+28+30+32+34+35+35+35+36}{10} = \frac{310}{10} = 31$$

A **weighted mean** is a mean computed by assigning weights to the data values. To find a weighted mean, do the following: First, multiply each data value by its assigned weight and then sum the results. Next, divide the sum obtained by the sum of the weights. Thus, for data values $x_1, x_2, ..., x_n$ with respective assigned weights $w_1, w_2, ..., w_n$, the weighted mean $= \dfrac{\sum w_i x_i}{\sum w_i}$. Here is an example.

> A student scores 80, 60, and 50 on three exams. Find the weighted mean of the student's three scores, where the score of 80 counts 20 percent, the score of 60 counts 20 percent, and the score of 50 counts 60 percent.

$$\text{weighted mean} = \frac{\sum w_i x_i}{\sum w_i} = \frac{20\%\,(80) + 20\%\,(60) + 60\%\,(50)}{20\% + 20\% + 60\%} = \frac{16 + 12 + 30}{100\%} = \frac{58}{1} = 58$$

# Median

The **median** is the middle value or the arithmetic average of the middle pair of values in an *ordered* set of data. For a small data set, you easily can determine a data set's median using a two-step process: First, put the data values in order from least to greatest (or greatest to least). Next, find the middle data value. If there is no single middle data value, find the arithmetic average of the middle pair of data values. When the number of data values is *odd,* the median is the middle value. When the number of data values is *even,* the median is the average of the middle pair of values. Here is an example.

> Find the median of the data set consisting of the 10 values 21, 35, 34, 30, 32, 36, 24, 35, 28, 35.

*Step 1.* Put the data values in order: 21, 24, 28, 30, 32, 34, 35, 35, 35, 36.

*Step 2.* The number of data values is even, so find the average of the middle pair of values: $\dfrac{32 + 34}{2} = 33$. Thus, the median is 33.

> **Tip: When you are finding a median, don't make the common mistake of neglecting to put the numbers in order first.**

In terms of position, the median is the $\dfrac{(n+1)}{2}$ data value in an ordered set of discrete values. You can find the median by counting up from the least data value to the $\dfrac{(n+1)}{2}$ position, which is the middle position of the ordered set of data. When $n$ is odd, there is one number at the $\dfrac{(n+1)}{2}$ position. When $n$ is even, the median is halfway between the two numbers on either side of the $\dfrac{(n+1)}{2}$ position. Here is an example.

> Find the median of the data in the following stem-and-leaf plot.
>
> **Ages of 40 Attendees at a Retirement Party**
>
> | Stem | Leaves |
> |------|--------|
> | 4 | 0 3 3 5 6 9 |
> | 5 | 3 4 4 5 6 6 7 7 7 7 7 8 8 8 9 |
> | 6 | 0 0 0 1 1 1 2 3 3 3 7 |
> | 7 | 1 4 7 8 |
> | 8 | 1 3 |
> | 9 | 0 1 |
> | Legend: 4|6 = 46 | |

The median for the stem-and-leaf plot shown is in the $\frac{(40+1)}{2} = 20.5$th position. Thus, the median is halfway between the 20th data value, 58, and the 21st data value, 59. The median is 58.5.

Tip: $\frac{(n+1)}{2}$ does not give a median's value; it gives the median's position in an ordered data set.

# Mode

The **mode** is the data value or values that occur with the highest frequency in a data set. A data set can have one mode, more than one mode, or no mode. If exactly two data values occur with the same frequency that is more often than that of any of the other data values, then the data set is bimodal. If three or more data values occur with the same frequency that is more often than that of any of the other data values, then the data set is multimodal. A data set in which each data value occurs the same number of times has no mode. Here is an example.

> Find the mode of the following data set: 21, 35, 34, 30, 32, 36, 24, 35, 28, 35.

The value 35 occurs three times, which is the highest frequency of occurrence for any one value in the data set. Thus, the mode is 35.

# Selecting the Most Appropriate Measure of Central Tendency

The mean, median, and mode are ways to describe a data set's central value. To know which of these measures of central tendency would be useful to describe a data set, consider the following information.

## Mean

- The mean is preferred when the distribution of the data has a symmetric shape (or close to it). *Tip:* A distribution is **symmetric** if its lower (left) half and upper (right) half are mirror images of each other.
- The actual data values are used in the computation of the mean. If any one number is changed, the mean's value will change. For example, the mean of the data set consisting of 50, 50, 87, 78, and 95 is 72. If the 95 in this set is changed to 100, the new data set's mean is 73.
- Although the mean represents a data set's central or typical value, the mean does not necessarily have the same value as one of the numbers in the set. For example, the mean of 50, 50, 87, 78, and 95 is 72, yet none of the five numbers in this data set equals 72.
- A disadvantage of the mean is that it is influenced by outliers, especially in a small data set. It tends to be "pulled" toward an extreme value, much more so than does the median. (An **outlier** is a data value that is extremely high or extremely low in comparison to most of the other data values.)
  - If a data set contains extremely high values that are not balanced by corresponding low values, the mean is misleadingly high. The mean of the data set consisting of 15, 15, 20, 25, and 25 is 20. If the 20 in this set is changed to 100, the mean of the new data set is 36. The value 36 does not represent the data set consisting of 15, 15, 100, 25, and 25 very well, since four of the data values are less than 30.
  - If a data set contains extremely low values that are not balanced by corresponding high values, the mean is misleadingly low. The mean of the data set consisting of 100, 100, 130, and 150 is 120. If the 150 in this set is changed to 10, the mean of the new data set is 85. The value 85 does not represent the data set consisting of 100, 100, 130, and 10 very well, since three of the data values are greater than or equal to 100.

## Median

- The median is the most useful alternative to the mean as a measure of central tendency. The median is preferred when the data distribution is "lopsided" with unbalanced extreme values or outliers on one side.
- Like the mean, the median does not necessarily have the same value as one of the numbers in the set. If the data set contains an odd number of data values, the median will be the middle number; however, for an even number of data values, the median is the arithmetic average of the middle pair of numbers.

- The median is not strongly influenced by outliers. For example, the median of the data set consisting of 10, 15, 20, 25, and 30 is 20. If the 30 in this set is changed to 100, the new data set's median remains 20.

- A disadvantage of the median as an indicator of a central value is that it is based on relative size, rather than on the actual numbers in the set. For example, a student who has test scores of 44, 47, and 98 shows improved performance that would not be reflected if the median of 47, rather than the mean of 63, was reported as the representative score.

## Mode

- The mode is the simplest measure of central tendency to calculate.

- If a data set has a mode, the mode (or modes) is one of the data values.

- The mode is the only appropriate measure of central tendency for data that are strictly nonnumeric, like data on ice cream flavor preferences (vanilla, chocolate, strawberry, and so on). Although it makes no sense to determine a mean or median ice cream flavor for the data, the ice cream flavor that was named most frequently would be the modal flavor.

- For quantitative data, the mode is not a preferred measure of central tendency.

- A disadvantage of the mode as an indicator of a central value is that it is based on relative frequency, rather than on all the values in the set. For example, a student who has test scores of 45, 45, and 99 shows improved performance that would not be reflected if the mode of 45, rather than the mean of 63, was reported as the representative score.

When you are summarizing data, you might want to report more than one measure of central tendency, if appropriate. For numeric data, if you select only one measure, the mean is preferred for data sets in which outliers are not present. The median is the preferred measure when outliers are present. The mode is the preferred measure for nonnumeric categorical data.

# Percentiles and Quartiles

Percentiles and quartiles are additional measures that are used to describe numerical data. The **Pth percentile** is a value at or below which $P$ percent of the data fall. At most $P$ percent of the data values are less than this value, and at most $P$ percent of the data values are greater. For example, the median is the 50th percentile because 50 percent of the data fall at or below the median. Percentiles split an ordered data set into hundredths. For example, 60 percent of the data values should fall at or below the 60th percentile.

**Quartiles** are values that divide an ordered data set into four portions, each of which contains approximately one-fourth of the data. About 25 percent of the data values are at or below the first quartile (also called the 25th percentile). About 50 percent of the data values are at or below the second quartile (also called the 50th percentile), which is the same as the median. About 75 percent of the data values are at or below the third quartile (also called the 75th percentile).

The **first quartile,** denoted $Q_1$, is the median of the lower half of an ordered data set, and the **third quartile,** denoted $Q_3$, is the median of the upper half. When the number of data values is odd, exclude the median to create the two halves of the data set. Here are examples.

Given the data set 21, 24, 28, 30, 32, 34, 35, 35, 35, 36, $Q_1$ is 28, the median is 33, and $Q_3$ is 35.

Given the data set 10, 12, 12, 13, 14, 15, 16, 17, 20, $Q_1$ is 12, the median is 14, and $Q_3$ is 16.5.

*Note:* Determining $Q_1$ and $Q_3$ by excluding the median to create the two halves when the number of data values is odd is not the only approach currently in use. You might encounter other methods for dividing the data set into two halves for the purposes of calculating $Q_1$ and $Q_3$ when the number of data values is odd.

Tip: Percentiles and quartiles are numbers along the horizontal axis. They are not percentages.

# Measures of Variability

This topic introduces measures of variability (spread). A **measure of variability** (also called **dispersion**) is a single number that describes the spread of a data set about its central value. Measures of center are important for describing data sets. However, their interpretation is enhanced when the variability about the central value is known. For example, one set of scores may be extremely consistent, with scores like 60, 62, 65, 68, 70, 70, 72, 75, 78, and 80; while another set of scores may be very erratic, with scores like 40, 40, 50, 55, 60, 80, 85, 90, 100, and 100. The scores in the first set cluster more closely together than do the scores in the second set. The scores in the second set are more spread out. The first data set has less variability than does the second data set.

Three measures that quantify variation in numerical data sets are the range, the mean absolute deviation (MAD), and the interquartile range (IQR).

## Range

The **range** of a data set is the difference between the **maximum value** (greatest value) and the **minimum value** (least value) in the data set. That is, range = maximum value – minimum value. The range describes how far apart the data are spread. *Tip:* The range should have the same units as those of the data values from which it is computed. If no units are specified, then the range will not specify units. Here is an example.

> Find the range of the following data set: 21, 35, 34, 30, 32, 36, 24, 35, 28, 35.

Range = maximum value – minimum value = 36 − 21 = 15.

The range gives an indication of the spread of the values in a data set, but its value is determined by only two of the data values. The extent of spread due to the other data values is not considered.

## MAD

The **MAD** is the average distance between each data value and the mean of the data values. Thus,

$$\text{MAD} = \frac{\text{sum of the absolute values of the differences between each data value and the mean}}{\text{number of data values}}.$$ The MAD should

have the same units as those of the data values from which it is computed. If no units are specified, then the MAD will not specify units.

The MAD is a measure of spread that takes into account all the data values in the data set. If there is no variability in a data set, each data value equals the mean, so the MAD for the data set is zero. The more the data values vary from the mean, the greater is the MAD. *Tip:* The MAD is used for distributions in which the mean is the appropriate measure of center.

To find the MAD of a data set, do four steps.

*Step 1.* Determine the mean for the data values.

*Step 2.* Find the absolute value of the difference between each data value and the mean.

*Step 3.* Sum the absolute values from step 2.

*Step 4.* Divide by the number of data values.

Here is an example.

> Find the MAD of the following data set: 21, 35, 34, 30, 32, 36, 24, 35, 28, 35. The mean (determined previously) is 31.

$$\text{MAD} = \frac{|21-31| + |35-31| + |34-31| + |30-31| + |32-31| + |36-31| + |24-31| + |35-31| + |28-31| + |35-31|}{10}$$

$$= \frac{10+4+3+1+1+5+7+4+3+4}{10} = \frac{42}{10} = 4.2$$

When you are given two data sets, the MAD of the one whose data values are clustered closer to the mean of the data is less than the MAD of the other data set. Here is an example.

The following two data sets both have a mean of 50.

Set 1: 30, 40, 50, 60, 70

Set 2: 10, 10, 50, 90, 90

The MAD of Set 1 is less than the MAD of Set 2. It is not necessary to calculate the MADs for the two data sets because, by inspection, the data values in Set 1 cluster more closely around the mean of 50 than do the data values in Set 2. Even though the two data sets have the same mean, the data in Set 2 have more spread than the data in Set 1 do.

Visually, in a manner of speaking, data sets whose distributions are "tall and thin" have MADs that are less than MADs of data sets whose distributions are "short and wide." Here is an example.

> The dot plots show the scores of 30 seventh graders on the mathematics beginning-of-year (BOY) assessment and on the mathematics end-of-year (EOY) assessment. Which set of scores has the lesser MAD?

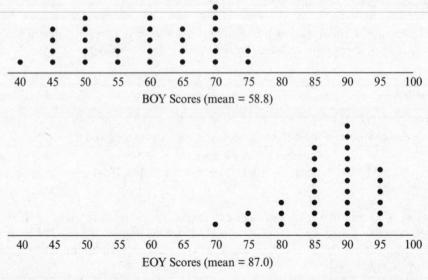

The BOY scores show more variability than do the EOY scores. The BOY distribution looks shorter and wider than the EOY distribution. The EOY scores are clustered more closely around the EOY mean of 87.0 than are the BOY scores around the BOY mean of 58.8. Therefore, by visual inspection, the MAD of the EOY scores is less than the MAD of the BOY scores.

# IQR

The **IQR** is the difference between the upper and lower quartiles of a data set. That is, $\text{IQR} = Q_3 - Q_1$.

The IQR is the range of the middle 50 percent of the data. A small IQR indicates the middle half of the data clusters around the median. A large IQR indicates the middle half of the data is spread out away from the median.

*Tip:* The IQR is used for data in which the median is the appropriate measure of center.

To determine the IQR, do three steps.

*Step 1.* Determine the data set's median.

*Step 2.* Determine the upper and lower quartiles.

*Step 3.* Compute the difference between the upper and lower quartiles.

Here are examples using the data sets given in "Percentiles and Quartiles" earlier in this chapter.

Given the data set 21, 24, 28, 30, 32, 34, 35, 35, 35, 36, $Q_1$ is 28, the median is 33, and $Q_3$ is 35. Thus, the IQR = 35 − 28 = 7.

Given the data set 10, 12, 12, 13, 14, 15, 16, 17, 20, $Q_1$ is 12, the median is 14, and $Q_3$ is 16.5. Thus, the IQR = 16.5 − 12 = 4.5.

# Five-Number Summary and Box Plots

For a set of data, the **five-number summary** consists of five measures: the minimum value (Min), the first quartile ($Q_1$), the median, the third quartile ($Q_3$), and the maximum value (Max), written in order from smallest to largest. A **box plot** (shown below) is a graphical representation of the five-number summary for a data set. Box plots are also called **box-and-whisker plots.** Here is an example. (*Note:* The dashed vertical lines are shown for clarity, but would not be included as part of the box plot.)

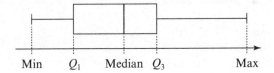

$$\text{Min} \qquad Q_1 \qquad \text{Median} \quad Q_3 \qquad\qquad \text{Max}$$

The box plot shows a rectangular box between $Q_1$ and $Q_3$, above the horizontal axis. The median is indicated with a vertical line in the interior of the box. The minimum value is at the end of the horizontal line extending from the left end of the box, and the maximum value is at the end of the horizontal line extending from the right end of the box. *Note:* Box plots also may be oriented vertically.

The box plot is a visual summary of the data. The five numbers of the five-number summary determine four groups from left to right, starting at the minimum value position in the box plot. Each group contains approximately 25% of the data values.

# Skewness

A data set can be described in terms of the skewness of its distribution. **Skewness** describes the "lopsidedness" of the distribution. In a skewed distribution, one tail of the distribution is considerably longer or drawn out relative to the other tail. A distribution that is **symmetric** has no skew. A distribution is **skewed to the right** (or **positively skewed**) if it has a longer tail to the right, toward larger values. A distribution is **skewed to the left** (or **negatively skewed**) if it has a longer tail to the left, toward smaller values. In a right-skewed distribution, the mean lies to the right of the median. In a left-skewed distribution, the mean lies to the left of the median. The mean and median coincide for a symmetric distribution (no skew).

Here are examples.

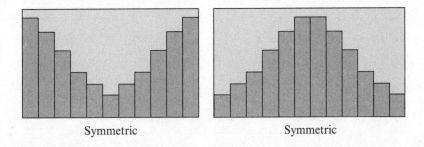

Symmetric                              Symmetric

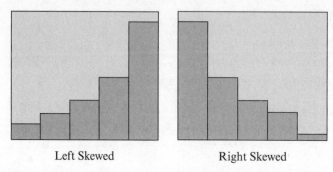

Left Skewed          Right Skewed

In box plots, skewness is detected by the position of the median. If the median is farther from the first quartile than it is from the third quartile, the distribution is skewed to the left. If the median is farther from the third quartile than it is from the first quartile, the distribution is skewed to the right. If the median is equidistant from the first and third quartiles, the distribution is symmetric. Here are examples.

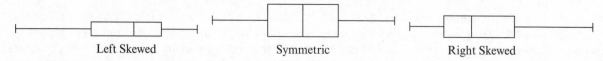

Left Skewed          Symmetric          Right Skewed

# Investigating Bivariate Data

For the Praxis MS Math test, you should have a basic understanding of how to detect relationships between two quantitative variables based on data that have been collected on both variables. These data are bivariate data. **Bivariate data** are paired values of data from two quantitative variables. The data are paired in a way that matches each value from one variable with a corresponding value from the other variable. Scatter plots, lines of best fit, simple linear regression, and correlation coefficients are used to investigate this type of data.

## Scatter Plots

A **scatter plot** is a graph of the ordered pairs of a set of bivariate data plotted on a coordinate grid. The scale for one of the variables is along the horizontal axis and the scale for the other variable is along the vertical axis. Each plotted ordered pair represents a **data point** in the scatter plot. (*Note:* Do not connect the data points in a scatter plot.) Always plot the **predictor variable** (also called the **explanatory variable** or **independent variable**), if there is one, on the horizontal axis and the **response variable** (also called the **dependent variable**) on the vertical axis. The scatter plot's pattern provides visual cues as to whether there is a relationship between the two variables, and, if there is, the nature of that relationship.

For the Praxis MS Math test, you should be able to examine scatter plots and distinguish between those that suggest linear relationships and those that suggest nonlinear relationships between two variables. The data points are often described as forming a "cloud." When the data points in a scatter plot appear to cluster around an imagined line passing through the points, the scatter plot suggests a **linear** relationship between the two variables. Here is an example.

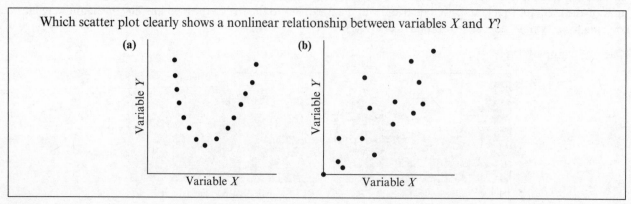

188

The scatter plot in (a) shows a recognizable curved pattern. This pattern suggests a curved relationship between the variables $X$ and $Y$. It is clearly nonlinear. The scatter plot in (b) shows a recognizable linear pattern. This pattern suggests a linear relationship between the variables $X$ and $Y$.

A scatter plot that has no recognizable pattern points to no relationship between the two variables. Here is an example.

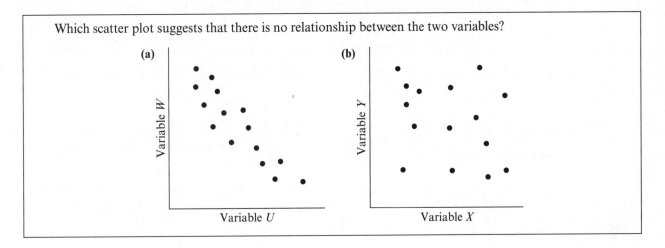

The scatter plot in (a) shows a recognizable linear pattern that suggests a linear relationship between variables $U$ and $W$. The scatter plot in (b) does not show a recognizable pattern to suggest a relationship between variables $X$ and $Y$.

If the relationship between two variables is linear, it can be positive or negative. For linear relationships, scatter plots that slant upward from left to right indicate positive linear relationships. In **positive linear relationships,** above-average values of one variable tend to be associated with above-average values of the other, and below-average values of the two variables also tend to be associated. Scatter plots that slant downward from left to right indicate negative linear relationships. In **negative linear relationships,** above-average values of one variable tend to be associated with below-average values of the other, and the reverse is true. Here is an example.

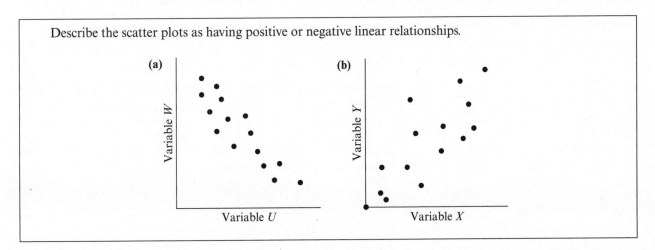

The scatter plot in (a) suggests a negative linear relationship between $U$ and $W$. The scatter plot in (b) suggests a positive linear relationship between $X$ and $Y$.

The closer the data points in a scatter plot cluster around an imagined line passing through the points, the stronger the linear relationship is between the two variables. Here is an example.

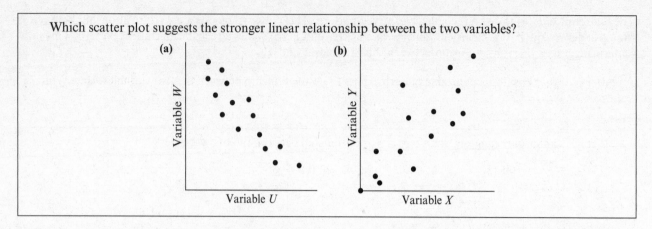

Which scatter plot suggests the stronger linear relationship between the two variables?

Both scatter plots indicate a linear relationship. The relationship between $U$ and $W$ is stronger than the relationship between $X$ and $Y$ because the data points in the scatter plot in (a) are clustered closer around an imagined line passing through the points than are the data points in the scatter plot in (b).

In a scatter plot, an **outlier** is a data point that is relatively far away from the rest of the points in the scatter plot. For example, in the scatter plot shown below, the data point marked with an asterisk is a noticeable outlier.

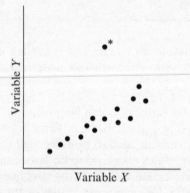

If you have *believable* information that an outlier doesn't belong with the other data points (perhaps it's the result of an error in collecting the data), you can exclude it when assessing linearity of the scatter plot.

Here are additional examples of scatter plots.

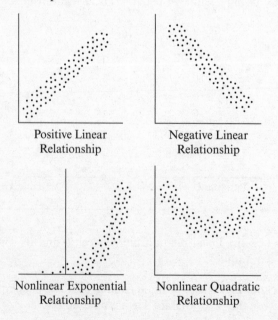

# Line of Best Fit and Simple Linear Regression

Suppose $X$ and $Y$ are the two variables under consideration, then the data points in the scatter plot consist of the ordered pairs, $(x_i, y_i)$, where $x_i \in X$ and $y_i \in Y$. If the scatter plot seems approximately linear, the **line of best fit** (or **regression line**) is a straight line that best represents the data points. It might pass through some of the points, none of the points, or even all of the points. It will always pass through the point whose coordinates are the means of the two variables.

The equation of the line of best fit is given by the **simple linear regression equation** $\widehat{Y} = a + bX$, where $\widehat{Y}$ (read as "$Y$-hat") is the predicted value of the response variable, $Y$, $a$ is a constant (corresponding to $X = 0$), and $b$ is the regression coefficient. For statistical reasons, to be safe, you should predict only within the range of the predictor variable. When you predict within the range of the plotted data, you are **interpolating.**

The coefficient $b$ is the **slope** of the regression line. The interpretation of the slope, $b$, is that if the $X$ variable increases by 1 unit, it is predicted that the $Y$ variable will change by $b$ units. The interpretation of the **intercept, $a$,** is that when the $X$ variable is zero, the $Y$ variable is $a$ units. However, if values for the $X$ variable near zero would not make sense, then typically the interpretation of the intercept will seem unrealistic in the real world. Nevertheless, the coefficient $a$ is a necessary part of the equation of the line of best fit.

The **residuals** are the differences between the actual $y$ values in the scatter plot and the $\widehat{Y}$ values predicted by the regression equation. Visually, they are the vertical distances of the data points from the regression line. The line of best fit minimizes the sum of the squares of the residuals and is the **least-squares regression line.** The closer the plotted data points are to the regression line, the smaller the residual sum of squares. Here is a detailed example to clarify your understanding of simple linear regression.

The following table contains 10 bivariate data points for the variables $X$ and $Y$.

| $X$ | 10 | 8 | 13 | 9 | 11 | 14 | 6 | 4 | 12 | 5 |
|-----|-----|-----|-----|-----|-----|-----|-----|-----|-----|-----|
| $Y$ | 8.1 | 6.9 | 7.5 | 8.8 | 8.3 | 9.9 | 7.2 | 4.3 | 10.8 | 5.7 |

The scatter plot and line of best fit are shown below.

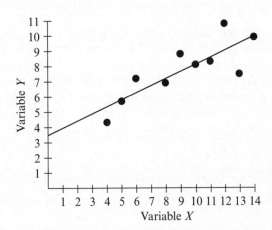

The linear regression equation of the line of best fit is $\widehat{Y} = 3.5 + 0.46X$. The interpretation of the slope of 0.46 is that if the $X$ variable increases by 1 unit, it is predicted that the $Y$ variable will increase by 0.46 units. The interpretation of the intercept, 3.5, is that when the $X$ variable is zero, the $Y$ variable is 3.5 units.

*Note:* The linear regression equation in this example is provided to you because it was obtained using technology that is unavailable to you when you take the Praxis MS Math test. The ETS graphing calculator does not have a menu for performing statistical analysis. Based on this fact, (currently) it is assumed you will not be expected to produce a regression equation when you take the test. However, it is important that you understand the function of a regression equation and that you can interpret its slope and intercept.

Now, of course, the regression equation does not perfectly predict the $Y$ value corresponding to a given $X$ value. In the case of $X = 12$, the predicted value is $\widehat{Y} = 3.5 + 0.46(12) = 9.0$, when the reality (according to the data table) is 10.8. There is an error in the prediction. This error is the residual for the data point (12, 10.8). This residual is $10.8 - 9.0 = 1.8$.

The regression equation allows you to predict $Y$ values for $X$ values not given in the table—provided you predict only within the range of the $X$ variable. For example, the predicted $Y$ value for $X = 7$ is $\widehat{Y} = 3.5 + 0.46(7) = 6.7$. The value 7 is not given as an $X$ value in the data table, but the value 7 is within the range of the available data, so it is permissible to predict its $Y$ value.

**Tip: Regression is strongly affected by outliers. Be cautious in your interpretation of regression results if the scatter plot shows clear-cut outliers.**

# Correlation Coefficient

Scatter plots visually show the direction, shape, and strength of the relationship between two quantitative variables. If the relationship is linear, the **correlation coefficient *r*** is a numerical measure that describes the direction and strength of the linear relationship between the two variables.

Correlation coefficients range from –1 to +1, with –1 indicating a "perfect" negative linear relationship and +1 indicating a "perfect" positive linear relationship. Correlation values very close to either –1 or +1 indicate very strong relationships, meaning the data points in the scatter plot lie close to a straight line. Correlations of precisely –1 or +1 occur only when the data points lie exactly along a straight line. If the two variables have no *relationship* to each other, then the correlation coefficient will be 0. The farther the correlation coefficient is from 0, the stronger the relationship. (Remember, however, that you cannot have correlation coefficients below –1 or above +1.)

The existence of a recognizable correlation between two variables does *not* imply that changes in one variable cause changes in the other variable. The correlation might be a reflection of outside variables that affect both variables under study. Simply put: Correlation does *not* imply causation.

In simple linear regression, the correlation coefficient is a measure of the strength of the linear relationship between the predictor variable and the response variable of the linear regression equation. Therefore, it can be used to assess the regression line's "goodness of fit." The closer $|r|$ is to 1, the more perfect the linear relationship is between $X$ and $Y$, and therefore, the better the regression line represents the data points. If $r$ is close to 0, there is little or no linear relationship, so the line is not a good fit for the data. For example, for the bivariate data shown previously in "Line of Best Fit and Simple Linear Regression," the correlation coefficient is 0.82, indicating a somewhat strong linear relationship between the variables $X$ and $Y$. This result suggests that the regression line is a good fit for the data.

**Tip: The correlation coefficient and the slope of the regression equation are not the same measure; however, their signs are always the same.**

# Sample Questions

Scores of 65 Tenth Graders on a Basic Arithmetic Skills Assessment

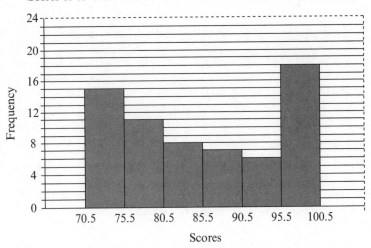

1. The histogram shows the distribution of scores of 65 tenth graders on a basic arithmetic assessment. Assuming the scores on the assessment are recorded as whole numbers, what percent of the tenth graders scored below 80.5?

   Ⓐ   26%
   Ⓑ   40%
   Ⓒ   60%
   Ⓓ   It cannot be determined from the information given in the graph.

**For the following question, select <u>all</u> that apply.**

2. For which of the following data sets is the mean clearly preferred over the median as a measure of central tendency?

   Ⓐ   The data set contains outliers.
   Ⓑ   The data set's distribution is symmetrical.
   Ⓒ   The data set consists of quantitative data.
   Ⓓ   The data set's distribution has no noticeable skewness.

**For the following question, enter your numeric answer in the box below the question.**

3. Jude has participated in eight track meets so far this season. His running times for the 400-meter race have been 73, 63, 68, 64, 69, 61, 66, and 64 seconds. What is Jude's mean running time for the eight meets?

                    [          ] seconds

**For the following question, enter your numeric answer in the box below the question.**

Social Studies Test Scores of 20 Sixth-Grade Students

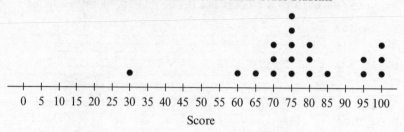

4. What is the range for the data shown in the dot plot?

5. What is the mean absolute deviation (MAD) for the data set consisting of 100, 100, 100, 100, 100, 100, 100, 100, 100, 100, 100, 100, 100, 100, 100, 100, 100, 100, and 100?

   Ⓐ  0
   Ⓑ  5
   Ⓒ  50
   Ⓓ  100

6. Loy scored at the 84th percentile on a multiple-choice statistics exam. The best interpretation of this information is that

   Ⓐ  Loy answered 84 percent of the questions on the test correctly.
   Ⓑ  Only 16 percent of the other students did worse on the test than did Loy.
   Ⓒ  Loy answered 84 questions correctly.
   Ⓓ  Loy did as well or better than 84 percent of the students who took the exam.

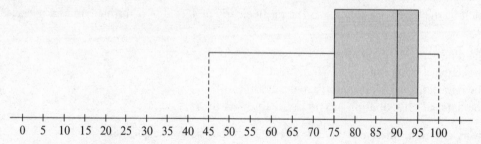

7. A box plot for the mathematics test scores of 200 sixth graders is shown above. What is the interquartile range for the students' test scores?

   Ⓐ  15
   Ⓑ  20
   Ⓒ  25
   Ⓓ  30

**For the following question, enter your numeric answer in the box below the question.**

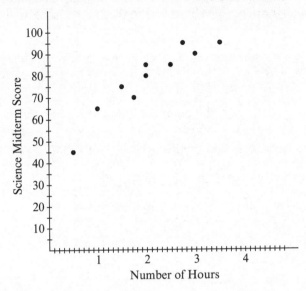

8. A scatter plot showing the linear relationship between the number of hours of study and the score on a science midterm exam of 10 eighth graders is shown above. The line of best fit for the data has equation $\hat{Y} = 16X + 46$. What is the predicted science midterm score for a student who studied $2\frac{1}{4}$ hours?

[     ]

# Answer Explanations

1. **B.** The graph shows the number of students who scored in each interval. To find the percent of students who scored below 80.5 will take two steps. First, find the number of students who scored below 80.5. Next, divide the result by 65, the total number of students, expressing the quotient as a percent.

   *Step 1.* From the histogram, 15 + 11 = 26 students scored below 80.5.

   *Step 2.* $\frac{26}{65} = 0.4 = 40\%$, choice B.

2. **B, D.** When a data set contains outliers, the median, which is not strongly influenced by outliers, is the preferred alternative to the mean, so eliminate choice A. For the data sets in choices B and D, the mean is the preferred measure of central tendency. Not enough information is provided in choice C to "clearly" prefer the mean over the median.

3. **66** mean $= \dfrac{\text{the sum of the running times}}{\text{number of running times}} = \dfrac{73 + 63 + 68 + 64 + 69 + 61 + 66 + 64}{8} = \dfrac{528}{8} = 66$

4. **70** According to the dot plot, the minimum value is 30 and the maximum value is 100. Thus, range = maximum value – minimum value = 100 – 30 = 70.

5. **A.** The data values are all the same, so there is no variability in the data set. Each data value equals the mean, so the MAD for the data set is 0, choice A.

6. **D.** The 84th percentile is a value at or below which 84 percent of the data fall. Therefore, the best interpretation of Loy's score is that she did as well or better than 84 percent of the students who took the exam, choice D.

**7. B.** The interquartile range (IQR) is the difference between the upper and lower quartiles of the students' test scores. The box plot shows the upper quartile is 95 and the lower quartile is 75.

$$IQR = 95 - 75 = 20$$

The interquartile range for the students' test scores is 20, choice B.

**8. 82**

$$2\frac{1}{4} \text{ hours} = 2.25 \text{ hours}$$

The predicted science midterm score for a student who studied 2.25 hours is

$$\widehat{Y} = 16(2.25) + 46 = 36 + 46 = 82$$

# Scoring Your Practice Tests

*Step 1*. Determine your raw score. Count how many questions you answered correctly. (***Remember:*** For selected-response questions with one or more correct answers, no credit is given unless <u>all</u> correct answers *and no others* are selected.)

*Step 2*. Determine your percent correct = $\dfrac{\text{raw score}}{55}$. ***Note:*** For the official exam, your percent correct is $\dfrac{\text{raw score}}{45}$ because 10 of the 55 test questions do not contribute toward your score.

*Step 3*. Use the table below to determine your approximate scaled score.*

| Percent Correct | Scaled Score | Percent Correct | Scaled Score |
|---|---|---|---|
| 0%–20% | 100 | 62% | 157 |
| 22% | 103 | 64% | 159 |
| 24% | 106 | 66% | 162 |
| 26% | 108 | 68% | 164 |
| 28% | 111 | 69% | 165 |
| 30% | 114 | 70% | 167 |
| 32% | 116 | 72% | 169 |
| 34% | 119 | 74% | 172 |
| 36% | 122 | 76% | 175 |
| 38% | 124 | 78% | 177 |
| 40% | 127 | 80% | 180 |
| 42% | 130 | 82% | 183 |
| 44% | 132 | 84% | 185 |
| 46% | 135 | 86% | 188 |
| 48% | 138 | 88% | 191 |
| 50% | 140 | 90% | 193 |
| 52% | 143 | 92% | 196 |
| 54% | 146 | 94% | 199 |
| 56% | 148 | 96% | 200 |
| 58% | 151 | 98% | 200 |
| 60% | 153 | 100% | 200 |

*The testing company does not reveal exactly how scaled scores are determined. The values in this table are approximate scaled scores only (current in 2016). Scaled scores for the official test may vary from form to form of the test.

***Caution:*** Do not let your scaled score give you a false sense of security. The practice tests in this book include questions similar to what might appear on the official test. However, you should not use your practice tests results to predict your score on the official test. You should try to achieve your personal best on the official test.

# Chapter 9

# Practice Test 1

**55 Questions**

**Time—2 Hours**

**Directions:** Read the directions for each question carefully. This test has several different question types. For each question, select the best single answer choice unless written instructions preceding the question state otherwise. For each selected-response question, select the best answer or answers from the choices given. For each numeric-entry question, enter an answer in the answer box. Enter the exact answer unless you are told to round your answer. If a question asks specifically for the answer as a fraction, there will be two boxes—a numerator box and a denominator box. Do not use decimal points in fractions.

---

1. Zoey and Jax both swam in the indoor pool at Gold Star Gym today. Zoey swims at Gold Star Gym every 12 days. Jax swims there every 15 days. If both continue with their regular swimming schedules at Gold Star Gym, the next time both will swim there on the same day is in how many days?

    Ⓐ 12
    Ⓑ 15
    Ⓒ 30
    Ⓓ 60

**For the following question, select <u>all</u> that apply.**

2. For which of the following expressions is $a - b$ a factor?

    Ⓐ $a^2 - b^2$
    Ⓑ $a^2 - ab + b^2$
    Ⓒ $a^3 - b^3$
    Ⓓ $a^3 - 3a^2b + 3ab^2 - b^3$

**For the following question, enter your numeric answer in the box below the question.**

| Determination of Course Grade | Percent |
|---|---|
| Average (mean) of three major exams | 50% |
| Average (mean) of weekly quizzes | 10% |
| Final exam score | 40% |

3. A student is trying to achieve an average of at least 80 to earn a grade of B in a college course. In determining the course grade, the instructor calculates a weighted average as shown in the table above. The student has scores of 72, 81, and 75 on the three major exams and an average of 92 on the weekly quizzes. To the nearest tenth, what is the *lowest* score the student can make on the final exam and still receive a B in the course?

    82

4. If $xy \neq 0$, then $\dfrac{3}{x} + \dfrac{4}{y} =$

    Ⓐ $\dfrac{12}{xy}$

    Ⓑ $\dfrac{7}{x + y}$

    Ⓒ $\dfrac{7}{xy}$

    Ⓓ $\dfrac{4x + 3y}{xy}$

GO ON TO THE NEXT PAGE

5. Which of the following expressions is equivalent to $(x^2 + 4)^{-\frac{1}{2}}$?

Ⓐ $-\dfrac{x^2 + 4}{2}$

Ⓑ $-\sqrt{x^2 + 4}$

Ⓒ $\dfrac{1}{\sqrt{x^2 + 4}}$

Ⓓ $\dfrac{1}{x + 2}$

6. A trip of 204 miles requires 8.5 gallons of gasoline. At this rate, how many gallons of gasoline would be required for a trip of 228 miles?

Ⓐ 9 gal

Ⓑ 9.5 gal

Ⓒ 10 gal

Ⓓ 10.5 gal

7. $4^x + 12^x =$

Ⓐ $4^x (1 + 3^x)$

Ⓑ $4(5^x)$

Ⓒ $16^x$

Ⓓ $16^{2x}$

**For the following question, select <u>all</u> that apply.**

8. If $x$ and $y$ are nonzero real numbers, which of the following statements must be true?

Ⓐ $|x| = -|-x|$

Ⓑ $\left|\dfrac{x}{y}\right| = \dfrac{|x|}{|y|}$

Ⓒ $|x| = \sqrt{(-x)^2}$

Ⓓ $|x + y| = |x| + |y|$

**For the following question, select <u>all</u> that apply.**

9. The whole number $y$ is exactly three times the whole number $x$. The whole number $z$ is the sum of $x$ and $y$. Which of the following could be the value of $z$?

Ⓐ 314

Ⓑ 416

Ⓒ 524

Ⓓ 1,032

10. $2x^3 y(x + 3)(3x - 1) =$

Ⓐ $3x^2 + 8x - 3$

Ⓑ $6x^5 y - 16x^4 y - 6x^3 y$

Ⓒ $6x^5 y + 16x^4 y - 6x^3 y$

Ⓓ $6x^6 y + 16x^5 y - 6x^3 y$

11. Solve $2x(x - 2) = 1$.

Ⓐ $x = \dfrac{1}{2}$ or $3$

Ⓑ $x = 1 \pm \sqrt{6}$

Ⓒ $x = \dfrac{-2 \pm \sqrt{6}}{2}$

Ⓓ $x = \dfrac{2 \pm \sqrt{6}}{2}$

$$3y = 2x - 16$$
$$4x + 5y = 10$$

12. What is the $y$ value of the ordered pair that is a solution to the system shown?

Ⓐ $-5$

Ⓑ $-2$

Ⓒ $2$

Ⓓ $5$

13. A pharmacist measures the mass of a medical substance and uses the appropriate number of significant figures to record the mass as 10 grams, to the nearest gram. Which of the following ways most accurately expresses the range of possible values of the mass of the substance?

Ⓐ $10 \text{ g} \pm 0.1 \text{ g}$

Ⓑ $10 \text{ g} \pm 0.5 \text{ g}$

Ⓒ $10 \text{ g} \pm 1.0 \text{ g}$

Ⓓ $10 \text{ g} \pm 0.0 \text{ g}$

GO ON TO THE NEXT PAGE

**14.** A carpenter needs to drill a hole in a triangular piece of wood so that the hole is equidistant from each side of the triangle. Which of the following constructions should the carpenter do to determine the location of the hole?

Ⓐ    Find the intersection of the bisectors of the three angles.

Ⓑ    Find the intersection of the three altitudes of the triangle.

Ⓒ    Find the intersection of the perpendicular bisectors of the three sides.

Ⓓ    Find the intersection of the three medians of the triangle.

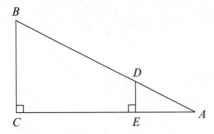

**15.** In the figure shown, $\overline{CE}$ has length 200 meters, $\overline{EA}$ has length 100 meters, and $\overline{DE}$ is perpendicular to $\overline{AC}$ and has length 50 meters. What is the area of $\triangle ABC$?

Ⓐ    7500 m$^2$

Ⓑ    15 000 m$^2$

Ⓒ    22 500 m$^2$

Ⓓ    45 000 m$^2$

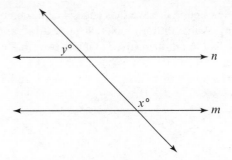

**16.** In the figure above, lines $m$ and $n$ are parallel and $x = 8y$. What is the value of $x$?

Ⓐ    10

Ⓑ    20

Ⓒ    160

Ⓓ    170

**For the following question, enter your numeric answer in the box below the question.**

**17.** A length of cable is attached to the top of a 15-foot vertical pole. The cable is anchored 8 feet from the base of the pole. What is the length, in feet, of the cable?

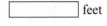 feet

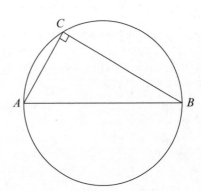

**18.** In the figure, the circle circumscribed about the right triangle has a radius of 5.5 centimeters. What is the length of the hypotenuse of the right triangle, in centimeters?

Ⓐ    11 cm

Ⓑ    5.5$\pi$ cm

Ⓒ    11$\pi$ cm

Ⓓ    It cannot be determined from the information given.

GO ON TO THE NEXT PAGE

**19.** A solid cube of silver has edges 4 centimeters long. A metallurgist melts the cube down and uses all the molten silver to make two smaller identical solid cubes. What is the length, in centimeters, of an edge of one of the smaller cubes?

Ⓐ   2 cm

Ⓑ   $2\sqrt{2}$ cm

Ⓒ   $2\sqrt[3]{2}$ cm

Ⓓ   $2\sqrt[3]{4}$ cm

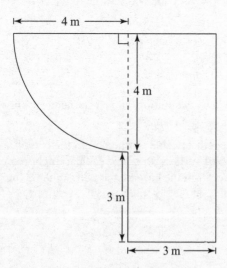

**20.** The figure in the diagram consists of a fourth of a circle and a rectangle with the dimensions shown. What is the approximate area of the figure, in square meters?

Ⓐ   21 m$^2$

Ⓑ   34 m$^2$

Ⓒ   41 m$^2$

Ⓓ   64 m$^2$

**21.** For disaster relief in a fire-damaged area, $1.6 billion is needed. This amount of money is approximately equivalent to spending $1 per second for how many years?

Ⓐ   10

Ⓑ   50

Ⓒ   100

Ⓓ   500

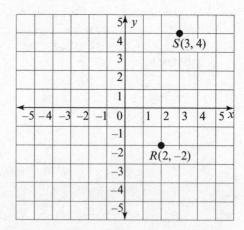

**22.** What is the midpoint of the line segment connecting the two points $R$ and $S$ shown above?

Ⓐ   (1, 6)

Ⓑ   (5, 2)

Ⓒ   (2.5, 1)

Ⓓ   (0.5, 3)

**For the following question, select <u>all</u> that apply.**

**23.** Which of the following sets of ordered pairs represents a function?

Ⓐ   {(4, 5), (3, 1), (3, 10), (−2, 0)}

Ⓑ   {(5, 5), ($5^2$, 5), ($5^3$, $5^3$), ($5^4$, $5^4$)}

Ⓒ   {(2, 3), (4, 3), (8, 3), (16, 3)}

Ⓓ   {(0, 0)}

GO ON TO THE NEXT PAGE

**24.** Solution A contains $3 \times 10^{-2}$ grams of salt. Solution B contains $6 \times 10^2$ grams of salt. The number of grams of salt in solution B is how many times the number of grams of salt in solution A?

Ⓐ   0.0002
Ⓑ   200
Ⓒ   2,000
Ⓓ   20,000

**25.** Determine the domain $D_f$ and the range $R_f$ of the function $y = \dfrac{x^2 + 40x - 500}{500}$, where $x$ is a real number between 500 and 750.

Ⓐ   $D_f = \{x \mid 500 < x < 750\}$;
       $R_f = \{y \mid 539 < y < 1{,}184\}$
Ⓑ   $D_f = \{x \mid x \text{ is a real number}\}$;
       $R_f = \{y \mid 539 < y < 1{,}184\}$
Ⓒ   $D_f = \{y \mid 539 < y < 1{,}184\}$;
       $R_f = \{x \mid 500 < x < 750\}$
Ⓓ   $D_f = \{x \mid 500 < x < 750\}$;
       $R_f = \{y \mid y \text{ is a real number}\}$

**26.** Using data collected through experimentation, a social scientist develops a function $y = f(x)$ that relates hours of sleep $y$ to age $x$. In addition to being a relation, which of the following statements MUST be true about the function?

Ⓐ   It has a smooth graph with no cusps or jagged edges.
Ⓑ   Every $y$ value has one and only one $x$ value.
Ⓒ   The graph of the function passes through the origin.
Ⓓ   It gives a single value for hours of sleep for each value in the age range.

**27.** How many different ways can four people sit in four of seven empty identical chairs that are placed in a row?

Ⓐ   24
Ⓑ   35
Ⓒ   840
Ⓓ   5,040

**28.** A line passes through the point $(0, 5)$ and is perpendicular to the line that has equation $x - 3y = 10$. Which of the following equations represents the line?

Ⓐ   $x + 3y = 5$
Ⓑ   $x - 3y = 5$
Ⓒ   $3x + y = 5$
Ⓓ   $-3x + y = 5$

**29.** Given the cubic function $f(x) = x^3$, which of the following best describes the function $f(x) = (x - 2)^3$?

Ⓐ   the same as the graph of $f(x) = x^3$ shifted up by 2 units
Ⓑ   the same as the graph of $f(x) = x^3$ shifted down by 2 units
Ⓒ   the same as the graph of $f(x) = x^3$ shifted right by 2 units
Ⓓ   the same as the graph of $f(x) = x^3$ shifted left by 2 units

**30.** If $f(x) = \dfrac{2x + 6}{x + 2}$ and $g(x) = x + 2$, then $(g \circ f)(x) = g(f(x)) =$

Ⓐ   $\dfrac{4x + 10}{x + 2}$

Ⓑ   $\dfrac{2x + 10}{x + 4}$

Ⓒ   $\dfrac{4x + 8}{x + 2}$

Ⓓ   $\dfrac{2x + 8}{x + 4}$

**31.** Blair has participated in eight track meets so far this season. His running times for the 400-meter race have been 73, 63, 68, 64, 69, 61, 66, and 64 seconds. What is Blair's median running time, in seconds, for the eight meets?

Ⓐ   64
Ⓑ   65
Ⓒ   66
Ⓓ   66.5

GO ON TO THE NEXT PAGE

**For the following question, enter your numeric answer in the box below the question.**

### Book Genre Preference

| Genre | Number of Students |
|-------|--------------------|
| Biography/Historical Nonfiction | 44 |
| Historical Fiction | 58 |
| Mystery | 64 |
| Science/Nature Informational | 50 |
| Science Fiction/Fantasy | 104 |
| **Total** | 320 |

**32.** The table shows the results of a poll of young readers regarding what genre of books they read most often. If a circle graph is constructed using the data in the table, what central angle should be used to represent the category Science Fiction/Fantasy?

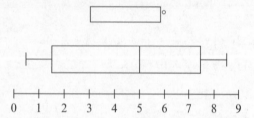

**33.** In the box plot shown above, the vertical line at 5 indicates that 5 is which of the following?

&#9424; the median
&#9425; the mean
&#9426; the first quartile
&#9427; the third quartile

| Grade Level | Cell Phone | No Cell Phone |
|-------------|-----------|---------------|
| Ninth | 55 | 45 |
| Tenth | 70 | 30 |
| Eleventh | 78 | 22 |
| Twelfth | 95 | 5 |

**34.** The data in the table above show cell phone status by grade level of 400 high school students. If one of the 400 students is randomly selected, what is the probability that the student has a cell phone, given that the student is a ninth grader?

&#9424; $\dfrac{149}{800}$

&#9425; $\dfrac{11}{100}$

&#9426; $\dfrac{11}{80}$

&#9427; $\dfrac{11}{20}$

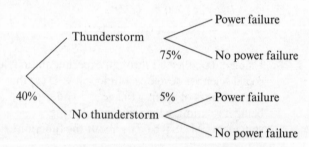

**35.** The partially completed probability diagram shown above represents the incidence of power failure during weather in which a thunderstorm might or might not develop. What is the probability that a thunderstorm develops and a power failure occurs?

&#9424; 2%
&#9425; 15%
&#9426; 65%
&#9427; 85%

GO ON TO THE NEXT PAGE

**36.** Only one of 10 remote controls in a box is defective. The remote controls are tested one at a time. If the first three remote controls tested are not defective, what is the probability that the fourth remote control tested is defective?

Ⓐ $\dfrac{1}{10}$

Ⓑ $\dfrac{1}{7}$

Ⓒ $\dfrac{7}{10}$

Ⓓ $\dfrac{9}{10}$

**For the following question, enter your numeric answer in the box below the question.**

**37.** Given the recursive sequence defined by

$f(0) = 5,$
$f(n) = 2f(n-1) + 1$ for $n \geq 1,$

what is the value of $f(3)$?

**38.** If both digits and letters can repeat, which of the following computations can be used to determine how many different license plate alphanumeric codes consisting of three digits followed by three uppercase letters of the English alphabet are possible?

Ⓐ $(3)(3)$

Ⓑ $(_{10}C_3)(_{26}C_3)$

Ⓒ $(10^3)(26^3)$

Ⓓ $36^6$

**For the following question, enter your numeric answer in the box below the question.**

**39.** A high school club has 50 members. A committee of four members is to be selected to attend a national conference. How many different committees could be formed?

**For the following question, enter your numeric answer in the box below the question.**

**40.** A small motor uses $3\dfrac{1}{4}$ gallons of gasoline every 15 hours. What is the motor's rate of gallons per day?

[　　　　] gal/day

**For the following question, select all that apply.**

**41.** Which of the following statements correctly describes the graph of the function $f$ defined by $5x - 3y = 15$?

Ⓐ The graph has slope of $-\dfrac{3}{5}$.

Ⓑ The graph has slope of $\dfrac{5}{3}$.

Ⓒ The $x$ intercept is 3.

Ⓓ The $y$ intercept is 5.

**42.** Set $A$ consists of all positive integers that are multiples of 4. Set $B$ consists of all 2-digit positive integers that are less than 100 and have a units digit of 8. How many integers are in the intersection of sets $A$ and $B$?

Ⓐ 2

Ⓑ 3

Ⓒ 4

Ⓓ 5

**43.** The sum of three consecutive odd integers is 40 less than 5 times the least of the integers. What is the value of the middle integer?

Ⓐ 21

Ⓑ 23

Ⓒ 25

Ⓓ 27

GO ON TO THE NEXT PAGE

**For the following question, select all that apply.**

**Social Studies Test Scores of 20 Sixth-Grade Students**

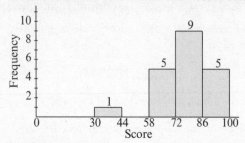

**44.** The histogram summarizes the scores of 20 sixth-grade students on a social studies test. Based on the histogram, which of the following statements about the social studies test scores can be determined conclusively to be correct?

    A   The mean score of the 20 students is less than their median score.

    B   The modal score of the 20 students is 79.

    C   The lowest score on the test was 30.

    D   The highest score on the test was 100.

**Weights, in Pounds, of 35 Members of a Fitness Club**

| Stem | Leaves |
|------|--------|
| 12 | 3 8 8 |
| 13 | 1 3 4 4 5 6 8 |
| 14 | 0 0 2 4 5 5 7 7 7 8 9 |
| 15 | 0 1 3 3 5 6 7 8 9 9 |
| 16 | 1 2 2 9 |
| Legend: 12\|3 = 123 | |

**45.** The stem-and-leaf plot above displays the weights of 35 members of a fitness club. What is the median weight of the 35 members?

    Ⓐ   137 lb

    Ⓑ   140 lb

    Ⓒ   147 lb

    Ⓓ   149 lb

**46.** The mean of six different positive integers is 73. Four of the integers are 48, 53, 61, and 82. What is the maximum possible value of the largest of the six integers?

    Ⓐ   82

    Ⓑ   83

    Ⓒ   193

    Ⓓ   194

**For the following question, enter your numeric answer in the box below the question.**

**47.** According to a survey of 200 students, 75 are enrolled in an English course and 52 are enrolled in a history course. Of those surveyed, 34 are enrolled in an English course, but not in a history course. How many students are enrolled in neither an English course nor a history course?

$$\boxed{\phantom{xxxxxxxx}}$$

**48.** Rose took a cab from the airport to her home. She gave the cab driver $38.50, which included the fare and a tip of $5. The cab company charges $3.50 for the first mile and $1.50 for each additional half-mile after that. How many miles is Rose's home from the airport?

    Ⓐ   10 miles

    Ⓑ   11 miles

    Ⓒ   20 miles

    Ⓓ   21 miles

**49.** Working alone at its constant rate, Machine 1 produces $40x$ electrical components in 10 hours. Working alone at its constant rate, Machine 2 produces $40x$ electrical components in 15 hours. How many hours does it take machines 1 and 2, working simultaneously at their respective constant rates, to produce $40x$ electrical components?

    Ⓐ   5 hours

    Ⓑ   6 hours

    Ⓒ   $8\frac{1}{4}$ hours

    Ⓓ   $12\frac{1}{2}$ hours

GO ON TO THE NEXT PAGE

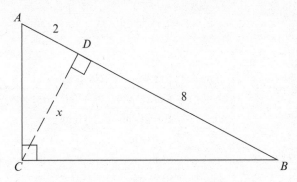

**50.** In the figure above, $\overline{CD}$ is an altitude of right triangle $ABC$, $AD = 2$, and $DB = 8$. Find the perimeter of triangle $ABC$.

Ⓐ $16\sqrt{5}$

Ⓑ $10 + 6\sqrt{5}$

Ⓒ $10 + 2\sqrt{5}$

Ⓓ It cannot be determined from the information given.

**51.** In the $xy$-plane, the graphs defined by $f(x) = \dfrac{x^2 + x - 6}{(x+3)}$ and $g(x) = 2.5x + 2.5$ intersect in how many distinct points?

Ⓐ 0

Ⓑ 1

Ⓒ 2

Ⓓ 4

**For the following question, enter your fractional answer in the boxes below the question.**

**52.** The enrollment at a small community college for the fall semester is 10% higher than the enrollment in the fall semester a year ago. The number of female students increased by 5% and the number of male students increased by 20%. Female students make up what fraction of the current enrollment at the community college? Give your answer as a fraction.

☐
☐

**For the following question, select __all__ that apply.**

**53.** The number 200 lies between $\dfrac{1}{4}x$ and $\dfrac{1}{3}x$. Which of the following numbers could be values of $x$?

Ⓐ 550

Ⓑ 650

Ⓒ 750

Ⓓ 850

**54.** If $\dfrac{1}{3^x} = \dfrac{1}{3^n} + \dfrac{1}{3^n} + \dfrac{1}{3^n}$, then $x$ expressed in terms of $n$ is

Ⓐ $n - 1$

Ⓑ $n + 1$

Ⓒ $3n$

Ⓓ $n^3$

**55.** In the equation $y = \dfrac{k}{x}$, $x$ and $y$ are both positive and $k$ is a constant. If $y$ increases by $\dfrac{1}{2}$ of its value, then the value of $x$ decreases by what fraction of its value?

Ⓐ $\dfrac{1}{4}$

Ⓑ $\dfrac{1}{3}$

Ⓒ $\dfrac{1}{2}$

Ⓓ $\dfrac{2}{3}$

STOP

# Answer Key

| Question Number | Correct Answer | Reference Chapter | Question Number | Correct Answer | Reference Chapter |
|---|---|---|---|---|---|
| 1. | D | Numbers and Operations | 29. | C | Functions and Their Graphs |
| 2. | A, C, D | Algebra | 30. | A | Functions and Their Graphs |
| 3. | 82 | Statistics | 31. | B | Statistics |
| 4. | D | Algebra | 32. | 117 | Statistics |
| 5. | C | Numbers and Operations | 33. | A | Statistics |
| 6. | B | Numbers and Operations | 34. | D | Probability |
| 7. | A | Numbers and Operations | 35. | B | Probability |
| 8. | B, C | Numbers and Operations | 36. | B | Probability |
| 9. | B, C, D | Numbers and Operations | 37. | 47 | Functions and Their Graphs |
| 10. | C | Algebra | 38. | C | Discrete Mathematics |
| 11. | D | Algebra | 39. | 230,300 | Discrete Mathematics |
| 12. | B | Algebra | 40. | 5.2 | Numbers and Operations |
| 13. | B | Measurement | 41. | B, C | Functions and Their Graphs |
| 14. | A | Geometry | 42. | C | Discrete Mathematics |
| 15. | C | Geometry | 43. | C | Algebra |
| 16. | C | Geometry | 44. | A | Statistics |
| 17. | 17 | Geometry | 45. | C | Statistics |
| 18. | A | Geometry | 46. | C | Statistics |
| 19. | D | Measurement | 47. | 114 | Discrete Mathematics |
| 20. | B | Measurement | 48. | B | Algebra |
| 21. | B | Measurement | 49. | B | Algebra |
| 22. | C | Algebra | 50. | B | Measurement |
| 23. | B, C, D | Functions and Their Graphs | 51. | A | Functions and Their Graphs |
| 24. | D | Numbers and Operations | 52. | $\dfrac{7}{11}$ | Numbers and Operations |
| 25. | A | Functions and Their Graphs | | | |
| 26. | D | Functions and Their Graphs | 53. | B, C | Algebra |
| 27. | C | Discrete Mathematics | 54. | A | Algebra |
| 28. | C | Algebra | 55. | B | Algebra |

# Answer Explanations

1. **D.** The number of days until the next time is the least common multiple of 12 and 15, which is 60. It will be 60 days before Zoey and Jax both will swim at Gold Star Gym on the same day, choice D.

2. **A, C, D.** Select choice A because $a^2 - b^2 = (a+b)(a-b)$. Eliminate choice B because $a^2 - ab + b^2$ is *not* factorable over the real numbers. Select choice C because $a^3 - b^3 = (a-b)(a^2 + ab + b^2)$. Select choice D because $a^3 - 3a^2b + 3ab^2 - b^3 = (a-b)^3$.

   *Tip:* If you have not memorized the special products given in Chapter 2, "Algebra," you should do so before the test.

3. **82** The question asks: What is the *lowest* score the student can make on the final exam and still receive a B in the course? Examine the table to review the instructor's grading guidelines.

   | Determination of Course Grade | Percent |
   |---|---|
   | Average (mean) of three major exams | 50% |
   | Average (mean) of weekly quizzes | 10% |
   | Final exam score | 40% |

   From the table, you can see that you first must calculate the mean of the student's three major exam scores:
   $$\text{mean} = \frac{72 + 81 + 75}{3} = 76 \;.$$
   Let $x$ = the lowest score the student can make on the final exam and still have at least an 80 average.

   Solve the following equation for $x$.
   $$50\%(76) + 10\%(92) + 40\%(x) = 80$$
   $$0.5(76) + 0.1(92) + 0.4(x) = 80$$
   $$38 + 9.2 + 0.4x = 80$$
   $$0.4x = 32.8$$
   $$x = 82$$

   The lowest score that will yield an average of at least 80 is 82.

4. **D.** $\dfrac{3}{x} + \dfrac{4}{y} = \dfrac{3y}{xy} + \dfrac{4x}{xy} = \dfrac{3y + 4x}{xy} = \dfrac{4x + 3y}{xy}$, choice D.

5. **C.** $(x^2 + 4)^{-\frac{1}{2}} = \dfrac{1}{(x^2 + 4)^{\frac{1}{2}}} = \dfrac{1}{\sqrt{x^2 + 4}}$, choice C.

6. **B.** The number of gallons needed for a 204-mile trip is 8.5 gallons. You want to know how many gallons are needed for a 228-mile trip. Set up a proportion and solve for $x$, the number of gallons needed for the 228-mile trip.
   $$\frac{x}{228 \text{ miles}} = \frac{8.5 \text{ gal}}{204 \text{ miles}}$$
   $$x = \frac{(8.5 \text{ gal})(228 \text{ miles})}{204 \text{ miles}}$$
   $$x = 9.5 \text{ gal, choice B}$$

   *Tip:* Check the units to make sure that (mathematically) they work out to be the desired units for the answer.

7. **A.** $4^x + 12^x = 4^x + (3 \cdot 4)^x = 4^x + 3^x \cdot 4^x = 4^x(1 + 3^x)$, choice A.

8. **B, C.** The absolute value of a nonzero number is always positive. Eliminate choice A because for any nonzero number, $|x|$ is positive and $-|-x|$ is negative, so the statement is always false. Eliminate choice D because, for example, $|-2 + 10| = |8| = 8$, but $|-2| + |10| = 2 + 10 = 12$.

   Select choice B. If the quotient of two numbers is positive, then both numbers are positive or both numbers are negative. If the quotient is negative, then the two numbers have opposite signs. Case 1: If $x$ and $y$ are both positive, then $\left|\dfrac{x}{y}\right| = \dfrac{x}{y} = \dfrac{|x|}{|y|}$. Similarly, if $x$ and $y$ are both negative, then $\left|\dfrac{x}{y}\right| = \dfrac{-x}{-y} = \dfrac{|x|}{|y|}$. Case 2: If $x$ and $y$ have opposite signs, with $x < 0$, then $\left|\dfrac{x}{y}\right| = -\dfrac{x}{y} = \dfrac{-x}{y} = \dfrac{|x|}{|y|}$. If $x$ and $y$ have opposite signs, with $y < 0$, then $\left|\dfrac{x}{y}\right| = -\dfrac{x}{y} = \dfrac{x}{-y} = \dfrac{|x|}{|y|}$. Thus, for all nonzero real numbers $x$ and $y$, choice B is true.

   Select choice C. The square root of a nonzero number is always positive: $\sqrt{(-x)^2} = \sqrt{x^2} = |x|$, so choice C is always true.

   *Tip:* Memorize the properties for absolute value given in Chapter 1, "Numbers and Operations" before you take the Praxis MS Math test.

9. **B, C, D.** Given that $x$ and $y$ are whole numbers and $z = x + y = x + 3x = 4x$, then $z$ is a multiple of 4. Therefore, $z$ represents a whole number that is divisible by 4. A number is divisible by 4 if and only if the last 2 digits form a number that is divisible by 4. Of the answer choices, only choice A fails the test for divisibility by 4—because the last two digits of 314 are 14, which is not divisible by 4. Choices B, C, and D are divisible by 4, so each could be the value of $z$.

10. **C.** $2x^3y(x + 3)(3x - 1) = 2x^3y(3x^2 + 8x - 3) = 6x^5y + 16x^4y - 6x^3y$, choice C.

11. **D.** Express $2x(x - 2) = 1$ in standard form.
    $$2x(x - 2) = 1$$
    $$2x^2 - 4x = 1$$
    $$2x^2 - 4x - 1 = 0$$

    Using the quadratic formula, $a = 2$, $b = -4$, $c = -1$ (include the $-$ signs).

    Plug into the formula.
    $$x = \frac{-(-4) \pm \sqrt{(-4)^2 - 4(2)(-1)}}{2(2)} = \frac{4 \pm \sqrt{16 + 8}}{4} = \frac{4 \pm \sqrt{24}}{4} = \frac{4 \pm 2\sqrt{6}}{4} = \frac{2 \pm \sqrt{6}}{2}, \text{ choice D}$$

12. **B.** Solve the system by the method of elimination.

    Write both equations in standard form (for convenience, the equations are numbered):
    $$(1)\ 2x - 3y = 16$$
    $$(2)\ 4x + 5y = 10$$

    Quick check: The system has exactly one solution because $\dfrac{2}{4} \neq \dfrac{-3}{5}$.

    To eliminate $x$, multiply equation (1) by $-2$ and add the result to equation (2).

    $$\begin{array}{l} 2x - 3y = 16 \\ 4x + 5y = 10 \end{array} \text{ implies } \begin{array}{l} -4x + 6y = -32 \\ 4x + 5y = 10 \end{array} \text{ implies } 11y = -22 \text{ implies } y = -2, \text{ choice B}$$

13. **B.** The maximum possible error of a measurement is half the magnitude of the smallest measurement unit used to obtain the measurement. The most accurate way of expressing the measurement is as a tolerance interval. Thus, a measurement of 10 grams, to the nearest gram, should be reported as 10 g ± 0.5 g, choice B.

14. **A.** The angle bisectors of a triangle are concurrent in a point that is equidistant from the three sides, making choice A the correct response.

15. **C.** From the figure, $\triangle ABC$ is a right triangle. To find the area of a right triangle, find $\frac{1}{2}$ the product of the lengths of the two legs. To find the area of $\triangle ABC$, take these three steps. First, determine $CA$, the length of leg $\overline{CA}$. Next, determine $BC$, the length of leg $\overline{BC}$. Then, find the area of $\triangle ABC$ by calculating $\frac{1}{2}bh = \frac{1}{2}(CA)(BC)$.

*Step 1.* Find $CA$ by adding the lengths of the two segments, $\overline{CE}$ and $\overline{EA}$.

$$CA = 200 \text{ m} + 100 \text{ m} = 300 \text{ m}$$

*Step 2.* Find $BC$. Right triangles $ABC$ and $ADE$ are similar triangles because they have two congruent right angles, and they have the acute angle $A$ in common. Determine $BC$ by using properties of similar triangles.

$$\frac{BC}{300 \text{ m}} = \frac{50 \text{ m}}{100 \text{ m}}$$
$$BC = \frac{(300 \text{ m})(50)}{100}$$
$$BC = 150 \text{ m}$$

*Step 3.* Find the area of $\triangle ABC$.

$$\text{area} = \frac{1}{2}bh = \frac{1}{2}(CA)(BC) = \frac{1}{2}(300 \text{ m})(150 \text{ m}) = 22\,500 \text{ m}^2, \text{ choice C}$$

16. **C.** The angles that measure $x°$ and $y°$ are angles formed when parallel lines are cut by a transversal. Use the properties of angles formed when parallel lines are cut by a transversal to find $x$ and $y$. The angle that measures $y°$ and the angle adjacent to the angle that measures $x°$ are congruent because they are corresponding angles. Thus, the angles that measure $x°$ and $y°$ are supplementary angles. Recall that the sum of supplementary angles is 180°. It is given that $x = 8y$, so $x + y = 180$, which implies that $8y + y = 180$. Solve for $y$, and then determine $x = 8y$.

$$8y + y = 180$$
$$9y = 180$$
$$y = 20$$
$$8y = 8(20) = 160, \text{ choice C}$$

*Tip:* Make sure you answer the question asked. This problem asks for the value of $x$, so after you find $y$, you keep going and find $x$.

**17.** 17 Sketch a diagram.

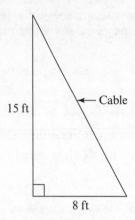

15 ft

← Cable

8 ft

The pole, the cable, and the ground form a right triangle. From the diagram, the cable is the hypotenuse of a right triangle that has legs of 15 feet and 8 feet. Use the Pythagorean theorem to find the length of the hypotenuse, denoted by $c$ (omit the units for convenience).

$$c^2 = a^2 + b^2$$
$$c^2 = 15^2 + 8^2$$
$$c^2 = 225 + 64$$
$$c^2 = 289$$
$$c = \sqrt{289} = 17$$

The length of the cable is 17 feet.

*Note:* The number $-17$ is also a solution, but it is rejected because length is nonnegative.

**18.** **A.** From the figure, right angle $ACB$ is an inscribed angle. The measure of an inscribed angle is half the degree measure of its intercepted arc. Thus, the degree measure of arc $AB$ is 180°, making the chord $AB$, which is the hypotenuse of right triangle $ABC$, a diameter of the circle. To find the length of the hypotenuse, multiply the radius by 2. The length of the hypotenuse = 2(5.5 cm) = 11 cm, choice A.

**19.** **D.** The volume $V$ of a cube with edge $s$ is given by $V = s^3$. The volume of the original cube will equal the sum of the volumes of the two smaller cubes. To find the length of an edge of one of the smaller cubes, take the following three steps: First, find the volume of the original cube. Next, find the volume of one of the smaller cubes. Finally, find the length of an edge of one of the smaller cubes.

*Step 1.* Find the volume $V_o$ of the original cube: $V_o = (4 \text{ cm})^3 = 64 \text{ cm}^3$.

*Step 2.* Find the volume $V_s$ of one of the smaller cubes: $V_s + V_s = V_o = 64 \text{ cm}^3$ implies that $2V_s = 64 \text{ cm}^3$. Thus, the volume of one of the smaller cubes is 32 cm³.

*Step 3.* Find the length, call it $e$, of an edge of one of the smaller cubes.

$$e^3 = 32 \text{ cm}^3$$
$$e = \sqrt[3]{32 \text{ cm}^3}$$
$$e = \sqrt[3]{(8 \text{ cm}^3)(4)}$$
$$e = 2\sqrt[3]{4} \text{ cm, choice D}$$

**20. B.** The area of the figure is the sum of the area of the fourth of the circle and the area of the rectangle. The formula for the area of a circle is $\pi r^2$ and the formula for the area of a rectangle is $lw$. From the diagram, you can determine that the radius of the fourth of the circle is 4 m and that the length of the rectangle is 4 m + 3 m = 7 m. Hence, the area of the figure equals $\frac{1}{4}\pi r^2 + lw = \frac{1}{4}\pi(4\text{ m})^2 + (7\text{ m})(3\text{ m}) = \frac{1}{4}\pi(16\text{ m}^2)$

$+ (21\text{ m}^2) \approx 34\text{ m}^2$, choice B.

**21. B.** You want to know how many years it would take to spend \$1.6 billion at the rate of \$1 per second $\left(\dfrac{\$1}{1\text{ s}}\right)$.

To determine which answer is correct, use dimensional analysis. Write \$1.6 billion as a fraction with denominator 1 and let unit analysis tell you which conversion fractions to multiply by, keeping in mind that you want years as your final answer.

$$\frac{\$1,600,000,000}{1} \times \frac{1\text{ s}}{\$1} \times \frac{1\text{ min}}{60\text{ s}} \times \frac{1\text{ h}}{60\text{ min}} \times \frac{1\text{ d}}{24\text{ h}} \times \frac{1\text{ yr}}{365\text{ d}} \approx 50\text{ years, choice B}$$

**22. C.** Plug into the midpoint formula to find the midpoint between (2, –2) and (3, 4).
$\left(\dfrac{x_1 + x_2}{2}, \dfrac{y_1 + y_2}{2}\right) = \left(\dfrac{2+3}{2}, \dfrac{-2+4}{2}\right) = (2.5, 1)$, choice C.

**23. B, C, D.** A function is a relation in which each first component is paired with *one and only one* second component. No two distinct ordered pairs have the same first components and different second components. Only the relation in choice A does not satisfies this requirement because the ordered pairs (3, 1) and (3, 10) have the same first component, 3, but different second components, 1 and 10. The sets of ordered pairs in choices B, C, and D represent functions.

**24. D.** Divide $6 \times 10^2$ grams by $3 \times 10^{-2}$ grams.

$$\frac{6 \times 10^2\text{ g}}{3 \times 10^{-2}\text{ g}} = \frac{\overset{2}{\cancel{6}} \times 10^2\ \cancel{g}}{\underset{1}{\cancel{3}} \times 10^{-2}\ \cancel{g}} = 2 \times 10^{2-(-2)} = 2 \times 10^{2+2} = 2 \times 10^4 = 20,000$$

The number of grams of salt in solution B is 20,000 times the number of grams of salt in solution A, choice D.

**25. A.** The function $y = \dfrac{x^2 + 40x - 500}{500}$ has no excluded values, so its domain is the set consisting of all its possible $x$ values; that is, $D_f = \{x \mid 500 < x < 750\}$. The range of $y = \dfrac{x^2 + 40x - 500}{500}$ is the set consisting of all its possible $y$ values. That is, $R_f = \left\{ y \,\middle|\, \dfrac{500^2 + 40(500) - 500}{500} < y < \dfrac{750^2 + 40(750) - 500}{500} \right\}$, which implies $R_f = \{y \mid 539 < y < 1,184\}$. Thus, choice A is the correct response.

**26. D.** The problem states that the relation is a function. Therefore, by definition, each first component (age value) is paired with one and only one second component (hours value). Thus, only the statement given in choice D will always be true about the social scientist's function. None of the other statements are guaranteed to be true about the social scientist's function.

**27. C.** There are two overall tasks to be accomplished. The first overall task is to select four of the seven chairs. Noting that different ordering of the chairs does not produce different arrangements, the number of ways to select four of seven chairs is $_7C_4$. The second overall task is to arrange the four people in the four chairs. Noting that different orderings of the people result in different arrangements, the number of different ways to seat four people in four chairs is $(4)(3)(2)(1) = 4!$. This is true because there are four ways to seat someone in the first chair, three ways to seat someone in the second chair, and so on. Therefore, by the fundamental counting principle, the total number of ways to seat four people in four of seven empty identical chairs is

$$_7C_4 \cdot 4! = \frac{7!}{4!3!} \cdot 4! = 35 \cdot 24 = 840, \text{ choice C}$$

**28.** **C.** You want to determine the equation of a line that passes through (0, 5) and is perpendicular to the line that has equation $x - 3y = 10$. When two lines are perpendicular, their slopes are negative reciprocals of each other. Use the slope-intercept form to write the equation. Observe that (0, 5) is the $y$-intercept of the line. You need two steps. First, find the slope of the desired equation by writing the equation $x - 3y = 10$ in slope-intercept form, and determining the negative reciprocal of its slope. Next, write the desired equation in slope-intercept form and then put it in standard form (because the answer choices are in standard form).

*Step 1.* Find the slope for the desired equation. Write $x - 3y = 10$ in slope-intercept form.

$$x - 3y = 10$$
$$-3y = -x + 10$$
$$y = \frac{1}{3}x - \frac{10}{3}$$

The slope of $x - 3y = 10$ is $\frac{1}{3}$, so the desired equation has slope $-3$.

*Step 2.* Write the equation and put it in standard form: $y = -3x + 5$ implies $3x + y = 5$, choice C.

**29.** **C.** Subtracting a positive constant $h$ from $x$ will result in a horizontal shift of $h$ units to the right. The graph of $f(x) = (x - 2)^3$ is the same as the graph of $f(x) = x^3$ shifted right by 2 units, choice C.

*Tip:* If you are unsure whether the shift is to the right or left, graph both functions on the ETS graphing calculator to check.

**30.** **A.** $(g \circ f)(x) = g(f(x)) = g\left(\frac{2x+6}{x+2}\right) = \frac{2x+6}{x+2} + 2 = \frac{2x+6}{x+2} + \frac{2(x+2)}{x+2} = \frac{2x+6}{x+2} + \frac{2x+4}{x+2} = \frac{4x+10}{x+2}$, choice A.

**31.** **B.** In an ordered set of numbers, the median is the middle number if there is a middle number; otherwise, the median is the arithmetic average of the pair of middle numbers. First, put the running times in order from smallest to largest: 61, 63, 64, 64, 66, 68, 69, 73. Since there is no middle number, average the two running times that are the middle pair in the list, 64 and 66.

$$\frac{64 + 66}{2} = \frac{130}{2} = 65, \text{ choice B}$$

**32.** **117** A circle graph is made by dividing the 360 degrees of the circle that makes the graph into portions that correspond to the proportion for each category. The central angle that should be used to represent the category Science Fiction/Fantasy is $\frac{104}{320}(360°) = 117°$.

**33.** **A.** A box plot graphically summarizes a data set by showing five numbers in the following order: the minimum value, the first quartile, the median, the third quartile, and the maximum value. Thus, the vertical line at 5 indicates that 5 is the median, choice A.

**34.** **D.** First, fill in the row and column totals for the table.

| Grade Level | Cell Phone | No Cell Phone | Row Total |
|-------------|-----------|---------------|-----------|
| Ninth | 55 | 45 | 100 |
| Tenth | 70 | 30 | 100 |
| Eleventh | 78 | 22 | 100 |
| Twelfth | 95 | 5 | 100 |
| **Column Total** | 298 | 102 | 400 |

This question asks you to find a conditional probability; that is, you are to find the probability when you already know that the student is a ninth grader. Thus, when computing the probability, the number of possible students under consideration is no longer 400, but is reduced to the total number of ninth graders, which is 100. According to the table, 55 of the 100 ninth graders have a cell phone.

Thus, $P$(the student has a cell phone given that the student is a ninth grader) $= \frac{55}{100} = \frac{11}{20}$, choice D.

**35. B.** Fill in the missing probabilities.

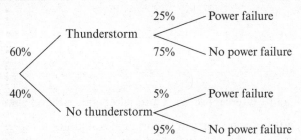

This problem requires an application of the multiplication rule, which states that $P(A$ and $B)$ $= P(A)P(B \mid A)$. $P$(thunderstorm and power failure) = $P$(thunderstorm) × $P$(power failure given a thunderstorm has developed) = $(60\%)(25\%) = 15\%$, choice B.

**36. B.** After three nondefective remote controls have been drawn, there are only seven remote controls left in the box, one of which is defective. Therefore, the probability that the next remote control is defective $= \dfrac{1}{7}$, choice B.

**37. 47** For the recursive formula given in the problem, you will need to find $f(1)$ and $f(2)$ before you can find $f(3)$. The problem tells you that $f(0) = 5$ and that $f(n) = 2f(n - 1) + 1$ for $n \ge 1$, then

$f(1) = 2f(0) + 1 = 2(5) + 1 = 10 + 1 = 11$

$f(2) = 2f(1) + 1 = 2(11) + 1 = 22 + 1 = 23$

$f(3) = 2f(2) + 1 = 2(23) + 1 = 46 + 1 = 47$

The value of $f(3)$ is 47.

**38. C.** Use the fundamental counting principle to work this problem. There are six slots to be filled, so to speak, on a license plate. There are 10 possibilities for each of the three digits and 26 possible values for each of the three letters, which means the total number of possible license plates is $10 \cdot 10 \cdot 10 \cdot 26 \cdot 26 \cdot 26 = (10^3)(26^3)$, choice C.

**39. 230,300** Noting that the order in which committee members are chosen does not make a difference regarding the composition of the committee, the number of different four-member committees that can be selected from the 50 members is the number of combinations of 4 people selected from 50 people, which is $_{50}C_4 = 230{,}300$.

**40. 5.2** First, change 15 hours to days.

$$15 \text{ hr} \times \frac{1 \text{ day}}{24 \text{ hr}} = \frac{\cancel{15}^{5} \text{ hr}}{1} \times \frac{1 \text{ day}}{\cancel{24}^{8} \text{ hr}} = \frac{5}{8} \text{ day}$$

The number of gallons per day is $\dfrac{3\frac{1}{4} \text{ gal}}{\frac{5}{8} \text{ day}} = \dfrac{\frac{13}{4}}{\frac{5}{8}} \cdot \dfrac{\text{gal}}{\text{day}} = \dfrac{8\left(\frac{13}{4}\right)}{8\left(\frac{5}{8}\right)} \cdot \dfrac{\text{gal}}{\text{day}} = \dfrac{26}{5} \dfrac{\text{gal}}{\text{day}} = 5.2 \text{ gal/day}.$

**41.** **B, C.** Write the equation in slope-intercept form.

$$5x - 3y = 15$$
$$-3y = -5x + 15$$
$$y = \frac{5}{3}x - 5$$

The graph has slope of $\frac{5}{3}$ and $y$ intercept of $-5$. Thus, select choice B and eliminate choices A and D. To find the $x$ intercept, let $y = 0$ and solve for $x$ in the original equation.

$$5x - 3y = 15$$
$$5x - 3(0) = 15$$
$$5x = 15$$
$$x = 3$$

Therefore, the $x$ intercept is 3, so select choice C.

**42.** **C.** The elements in set $A$ are 4, 8, 12, 16, 20, 24, 28, and so on. The elements in set $B$ are 18, 28, 38, 48, 58, 68, 78, 88, and 98. Of the numbers in set $B$, 28, 48, 68, and 88 are multiples of 4 and therefore in set $A$ as well. Thus, 4 numbers are in the intersection of sets $A$ and $B$, choice C.

**43.** **C.** Let $n$, $n + 2$, and $n + 4$ be the three consecutive odd integers. Solve the following equation for $n + 2$, the middle integer.

$$n + (n + 2) + (n + 4) = 5n - 40$$
$$n + n + 2 + n + 4 = 5n - 40$$
$$3n + 6 = 5n - 40$$
$$-2n = -46$$
$$n = 23$$
$$n + 2 = 25$$

The middle integer is 25, choice C.

**44.** **A.** Because of the grouping of data into intervals, the exact data values are not displayed in a histogram. Thus, histograms do not provide high levels of specific information about data values. For example, you know there is one data value in the interval "30 to less than 44," but without further information, you cannot determine its exact value (eliminate choice C). For the same reason, the maximum value and the mode cannot be identified (eliminate choices D and B). However, the histogram does give information about the shape of the distribution. The distribution has a tail to the left, indicating negative skewness. Therefore, the mean score of the data lies to the left of the median score (select choice A).

**45.** **C.** In an ordered set of data values, the median is the $\left(\frac{n+1}{2}\right)$ data value. There are 35 data values, so the median is the $\frac{35+1}{2} = \frac{36}{2} = 18$th data value. Counting from the least weight, the 18th weight in the stem-and-leaf plot is 147 pounds, choice C.

**46.** **C.** Let $x$ and $y$ be the two positive integers whose values you are not given and, for convenience, let $x < y$. Given that 73 is the mean of the six numbers, $\frac{48 + 53 + 61 + 82 + x + y}{6} = 73$. Solve this equation for $x + y$.

$$\frac{48 + 53 + 61 + 82 + x + y}{6} = 73$$
$$48 + 53 + 61 + 82 + x + y = (6)(73)$$
$$244 + x + y = 438$$
$$x + y = 194$$

Because $x$ and $y$ are positive integers, the least that $x$ can be is 1. Therefore, the greatest that $y$ can be is 193, choice C.

**47.** **114** Of the 75 students who are enrolled in an English course, 34 are not enrolled in a history course. Thus, $75 - 34 = 41$ students are enrolled in both English and history. Of the 52 students who are enrolled in history, $52 - 41 = 11$ are enrolled in history only. Sketch a Venn diagram to illustrate the information.

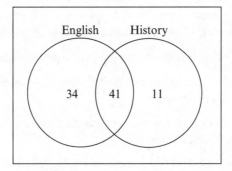

The entire rectangle represents the 200 students. The region that is outside the two intersecting circles represents the students who are enrolled in neither an English course nor a history course. From the diagram, the number of students who are enrolled in neither an English course nor a history course is $200 - (34 + 41 + 11) = 200 - 86 = 114$.

**48.** **B.** The fare is $3.50 for the first mile plus $1.50 for each additional half-mile.

**Method 1:** To solve the problem, break the distance into a 1-mile portion plus a portion composed of half-mile segments. Then write and solve an equation that models the situation.

Let $n$ = the number of half-mile segments.

Distance from the airport to Rose's home = 1 mile + $n$ half-miles

$$\text{Fare} = \$3.50 \text{ (for the first mile)} + n \cdot \frac{\$1.50}{\text{half-mile}}$$

Write an equation that represents the facts given.

$$\text{Fare} + \text{Tip} = \$38.50$$

$$\left(\$3.50 + n \cdot \frac{\$1.50}{\text{half-mile}}\right) + \$5 \text{ (tip)} = \$38.50$$

Solve the equation, omitting the units for convenience.

$$(3.50 + n \cdot 1.50) + 5 = 38.50$$
$$3.50 + 1.5n + 5 = 38.50$$
$$1.5n = 30$$
$$n = \frac{30}{1.5}$$
$$n = 20 \text{ half-mile segments}$$

Distance from the airport to Rose's home = 1 mile + 20 half-miles = 1 mile + 10 miles = 11 miles, choice B.

**Method 2:** Check the answer choices (a handy test-taking strategy for multiple-choice questions).

Check A: If the distance to Rose's home is 10 miles, then the trip is broken into a 1-mile portion plus 9 miles = 1 mile + 18 half-miles. The fare for the trip = $3.50 (for the first mile) + (18 half-miles)$\left(\dfrac{\$1.50}{\text{half-mile}}\right)$ = $3.50 + $27.00 = $30.50. When you add the $5 tip, the total is $35.50, which is not equal to $38.50, so eliminate A.

Check B: If the distance to Rose's home is 11 miles, then the trip is broken into a 1-mile portion plus 10 miles = 1 mile + 20 half-miles. The fare for the trip = $3.50 (for the first mile) + (20 half-miles)$\left(\dfrac{\$1.50}{\text{half-mile}}\right)$ = $3.50 + $30.00 = $33.50. When you add the $5 tip, the total is $38.50, which is correct. Choice B is the correct response.

In a test situation, go on to the next question because you have found the correct answer. You would not check choices C and D; but for your information, choice C gives $65.50 and choice D gives $68.50, both of which are too high.

**49. B.** You have two "workers" (in this problem, the two machines) that can do the same job (in this problem, produce $40x$ electrical components), so use the quick solution method. Multiply their individual times, then divide this product by the sum of their individual times. Omitting the units, calculate $\dfrac{(10)(15)}{10+15} = \dfrac{150}{25} = 6$. The time it takes machines 1 and 2, working simultaneously at their respective constant rates, to produce $40x$ electrical components is 6 hours, choice B.

*Tip:* You should eliminate choice D at the outset because the time for the two machines working together should be less than either of their times working alone.

**50. B.** The perimeter of $\triangle ABC = \left(\text{length of } \overline{AB}\right) + \left(\text{length of } \overline{BC}\right) + \left(\text{length of } \overline{AC}\right) = AB + BC + AC$.

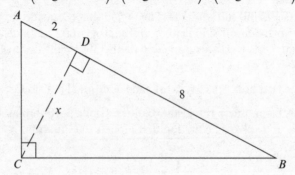

From the information given, $AB = AD + DB = 2 + 8 = 10$. Now, determine $BC$ and $AC$ to find the perimeter. The altitude to the hypotenuse of a right triangle is the geometric mean of the lengths of the two segments into which it separates the hypotenuse. Therefore, $\dfrac{AD}{x} = \dfrac{x}{DB}$. Substitute $AD = 2$ and $DB = 8$ and solve for $x$.

$$\frac{2}{x} = \frac{x}{8}$$
$$x^2 = 16$$
$$x = 4$$

*Tip:* The number $-4$ is also a solution, but it is rejected because length is nonnegative.

Use the Pythagorean theorem to solve for $BC$ and $AC$.

$$BC = \sqrt{4^2 + 8^2} = \sqrt{80} = 4\sqrt{5} \text{ and } AC = \sqrt{4^2 + 2^2} = \sqrt{20} = 2\sqrt{5}$$

Thus, the perimeter of $\triangle ABC = 10 + 4\sqrt{5} + 2\sqrt{5} = 10 + 6\sqrt{5}$, choice B.

**51. A.** The rational function $f$ defined by $f(x) = \dfrac{x^2 + x - 6}{(x+3)} = \dfrac{(x+3)(x-2)}{(x+3)}$ is undefined when $x = -3$. Simplified, $f(x) = \dfrac{(x+3)(x-2)}{(x+3)} = x - 2$, so the graph of $f$ is the line whose equation is $y = x - 2$, but with a "hole" at the point $(-3, -5)$. The graph of the linear function $g$ defined by $g(x) = 2.5x + 2.5$ is the line $y = 2.5x + 2.5$ that intersects the line $y = x - 2$ at $(-3, -5)$. That is, $(-3, -5)$ satisfies both $y = x - 2$ and $y = 2.5x + 2.5$. However, $-3$ is not in the domain of $f$, so the graphs of $f$ and $g$ do not intersect, choice A.

*Caution:* Using the ETS graphing calculator for problems involving holes in graphs can lead to incorrect answer choices.

**52.** $\dfrac{7}{11}$ Let $f$ = the number of female students enrolled in the fall semester a year ago. Then, $f + 0.05f = 1.05f$ = the number of female students currently enrolled.

Let $m$ = the number of male students enrolled in the fall semester a year ago. Then, $m + 0.20m = 1.20m$ = the number of male students currently enrolled.

$f + m$ = the total enrollment in the fall semester a year ago, and $(f + m) + 0.10(f + m) = 1.10(f + m)$ = the current enrollment at the community college.

The current enrollment also equals $1.05f + 1.20m$.

Therefore, $1.05f + 1.20m = 1.10(f + m)$, which implies that $0.10m = 0.05f$, or equivalently, $2m = f$. This result tells you that in the fall semester a year ago, there were twice as many female students as male students. Pick convenient values for $m$ and $f$ that satisfy this relationship. For example, let $m = 100$ and $f = 200$. With these values, the total enrollment a year ago is 300. *Tip:* You can check that $1.20(100) + 1.05(200) = 120 + 210 = 330$, which is the same as $1.10(300)$.

Thus, the fraction of the current enrollment at the community college that is female students is $\dfrac{1.05(200)}{1.10(300)} = \dfrac{210}{330} = \dfrac{7}{11}$.

*Tip:* When you work with ratios (fractions), proportions, and percents, you often can pick convenient numbers to work with. Just make sure the numbers you pick satisfy all the conditions of the problem.

**53. B, C.** $\dfrac{1}{4}x < 200 < \dfrac{1}{3}x$ implies that $12\left(\dfrac{1}{4}x\right) < 12(200) < 12\left(\dfrac{1}{3}x\right)$, which is equivalent to $3x < 2,400 < 4x$. Check the answer choices for numbers that satisfy this double inequality.

Check A: $3(550) = 1,650$ and $4(550) = 2,200$, so reject choice A because 550 is too low.

Check B: $3(650) = 1,950$ and $4(650) = 2,600$, so select choice B because $x = 650$ satisfies the double inequality.

Check C: $3(750) = 2,250$ and $4(750) = 3,000$, so select choice C because $x = 750$ satisfies the double inequality.

Check D: $3(850) = 2,550$, so reject choice D because $x = 850$ is too high.

*Tip:* Eliminating fractions at the outset simplifies the calculations for this problem.

**54. A.** Simplify the equation.

$$\frac{1}{3^x} = \frac{1}{3^n} + \frac{1}{3^n} + \frac{1}{3^n}$$

$$\frac{1}{3^x} = \frac{3}{3^n}$$

$$\frac{1}{3^x} = \frac{1}{3^{n-1}}, \text{ which implies } x = n - 1, \text{ choice A}$$

**55. B.** Given that $y = \dfrac{k}{x}$, then $xy = k$, where $k$ is a constant. If $y$ is increased by $\dfrac{1}{2}$ of its value to $\dfrac{3}{2}y$, then $x$ must be decreased to $\dfrac{2}{3}x$ so that the product $\left(\dfrac{2}{3}x\right)\left(\dfrac{3}{2}y\right) = xy = k$ remains constant. Thus, if $y$ is increased by $\dfrac{1}{2}$ of its value, then $x$ is decreased by $\dfrac{1}{3}$ of its value, choice B. For example, suppose $x = 3$, $y = 6$, and $k = 18$; then $(3)(6) = 18$. Suppose 6 increases by $\dfrac{1}{2}$ of 6; that is, suppose 6 increases to 9. Then 3 must decrease to 2, to keep the product $xy$ equal to 18. So, 3 must decrease by 1, which is $\dfrac{1}{3}$ of its value.

# Chapter 10

# Practice Test 2

**55 Questions**

**Time—2 Hours**

**Directions:** Read the directions for each question carefully. This test has several different question types. For each question, select the best single answer choice unless written instructions preceding the question state otherwise. For each selected-response question, select the best answer or answers from the choices given. For each numeric-entry question, enter an answer in the answer box. Enter the exact answer unless you are told to round your answer. If a question asks specifically for the answer as a fraction, there will be two boxes—a numerator box and a denominator box. Do not use decimal points in fractions.

1. Which of the following equations defines $y$ as a function of $x$?

   Ⓐ  $9x - 16y^2 = 9$
   Ⓑ  $x^2 + y^2 = 100$
   Ⓒ  $5y - 125x^2 = 10$
   Ⓓ  $x = |y|$

**Categories of 1,200 Books Sold
at The World of Books in December**

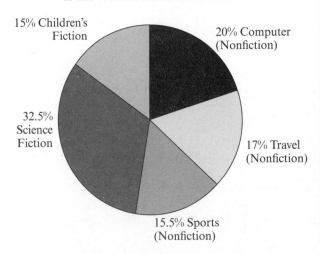

15% Children's Fiction

20% Computer (Nonfiction)

32.5% Science Fiction

17% Travel (Nonfiction)

15.5% Sports (Nonfiction)

2. The circle graph displays the categories, by percentages, of 1,200 books sold at The World of Books bookstore. According to the information in the graph, how many fiction books were sold in December?

   Ⓐ  180
   Ⓑ  390
   Ⓒ  570
   Ⓓ  630

**For the following question, select <u>all</u> that apply.**

3. A student solved a word problem and correctly gave the numerical part of the solution as 7.3. Which of the following questions could have been asked in the word problem?

   Ⓐ  How many buses are needed to transport the students?
   Ⓑ  What is the average time, in minutes, that customers spent waiting in line?
   Ⓒ  What is the length, in centimeters, of each piece of ribbon?
   Ⓓ  How many possible ways can the three different letters be arranged?

   1 cup = 16 tablespoons (T)

   1 tablespoon = 3 teaspoons (tsp)

4. A punch recipe calls for $2\frac{3}{4}$ cups of cranberry juice, $1\frac{1}{2}$ cups of orange juice, $\frac{3}{4}$ cup of water, 1 teaspoon cinnamon, and 3 tablespoons of sugar. What is the ratio of the total amount of fruit juice to the total amount of cinnamon and sugar called for in the recipe?

   Ⓐ  1 to 20
   Ⓑ  68 to 1
   Ⓒ  102 to 5
   Ⓓ  227 to 1

GO ON TO THE NEXT PAGE

**5.** Maria withdrew 25 percent of her money from her savings account. Later she withdrew another $150, leaving a balance of $975. How much money was in Maria's account originally if no other transactions were posted to her account?

   Ⓐ   $1,125.00

   Ⓑ   $1,500.00

   Ⓒ   $1,968.75

   Ⓓ   $4,500.00

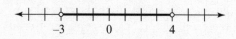

**6.** The graph on the number line shown represents the set of values of $x$ satisfying which of the following inequalities?

   Ⓐ   $\left| x - \dfrac{1}{2} \right| < \dfrac{7}{2}$

   Ⓑ   $\left| x - \dfrac{1}{2} \right| > \dfrac{7}{2}$

   Ⓒ   $\left| x - \dfrac{1}{2} \right| \le \dfrac{7}{2}$

   Ⓓ   $\left| x - \dfrac{1}{2} \right| \ge \dfrac{7}{2}$

| $n$ | 1 | 2 | 3 | 4 | ... |
|-----|---|---|---|---|-----|
| $m$ | 0 | 1 | 4 | 9 | ... |

**7.** If the pattern shown in the table continues indefinitely, which of the following expressions should be used to find $m$ for a given value of $n$?

   Ⓐ   $\sqrt{n}$

   Ⓑ   $n^2$

   Ⓒ   $n^2 - 1$

   Ⓓ   $(n-1)^2$

**For the following question, select __all__ that apply.**

**8.** Which of the following figures is a net of a cube?

Ⓐ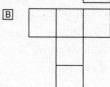

Ⓑ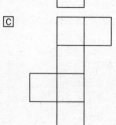

Ⓒ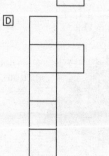

Ⓓ

**9.** Given: $\dfrac{a}{b} = 10$ and $\dfrac{b}{c} = 5$, where $bc \ne 0$. What is the value of $\dfrac{a}{b+c}$?

   Ⓐ   $\dfrac{25}{6}$

   Ⓑ   $\dfrac{25}{3}$

   Ⓒ   $\dfrac{5}{3}$

   Ⓓ   12

GO ON TO THE NEXT PAGE

**10.** Which of the following sets is closed with respect to the given operation?

    Ⓐ   the set of perfect squares with respect to multiplication

    Ⓑ   the set of whole numbers with respect to subtraction

    Ⓒ   the set of odd numbers with respect to addition

    Ⓓ   the set of integers with respect to division

**For the following question, select <u>all</u> that apply.**

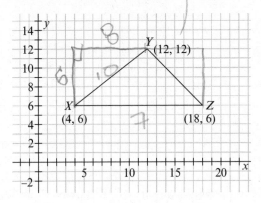

**11.** Which of the following properties associated with $\triangle XYZ$ is a rational quantity?

    Ⓐ   perimeter of $\triangle XYZ$

    Ⓑ   area of $\triangle XYZ$

    Ⓒ   length of side $\overline{XY}$

    Ⓓ   midpoint of side $\overline{XZ}$

**For the following question, enter your numeric answer in the boxes below the question.**

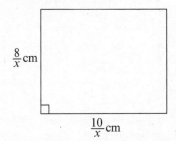

**12.** If the perimeter of the rectangle shown is 18 centimeters, what are the dimensions of the rectangle, in centimeters? (List the shorter dimension first.)

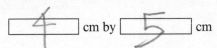

    [ 4 ] cm by [ 5 ] cm

**13.** Measured to the nearest meter, the length of a rectangular yard is 60 meters and its width is 30 meters. Which of the following is the most accurate way to express the area, $A$, of the yard?

    Ⓐ   $1755.25 \text{ m}^2 \le A \le 1845.25 \text{ m}^2$

    Ⓑ   $1784.75 \text{ m}^2 \le A \le 1814.75 \text{ m}^2$

    Ⓒ   $1711 \text{ m}^2 \le A \le 1891 \text{ m}^2$

    Ⓓ   $A = 1800 \text{ m}^2$

**14.** To estimate the population of fish in a lake, a parks and recreation team captures and tags 500 fish and then releases the tagged fish back into the lake. One month later, the team returns and captures 100 fish from the lake, 20 of which bear tags that identify them as being among the previously captured fish. If all the tagged fish are still active in the lake when the second group of fish is captured, what is the best estimate of the fish population in the lake based on the information obtained through this capture-recapture strategy?

    Ⓐ   100 fish

    Ⓑ   1,500 fish

    Ⓒ   2,500 fish

    Ⓓ   3,000 fish

GO ON TO THE NEXT PAGE

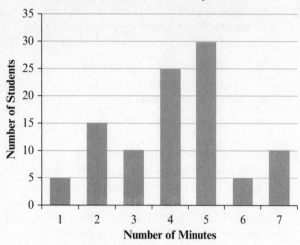

**Number of Minutes Predicted by Students**

**15.** A science teacher asked 100 students to predict the number of minutes it would take a chemical reaction to reach completion. The graph shown displays the students' responses. To the nearest tenth, what is the mean (arithmetic average) number of minutes predicted by the students?

Ⓐ  4.0
Ⓑ  4.2
Ⓒ  4.8
Ⓓ  5.0

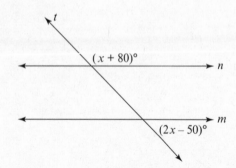

**16.** In the figure, line $t$ is a transversal of lines $m$ and $n$. For what value of $x$ will lines $m$ and $n$ be parallel?

Ⓐ  $16\dfrac{2}{3}$
Ⓑ  50
Ⓒ  100
Ⓓ  130

**17.** A length of cable is attached to the top of a 12-foot vertical pole. The cable is anchored 5 feet from the base of the pole. What is the length of the cable, in feet?

Ⓐ  7 ft
Ⓑ  13 ft
Ⓒ  17 ft
Ⓓ  169 ft

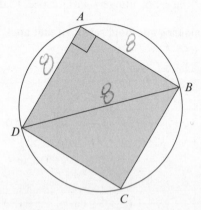

**18.** In the figure, the circle circumscribed about the square $ABCD$ has a circumference of $8\pi$ cm. Find the area of the square $ABCD$.

Ⓐ  $4\sqrt{2}$ cm$^2$
Ⓑ  32 cm$^2$
Ⓒ  $32\pi$ cm$^2$
Ⓓ  It cannot be determined from the information given.

**19.** The density of silver is 10.5 grams per cubic centimeter. What is the mass, in grams, of a cube of silver that measures 2 centimeters on an edge?

Ⓐ  21 g
Ⓑ  42 g
Ⓒ  84 g
Ⓓ  168 g

**For the following question, enter your numeric answer in the box below the question.**

**20.** Tara bought a precious stone pendant in 2008 for $500. By 2011, the pendant had lost 10 percent of its value. In 2013, it was worth 10 percent more than in 2011. By 2016 it had lost 20 percent of its value from 3 years previously. What was the pendant worth in 2016?

$ _____

GO ON TO THE NEXT PAGE

**21.** A national health study estimates that 35 percent of the people over the age of 65 in the United States will get flu shots this year. According to the study, of the people who get flu shots, an estimated 2 percent will have some sort of adverse reaction. If $N$ represents the number of people over the age of 65 in the United States, estimate how many people over age 65 will have an adverse reaction after getting flu shots this year.

   Ⓐ   $0.007N$
   Ⓑ   $0.02N$
   Ⓒ   $0.35N$
   Ⓓ   $0.37N$

**22.** For what value of $k > 0$ will the function defined by $y = 16x^2 - kx + 25$ have exactly one real zero?

   Ⓐ   4
   Ⓑ   8
   Ⓒ   20
   Ⓓ   40

**For the following question, select all that apply.**

**23.** Which two of the following functions have the same domain and the same range?

   Ⓐ   $\{(0, 0), (1, 1), (2, 4), (3, 9), (4, 16)\}$
   Ⓑ   $\{(x, y) \mid y = x^2\}$
   Ⓒ   $\{(0, 0), (1, 1), (2, 4), (3, 9), (4, 16), \ldots\}$
   Ⓓ   $\{(x, y) \mid y = |x|\}$

**24.** A team of biologists introduces a herd of 100 deer onto an uninhabited island. If the deer population doubles every 8 years, which of the following functions models the growth of the deer population on the island if $t$ is the time in years?

   Ⓐ   $(100)^{0.125t}$
   Ⓑ   $(100)2^{0.125t}$
   Ⓒ   $(100)^{8t}$
   Ⓓ   $(100)2^{8t}$

**25.** What is the equation of the line that is perpendicular to the line whose equation is $5x - 6y = 4$ and passes through the point $(3, 1)$?

   Ⓐ   $5x - 6y = 9$
   Ⓑ   $-6x + 5y = -13$
   Ⓒ   $6x + 5y = 23$
   Ⓓ   $6x + 5y = 21$

**26.** The exterior of a spherical tank with radius 12 feet is to be painted with one coat of paint. The paint sells for $24.50 per gallon and can be purchased in 1-gallon cans only. If a can of paint will cover approximately 400 square feet, what is the cost of the paint needed to paint the exterior of the tank?

   Ⓐ   $24.50
   Ⓑ   $98.00
   Ⓒ   $110.25
   Ⓓ   $122.50

**27.** An experiment consists of flipping a coin five times and observing the up face of the coin. Which of the following expressions gives the number of different outcomes in the sample space for this experiment?

   Ⓐ   $2^5$
   Ⓑ   $_5P_2$
   Ⓒ   $5^2$
   Ⓓ   $_5C_2$

| $\otimes$ | $a$ | $b$ |
|---|---|---|
| $a$ | $a$ | $b$ |
| $b$ | $b$ | $b$ |

**For the following question, select all that apply.**

**28.** The table shown defines an operation $\otimes$ on the set $S = \{a, b\}$. Which of the following statements about set $S$ with respect to $\otimes$ are true?

   Ⓐ   Set $S$ is closed.
   Ⓑ   Set $S$ is commutative.
   Ⓒ   Set $S$ contains an identity element.
   Ⓓ   Set $S$ contains inverses for all elements in set $S$.

**GO ON TO THE NEXT PAGE**

**For the following question, select all that apply.**

29. Which of the following statements about the function $y = 3.8x + 1$ are true?

   A   For every 1-unit change in the input, there is a 3.8-unit change in the output.

   B   For every 1-unit change in the input, there is a 4.8-unit change in the output.

   C   For every 1-unit change in the output, there is a 3.8-unit change in the input.

   D   For every 1-unit change in the output, there is a 4.8-unit change in the input.

**Weights (in pounds) of the 36 Members of a Middle School Track Team**

| Stem | Leaves | | | | |
|------|------|------|------|------|------|
| 10 | 0 | 3 | 3 | 7 | 8 |
| 11 | 1 | 1 | 1 | 4 | 7 | 8 |
| 12 | 2 | 6 | 8 | 8 | 9 |
| 13 | 2 | 6 | 6 | 8 |
| 14 | 1 | 2 | 4 |
| 15 | 3 | 4 | 7 | 7 | 7 |
| 16 | 3 | 7 | 8 |
| 17 | 2 | 4 | 8 |
| 18 | 3 | 6 |

30. The graph shown is a stem-and-leaf plot of the weights of 36 students who make up the membership of a middle school track team. What percent of the students on the track team weigh less than 115 pounds?

   Ⓐ   10%
   Ⓑ   15%
   Ⓒ   25%
   Ⓓ   30%

31. At a grand-opening sale of an appliance store, 152 customers bought a washer or a dryer. Looking at the inventory, the store manager found that 94 washers and 80 dryers were sold. Of the 152 customers, how many bought only a washer?

   Ⓐ   22
   Ⓑ   58
   Ⓒ   72
   Ⓓ   130

32. $\dfrac{a}{a^2 - b^2} - \dfrac{b}{a^2 + ab} =$

   Ⓐ   $\dfrac{a - b}{b(a + b)}$

   Ⓑ   $\dfrac{a - b}{a(a + b)}$

   Ⓒ   $\dfrac{a^2 - ab + b^2}{a(a + b)(a - b)}$

   Ⓓ   $\dfrac{a^2 - ab - b^2}{a(a + b)(a - b)}$

33. What are the units of the quantity $Y = \dfrac{Adv}{t}$, where $A$ is measured in square centimeters ($cm^2$), $d$ is expressed in grams per $cm^3$ $\left(\dfrac{g}{cm^3}\right)$, $v$ is expressed in centimeters per second $\left(\dfrac{cm}{s}\right)$, and $t$ is given in seconds (s)?

   Ⓐ   g

   Ⓑ   $\dfrac{g}{s^2}$

   Ⓒ   $\dfrac{g\text{-cm}}{s}$

   Ⓓ   $\dfrac{g\text{-cm}}{s^2}$

**Resident Status of Second-Year Students ($n = 500$)**

| | On-Campus | Off-Campus |
|------|------|------|
| Male | 114 | 135 |
| Female | 156 | 95 |

34. The table shows the resident status, by gender, of 500 second-year students at a small community college. If one of the 500 students is randomly selected, what is the probability that the student resides off-campus given that the student is a female?

   Ⓐ   $\dfrac{86}{125}$

   Ⓑ   $\dfrac{95}{251}$

   Ⓒ   $\dfrac{19}{100}$

   Ⓓ   $\dfrac{4,769}{50,000}$

GO ON TO THE NEXT PAGE

**35.** What is the approximate volume of a right triangular prism that is 20 inches in height and whose bases are equilateral triangles that are 4 inches on a side?

Ⓐ   $7 \text{ in}^3$

Ⓑ   $46 \text{ in}^3$

Ⓒ   $80 \text{ in}^3$

Ⓓ   $139 \text{ in}^3$

**For the following question, enter your numeric answer in the box below the question.**

**36.** A collection of dimes and quarters has a value of $22.50. Ten times as many dimes as quarters are in the collection of coins. How many dimes are in the collection?

⬚ dimes

**37.** In a coordinate plane, triangle $ABC$ has vertices $A(2, 1)$, $B(2, 5)$, and $C(5, 2)$. Triangle $A'B'C'$ is the image of triangle $ABC$ after a reflection over the $y$-axis followed by a translation of 4 units to the right and 6 units down. What are the coordinates of $B'$?

Ⓐ   $(-2, 5)$

Ⓑ   $(2, -1)$

Ⓒ   $(6, -1)$

Ⓓ   $(6, 1)$

**38.** The scatter plot shows the linear relationship between the number of hours of study and the number of questions missed on a mathematics midterm exam by 10 eighth graders. If you were to use the scatter plot to predict the number of questions missed based on the number of hours of study, you should limit the number of hours to between

Ⓐ   1 and 4 hours

Ⓑ   1 and 5 hours

Ⓒ   1 and 6 hours

Ⓓ   1 and 7 hours

**For the following question, select all that apply.**

**39.** The lengths of two sides of a triangle are 7 and 19. Which of the following could be the length of the third side?

Ⓐ   11

Ⓑ   13

Ⓒ   25

Ⓓ   27

**40.** The probability is $\frac{1}{6}$ that a number cube, with faces numbered 1 to 6, will show the number 3 on the up face in one toss of the cube. In three tosses of the number cube, what is the probability that the number 3 will appear on the up face on at least one of the tosses?

Ⓐ   $\dfrac{91}{216}$

Ⓑ   $\dfrac{125}{216}$

Ⓒ   $\dfrac{5}{6}$

Ⓓ   $\dfrac{17}{18}$

**GO ON TO THE NEXT PAGE**

**41.** Which of the following scenarios has the greatest number of possible outcomes?

Ⓐ the number of ways three different prizes can be awarded among 10 people if no one person can receive more than one prize

Ⓑ the number of different three-letter arrangements of the 10 uppercase letters, A through J, if no letter can repeat

Ⓒ the number of different committees of three people that can be formed from among a group of 10 people

Ⓓ the number of different three-digit passcodes that can be formed using the 10 digits 0 through 9, if digits can repeat

**For the following question, enter your fractional answer in the boxes below the question.**

**42.** The ratio of $x$ to $y$ is 20 to 11, and the ratio of $y$ to $z$ is 3 to 5. What is the ratio of $x$ to $z$? Give your answer as a fraction.

$$y = 4(x + 3) + 5$$

**43.** If the value of $x$ in the equation above is increased by 1, the value of $y$ will increase by

Ⓐ 4

Ⓑ 5

Ⓒ 17

Ⓓ 21

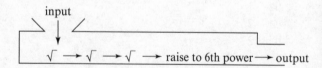

**44.** If a positive number $x$ is used as the input for the function machine shown, which of the following expressions is equivalent to the output?

Ⓐ $x^{\frac{1}{24}}$

Ⓑ $x^{\frac{3}{4}}$

Ⓒ $x$

Ⓓ $x^{\frac{3}{2}}$

**45.** The operation $\oplus$ is defined on the set $R$ of real numbers by $x \oplus y = 3x + xy$, where $x$ and $y$ are real numbers and the operations on the right side of the equal sign denote the standard operations for the real number system. Which of the following questions tests whether the operation $\oplus$ is commutative?

Ⓐ Does $x + y = y + x$ for all real numbers $x$ and $y$?

Ⓑ Does $3x + xy = 3x + yx$ for all real numbers $x$ and $y$?

Ⓒ Does $3x + x^2 = 3y + y^2$ for all real numbers $x$ and $y$?

Ⓓ Does $3x + xy = 3y + yx$ for all real numbers $x$ and $y$?

**For the following question, enter your numeric answer in the box below the question.**

**46.** The original price of a sofa was 30 percent less than the sofa's suggested retail price of $500. The price at which the sofa was sold was 30 percent more than the original price. What is the price at which the sofa was sold?

**For the following question, select all that apply.**

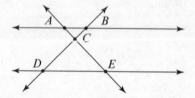

**47.** In the figure shown, above, $\overrightarrow{AB} \parallel \overrightarrow{DE}$, which of the following geometric theorems would most likely be used to prove that $\triangle ABC \sim \triangle EDC$?

Ⓐ Vertical angles of intersecting lines are congruent.

Ⓑ If two parallel lines are cut by a transversal, then any pair of alternate interior angles is congruent.

Ⓒ If two angles of one triangle are congruent to two corresponding angles of another triangle, then the triangles are similar.

Ⓓ The measure of an exterior angle of a triangle equals the sum of the measures of the remote interior angles.

GO ON TO THE NEXT PAGE

**For the following question, enter your fractional answer in the boxes below the question.**

**48.** Squaring both sides of the equation $2x = \sqrt{3x+1}$ and then solving for $x$ gives rise to what extraneous solution?

**49.** If a prime number $p$ is a factor of both $(14n + 13)$ and $(7n + 1)$, what is the value of $p$?

Ⓐ 7

Ⓑ 11

Ⓒ 13

Ⓓ It cannot be determined from the information given.

**50.** What is the third term in the binomial expansion of $(x + 2y)^5$?

Ⓐ $10x^2y^3$

Ⓑ $10x^3y^2$

Ⓒ $40x^3y^2$

Ⓓ $80x^2y^3$

**51.** If the function $f$ is defined by

$f(x) = \dfrac{x+1}{x-2}$, $x \neq 2$, then $f^{-1}$, the inverse of $f$, is

defined by which of the following equations?

Ⓐ $f^{-1}(x) = -\dfrac{x-1}{x+2}$, $x \neq -2$

Ⓑ $f^{-1}(x) = \dfrac{x-2}{x+1}$, $x \neq -1$

Ⓒ $f^{-1}(x) = -\dfrac{2x+1}{x-1}$, $x \neq 1$

Ⓓ $f^{-1}(x) = \dfrac{2x+1}{x-1}$, $x \neq 1$

Scores of 20 Students on Biology Exam

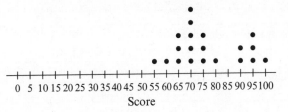

**52.** The dot plot shown above displays the scores of 20 students on a biology exam. The mean absolute deviation of these data is approximately 11. Determine the number of students whose scores are within one mean absolute deviation of the mean.

Ⓐ 9

Ⓑ 10

Ⓒ 11

Ⓓ 12

**For the following question, enter your numeric answer in the box below the question.**

**53.** Given $x^2 + kx + c = (x + h)^2$, where $c$, $k$, and $h$ are real numbers, if $k = 6$, what is the value of $c$?

**54.** Treasure coins in a video game are distributed among five locations in the ratio 1:2:3:4:5. To win the game, a player must acquire at least half of the number of coins in at least three of the five locations. To win, a player must acquire what minimum percent of the total coins?

Ⓐ 10%

Ⓑ 15%

Ⓒ 20%

Ⓓ 25%

**For the following question, select <u>all</u> that apply.**

**55.** If $f$ is a real-valued function, which of the following values are NOT in the domain of $f$,

where $f(x) = \dfrac{\sqrt{x+2}}{2x^3 + x^2 - 2x - 1}$?

Ⓐ $-3$

Ⓑ $-1$

Ⓒ $-\dfrac{1}{2}$

Ⓓ $1$

# Answer Key

| Question Number | Correct Answer | Reference Chapter | Question Number | Correct Answer | Reference Chapter |
|---|---|---|---|---|---|
| 1. | C | Functions and Their Graphs | 30. | C | Statistics |
| 2. | C | Statistics | 31. | C | Discrete Mathematics |
| 3. | B, C | Algebra | 32. | C | Algebra |
| 4. | C | Numbers and Operations | 33. | B | Measurement |
| 5. | B | Numbers and Operations | 34. | B | Probability |
| 6. | A | Algebra | 35. | D | Measurement |
| 7. | D | Discrete Mathematics | 36. | 180 | Algebra |
| 8. | A, C | Geometry | 37. | B | Geometry |
| 9. | B | Algebra | 38. | A | Statistics |
| 10. | A | Numbers and Operations | 39. | B, C | Geometry |
| 11. | B, C, D | Measurement | 40. | A | Probability |
| 12. | 4, 5 | Measurement | 41. | D | Discrete Mathematics |
| 13. | A | Measurement | 42. | $\dfrac{12}{11}$ | Numbers and Operations |
| 14. | C | Numbers and Operations | | | |
| 15. | B | Statistics | 43. | A | Functions and Their Graphs |
| 16. | B | Geometry | 44. | B | Functions and Their Graphs |
| 17. | B | Geometry | 45. | D | Numbers and Operations |
| 18. | B | Measurement | 46. | 455 | Numbers and Operations |
| 19. | C | Measurement | 47. | A, B, C | Geometry |
| 20. | 396 | Numbers and Operations | 48. | $-\dfrac{1}{4}$ | Algebra |
| 21. | A | Numbers and Operations | | | |
| 22. | D | Algebra | 49. | B | Numbers and Operations |
| 23. | B, D | Functions and Their Graphs | 50. | C | Discrete Mathematics |
| 24. | B | Functions and Their Graphs | 51. | D | Functions and Their Graphs |
| 25. | C | Algebra | 52. | A | Statistics |
| 26. | D | Algebra | 53. | 9 | Algebra |
| 27. | A | Discrete Mathematics | 54. | C | Numbers and Operations |
| 28. | A, B, C | Numbers and Operations | 55. | A, B, C, D | Functions and Their Graphs |
| 29. | A | Functions and Their Graphs | | | |

# Answer Explanations

1. **C.** Recall that a function is a set of ordered pairs in which each first component is paired with *one and only one* second component; that is, each $x$ value is paired with one and only one $y$ value. Eliminate choices by showing an example that violates the definition of a function. Eliminate choice A because (17, –3) and (17, 3) satisfy the equation. Eliminate choice B because (6, –8) and (6, 8) satisfy the equation. Eliminate choice D because (2, 2) and (2, –2) satisfy the equation. Thus, choice C is the correct response. You should go on to the next question; but just so you know, for choice C, $y = 25x^2 + 2$, which yields exactly one value of $y$ for every $x$.

   *Tip:* When $y$ is squared, the equation will *not* define a function.

2. **C.** The graph shows the percentage of children's fiction books and the percentage of science fiction books sold in December. To find how many fiction books were sold, do two steps. First, find the total percentage of fiction books sold. Next, find the total number of fiction books sold.

   *Step 1.* 15% + 32.5% = 47.5%

   *Step 2.* 47.5% of 1,200 books = (0.475)(1,200 books) = 570 books, choice C

3. **B, C.** Eliminate choice A because the number of buses must be a whole number. Select choice B; the average time could be 7.3 minutes. Select choice C; the length of each piece of ribbon could be 7.3 centimeters. Eliminate choice D because the number of possible ways must be a whole number.

4. **C.** The question asks: What is the ratio of the total amount of fruit juice to the total amount of cinnamon and sugar called for in the recipe? The amount of each kind of fruit juice is given in cups. The cinnamon is given in teaspoons, and the sugar, in tablespoons. To compare the total amount of fruit juice to the total amount of cinnamon and sugar, both amounts will need to be in the same units. To answer the question, do three steps. First, find the total amount of fruit juice in cups; then, using the conversion table, convert the answer to tablespoons. Next, using the conversion table, convert the amount of cinnamon into tablespoons. Then find the total amount of cinnamon and sugar in tablespoons. Finally, find the ratio of the total amount of fruit juice to the total amount of cinnamon and sugar.

   *Step 1.* $2\frac{3}{4}$ c $+ 1\frac{1}{2}$ c $= 4\frac{1}{4}$ c; $4\frac{1}{4}$ c $\times \dfrac{16\text{ T}}{\text{c}} = 68$ T fruit juice

   *Step 2.* 1 tsp cinnamon $= \dfrac{1}{3}$ T cinnamon; $\dfrac{1}{3}$ T cinnamon $+ 3$ T sugar $= 3\frac{1}{3}$ T cinnamon and sugar

   *Step 3.* The ratio of the total amount of fruit juice to the total amount of cinnamon and sugar is

   $$\frac{68\text{ T}}{3\frac{1}{3}\text{ T}} = \frac{68\ \cancel{T}}{\frac{10}{3}\ \cancel{T}} = \frac{3(68)}{\cancel{3}\left(\frac{10}{\cancel{3}}\right)} = \frac{204}{10} = \frac{102}{5}, \text{ choice C.}$$

5. **B.** Let $x =$ the original amount in Maria's account. Write an equation that represents the transactions and solve for $x$.

   $$x - 0.25x - \$150 = \$975$$
   $$0.75x = \$1{,}125$$
   $$x = \$1{,}500$$

   The original amount in Maria's account was $1,500, choice B.

6. **A.** From your knowledge of solving inequalities, you know the open circles at –3 and 4 mean that –3 and 4 are not included in the solution set. Thus, the inequality symbol in the answer must be either < or >, so eliminate choices C and D.

   **Method 1.** Test a number from the interval shown in the graph in each of the inequalities given in choices A and B. For convenience and ease of calculation, select 0 as your test number.

   Check A: When $x = 0$, $\left|x - \dfrac{1}{2}\right| = \left|0 - \dfrac{1}{2}\right| = \left|-\dfrac{1}{2}\right| = \dfrac{1}{2} < \dfrac{7}{2}$, which is true. Thus, choice A is the correct response.

Check B: You have determined that choice A is the correct response, so go on to the next problem. However, you can easily see that $x = 0$ does not satisfy the inequality in choice B because $\frac{1}{2} > \frac{7}{2}$ is false.

***Tip:*** You also can use this method for testing a number in inequalities that contain the symbols $\leq$ or $\geq$. When you test a number from a given interval in these inequalities, do not select one of the endpoints of the interval as your test number because doing so might lead you to make a wrong decision about which inequality is the correct answer.

**Method 2.** Solve the inequalities given in choices A and B.

Check A:

$$\left| x - \frac{1}{2} \right| < \frac{7}{2}$$
$$-\frac{7}{2} < x - \frac{1}{2} < \frac{7}{2}$$
$$-\frac{7}{2} + \frac{1}{2} < x < \frac{7}{2} + \frac{1}{2}$$
$$-\frac{6}{2} < x < \frac{8}{2}$$
$$-3 < x < 4$$

This inequality is illustrated in the graph shown. Thus, choice A is the correct response.

Check B: You have determined that choice A is the correct response, so go on to the next problem. However, for your information, the solution to choice B is $x < -3$ or $x > 4$.

7. **D.** Check the formulas given in the answer choices using the values in the table.

Check A: When $n = 1$, $\sqrt{n} = \sqrt{1} = 1$, not 0; eliminate choice A.

Check B: When $n = 1$, $n^2 = 1^2 = 1$, not 0; eliminate choice B.

Check C: When $n = 1$, $n^2 - 1 = 1^2 - 1 = 0$ ✓; when $n = 2$, $n^2 - 1 = 2^2 - 1 = 3$, not 1; eliminate choice C. Therefore, you know that choice D is the correct response. You should go on to the next problem.

For your information, here is the check for choice D: When $n = 1$, $(n - 1)^2 = (1 - 1)^2 = 0$ ✓; when $n = 2$, $(n - 1)^2 = (2 - 1)^2 = 1$ ✓; when $n = 3$, $(n - 1)^2 = (3 - 1)^2 = 4$ ✓; and when $n = 4$, $(n - 1)^2 = (4 - 1)^2 = 9$ ✓.

***Tip:*** When simple math is involved, do the checks mentally to save time.

8. **A, C.** A net is a two-dimensional figure that can be formed into a three-dimensional solid. The net of a cube has six congruent square faces. Eliminate choice B because this figure has only five faces. Choices A, C, and D have six congruent square faces, but only choices A and C can be formed into a cube. Eliminate choice D because two faces will overlap when the figure is folded into three dimensions.

9. **B. Method 1.** Express $\dfrac{a}{b + c}$ in terms of $\dfrac{a}{b}$ and $\dfrac{b}{c}$ by dividing each term in its numerator and denominator by $b$.

$$\frac{a}{b + c} = \frac{\dfrac{a}{b}}{\dfrac{b}{b} + \dfrac{c}{b}} = \frac{\dfrac{a}{b}}{\dfrac{b}{b} + \dfrac{1}{\frac{b}{c}}} = \frac{10}{1 + \dfrac{1}{5}} = \frac{10}{\dfrac{6}{5}} = \frac{50}{6} = \frac{25}{3}, \text{ choice B}$$

**Method 2.** Substitute values for $a$, $b$, and $c$ that satisfy the conditions given, and then work with your substituted numbers.

Let $a = 100$, $b = 10$, and $c = 2$. Then $\dfrac{a}{b} = \dfrac{100}{10} = 10$ ✓, $\dfrac{10}{2} = 5$ ✓, and $\dfrac{a}{b + c} = \dfrac{100}{10 + 2} = \dfrac{100}{12} = \dfrac{25}{3}$, choice B.

***Tip:*** As shown above, when you substitute values for the variables, always check to make sure the values satisfy the conditions given in the problem.

**10. A.** A set is closed with respect to an operation if the result of performing the operation with any pair of elements in the set yields an element contained in the set. Choice A is the correct response. To show that the set of perfect squares is closed with respect to multiplication, let $a^2$ and $b^2$ be any two perfect squares. Then $(a^2)(b^2) = (ab)^2$, which is also a perfect square. You should move on to the next problem. But for your information, to show a set is *not* closed, you need to find just *one* pair of elements that does not yield an element in the set when the operation is performed with that pair of elements. Eliminate answer choices that are *not* closed by selecting arbitrary pairs of values and testing them with the given operation. ***Tip:*** Use mental math to save time.

Eliminate choice B because 5 and 9 are whole numbers, but $5 - 9 = -4$, which is not a whole number. Eliminate choice C because 3 and 5 are odd numbers, but $3 + 5 = 8$, which is not an odd number. Eliminate choice D because 1 and 2 are integers, but $1 \div 2 = 0.5$, which is not an integer.

**11. B, C, D.** Make a sketch. Draw the altitude from vertex $Y$ to side $\overline{XZ}$ and label the point of intersection $P$ as shown here.

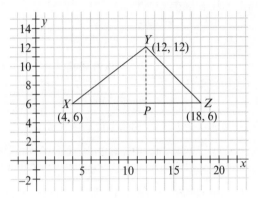

From the figure, you can determine that the length of side $\overline{XZ}$ is 14 units and that the altitude of triangle $XYZ$, from the vertex $Y$ to side $\overline{XZ}$, is 6 units. The line segment $\overline{YP}$ creates two right triangles: triangles $XPY$ and $ZPY$. Use the information given and the properties of right triangles to check the answer choices. Start by selecting answer choices that are obviously rational quantities.

Select choice B because the area of triangle $XYZ$ is $\frac{1}{2}(XZ)(YP) = \frac{1}{2}(14 \text{ units})(6 \text{ units})$, which is a rational quantity. Select choice C because $\overline{XY}$ is the hypotenuse of a right triangle whose legs are 8 units and 6 units; thus, the length of $\overline{XY}$ is 10 units, a rational quantity. Select choice D because the length of $\overline{XZ}$ is 14 units, a rational quantity, so its midpoint is a rational quantity as well. Eliminate choice A. The perimeter of triangle $XYZ$ is irrational because it has a portion, namely $\overline{YZ}$, that is the hypotenuse of a right triangle whose legs are each 6 units; thus, the length of $\overline{YZ} = \sqrt{6^2 + 6^2} = \sqrt{72}$ units, an irrational quantity.

**12. 4, 5** In terms of $x$, the dimensions of the rectangle are $\frac{8}{x}$ cm by $\frac{10}{x}$ cm. Write an equation that represents the facts given.

$$2\left(\frac{8}{x} \text{ cm}\right) + 2\left(\frac{10}{x} \text{ cm}\right) = 18 \text{ cm}$$

Solve the equation for $x$ (omitting the units for convenience) and then compute $\frac{8}{x}$ cm and $\frac{10}{x}$ cm.

$$2\left(\frac{8}{x}\right) + 2\left(\frac{10}{x}\right) = 18$$
$$x\left(\frac{16}{x}\right) + x\left(\frac{20}{x}\right) = x(18)$$
$$16 + 20 = 18x$$
$$36 = 18x$$
$$2 = x$$

Thus, $\dfrac{8}{x}$ cm $= \dfrac{8}{2}$ cm $= 4$ cm and $\dfrac{10}{x}$ cm $= \dfrac{10}{2}$ cm $= 5$ cm.

The dimensions of the rectangle are 4 cm by 5 cm.

**13.** **A.** The maximum possible error of a measurement is half the magnitude of the smallest measurement unit used to obtain the measurement. Therefore, the most accurate way of expressing the dimensions of the yard is as tolerance intervals. Thus, it is more accurate to express the length of the yard as 60 m $\pm$ 0.5 m and its width as 30 m $\pm$ 0.5 m, and to determine the area as a tolerance interval based on these intervals (eliminate choice D). Area equals length times width. The tolerance interval for the area, $A$, of the yard is obtained as follows: (60 m − 0.5 m)(30 m − 0.5 m) $\le A \le$ (60 m + 0.5 m)(30 m + 0.5 m) = (59.5 m)(29.5 m) $\le A \le$ (60.5 m)(30.5 m) = 1755.25 m$^2$ $\le A \le$ 1845.25 m$^2$, choice A.

**14.** **C.** If all the tagged fish are still active in the lake when the second group of fish is captured, the proportion of tagged fish in the second group should equal the proportion of tagged fish in the whole population, $P$, of fish in the lake. Set up a proportion and solve for $P$.

$$\frac{20}{100} = \frac{500}{P}$$
$$P = \frac{(100)(500)}{20}$$
$$P = 2{,}500$$

The best estimate of the fish population is 2,500 fish, choice C.

**15.** **B.** To find the mean, multiply each of the number of minutes by the number of students who predicted that many minutes and divide the result by 100 (the total number of students).

$$\text{mean} = \frac{5(1)+15(2)+10(3)+25(4)+30(5)+5(6)+10(7)}{100} = \frac{415}{100} = 4.15 \approx 4.2, \text{ choice B}$$

**16.** **B.** From the properties of parallel lines cut by a transversal, you know that one way lines $m$ and $n$ will be parallel is for a pair of corresponding angles for the transversal $t$ to be congruent. In the figure, the angle that measures $(x + 80)°$ corresponds to the angle above line $m$ that is supplementary to the angle that measures $(2x − 50)°$. Label this angle $\theta$.

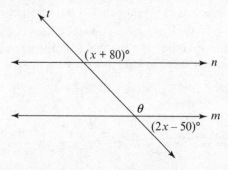

To find the value of $x$ for which lines $m$ and $n$ are parallel, do two steps. First, find the measure of angle $\theta$ in terms of $x$. Next, write and solve an equation that ensures that angle $\theta$ and the angle that measures $(x + 80)°$ are congruent.

*Step 1.* Recall that the sum of supplementary angles is 180°. Thus, angle $\theta$ measures $180° − (2x − 50)°$.

*Step 2.* Lines $m$ and $n$ are parallel when $(x + 80)° = 180° − (2x − 50)°$. Solve for $x$ (omitting the units for convenience).

$$(x+80) = 180 - (2x - 50)$$
$$x + 80 = 180 - 2x + 50$$
$$3x = 150$$
$$x = 50, \text{ choice B}$$

**17. B.** Make a sketch.

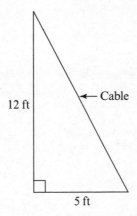

The pole, the cable, and the ground form a right triangle. From the sketch, the cable is the hypotenuse of a right triangle that has legs of 12 feet and 5 feet. Use the Pythagorean theorem to find the length of the hypotenuse, denoted by $c$ (omit the units for convenience).

$$c^2 = a^2 + b^2$$
$$c^2 = (12)^2 + (5)^2$$
$$c^2 = 144 + 25$$
$$c^2 = 169$$
$$c = \sqrt{169}$$
$$c = 13$$

The length of the cable is 13 feet, choice B.

*Tip:* The number $-13$ is also a solution, but is rejected because length is nonnegative.

**18. B.** From the figure, right angle $DAB$ is an inscribed angle. The measure of an inscribed angle is half the degree measure of its intercepted arc. Thus, the degree measure of arc $DB$ is 180°. Therefore, chord $\overline{DB}$ is a diameter of the circle that has circumference $8\pi$ cm. Also, chord $\overline{DB}$ is the diagonal of the square $ABCD$ and the hypotenuse of right triangle $DAB$. The area of square $ABCD$ is $x \cdot x = x^2$. To find the area of square $ABCD$, do three steps. First, use the formula for the circumference of a circle to find the length of chord $\overline{DB}$, which is the same as $d$, the diameter of the circle. Next, use the Pythagorean theorem to find the length of $x$, a side of the square. Finally, use the value obtained for $x$ to find the area of the square.

*Step 1.* Using $C = \pi d$, solve for the length of chord $DB = d$.

$$C = \pi d$$
$$\pi d = 8\pi \text{ cm}$$
$$d = 8 \text{ cm} = \text{the length of chord } \overline{DB}$$

*Step 2.* Apply the Pythagorean theorem in right triangle $DAB$ to find the length of $x$ (omit the units for convenience).

$$x^2 + x^2 = (8)^2$$
$$2x^2 = 64$$
$$x^2 = 32$$
$$x = \sqrt{32}$$

*Step 3.* Find the area of square $ABCD$.

$$\left(\sqrt{32} \text{ cm}\right)\left(\sqrt{32} \text{ cm}\right) = 32 \text{ cm}^2, \text{ choice B}$$

*Note:* Notice that in Step 2, you determine $x^2$, the area of the square, just before you obtain $x$. You actually can skip Step 3 in this problem by stopping when you find $x^2$.

*Tip:* In an isosceles right triangle, the square of the length of the hypotenuse is always twice the square of the length of a leg of the triangle.

**19.** **C.** You are to find the mass, in grams, of the cube. The units for density are grams per cubic centimeter $\left(\dfrac{g}{cm^3}\right)$, so dimensional analysis tells you that if you want to have grams as the units of the answer, then you will need to "cancel" $cm^3$ from the denominator of the density quantity. Cubic centimeters are units of volume. To find the mass of the silver cube, do two steps. First, find the volume of the cube, and then multiply by the density of silver.

*Step 1.* Volume of cube $= (2\text{ cm})^3 = 8\text{ cm}^3$

*Step 2.* Mass of cube $= \left(8\ \cancel{cm^3}\right)\left(\dfrac{10.5\text{ g}}{\cancel{cm^3}}\right) = 84\text{ g}$

The mass of the cube is 84 grams, choice C.

**20.** **396** You are asked to find the value of the pendant after a series of percent increases and decreases. Systematically calculate the percent increases and decreases from year to year.

In 2008, the value is $500. In 2011, the value is $500 − 10\%(\$500) = 90\%(\$500) = 0.90(\$500) = \$450$. In 2013, the value is $\$450 + 10\%(\$450) = \$450 + 0.10(\$450) = \$495$. In 2016, the value is $\$495 − 20\%(\$495) = 80\%(\$495) = 0.80(\$495) = \$396$.

**21.** **A.** The number of people over age 65 who get a flu shot is $35\%N = 0.35N$. Of this number, 2 percent will have an adverse reaction. Thus, the estimated number of people over age 65 who will have an adverse reaction after getting flu shots is $(0.02)(0.35)N = 0.007N$, choice A.

**22.** **D.** The quadratic function defined by $y = 16x^2 − kx + 25$ will have exactly one real zero when the discriminant of $16x^2 − kx + 25 = 0$ is zero. The coefficients for $16x^2 − kx + 25 = 0$ are $a = 16$, $b = −k$, and $c = 25$. The discriminant is $b^2 − 4ac$. Set this quantity equal to zero and solve for $k$.

$b^2 − 4ac = (−k)^2 − 4(16)(25) = 0$, which implies $k^2 − 1{,}600 = 0$. Thus, the positive value $k = \sqrt{1{,}600} = 40$, choice D.

**23.** **B, D.** The function given in choice A is a finite function. None of the other functions are finite, so eliminate choice A. Compare the domains of the functions, and then compare the ranges. The domain of each of the functions given in choices B and D is the set of real numbers; however, the domain in choice C is the set of whole numbers, so eliminate choice C. The range of each of the functions in choices B and D is the nonnegative real numbers, so the two correct choices are B and D.

**24.** **B.** Make a chart that shows the growth of the deer population as a function of time, $t$, at 8-year intervals.

| Time in years | $t = 0$ | $t = 8$ | $t = 16$ | $t = 24$ | ... |
|---|---|---|---|---|---|
| Deer population | 100 | $(100)2$ | $(100)2^2$ | $(100)2^3$ | ... |

From your table, you can see that at 8-year intervals, you are multiplying by a power of 2. Therefore, the function that models the population growth must have an exponential factor that has base 2 in it, so eliminate choices A and C, which do not have an exponential factor with base 2. Now decide whether the exponent for 2 in the expression should be $0.125t$ (choice B) or $8t$ (choice D). Again, use your table to help you decide. When $t = 0$, $(100)2^{0.125t}$ and $(100)2^{8t}$ both equal $(100)2^0 = (100)1 = 100$, which matches the table. When $t = 8$, $(100)2^{0.125t} = (100)2^{0.125(8)} = (100)2$, which matches the table; however, $(100)2^{8t} = (100)2^{8(8)} = (100)2^{64}$, which does not match the table. Therefore, choice B is the correct response.

**25.** **C.** When two lines are perpendicular, their slopes are negative reciprocals of each other. You can write the equation of a line when you know the slope of the line and a point on the line. To find the equation of the line that is perpendicular to the line whose equation is $5x − 6y = 4$ and passes through the point $(3, 1)$, do three steps. First, find the slope, $m$, of the line whose equation is $5x − 6y = 4$. Next, find the negative reciprocal of $m$, which is $-\dfrac{1}{m}$. Then use the point-slope form to determine the equation of the line with slope $-\dfrac{1}{m}$ that passes through the point $(3, 1)$.

*Step 1.* Rewrite $5x - 6y = 4$ as $y = \dfrac{5}{6}x - \dfrac{2}{3}$, which shows the slope of this line is $\dfrac{5}{6}$.

*Step 2.* The negative reciprocal of $\dfrac{5}{6}$ is $-\dfrac{6}{5}$.

*Step 3.* Use the point-slope form to write the equation of the line.

$$y - 1 = -\frac{6}{5}(x - 3)$$

$$y = -\frac{6}{5}x + \frac{18}{5} + 1$$

$$5(y) = 5\left(-\frac{6}{5}x + \frac{23}{5}\right)$$

$$5y = -6x + 23$$

$$6x + 5y = 23, \text{ choice C}$$

**26. D.** To determine the cost of the paint, do three steps. First, find the surface area (*S.A.*) of the sphere. Next, find the number of gallons of paint needed. Then find the cost of the paint.

*Step 1.* $S.A. = 4\pi r^2 = 4\pi(12 \text{ ft})^2 = 1{,}809.5575 \ldots \text{ ft}^2$ (Don't round this answer.)

*Step 2.* Number of gallons needed $= 1{,}809.5575 \ldots \; \cancel{\text{ft}^2} \times \dfrac{1 \text{ gal}}{400 \; \cancel{\text{ft}^2}} \approx 4.5 \text{ gal}$, so 5 gallons will need to be purchased (because the paint is sold in gallon containers only).

*Step 3.* Cost of 5 gallons of paint $= 5 \; \cancel{\text{gal}} \times \dfrac{\$24.50}{1 \; \cancel{\text{gal}}} = \$122.50$, choice D.

**27. A.** The coin is to be flipped five times, so work this problem by using the fundamental counting principle. There are two possibilities for each of the five coin flips, which means the total number of possible outcomes in the sample space is $2 \cdot 2 \cdot 2 \cdot 2 \cdot 2 = 2^5$, choice A.

**28. A, B, C.** You want to determine which of the given properties hold for set $S$ with respect to $\otimes$. Using the table, list the possible "products" and check for the properties given in the answer choices.

From the table, you have $a \otimes a = a$, $a \otimes b = b$, $b \otimes a = b$, and $b \otimes b = b$.

Select choice A: Set $S$ is closed with respect to $\otimes$ because when $\otimes$ is performed on any two elements in set $S$, the result is an element in set $S$. Select choice B: Because $a \otimes b = b$ and $b \otimes a = b$, set $S$ is commutative with respect to $\otimes$. Select choice C: Given that $a \otimes a = a$, $a \otimes b = b$, and $b \otimes a = b$, set $S$ contains an identity element, namely $a$, with respect to the operation of $\otimes$. Eliminate choice D: Set $S$ does not contain an inverse for every element in set $S$. In particular, the element $b$ does not have an inverse because there is no element in set $S$ such that $b \otimes$ (that element) $= a$ (the identity element).

**29. A.** The rate of change of $y = 3.8x + 1$ is 3.8. Thus, for every 1-unit change in the input, there is a 3.8-unit change in the output, choice A. None of the other options contains a true statement about the function.

**30. C.** To find the percent of students who weigh less than 115 pounds, do two steps. First, read the information in the stem-and-leaf plot to determine how many students weigh less than 115 pounds. Next, use the result to find the percent of students who weigh less than 115 pounds.

*Step 1.* Using the stem-and-leaf plot, count how many students weigh less than 115 pounds. There are nine weights that are less than 115 pounds (100, 103, 103, 107, 108, 111, 111, 111, and 114).

*Tip:* Do this step mentally. Don't waste time writing down the weights.

*Step 2.* The percent of students who weigh less than 115 pounds is $\dfrac{9}{36} = 25\%$, choice C.

**31.** **C.** Let $W$ = the set of customers who bought washers and $D$ = the set of customers who bought dryers. Using the notation $|X|$ to represent the number of elements in a set, you have $|W| = 94$ and $|D| = 80$. Because $|W| + |D| = 94 + 80 = 174$, which is greater than 152, the total number of customers, you logically can conclude that some customers bought both a washer and a dryer. Draw a Venn diagram showing two overlapping circles representing $W$ and $D$. Label the intersection $W \cap D$.

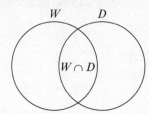

The intersection $W \cap D$ represents the set of customers who bought both a washer and a dryer. From the diagram and the information given in the problem, you have the following equation:

$$152 = |W| + |D| - |W \cap D|$$

Thus, $152 = 94 + 80 - |W \cap D|$

Solving for $|W \cap D|$ yields

$$|W \cap D| = 94 + 80 - 152 = 22$$

Therefore, the number of customers who bought only a washer is $|W| - |W \cap D| = 94 - 22 = 72$, choice C.

**32.** **C.** $\dfrac{a}{a^2 - b^2} - \dfrac{b}{a^2 + ab} = \dfrac{a}{(a+b)(a-b)} - \dfrac{b}{a(a+b)} = \dfrac{a \cdot a}{a(a+b)(a-b)} - \dfrac{b(a-b)}{a(a+b)(a-b)} =$

$\dfrac{a^2}{a(a+b)(a-b)} - \dfrac{ab-b^2}{a(a+b)(a-b)} = \dfrac{a^2 - ab + b^2}{a(a+b)(a-b)}$, choice C

*Tip:* Watch your signs! A minus sign before a fraction applies to the entire numerator, not just to the first term.

**33.** **B.** Plug the units into the formula and simplify as you would for variable quantities.

$$Y = \frac{Adv}{t} = \frac{\left(cm^2\right)\left(\dfrac{g}{cm^3}\right)\left(\dfrac{cm}{s}\right)}{s} = \frac{\dfrac{g}{s}}{s} = \frac{g}{s^2}, \text{ choice B}$$

**34.** **B.** You are to find a conditional probability. That is, you want to find the probability when you already know the student is female. Thus, when computing the probability, the number of possible students under consideration is no longer 500, but is reduced to the total number of female students. Specifically, once you know that the selected person is a female student, you are dealing only with the students in the second row of the table. First, find the total number of female students. Next, among those, determine the number who reside off-campus, and then compute the conditional probability.

*Step 1.* Total female students is $156 + 95 = 251$.

*Step 2.* Among the 251 female students, 95 reside off-campus. Thus, $P$(resides off-campus | given student is female) $= \dfrac{95}{251}$, choice B.

**35.** **D.** The volume of a right prism is given by $V = Bh$. To find the volume of the right triangular prism, do two steps. First, find the area, $B$, of one of the equilateral triangular bases. Next, find the volume by multiplying $B$ by 20 inches, the height ($h$) of the prism.

*Step 1.* The area of an equilateral triangle with sides of 4 inches is $\dfrac{\sqrt{3}}{4} s^2 = \dfrac{\sqrt{3}}{4}(4 \text{ in})^2 = 4\sqrt{3} \text{ in}^2$.

*Tip:* If you forget the formula for the area of an equilateral triangle, you can derive it by using the Pythagorean theorem to determine the height (altitude) of the triangle, and then using the formula area = $\dfrac{1}{2}bh$ to find the area of the equilateral triangle.

*Step 2.* Volume = $(4\sqrt{3} \text{ in}^2)(20 \text{ in}) \approx 139 \text{ in}^3$, choice D.

**36.** **180** Let $q$ = the number of quarters and $10q$ = the number of dimes.

Make a table to organize the coin information.

| Denomination | Dimes | Quarters | Total |
|---|---|---|---|
| Face Value per Coin | $0.10 | $0.25 | N/A |
| Number of Coins | $10q$ | $q$ | Not given |
| Value of Coins | $0.10(10q)$ | $0.25q$ | $22.50 |

Using the table information, write an equation that represents the facts.

$$\$0.10(10q) + \$0.25q = \$22.50$$

Solve the equation for $q$, the number of quarters, omitting the units for convenience. Then compute $10q$, the number of dimes.

$$0.10(10q) + 0.25q = 22.50$$
$$q + 0.25q = 22.50$$
$$1.25q = 22.50$$
$$q = 18$$
$$10q = 10(18) = 180$$

There are 180 dimes in the collection.

*Tip:* Be sure to answer the question asked. After you determine the number of quarters, use the result to determine the number of dimes.

**37.** **B.** Under a reflection over the $y$-axis, $(2, 5) \rightarrow (-2, 5)$. Under a translation of 4 units right and 6 units down, $(-2, 5) \rightarrow (-2 + 4, 5 - 6) = (2, -1)$. The coordinates of $B'$ are $(2, -1)$, choice B.

**38.** **A.** For statistical reasons, you should predict only within the range of the predictor variable, which is the number of hours in this case. The minimum number of hours of study is 1, and the maximum number is 4. You should restrict the number of hours to between 1 and 4, choice A.

**39.** **B, C.** The sum of the lengths of any two sides of a triangle must be greater than the third side. It follows that given two sides of lengths $x$ and $y$, where $x > y$, the length of the third side, call it $z$, satisfies the inequality $(x - y) < z < (x + y)$. Thus, if two sides have lengths of 7 and 19, then the length of the third side must be greater than $19 - 7 = 12$ and less than $19 + 7 = 26$. Select choices B and C because 13 and 25 fall between 12 and 26. Choice A is too short, and choice D is too long.

**40.** **A.** The probability of at least one 3 appearing on the up face in three tosses of the number cube is 1 minus the probability of no 3s appearing in three tosses. The probability of no 3 in one toss of the number cube is $1 - \frac{1}{6} = \frac{5}{6}$. The probability of no 3s in three tosses is $\frac{5}{6} \cdot \frac{5}{6} \cdot \frac{5}{6} = \frac{125}{216}$. Therefore, the probability of at least one 3 in three tosses of the number cube is $1 - \frac{125}{216} = \frac{91}{216}$, choice A.

**41.** **D.** Calculate the result in each scenario. For choice A, using the fundamental counting principle (FCP), there are 10 ways to award the first prize; following that award, there are 9 ways to award the second prize (because no one can receive more than one prize); and following that award, there are 8 ways to award the third prize. Thus, the number of ways to award the three prizes is $(10)(9)(8) = 720$. For choice B, using the FCP, there are 10 ways to choose the first letter; following that selection, there are 9 ways to choose the second letter (because letters cannot repeat); and following that selection, there are 8 ways to select the third letter. Thus, the number of arrangements is $(10)(9)(8) = 720$. Eliminate choices A and B because these two scenarios result in an equal number of outcomes, so neither can be the correct answer. For choice C, the number of different committees is $_{10}C_3 = \frac{10!}{3!7!} = 120$. Eliminate C because the result is less than A or B, so choice C cannot be the correct answer. Therefore, you know that choice D is the correct response. You should go on to the next problem. For your information, using the FCP, there are 10 ways to select the first digit, 10 ways to select the second digit (because digits can repeat), and 10 ways to select the third digit. Thus, the number of different passcodes is $(10)(10)(10) = 1,000$, which is greater than any of the results in the other answer choices.

**42.** $\dfrac{12}{11}$ The ratio of $x$ to $y$ is 20 to 11, so $\dfrac{x}{y} = \dfrac{20}{11}$. The ratio of $y$ to $z$ is 3 to 5, $\dfrac{y}{z} = \dfrac{3}{5}$. The product of $\dfrac{x}{y}$ and $\dfrac{y}{z}$ is

$\dfrac{x}{y} \cdot \dfrac{y}{z} = \dfrac{x}{\cancel{y}} \cdot \dfrac{\cancel{y}}{z} = \dfrac{x}{z}$, which is the ratio of $x$ to $z$. Therefore, the ratio of $x$ to $z$ is $\dfrac{x}{y} \cdot \dfrac{y}{z} = \dfrac{\cancel{20}^{4}}{11} \cdot \dfrac{3}{\cancel{5}^{1}} = \dfrac{12}{11}$.

**43. A.** The equation $y = 4(x + 3) + 5$ is equivalent to $y = 4x + 17$. The rate of change for this equation is 4. Therefore, for every 1-unit change in $x$, there is a 4-unit change in $y$, choice A.

**44. B.** The answer choices are given as exponential expressions, so a logical way to work this problem is to perform on $x$ the sequence of operations indicated by the function machine, using the exponential form for the operation.

$$\left(\left(\left((x)^{\frac{1}{2}}\right)^{\frac{1}{2}}\right)^{\frac{1}{2}}\right)^{6} = x^{\frac{1}{2} \cdot \frac{1}{2} \cdot \frac{1}{2} \cdot 6} = x^{\frac{6}{8}} = x^{\frac{3}{4}}, \text{ choice B}$$

**45. D.** The operation $\oplus$ is commutative on the set $R$ of real numbers if $x \oplus y = y \oplus x$ for all real numbers $x$ and $y$. By the definition of the operation, $x \oplus y = 3x + xy$ and $y \oplus x = 3y + yx$, so the question that tests commutativity is "Does $3x + xy = 3y + yx$ for all real numbers $x$ and $y$?", choice D.

**46.** 455 The sofa's original price was 70% of $500, which is $0.7(\$500) = \$350$. The sofa's selling price was 130% of $350, which is $1.3(\$350) = \$455$.

**47. A, B, C.** Considering the theorems given in the answer options, only choice D would be eliminated from the proof. A simple way to show that two triangles are similar is to show that two angles of one triangle are congruent to two corresponding angles of the other triangle (choice C). You could proceed by showing that $\angle ACB$ is congruent to $\angle ECD$ because these angles are vertical angles of intersecting lines (choice A), and then showing $\angle ABC$ is congruent to $\angle EDC$ because these angles form a pair of alternate-interior angles of two parallel lines cut by a transversal (choice B).

**48.** $-\dfrac{1}{4}$ Square both sides of the equation $2x = \sqrt{3x + 1}$ and solve for $x$.

$$(2x)^2 = \left(\sqrt{3x + 1}\right)^2$$
$$4x^2 = 3x + 1$$
$$4x^2 - 3x - 1 = 0$$
$$(4x + 1)(x - 1) = 0$$
$$x = -\frac{1}{4}(\text{extraneous}) \text{ or } x = 1$$

$-\dfrac{1}{4}$ is an extraneous solution because it makes the left side of the original equation negative, so it cannot equal $\sqrt{3x + 1}$, which is always nonnegative.

Checking $x = 1$ shows 1 satisfies the original equation.

$$2(1) \overset{?}{=} \sqrt{3(1) + 1}$$
$$2 \overset{?}{=} \sqrt{4}$$
$$2 \overset{\checkmark}{=} 2$$

*Tip:* Remember to answer the question posed. The question asks for the extraneous solution.

**49.** **B.** If an integer is a factor of both of the integers $x$ and $y$, then it is a factor of $ax + by$, for any integers $a$ and $b$. Let $x = (14n + 13)$ and $y = (7n + 1)$. Because $p$ is a factor of both $x = (14n + 13)$ and $y = (7n + 1)$, then $p$ is a factor of $1x - 2y = (1)(14n + 13) - 2(7n + 1) = 14n + 13 - 14n - 2 = 11$. The only positive factors of 11 are 1 and 11. Given that $p$ is prime, it follows that $p$ equals 11, choice B.

**50.** **C.** Use the binomial theorem, $(x + y)^n = \sum_{k=0}^{n} \binom{n}{k} x^{n-k} y^k$. For this problem, $(x + 2y)^5 = \sum_{k=0}^{5} \binom{5}{k} x^{5-k} (2y)^k$.

The third term is $\binom{5}{2} x^{5-2} (2y)^2 = 10(x^3)(2y)^2 = 10(x^3)(4y^2) = 40x^3 y^2$, choice C.

*Tip:* You can use the ETS graphing calculator to compute $\binom{5}{2} = {_5}C_2$. Keying in nCr(5,2) returns 10.

**51.** **D.** Let $y = f(x) = \dfrac{x+1}{x-2}$. Interchange $x$ and $y$ in $y = f(x)$, and then solve for $y$.

$$x = \frac{y+1}{y-2}$$
$$xy - 2x = y + 1$$
$$xy - y = 2x + 1$$
$$y(x - 1) = 2x + 1$$
$$y = \frac{2x+1}{x-1}$$
$$f^{-1}(x) = \frac{2x+1}{x-1}, \text{ choice D}$$

**52.** **A.** The mean of the scores is $\dfrac{55 + 60 + 3(65) + 5(70) + 3(75) + 80 + 2(90) + 3(95) + 100}{20} = \dfrac{1,530}{20} = 76.5$. One mean absolute deviation below the mean is $76.5 - 11 = 65.5$, and one mean absolute deviation above the mean is $76.5 + 11 = 87.5$. Exactly 9 scores fall between these two values, meaning 9 scores are within one mean absolute deviation of the mean, choice A.

**53.** **9** Given $x^2 + 6x + c = (x + h)^2$ or equivalently $x^2 + 6x + c = x^2 + 2xh + h^2$, then $6 = 2h$ and $c = h^2$ (because corresponding coefficients are equal). Thus, $h = 3$ and $c = 3^2 = 9$.

**54.** **C.** For convenience, designate the locations L1, L2, L3, L4, and L5, with treasure coins in the ratio 1:2:3:4:5, respectively. Let $n =$ the number of coins in L1, then L1, L2, L3, L4, and L5 have $n$, $2n$, $3n$, $4n$, and $5n$ coins, respectively. The minimum number of coins needed to win is half of the combined number of coins in L1, L2, and L3 (because these locations have the fewest number of coins). This minimum number is $\dfrac{1}{2}(n + 2n + 3n) = \dfrac{1}{2}(6n) = 3n$. The total number of coins is $n + 2n + 3n + 4n + 5n = 15n$. The minimum percent to win is $\dfrac{3n}{15n} = \dfrac{1}{5} = 20\%$, choice C.

*Tip:* Notice that you do not need to know the actual number of coins at any of the locations or the actual total number of coins. Instead, you can work with the ratio relationships to answer the question.

**55.** **A, B, C, D.** Any value of $x$ for which $f(x) = \dfrac{\sqrt{x+2}}{2x^3 + x^2 - 2x - 1}$ is undefined over the real numbers is not in the domain of $f$. Therefore, you must exclude from the domain values for which $(x + 2) < 0$ (or equivalently $x < -2$) and values for which the denominator evaluates to zero.

First, check the answer choices for values less than $-2$. Only $-3$ (choice A) is less than $-2$, so $-3$ is not in the domain of $f$.

Next, check whether any of the values given in choices B, C, or D results in a 0 denominator.

Check B: If $x = -1$, then $2x^3 + x^2 - 2x - 1 = 2(-1)^3 + (-1)^2 - 2(-1) - 1 = -2 + 1 + 2 - 1 = 0$. Thus, $f$ is undefined when $x = -1$, so $-1$ is not in the domain of $f$.

Check C: If $x = -\dfrac{1}{2}$, then $2x^3 + x^2 - 2x - 1 = 2\left(-\dfrac{1}{2}\right)^3 + \left(-\dfrac{1}{2}\right)^2 - 2\left(-\dfrac{1}{2}\right) - 1 = 2\left(-\dfrac{1}{8}\right) + \dfrac{1}{4} + 1 - 1 = -\dfrac{1}{4} + \dfrac{1}{4} + 1 - 1 = 0.$

Thus, $f$ is undefined when $x = -\dfrac{1}{2}$, so $-\dfrac{1}{2}$ is not in the domain of $f$.

Check D: If $x = 1$, then $2x^3 + x^2 - 2x - 1 = 2(1)^3 + (1)^2 - 2(1) - 1 = 2 + 1 - 2 - 1 = 0$. Thus, $f$ is undefined when $x = 1$, so 1 is not in the domain of $f$.

Select choices A, B, C, and D because none of these answer choices are in the domain of $f$.

# Chapter 11

# Practice Test 3

**55 Questions**

**Time—2 Hours**

**Directions:** Read the directions for each question carefully. This test has several different question types. For each question, select the best single answer choice unless written instructions preceding the question state otherwise. For each selected-response question, select the best answer or answers from the choices given. For each numeric-entry question, enter an answer in the answer box. Enter the exact answer unless you are told to round your answer. If a question asks specifically for the answer as a fraction, there will be two boxes—a numerator box and a denominator box. Do not use decimal points in fractions.

1. A family on vacation in an RV leaves home at 9 a.m., travels at an average speed of 50 miles per hour, and arrives at the vacation destination at 2 p.m., with no stops along the way. At approximately what time would the family have arrived if the average speed of the trip had been 65 miles per hour?

   Ⓐ 12:24 p.m.
   Ⓑ 12:51 p.m.
   Ⓒ 1:24 p.m.
   Ⓓ 1:51 p.m.

2. Which of the following graphs illustrates the solution to $\dfrac{2-x}{5} < 1$?

   Ⓐ 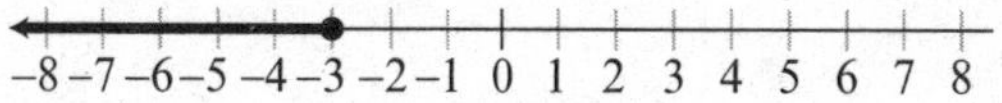
   Ⓑ 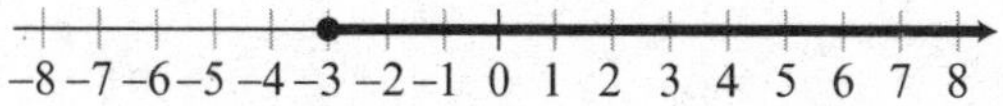
   Ⓒ 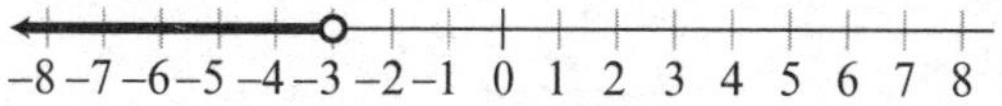
   Ⓓ

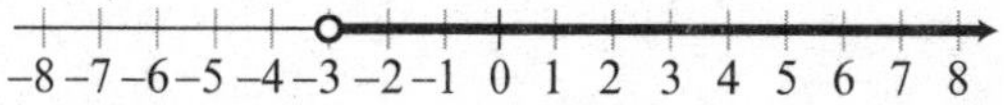

GO ON TO THE NEXT PAGE

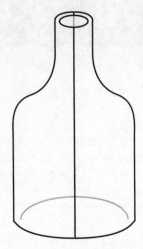

**3.** Water is poured at a constant rate into the container shown in the diagram. Which of the following graphs best represents the height of the water in the container as a function of time?

Ⓐ

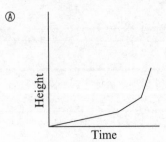

Ⓑ

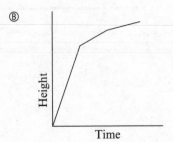

Ⓒ

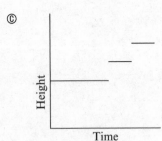

Ⓓ

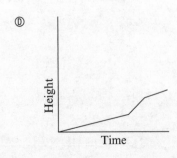

**4.** Using a protractor, a student measures the acute angles in a right triangle and then adds the two measurements to obtain a sum of 81°. What is the percent error of the sum?

Ⓐ  0.10%

Ⓑ  0.11%

Ⓒ  10%

Ⓓ  11%

**5.** For calls to a foreign country, a long-distance phone service charges $3.75 for the first minute (or fraction thereof) and $0.55 for each additional minute. Suppose that a customer using the service is charged $11.45 for a call. For how many minutes did the customer's phone call last?

Ⓐ  12 minutes

Ⓑ  13 minutes

Ⓒ  14 minutes

Ⓓ  15 minutes

**6.** The number 144 has how many positive factors?

Ⓐ  6

Ⓑ  8

Ⓒ  15

Ⓓ  30

**For the following question, enter your numeric answer in the box below the question.**

**7.** What is the least positive integer $k$ such that $\dfrac{1}{4^k} < 0.001?$

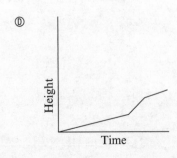

**8.** Grace runs the same distance each morning before going to work. For 10 days, she records her running times for her target distance. Her recorded running times are 21 minutes, 35 minutes, 34 minutes, 30 minutes, 32 minutes, 36 minutes, 24 minutes, 35 minutes, 28 minutes, and 35 minutes. What is the difference, in minutes, between Grace's median running time and her mean running time for the 10 days?

Ⓐ  0 minutes

Ⓑ  2 minutes

Ⓒ  3 minutes

Ⓓ  4 minutes

GO ON TO THE NEXT PAGE

**9.** $(a^{-1} + b^{-1})^{-1} =$

Ⓐ   $a + b$

Ⓑ   $\dfrac{1}{a} + \dfrac{1}{b}$

Ⓒ   $\dfrac{ab}{a + b}$

Ⓓ   $\dfrac{2}{a + b}$

**10.** In a mixture, the ratio of cornmeal to wheat bran, by weight, is 2 to 3. Find the amount (in ounces) of a mixture that contains 30 ounces of cornmeal.

Ⓐ   30 oz

Ⓑ   40 oz

Ⓒ   50 oz

Ⓓ   75 oz

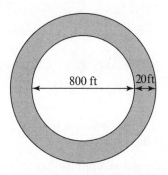

**11.** The figure above shows two concentric circles. Find the area of the shaded region, in square feet.

Ⓐ   $8{,}100\pi$ ft$^2$

Ⓑ   $16{,}400\pi$ ft$^2$

Ⓒ   $32{,}400\pi$ ft$^2$

Ⓓ   $65{,}600\pi$ ft$^2$

**12.** On a number line, line segment $x$ has endpoints $6\dfrac{1}{4}$ and $6\dfrac{1}{2}$, and line segment $y$ has endpoints $\dfrac{5}{\sqrt{8}}$ and $\dfrac{3}{\sqrt{2}}$. What is the ratio of the length of $y$ to the length of $x$?

Ⓐ   $\dfrac{1}{\sqrt{2}}$

Ⓑ   $\sqrt{2}$

Ⓒ   $\dfrac{4}{\sqrt{2}}$

Ⓓ   $4\sqrt{2}$

**13.** The ratio of the volume of sphere $A$ to the volume of sphere $B$ is 27 to 1. What is the ratio of the surface area of sphere $A$ to the surface area of sphere $B$?

Ⓐ   3 to 1

Ⓑ   6 to 1

Ⓒ   9 to 1

Ⓓ   27 to 1

**14.** $(2x^2 - 3x - 2)^{-1}(2x^2 + 7x + 3)(x^2 - x - 2)$ $(x^2 - 9)^{-1} =$

Ⓐ   $\dfrac{x + 1}{x - 3}$

Ⓑ   $\dfrac{x - 1}{x + 3}$

Ⓒ   $\dfrac{(x + 7)(x + 1)}{(x + 3)(x - 3)}$

Ⓓ   $-\dfrac{1}{3}$

**15.** $\dfrac{ab - b^2}{ab - a^2} - \dfrac{a^2 b - b^2}{ab} =$

Ⓐ   $-\dfrac{1}{a}$

Ⓑ   $-a$

Ⓒ   $a$

Ⓓ   $-\dfrac{a^2 + 2b}{a}$

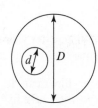

**16.** In the picture shown above, the diameter, $D$, of the larger circle is four times the diameter, $d$, of the smaller circle. What is the ratio of the area of the smaller circle to the area of the larger circle?

Ⓐ   $\dfrac{1}{16}$

Ⓑ   $\dfrac{1}{8}$

Ⓒ   $\dfrac{1}{4}$

Ⓓ   $\dfrac{1}{2}$

GO ON TO THE NEXT PAGE

**17.** A 40-foot cable is attached to the outside wall of a four-story building. One end of the cable is anchored 24 feet from the base of the building. How high up (in feet) on the outside wall of the building does the other end of the cable reach?

Ⓐ   16 ft
Ⓑ   32 ft
Ⓒ   36 ft
Ⓓ   47 ft

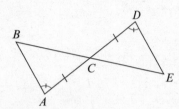

**18.** In the figure above, $\angle A \cong \angle D$ and $\overline{BE}$ bisects $\overline{AD}$. Which of the following methods should be used to show triangle $ABC$ is congruent to triangle $DEC$?

Ⓐ   SSS
Ⓑ   SAS
Ⓒ   AAA
Ⓓ   ASA

**19.** If the surface area of a sphere is $144\pi$ cm$^2$, find the volume of the sphere.

Ⓐ   36 cm$^3$
Ⓑ   288 cm$^3$
Ⓒ   $216\pi$ cm$^3$
Ⓓ   $288\pi$ cm$^3$

**For the following question, enter your numeric answer in the box below the question.**

**20.** Two identical machines can do a job in 10 days. How many days will it take five such machines to do the same job?

⬚ days

**21.** Two vehicles leave the same location at 10:45 a.m., one traveling due north at 70 miles per hour and the other due south at 60 miles per hour. If the vehicles maintain their respective speeds, at what time will they be 325 miles apart?

Ⓐ   12:15 p.m.
Ⓑ   1:15 p.m.
Ⓒ   2:15 p.m.
Ⓓ   3 p.m.

**For the following question, enter your numeric answer in the box below the question.**

**22.** A scientist wants to divide a rectangular field that measures 24 feet by 36 feet into equal square plots with no land left over. What is the greatest length, in feet, for each side of the square plots?

⬚ feet

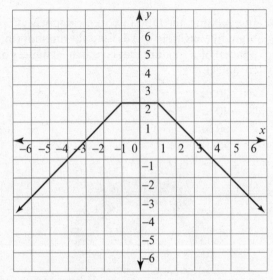

**23.** Which of the following sets is the range of the function shown above?

Ⓐ   $\{y \mid y \text{ is a real number}\}$
Ⓑ   $\{y \mid y \text{ is a real number}, y \le 2\}$
Ⓒ   $\{y \mid y \text{ is a real number}, -3 \le y \le 3\}$
Ⓓ   $\{y \mid y \text{ is a real number}, -6 \le y \le 6\}$

**For the following question, select all that apply.**

**24.** Which of the following polynomial functions have zeros at $-4, -1, \frac{1}{2}$, and 2?

Ⓐ   $P(x) = x(x+4)\left(x - \dfrac{1}{2}\right)(x-2)(x+1)$

Ⓑ   $P(x) = (x-4)(2x+1)(x+2)(x-1)$

Ⓒ   $P(x) = (x+4)(2x-1)(x-2)(x+1)$

Ⓓ   $P(x) = 2x(x+4)\left(x - \dfrac{1}{2}\right)(x-2)(x+1)$

GO ON TO THE NEXT PAGE

**25.** A candy store owner mixes candy that normally sells for $5.00 per pound and candy that normally sells for $7.50 per pound to make a 90-pound mixture to sell at $6.00 per pound. To make sure that $6.00 per pound is a fair price, how many pounds of the $5.00 candy should the owner use?

Ⓐ   36 lb
Ⓑ   42 lb
Ⓒ   50 lb
Ⓓ   54 lb

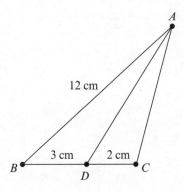

**26.** In triangle $ABC$, $\angle DAB \cong \angle DAC$. What is the length of $\overline{AC}$, in centimeters?

Ⓐ   6 cm
Ⓑ   7 cm
Ⓒ   8 cm
Ⓓ   It cannot be determined from the information given.

**27.** Candi scored at the 85th percentile on a multiple-choice exam. The best interpretation of this information is that

Ⓐ   Candi answered 85 percent of the questions on the test correctly.
Ⓑ   Only 15 percent of the other students did worse on the test than Candi.
Ⓒ   Candi answered 85 questions correctly.
Ⓓ   Candi did as well or better than 85 percent of the students who took the exam.

**28.** A water tank can be filled in 6 hours when the input valve is open and the outlet valve is closed. When the input valve is closed and the outlet valve is open, the same tank can be emptied in 10 hours. If a tank is filled with both valves open, how long will it take to fill the tank?

Ⓐ   4 hours
Ⓑ   $7\frac{1}{2}$ hours
Ⓒ   15 hours
Ⓓ   16 hours

**29.** Given the cubic function $f(x) = x^3$, which of the following best describes the function $g(x) = (x - 5)^3 + 2$?

Ⓐ   the same as the graph of $f(x) = x^3$ shifted right by 5 units and up by 2 units
Ⓑ   the same as the graph of $f(x) = x^3$ shifted left by 5 units and up by 2 units
Ⓒ   the same as the graph of $f(x) = x^3$ shifted right by 5 units and down by 2 units
Ⓓ   the same as the graph of $f(x) = x^3$ shifted left by 5 units and down by 2 units

**30.** A realtor who is selling houses located in an upscale housing development has determined the following probabilities for two neighboring houses, one of which is a model home: The probability that the model home will be sold is 0.50, the probability that the house next door will be sold is 0.40, and the probability that at least one of the two houses will be sold is 0.80. Find the probability that the house next door will be sold given that the model home has already been sold.

Ⓐ   10%
Ⓑ   20%
Ⓒ   30%
Ⓓ   40%

GO ON TO THE NEXT PAGE

**31.** First prize for a television show's promotional drawing is a 24 × 16 × 8 inch rectangular box stuffed to capacity with U.S. $20 bills. On average, U.S. $20 bills measure 6.14 inches long and 2.61 inches wide, and a stack of one hundred $20 bills is about 0.43 inch thick. What is the approximate total value of money in the first-prize box of $20 bills?

Ⓐ $45,000

Ⓑ $890,000

Ⓒ $1,160,000

Ⓓ $8,920,000

**32.** The compound interest formula is $P = P_0(1 + r)^t$, where $r$ is the rate, compounded annually, and $P$ is the value after $t$ years of an initial investment of $P_0$. Suppose a couple establishes a savings account for their child with an investment of $10,000. Assuming no withdrawals and no additional deposits are made, approximately what interest rate compounded annually is needed to double the investment in 20 years?

Ⓐ 3.5%

Ⓑ 5.5%

Ⓒ 10.0%

Ⓓ 103.5%

**33.** The formula for the distance from point $(x_1, y_1)$ to line $Ax + By + C = 0$ is given by $d = \dfrac{|Ax_1 + By_1 + C|}{\sqrt{A^2 + B^2}}$. What is the distance from the point $(-3, 7)$ to the line that has equation $4x + 3y = -5$?

Ⓐ 0.6

Ⓑ 0.8

Ⓒ 2.0

Ⓓ 2.8

### Library Users by Gender ($N = 200$)

|  | Female | Male |
|---|---|---|
| **Former Student** | 25 | 5 |
| **Current Student** | 93 | 77 |

**34.** The data in the table show the student status, by gender, of 200 library users at a small college for a given day. If one of the 200 students is randomly selected, what is the probability that the student is a male former student?

Ⓐ $\dfrac{1}{40}$

Ⓑ $\dfrac{1}{8}$

Ⓒ $\dfrac{5}{8}$

Ⓓ $\dfrac{5}{6}$

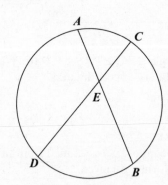

**35.** In the circle shown, chords $\overline{AB}$ and $\overline{CD}$ intersect at point $E$ such that the length of $\overline{AE}$ is one-half the length of $\overline{EB}$. If the length of $\overline{CE}$ is 2 centimeters and the length of $\overline{ED}$ is 6 centimeters, find the length (in centimeters) of chord $\overline{AB}$.

Ⓐ $\sqrt{6}$ cm

Ⓑ 4 cm

Ⓒ $2\sqrt{6}$ cm

Ⓓ $3\sqrt{6}$ cm

**36.** Which equation has both −4 and 4 in the solution set?

Ⓐ $x = \sqrt[3]{64}$

Ⓑ $x = \sqrt{16}$

Ⓒ $x^2 = 16$

Ⓓ $x^3 = 64$

GO ON TO THE NEXT PAGE

**37.** A small town has one area code and four prefixes available—560, 562, 564, and 569—for the ten-digit telephone numbers in the town. Which of the following computations will yield the number of different telephone numbers that are possible if all four prefixes are used?

Ⓐ  $4(_{10}C_4)$

Ⓑ  $4(10^4)$

Ⓒ  $10^8$

Ⓓ  $10^{16}$

**38.** If $f(x) = -16x^{-4}$, then $f(-2)$ is

Ⓐ  $-1$

Ⓑ  $1$

Ⓒ  $128$

Ⓓ  $256$

**39.** A box contains 25 wooden tiles of identical size and shape, which are numbered 1 through 25. If one tile is drawn at random from the box, what is the probability that the number on the tile is a prime number?

Ⓐ  $\dfrac{1}{25}$

Ⓑ  $\dfrac{9}{25}$

Ⓒ  $\dfrac{2}{5}$

Ⓓ  $\dfrac{12}{25}$

**For the following question, enter your numeric answer in the box below the question.**

**40.** If $x^2 - 13 = 12x$, what is the value of $|x - 6|$?

☐

**41.** If $p(x) = (2x - 3)(x + k)$, and $-3$ is the remainder when $p(x)$ is divided by $(x - 1)$, what is the value of $k$?

Ⓐ  $-6$

Ⓑ  $-3$

Ⓒ  $2$

Ⓓ  $6$

| Mean Score | 65 |
|---|---|
| Median Score | 73 |
| Modal Score | 77 |
| Range | 52 |
| Mean Absolute Deviation | 15 |
| Number of Students | 50 |

**42.** The data in the table summarize the scores of 50 students on a social studies exam. Which of the following statements best describes the distribution of the scores?

Ⓐ  The distribution is positively skewed.

Ⓑ  The distribution is negatively skewed.

Ⓒ  The distribution is symmetric.

Ⓓ  The distribution is bimodal.

**43.** What is the inverse of the function defined by $y = x^5 - 3$?

Ⓐ  $y = \dfrac{1}{\sqrt[5]{x - 3}}$

Ⓑ  $y = \dfrac{1}{x^5 - 3}$

Ⓒ  $y = \sqrt[5]{x} + 3$

Ⓓ  $y = \sqrt[5]{x + 3}$

GO ON TO THE NEXT PAGE

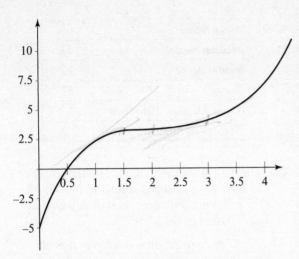

**44.** The graph shown is the graph of $y = x^3 - 6x^2 + 12x - 5$. The rate of change of a curve at a point is described by the slope of the tangent to the curve at the point. Which of the following statements is true about the rate of change of $y$ with respect to $x$?

Ⓐ The rate of change is constant between 0 and 0.5.

Ⓑ The rate of change is increasing between 0.5 and 1.5.

Ⓒ The rate of change is decreasing between 2 and 3.

Ⓓ The rate of change is increasing between 3 and 3.5.

**45.** Which of the following sets is the solution to $2x^2 - x < 1$?

Ⓐ $\left\{ x \in \text{reals},\ x < -1 \text{ or } x > \dfrac{1}{2} \right\}$

Ⓑ $\left\{ x \in \text{reals},\ x < \dfrac{1}{2} \text{ or } x > 1 \right\}$

Ⓒ $\left\{ x \in \text{reals},\ -\dfrac{1}{2} < x < 1 \right\}$

Ⓓ $\left\{ x \in \text{reals},\ -1 < x < \dfrac{1}{2} \right\}$

**46.** A bag contains 10 blue marbles, 7 red marbles, 5 green marbles, and 3 yellow marbles. If two marbles are randomly drawn from the bag, one after the other, without replacement after the first draw, what is the probability that both marbles will be yellow?

Ⓐ $\dfrac{9}{625}$

Ⓑ $\dfrac{1}{100}$

Ⓒ $\dfrac{3}{25}$

Ⓓ $\dfrac{2}{24}$

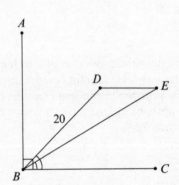

**47.** In the figure shown, $\overline{AB} \perp \overline{BC}$, $\overline{DE} \parallel \overline{BC}$, $m\angle DBC = 45°$, $m\angle EBC = 30°$, and $BD = 20$. What is the perimeter of triangle $DBE$?

Ⓐ $10\left(2 + \sqrt{2} + 3\right)$

Ⓑ $10\left(2 + \sqrt{2} + \sqrt{6}\right)$

Ⓒ $20\left(2 + \sqrt{2} + \sqrt{3}\right)$

Ⓓ $20\left(2 + 2\sqrt{2}\right)$

**For the following question, enter your numeric answer in the box below the question.**

Total Savings and Investments
of 3,000 Workers, Ages 30 to 50

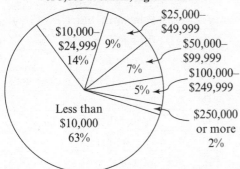

**48.** The circle graph above shows the distribution of 3,000 workers, ages 30 to 50, according to their total savings and investments. According to the graph, the number of workers who have less than \$10,000 in savings and investments is what percent of the number of workers who have \$100,000 or more in savings and investments?

[ ]%

**For the following question, select all that apply.**

**49.** Suppose $a = \dfrac{x}{4} + \dfrac{y}{4^2} + \dfrac{z}{4^3}$, where $x$, $y$, and $z$ are each either 0 or 1. Which of the following fractions are possible values of $a$?

A  $\dfrac{5}{64}$

B  $\dfrac{13}{64}$

C  $\dfrac{3}{16}$

D  $\dfrac{5}{16}$

**50.** Given $3x + 2y + 6z = 50$ and $7x + 8y + 4z = 70$, what is the arithmetic average of $x$, $y$, and $z$?

Ⓐ 4
Ⓑ 10
Ⓒ 12
Ⓓ It cannot be determined from the information given.

**Answer the question by selecting all that apply.**

**51.** The square root of the product of $p$ and $q$ is 14, where $p$ and $q$ are two positive integers. Which of the following integers could be a sum for $(p + q)$?

A  35
B  54
C  100
D  197

**For the following question, enter your numeric answer in the box below the question.**

**52.** One of the interior angles of a regular polygon measures 140°. What is the sum of the measures of the polygon's interior angles?

[ ]°

**53.** Two boxes each contain four tiles, numbered 1, 2, 3, and 4. The tiles are identical in shape and size. A student randomly draws one tile from each box and calculates the product of the two numbers on the tiles. Which of the following products is most likely to occur?

Ⓐ 2
Ⓑ 4
Ⓒ 6
Ⓓ 8

**54.** The graph of the function $f$ defined by $f(x) = 3^x$ is reflected over the $x$-axis and translated 5 units to the right to become the function $g$. Which of the following equations defines $g$?

Ⓐ  $g(x) = -3^{x-5}$
Ⓑ  $g(x) = -3^x - 5$
Ⓒ  $g(x) = 3^{-(x+5)}$
Ⓓ  $g(x) = 3^{-x} - 5$

**For the following question, select all that apply.**

**55.** A camper leaves camp and jogs 3 miles to a river, rests for a while, and then jogs 4 more miles. At this point which of the following could be the jogger's distance from camp?

A  1 mile
B  5 miles
C  7 miles
D  9 miles

# Answer Key

| Question Number | Correct Answer | Reference Chapter | Question Number | Correct Answer | Reference Chapter |
|---|---|---|---|---|---|
| 1. | B | Algebra | 29. | A | Functions and Their Graphs |
| 2. | D | Algebra | 30. | B | Probability |
| 3. | A | Functions and Their Graphs | 31. | B | Measurement |
| 4. | C | Measurement | 32. | A | Numbers and Operations |
| 5. | D | Algebra | 33. | D | Algebra |
| 6. | C | Numbers and Operations | 34. | A | Probability |
| 7. | 5 | Algebra | 35. | D | Geometry |
| 8. | B | Statistics | 36. | C | Algebra |
| 9. | C | Algebra | 37. | B | Discrete Mathematics |
| 10. | D | Numbers and Operations | 38. | A | Functions and Their Graphs |
| 11. | B | Measurement | 39. | B | Probability |
| 12. | B | Numbers and Operations | 40. | 7 | Algebra |
| 13. | C | Measurement | 41. | C | Functions and Their Graphs |
| 14. | A | Algebra | 42. | B | Statistics |
| 15. | B | Algebra | 43. | D | Functions and Their Graphs |
| 16. | A | Measurement | 44. | D | Functions and Their Graphs |
| 17. | B | Geometry | 45. | C | Algebra |
| 18. | D | Geometry | 46. | B | Probability |
| 19. | D | Measurement | 47. | B | Geometry |
| 20. | 4 | Algebra | 48. | 900 | Statistics |
| 21. | B | Algebra | 49. | A, D | Algebra |
| 22. | 12 | Numbers and Operations | 50. | A | Algebra |
| 23. | B | Functions and Their Graphs | 51. | A, C, D | Numbers and Operations |
| 24. | A, C, D | Functions and Their Graphs | 52. | 1,260 | Geometry |
| 25. | D | Algebra | 53. | B | Probability |
| 26. | C | Geometry | 54. | A | Functions and Their Graphs |
| 27. | D | Statistics | 55. | A, B, C | Algebra |
| 28. | C | Algebra | | | |

# Answer Explanations

1. **B.** At 50 miles per hour, it took the family 5 hours (9 a.m. to 2 p.m.) to reach their destination. The distance traveled is $\left(5 \cancel{hr}\right)\left(50 \dfrac{miles}{\cancel{hr}}\right) = 250$ miles. At an average speed of 65 miles per hour, the trip would have taken $\dfrac{250 \cancel{miles}}{65 \dfrac{\cancel{miles}}{hr}} \approx 3.85$ hours $= 3$ hours 51 minutes. Therefore, if the family left at 9 a.m. and traveled at an average speed of 65 miles per hour, they would have arrived at (approximately) 9 a.m. plus 3 hours 51 minutes, which is 12:51 p.m., choice B.

2. **D.** Solve the inequality.

$$\frac{2-x}{5} < 1$$
$$2 - x < 5$$
$$-x < 3$$
$$x > -3$$

The graph for this inequality is a ray extending to the right from the point $-3$ with an open dot at the point $-3$, choice D.

*Tip:* Remember to reverse the direction of the inequality when you multiply both sides by a negative quantity.

3. **A.** Analyze the figure. As water is poured into the container at a constant rate, the height of the water rises at a constant rate until it reaches the point near the top where the bottle narrows. At that point, the water rises at a faster (but still constant) rate until it reaches the bottle's neck, where it rises at an even faster rate.

   The graph that corresponds to this analysis is given in choice A. Choice B is incorrect because it indicates that the rate at which the water rises slows down as the water reaches the top of the bottle. Choice C is incorrect because it indicates that the height of the water in the bottle is constant at first, then suddenly leaps to a higher level and remains constant at that level for a while and, finally, leaps to an even higher level, where it remains constant. Choice D is incorrect because it indicates that the rate at which the water rises initially is the same as the rate at which it rises when it reaches the bottle's neck.

4. **C.** The sum of the acute angles of a right triangle is 90°. To find the percent error of the student's sum, do two steps. First, find the absolute error by finding the difference between 90° and the student's sum. Next, find the percent error by dividing the difference by 90°.

   *Step 1.* The absolute error is $90° - 81° = 9°$.

   *Step 2.* The percent error is $\dfrac{9°}{90°} = 0.10 = 10\%$, choice C.

5. **D.** Suppose $x$ is the total number of minutes that the call lasted. Then $x$ is the sum of the first minute and the total number of minutes talked after the first minute, which is $x - 1$. The charge for the first minute, \$3.75, plus the charge for the additional minutes, \$0.55($x - 1$), equals the total charge for the call, \$11.45. Write an equation to represent the facts and solve for $x$ (omitting the units for convenience).

$$3.75 + 0.55(x - 1) = 11.45$$
$$3.75 + 0.55x - 0.55 = 11.45$$
$$0.55x = 8.25$$
$$x = 15$$

The call lasted 15 minutes, choice D.

**6.** **C.** The prime factorization of 144 is $2^4 \cdot 3^2$. Therefore, the number 144 has $(4+1)(2+1) = (5)(3) = 15$ positive factors, choice C.

**7.** **5** The inequality $\dfrac{1}{4^k} < 0.001$ implies that $4^k > 1,000$. Substitute possible values of $k$ until you obtain one that satisfies this inequality: $4^1 = 4$, $4^2 = 16$, $4^3 = 64$, $4^4 = 256$, $4^5 = 1,024$. Thus, $k = 5$ is the least integer that satisfies the inequality.

**8.** **B.** To find the difference between the median and the mean, do three steps. First, calculate the mean. Next, calculate the median. Then compute the difference, median − mean.

*Step 1.* Omitting the units for convenience, the mean is

$$\frac{21+24+28+30+32+34+35+35+35+36}{10} = 31$$

*Step 2.* Omitting the units, put the times in order: 21, 24, 28, 30, 32, 34, 35, 35, 35, 36. Average the middle pair: $\dfrac{32+34}{2} = 33$.

*Step 3.* The difference is 33 minutes − 31 minutes = 2 minutes, choice B.

**9.** **C.** $\left(a^{-1} + b^{-1}\right)^{-1} = \dfrac{1}{\left(a^{-1} + b^{-1}\right)} = \dfrac{1}{\left(\dfrac{1}{a} + \dfrac{1}{b}\right)} = \dfrac{ab \cdot 1}{ab\left(\dfrac{1}{a} + \dfrac{1}{b}\right)} = \dfrac{ab}{b+a} = \dfrac{ab}{a+b}$, choice C.

**10.** **D.** The amount (in ounces) in the mixture is the sum of the amount (in ounces) of cornmeal in the mixture and the amount (in ounces) of wheat bran in the mixture. You know how much cornmeal is in the mixture. You will need to find the amount of wheat bran in the mixture. To find the total number of ounces in the mixture, do two steps. First, set up a proportion and find the amount (in ounces) of wheat bran in the mixture. Next, find the total amount (in ounces) of the mixture.

*Step 1.* Omitting the units, solve the following proportion:

$$\frac{30}{x} = \frac{2}{3}$$
$$x = \frac{(30)(3)}{2}$$
$$x = 45$$

The amount of wheat bran in the mixture is 45 ounces.

*Step 2.* The total amount of the mixture is 30 ounces + 45 ounces = 75 ounces, choice D.

**11.** **B.** The shaded region is the difference between the area of the larger circle and the area of the smaller circle. The formula for the area of a circle is $\pi r^2$. Calculate the two areas and subtract. From the figure, you have the diameter of the larger circle is 800 ft + 2(20 ft) = 840 ft, and the diameter of the smaller circle is 800 ft. Thus, the radius of the larger circle is $\dfrac{1}{2}(840 \text{ ft}) = 420$ ft, and the radius of the smaller circle is $\dfrac{1}{2}(800 \text{ ft}) = 400$ ft.

The area of the shaded region is $\pi(420 \text{ ft})^2 - \pi(400 \text{ ft})^2 = 16,400\pi \text{ ft}^2$, choice B.

**12. B.** You are given the endpoints of segments $x$ and $y$, so you can find their lengths by subtracting endpoints. To find the ratio of the length of $y$ to the length of $x$, do two steps. First, find the lengths of each of the line segments. Next, find the ratio of the length of $y$ to the length of $x$.

*Step 1.* The length of segment $x$ is $6\frac{1}{2} - 6\frac{1}{4} = \frac{1}{4}$; the length of segment $y$ is

$$\frac{3}{\sqrt{2}} - \frac{5}{\sqrt{8}} = \frac{3}{\sqrt{2}} - \frac{5}{\sqrt{4 \cdot 2}} = \frac{3}{\sqrt{2}} - \frac{5}{2\sqrt{2}} = \frac{6}{2\sqrt{2}} - \frac{5}{2\sqrt{2}} = \frac{1}{2\sqrt{2}} = \frac{1 \cdot \sqrt{2}}{2\sqrt{2}\sqrt{2}} = \frac{\sqrt{2}}{4}.$$

*Step 2.* $\dfrac{y}{x} = \dfrac{\frac{\sqrt{2}}{4}}{\frac{1}{4}} = \dfrac{4\left(\frac{\sqrt{2}}{4}\right)}{4\left(\frac{1}{4}\right)} = \dfrac{\sqrt{2}}{1} = \sqrt{2}$, choice B.

**13. C.** Upon first reading, you might think this problem will take some time to work out. However, recall that when the dimensions of a solid figure are multiplied by a scale factor, the surface area and volume are multiplied by the scale factor raised to the second power and third power, respectively. To find the ratio of the surface areas of the spheres, do two steps. First, using the ratio of the volumes, determine the scale factor. Next, find the ratio of the surface areas by squaring the scale factor.

*Step 1.* The ratio of the volumes is $\dfrac{27}{1}$, which implies (scale factor)$^3 = 27$. Thus, the scale factor is 3.

*Step 2.* The ratio of the surface areas is $3^2$ to 1, which is 9 to 1, choice C.

*Tip:* Knowing how scale factors impact area and volume can be very helpful to you on the test.

**14. A.** Simplify the expression.

$$(2x^2 - 3x - 2)^{-1}(2x^2 + 7x + 3)(x^2 - x - 2)(x^2 - 9)^{-1} = \frac{(2x^2 + 7x + 3)(x^2 - x - 2)}{(2x^2 - 3x - 2)(x^2 - 9)}$$

$$= \frac{(2x + 1)(x + 3)(x + 1)(x - 2)}{(2x + 1)(x - 2)(x + 3)(x - 3)}$$

$$= \frac{\cancel{(2x+1)}\;\cancel{(x+3)}(x+1)\cancel{(x-2)}}{\cancel{(2x+1)}\;\cancel{(x-2)}\;\cancel{(x+3)}(x-3)}$$

$$= \frac{x + 1}{x - 3}, \text{ choice A}$$

**15. B.** Simplify the expression.

$$\frac{ab - b^2}{ab - a^2} - \frac{a^2b - b^2}{ab} = \frac{b(a - b)}{a(b - a)} - \frac{b(a^2 - b)}{ab} = \frac{-b}{a} - \frac{(a^2 - b)}{a} = \frac{-b - a^2 + b}{a} = \frac{-a^2}{a} = -a, \text{ choice B}$$

*Tip:* Watch your signs! A minus sign before a fraction applies to all terms in the numerator, not just to the first term.

**16. A.** The diameter, $D$, of the larger circle is four times the diameter, $d$, of the smaller circle. One way to work the problem is to use the formula $A = \pi r^2$ to find the areas of the two circles in terms of $D$, and then find the ratio of the area of the smaller circle to the larger circle. However, you should remember that when the dimensions of a two-dimensional figure are multiplied by a scale factor, $s$, the area of the figure produced is $s^2$ times the area of the original figure. Therefore, the area of the larger circle in the diagram is $4^2 = 16$ times the area of the smaller circle. Hence, the ratio of the area of the smaller circle to the larger circle is $\dfrac{1}{16}$, choice A.

*Tip:* Knowing how scale factors impact area and volume can save you time on the test.

**17. B.** Make a sketch.

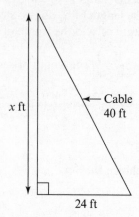

The building, the cable, and the ground form a right triangle. From the sketch, the length of the cable, 40 feet, is the length of the hypotenuse of a right triangle that has legs of 24 feet and $x$ feet. Use the Pythagorean theorem to find the missing leg, $x$.

**Method 1.** $c = 40$ ft, $a = 24$ ft, and $b = x$

Omitting the units, substitute into the Pythagorean theorem and solve for $x$.

$$a^2 + b^2 = c^2$$
$$(24)^2 + x^2 = (40)^2$$
$$576 + x^2 = 1{,}600$$
$$x^2 = 1{,}600 - 576$$
$$x^2 = 1{,}024$$
$$x = \sqrt{1{,}024}$$
$$x = 32$$

The cable reaches 32 feet up the wall, choice B.

*Tip:* The number −32 is also a solution, but it is rejected because length is nonnegative.

**Method 2.** The Pythagorean triple (3, 4, 5) and its multiples (6, 8, 10), (9, 12, 15), ..., (24, 32, 40), and so on, satisfy the Pythagorean theorem. The length of the hypotenuse is 40 and one of the legs has length of 24. Therefore, you know that the length of the third leg of the right triangle must be 32. Thus, $x = 32$ feet, choice B.

**18. D.** Eliminate choice C because this is not a method for proving congruence. Looking at the figure, you have $\angle ACB \cong \angle DCE$ because they are vertical angles. You know that $\overline{AC} \cong \overline{DC}$ because $\overline{BE}$ bisects $\overline{AD}$. You are given that $\angle A \cong \angle D$. Thus, you have two angles and the included side of triangle $ABC$ congruent to two angles and the included side of triangle $DEC$. Therefore, ASA, choice D, is the correct response.

**19. D.** The formula for the surface area of a sphere is $S.A. = 4\pi r^2$. The formula for the volume, $V$, of a sphere is $\frac{4}{3}\pi r^3$. To find the volume of the sphere, do two steps. First, find the radius of the sphere using the formula for surface area. Next, use the radius to find the volume.

*Step 1.* $S.A. = 4\pi r^2 = 144\pi$ cm$^2$ implies $r^2 = 36$ cm$^2$. Thus, $r = 6$ cm.

*Step 2.* $V = \frac{4}{3}\pi r^3 = \frac{4}{3}\pi (6 \text{ cm})^3 = \frac{4}{3}\pi \left(216 \text{ cm}^3\right) = 288\pi \text{cm}^3$, choice D.

*Tip:* Be sure to memorize the basic geometry formulas for area and volume before taking the test.

**20.** **4** Use logical reasoning to reach the solution. The machines are identical, so if two machines can do the job in 10 days, then it should take twice as long for one machine to do the same job. So one machine can do the job in 20 days. If five such machines do the job together, they should take $\frac{1}{5}$ as long as it takes for one machine. Therefore, five machines can do the same job in $\frac{1}{5}(20 \text{ days}) = 4$ days.

**21.** **B.** Recall that distance = (rate)(time). The key idea in problems involving the distance formula is that a given distance is determined by a uniform rate and the time traveled at that rate. For the situation in this problem, the two vehicles will travel the same amount of time. To determine the time at which the two vehicles will be 325 miles apart, do two steps. First, Let $t$ be the time traveled by the two vehicles. Write an equation and solve for $t$. Next, determine the time of day by adding the time traveled to the time of departure.

*Step 1.* Let $t$ = the time (in hours) it will take for the two vehicles to be 325 miles apart.

Distance traveled by vehicle traveling north = (rate)(time) = $\left(70\frac{\text{miles}}{\text{hr}}\right)(t)$

Distance traveled by vehicle traveling south = (rate)(time) = $\left(60\frac{\text{miles}}{\text{hr}}\right)(t)$

The two vehicles are traveling in opposite directions, so the total distance traveled is

$$70\frac{\text{miles}}{\text{hr}}t + 60\frac{\text{miles}}{\text{hr}}t = 325 \text{ miles}$$

Solve for $t$ (omitting the units for convenience).

$$70t + 60t = 325$$
$$130t = 325$$
$$t = 2.5$$

The time it will take for the two vehicles to be 325 miles apart is 2.5 hours or 2 hours 30 minutes.

*Step 2.* The clock time is 10:45 a.m. + 2 hours 30 minutes = 1:15 p.m., choice B.

**22.** **12** The greatest length for each side of the square plots is the greatest common factor of 24 and 36. Because $24 = 2 \cdot 2 \cdot 2 \cdot 3$ and $36 = 2 \cdot 2 \cdot 3 \cdot 3$, the gcf $(24, 36) = 2 \cdot 2 \cdot 3 = 12$. Therefore, the greatest length for each side of the square plots is 12 feet.

**23.** **B.** The range of a function is the set of possible second components of the ordered pairs that compose the function. From the graph, the values of $y$ are less than or equal to 2. Thus, choice B is the correct response.

**24.** **A, C, D.** If $x - r$ is a factor of $P(x)$, then the number $r$ is a zero of $P(x)$. By inspection, choices A and D have the desired zeros plus an additional zero of 0. Choice C also has the desired zeros because the factor $(2x - 1)$ would yield a zero of $\frac{1}{2}$. Select choices A, C, and D. Eliminate choice B because this function does not have the desired zeros.

**25. D.** Let $x$ = the number of pounds of the candy priced at $5.00 per pound needed. Then $90 - x$ = the number of pounds of the candy priced at $7.50 per pound needed. Make a table to organize the information given.

| When | Price per Pound | Number of Pounds | Value |
|---|---|---|---|
| Before mixed | $5.00 | $x$ | $5.00x$ |
| | $7.50 | $90 - x$ | $7.50(90 - x)$ |
| After mixed | $6.00 | 90 | $6.00(90)$ |

The value of the candy before it is mixed should equal the value after it is mixed. Using the information in the table, write an equation that represents the facts given (omitting "pounds" and "per pound" because these units cancel each other).

$$\$5.00x + \$7.50(90 - x) = \$6.00(90)$$

Solve the equation, omitting the units for convenience.

$$5.00x + 7.50(90 - x) = 6.00(90)$$
$$5.00x + 675 - 7.50x = 540$$
$$-2.50x = -135$$
$$x = 54$$

The owner should use 54 pounds of the $5.00 candy, choice D.

*Tip:* Use logical reasoning when you are problem solving. If the owner used half of each type of candy, then the price should be the average of $5.00 and $7.50, which is $6.25. So, you know that to bring the price down to $6.00 per pound will require more than 45 pounds (half) of the lower-priced candy. Therefore, eliminate choices A and B at the start.

**26. C.** $\angle DAB \cong \angle DAC$; therefore, $\overline{AD}$ bisects $\angle A$. Recall that the angle bisector of an angle of a triangle divides the opposite side in the ratio of the sides that form the angle bisected. Thus, $\dfrac{BD}{DC} = \dfrac{AB}{AC}$. Substitute the values given into this proportion and solve for $AC$.

$$\frac{BD}{DC} = \frac{AB}{AC}$$
$$\frac{3 \text{ cm}}{2 \text{ cm}} = \frac{12 \text{ cm}}{AC}$$
$$AC = \frac{(2)(12 \text{ cm})}{3}$$
$$AC = 8 \text{ cm, choice C}$$

**27. D.** The 85th percentile is a value at or below which 85 percent of the data fall. Therefore, the best interpretation of Candi's score is that she did as well or better than 85% of the students who took the exam, choice D.

**28. C.** This problem is best analyzed as a "work problem." The key idea in a work problem is that the rate at which work is done equals the amount of work accomplished divided by the amount of time worked: $\text{rate} = \dfrac{\text{amount of work done}}{\text{time worked}}$. For the situation in this problem, the work to be done is to fill the tank. However, only the input valve works to fill the tank. The output valve works counter to the input valve because it works to empty the tank. Let $t$ = the time (in hours) it will take to fill the tank with both valves open.

To find $t$, do two steps. First, determine the rate, $R$, at which the tank can be filled when the input valve is open and the outlet valve is closed, and the rate, $r$, at which the tank can be emptied when the input valve is closed and the outlet valve is open. Next, write an equation and solve for $t$.

*Step 1.* The rate for filling the tank is $R = \dfrac{1 \text{ full tank}}{6 \text{ hr}} = \dfrac{1}{6}$ tank per hr. The rate for emptying the tank is

$r = \dfrac{1 \text{ full tank}}{10 \text{ hr}} = \dfrac{1}{10}$ tank per hr.

*Step 2.* $\left(\dfrac{1}{6} \text{ tank per hr}\right)(t) - \left(\dfrac{1}{10} \text{ tank per hr}\right)(t) = 1$ full tank

Omit the units and solve for $t$.

$$\left(\frac{1}{6}\right)(t) - \left(\frac{1}{10}\right)(t) = 1$$

$$30\left(\frac{1}{6}\right)(t) - 30\left(\frac{1}{10}\right)(t) = 30(1)$$

$$5t - 3t = 30$$

$$2t = 30$$

$$t = 15$$

With both valves open, it will take 15 hours to fill the tank, choice C.

29. **A.** Subtracting 5 from $x$ will result in a horizontal shift of 5 units to the right. Adding 2 to $f(x)$ will result in a vertical shift of 2 units up. Thus, the graph of $g(x) = (x-5)^3 + 2$ is the same as the graph of $f(x) = x^3$ shifted right by 5 units and up by 2 units, choice A.

*Tip:* If you are unsure about the shifts, graph the two functions on the ETS graphing calculator to check.

30. **B.** The problem asks: Find the probability that the house next door will be sold given that the model home has already been sold. This probability is a conditional probability. If $A$ is the event that the model home will be sold and $B$ is the event that the house next door will be sold, then find $P(B \mid A) = \dfrac{P(A \cap B)}{P(A)}$. Looking at the formula, you see that you are given $P(A) = 0.50$, but you are not given $P(A \cap B)$, which is the probability that both houses are sold. The problem states "the probability that at least one of the two houses will be sold is 0.80." The probability that at least one of the two houses will be sold is $P(A \cup B)$. Recall that $P(A \cup B) = P(A) + P(B) - P(A \cap B)$. Thus, given $P(A) = 0.50$, $P(B) = 0.40$, and $P(A \cup B) = 0.80$, you can determine $P(A \cap B)$. To find $P(B \mid A)$, do two steps. First, determine $P(A \cap B)$. Next, use the information obtained and information given in the problem to calculate $P(B \mid A)$.

*Step 1.* $P(A \cup B) = P(A) + P(B) - P(A \cap B)$ implies $0.80 = 0.50 + 0.40 - P(A \cap B)$. Thus, $P(A \cap B) = 0.90 - 0.80 = 0.10$.

*Step 2.* $P(B \mid A) = \dfrac{P(A \cap B)}{P(A)} = \dfrac{0.10}{0.50} = 0.20 = 20\%$, choice B.

31. **B.** The capacity of the box is its volume, which equals $(24 \text{ in})(16 \text{ in})(8 \text{ in})$. The thickness of a single U.S. \$20 bill is $\dfrac{0.43 \text{ in}}{100} = 0.0043$ in, so the dimensions of a U.S. \$20 bill are $6.14 \times 2.61 \times 0.0043$ inches. Thus, the approximate total value of money in the first-prize box of \$20 bills is

$$\frac{(24 \text{ in})(16 \text{ in})(8 \text{ in})}{(6.14 \text{ in})(2.61 \text{ in})(0.0043 \text{ in})} \cdot \$20 = \frac{3{,}072 \text{ in}^3}{0.06890922 \text{ in}^3} \cdot \$20 = \$891{,}607.83 \approx \$890{,}000, \text{ choice B.}$$

**32.** **A.** Find the rate, compounded annually, that will double an investment of $10,000 in 20 years. That is, find the rate $r$, compounded annually, that will yield a value of $20,000 for $P$ in 20 years.

Therefore, (omitting the units) find $r$, so that $10,000(1 + r)^{20} = 20,000$.

Work this problem by checking the answer choices.

Checking A: $10,000(1 + 0.035)^{20} = 19,897.8886\ldots$ or approximately 20,000, indicating choice A is the correct response.

In a test situation, you should go on to the next question since you have obtained the correct answer. You would not have to check the other answer choices. For your information, choice B yields approximately 29,000; choice C yields approximately 67,000; and choice D yields approximately $1.6 \times 10^{10}$.

*Tip:* When feasible, working backward by checking answer choices is a clever strategy for multiple-choice questions on the test.

**33.** **D.** First, rewrite $4x + 3y = -5$ as $4x + 3y + 5 = 0$, and then apply the formula using the point $(-3, 7)$.
$$d = \frac{|Ax_1 + By_1 + C|}{\sqrt{A^2 + B^2}} = \frac{|4(-3) + 3(7) + 5|}{\sqrt{4^2 + 3^2}} = \frac{|-12 + 21 + 5|}{\sqrt{25}} = \frac{|14|}{5} = \frac{14}{5} \text{ or } 2.8, \text{ choice D.}$$

**34.** **A.** From the table, you can determine that of the 200 students, 5 are male former students. Thus, $P$(male former student) $= \dfrac{5}{200} = \dfrac{1}{40}$, choice A.

**35.** **D.** Recall that if two chords intersect within a circle, the product of the lengths of the segments of one chord equals the product of the lengths of the segments of the other. Therefore, $(AE)(EB) = (CE)(ED)$. Let $x = AE$. Then $2x = EB$. To determine $AB$, do two steps. First, use $(AE)(EB) = (CE)(ED)$ to determine $AE$ and $EB$. Next, add $AE$ and $EB$.

*Step 1.* Solve for $x$ and $2x$.

$$
\begin{aligned}
(x)(2x) &= (2 \text{ cm})(6 \text{ cm}) \\
2x^2 &= 12 \text{ cm}^2 \\
x^2 &= 6 \text{ cm}^2 \\
x &= \sqrt{6} \text{ cm} \\
2x &= 2\sqrt{6} \text{ cm}
\end{aligned}
$$

Thus, $AE = \sqrt{6}$ cm and $EB = 2\sqrt{6}$ cm.

*Step 2:* The length of chord $\overline{AB}$ is $\sqrt{6}$ cm $+ 2\sqrt{6}$ cm $= 3\sqrt{6}$ cm, choice D.

*Tip:* Make sure you answer the question asked.

**36.** **C.** Check the answer choices.

Check A: The solution of $x = \sqrt[3]{64}$ is 4. Eliminate choice A.

Check B: The solution of $x = \sqrt{16}$ is 4. Eliminate choice B. *Tip:* The square root symbol $\left(\sqrt{\phantom{x}}\right)$ always returns the principal square root, which is nonnegative.

Check C: The solution of $x^2 = 16$ is $x = \sqrt{16} = 4$ or $x = -\sqrt{16} = -4$. Choice C is the correct response.

In a test situation, you should move on to the next question. For your information, the check for choice D is shown below.

Check D: The solution of $x^3 = 64$ is $x = \sqrt[3]{64} = 4$.

**37. B.** Use the fundamental counting principle to determine the number of possible telephone numbers for each prefix. After the prefix, there are four slots to fill. For each slot, 10 digits are available, which means the number of possible telephone numbers for each prefix is $10 \cdot 10 \cdot 10 \cdot 10 = 10^4$. By the addition principle, the total number of possible telephone numbers if all four prefixes are used is $10^4 + 10^4 + 10^4 + 10^4 = 4(10^4)$, choice **B**.

**38. A.** Evaluate the function.

$$f(-2) = -16(-2)^{-4} = -16\frac{1}{(-2)^4} = \frac{-16}{16} = -1, \text{ choice A}$$

**39. B.** To find the probability the number on the tile is prime, do two steps. First, count how many numbers between 1 and 25 are prime. Then, divide this answer by 25 and simplify, if possible.

*Step 1.* The primes between 1 and 25 are 2, 3, 5, 7, 11, 13, 17, 19, and 23, which is a total of 9 primes. (Remember, the number 1 is neither prime nor composite.)

*Step 2.* The probability is $\frac{9}{25}$, choice **B**.

**40. 7** First, rearrange the terms so that only $x$ terms are on the left side of the equation. Next, complete the square for the $x$ terms. Then take the square root of both sides of the equation. Remember, $\sqrt{(x)^2} = |x|$.

$$x^2 - 13 = 12x$$
$$x^2 - 12x = 13$$
$$x^2 - 12x + 36 = 13 + 36$$
$$(x-6)^2 = 49$$
$$|x-6| = 7$$

**41. C.** By the remainder theorem, $p(1) = -3$. Substitute into $p(x)$ and solve for $k$.

$$p(x) = (2x - 3)(x + k)$$
$$p(1) = (2(1) - 3)((1) + k)$$
$$-3 = (-1)(1 + k)$$
$$-3 = -1 - k$$
$$k = 2, \text{ choice C}$$

**42. B.** If the data were represented using a histogram, the mean would lie to the left of both the median and the mode on the horizontal axis, indicating that the data are skewed, with a tail on the left. Thus, the distribution is negatively skewed, choice **B**.

**43. D.** Interchange $x$ and $y$ in $y = x^5 - 3$, and then solve for $y$.

$$x = y^5 - 3$$
$$x + 3 = y^5$$
$$\sqrt[5]{x+3} = y$$
$$y = \sqrt[5]{x+3}, \text{ choice D}$$

**44. D.** Check each statement against the behavior of the graph of the function. Choice A is incorrect because the slope of the tangent line is decreasing between 0 and 0.5, not constant. Choice B is incorrect because the slope of the tangent line is decreasing between 0.5 and 1.5. Choice C is incorrect because the slope of the tangent line is increasing between 2 and 3. Choice D is correct because the slope of the tangent line is increasing between 3 and 3.5.

**45.** **C.** Rewrite $2x^2 - x < 1$ as $2x^2 - x - 1 < 0$.

Factor the left side of the inequality to obtain $(2x + 1)(x - 1) < 0$. Now determine when the product $(2x + 1)$ $(x - 1)$ is negative. First, find the values for $x$ at which the factors change sign; that is, find the zero for each factor.

Set each factor equal to 0 and solve for $x$.

$2x + 1 = 0$ yields $x = -\dfrac{1}{2}$ and $x - 1 = 0$ yields $x = 1$.

The two values $-\dfrac{1}{2}$ and 1 divide the number line into three intervals: $\left(-\infty, -\dfrac{1}{2}\right)$, $\left(-\dfrac{1}{2}, 1\right)$, and $(1, \infty)$.

Next, determine in which interval(s) the product of the two factors is negative.

**Method 1.** Make an organized table to determine the sign of $(2x + 1)(x - 1)$ for each of these intervals.

| Interval | Sign of $(2x + 1)$ | Sign of $(x - 1)$ | Sign of $(2x + 1)(x - 1)$ |
|---|---|---|---|
| $\left(-\infty, -\dfrac{1}{2}\right)$ | negative | negative | positive |
| $\left(-\dfrac{1}{2}, 1\right)$ | positive | negative | negative |
| $(1, \infty)$ | positive | positive | positive |

Thus, $(2x + 1)(x - 1)$ is negative only in the interval $\left(-\dfrac{1}{2}, 1\right)$, choice C.

**Method 2.** Use the ETS graphing calculator to graph $y = 2x^2 - x - 1$.

The graph intersects the $x$-axis at $x = -\dfrac{1}{2}$ and $x = 1$. You can see that the graph is below the $x$-axis (and, therefore, negative) between these two points and above the $x$-axis otherwise. Thus, $2x^2 - x - 1$ is negative only in the interval $\left(-\dfrac{1}{2}, 1\right)$, choice C.

**46.** **B.** By the multiplication rule, $P(A \cap B) = P(A)P(B|A)$. The probability that a yellow marble is drawn on the first draw is

$$P(\text{yellow on first draw}) = \frac{\text{Number of yellow marbles in bag}}{\text{Total number of marbles}} = \frac{3}{25}$$

After this event occurs, since the yellow marble drawn first is not put back in the bag, the probability that a yellow marble will be drawn on the second draw is

$$P(\text{yellow on second draw given first draw is yellow}) = \frac{2}{24} = \frac{1}{12}$$

Hence, the probability that both marbles will be yellow when two marbles are randomly drawn from the bag without replacement is

$$\frac{3}{25} \cdot \frac{1}{12} = \frac{1}{100}, \text{ choice B}$$

**47. B.** Make a sketch. Construct a perpendicular segment from $D$ to $\overline{AB}$. Label the point of intersection $F$.

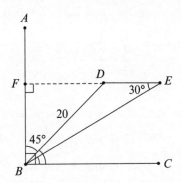

Angle $FBD$ is a 45° angle because its measure is $90° - m\angle DBC = 90° - 45° = 45°$. Given that $\overline{DE} \parallel \overline{BC}$, $\angle FEB$ is congruent to $\angle EBC$ because they are alternate interior angles of parallel lines. Angle $FEB$ is a 30° angle because it is congruent to angle $\angle EBC$ that has a measure of 30°.

The perimeter of triangle $DBE$ is $DB + BE + ED = 20 + BE + ED$. You need $BE + ED$. First, find $BF$ and $DF$, the lengths of the legs of the 45°-45°-90° right triangle $DFB$, which has hypotenuse of length 20. Use $BF$ to find $BE$, which is the length of the hypotenuse of the 30°-60°-90° right triangle $EFB$. Next, use $BF$ to find $EF$, which is the length of the side opposite the 60° angle in the 30°-60°-90° right triangle $EFB$. Use $EF$ and $DF$ to find $ED$, which is $EF - DF$. Then, find the perimeter.

*Step 1.* Find $BF$ and $DF$.

The lengths of the sides of a 45°-45°-90° right triangle are in the ratio $\dfrac{1}{\sqrt{2}} : \dfrac{1}{\sqrt{2}} : 1$. Hence,

$$BF = DF = 20\left(\frac{1}{\sqrt{2}}\right) = \frac{20}{\sqrt{2}} = 10\sqrt{2}.$$

*Step 2.* Use $BF$ to find $BE$.

In the 30°-60°-90° right triangle $EFB$, $BF$ is the side opposite the 30° angle and $BE$ is the hypotenuse. The lengths of the sides of a 30°-60°-90° right triangle are in the ratio $1 : \sqrt{3} : 2$. So
$BE = (BF)(2) = \left(10\sqrt{2}\right)(2) = 20\sqrt{2}.$

*Step 3.* Use $BF$ to find $EF$.

In the 30°-60°-90° right triangle $EFB$, $EF$ is the length of the side opposite the 60° angle and $BF$ is the length of the other leg. The lengths of the sides of a 30°-60°-90° right triangle are in the ratio $1 : \sqrt{3} : 2$. So
$EF = (BF)\left(\sqrt{3}\right) = \left(10\sqrt{2}\right)\left(\sqrt{3}\right) = 10\sqrt{6}.$

*Step 4.* Use $EF$ and $DF$ to find $ED$.

$$ED = EF - DF = 10\sqrt{6} - 10\sqrt{2}$$

*Step 5.* Find the perimeter.

Perimeter $= 20 + BE + ED = 20 + 20\sqrt{2} + 10\sqrt{6} - 10\sqrt{2} = 20 + 10\sqrt{2} + 10\sqrt{6} = 10\left(2 + \sqrt{2} + \sqrt{6}\right)$, choice B

*Tip:* When a figure has angles of 30° or 45°, consider constructions that will result in 30°-60°-90° or 45°-45°-90° right triangles.

The explanation for this question might seem lengthy (and, perhaps, complicated) to you. Actually, after you have created the two special right triangles, the computations are straightforward and can be done without a calculator.

**48.** **900** All of the percentages in the circle graph have the same base (3,000 workers), so work with the percents rather than the actual number of workers. The percent of workers who have less than $10,000 in savings and investments is 63%. The percent of workers who have $100,000 or more in savings and investments is 5% + 2% = 7%.

To answer the question, determine what percent 63% is of 7%.

$$\frac{63\%}{7\%} = 9 = 900\%$$

**49.** **A, D.** There are eight possibilities for $x$, $y$, and $z$. Written as ordered triples, the eight possibilities are $(0, 0, 0)$, which yields $a = 0$; $(0, 0, 1)$, which yields $a = \frac{1}{4^3} = \frac{1}{64}$; $(0, 1, 0)$, which yields $a = \frac{1}{4^2} = \frac{1}{16}$; $(0, 1, 1)$, which yields $a = \frac{1}{4^2} + \frac{1}{4^3} = \frac{1}{16} + \frac{1}{64} = \frac{5}{64}$ (select choice A); $(1, 0, 0)$, which yields $a = \frac{1}{4}$; $(1, 0, 1)$, which yields $a = \frac{1}{4} + \frac{1}{4^3} = \frac{1}{4} + \frac{1}{64} = \frac{17}{64}$; $(1, 1, 0)$, which yields $a = \frac{1}{4} + \frac{1}{4^2} = \frac{1}{4} + \frac{1}{16} = \frac{5}{16}$ (select choice D); and $(1, 1, 1)$, which yields $a = \frac{1}{4} + \frac{1}{4^2} + \frac{1}{4^3} = \frac{1}{4} + \frac{1}{16} + \frac{1}{64} = \frac{21}{64}$. The fractions in choices B and C are not possible values of $a$. Only the fractions in choices A and D are possible values of $a$.

**50.** **A.** The average is $\frac{x + y + z}{3}$. You have three variables and only two equations, so finding specific values for $x$, $y$, and $z$ is problematic. Notice that if you can determine the sum $x + y + z$, you can answer the question. Observe that corresponding coefficients in the two equations add to 10. Add the two equations and solve for $(x + y + z)$.

$$3x + 2y + 6z = 50$$
$$7x + 8y + 4z = 70$$
$$10x + 10y + 10z = 120$$
$$10(x + y + z) = 120$$
$$(x + y + z) = 12$$

Thus, the average is $\frac{12}{3} = 4$, choice A.

**51.** **A, C, D.** $\sqrt{pq} = 14$ implies $pq = 196$. The positive factors of 196 are 1, 2, 4, 7, 14, 28, 49, 98, and 196. The possible two-factor combinations for $p$ and $q$ are 1 and 196, 2 and 98, 4 and 49, 7 and 28, and 14 and 14. The possible sums for these two-factor combinations are 197 (select choice D), 100 (select choice C), 53, 35 (select choice A), and 28. Choice B is not a possible sum.

**52.** **1,260** The measure of an exterior angle of the regular polygon is 180° − 140° = 40°. The sum of the measures of the exterior angles of a polygon is 360°, no matter how many sides the polygon has. Because the polygon is a regular polygon, its number of sides is $\frac{360°}{40°} = 9$. The polygon has 9 sides and 9 congruent interior angles. The sum of the measures of the interior angles is $(9)(140°) = 1,260°$.

**53.** **B.** Show the sample space in a table.

| | | Box 1 | | | |
|---|---|---|---|---|---|
| | | 1 | 2 | 3 | 4 |
| **Box 2** | 1 | 1 | 2 | 3 | 4 |
| | 2 | 2 | 4 | 6 | 8 |
| | 3 | 3 | 6 | 9 | 12 |
| | 4 | 4 | 8 | 12 | 16 |

The possible products and their frequencies are 1 (1 time), 2 (2 times), 3 (2 times), 4 (3 times), 6 (2 times), 8 (2 times), 9 (1 time), 12 (2 times), and 16 (1 time). The product 4 (choice B) occurs three times, and, thus, is most likely to occur.

**54. A.** The function $-f(x)$ reflects $f(x)$ over the $x$-axis, and the function $f(x-5)$ is a horizontal shift of 5 units to the right. Applying both of these transformations to $f$ defined by $f(x) = 3^x$ results in the new function $g$ defined by $g(x) = -3^{x-5}$, choice A.

**55. A, B, C.** Do not assume that the jogger went in a straight line in one direction. Let $x$ be the jogger's distance from camp. Make a sketch. Show the camp and river as 3 miles apart. Construct a circle at the river with radius 4 miles.

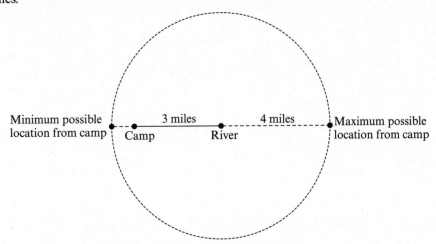

From the sketch, you can determine that $1 \le x \le 7$. Select choices A, B, and C because each falls in this interval. Eliminate choice D because it is too far.

# Appendix A

# Simplifying Radicals

A radical is simplified when

- the radicand contains no variable factor raised to a power equal to or greater than the index of the radical;
- the radicand contains no constant factor that can be expressed as a power equal to or greater than the index of the radical;
- the radicand contains no fractions;
- no fractions contain radicals in the denominator;
- and the index of the radical is reduced to its lowest value.

Here are examples.

$$\sqrt[3]{24a^5b^6} = \left(\sqrt[3]{8a^3b^6}\right)\left(\sqrt[3]{3a^2}\right) = 2ab^2\left(\sqrt[3]{3a^2}\right) \text{ is simplified.}$$

$$\sqrt{12} = \left(\sqrt{4}\right)\left(\sqrt{3}\right) = 2\left(\sqrt{3}\right) \text{ is simplified.}$$

$$\frac{\sqrt{54}}{\sqrt{6}} = \sqrt{9} = 3 \text{ is simplified.}$$

$$\frac{1}{\sqrt{2}} = \left(\frac{1}{\sqrt{2}}\right)\left(\frac{\sqrt{2}}{\sqrt{2}}\right) = \frac{\sqrt{2}}{2} \text{ is simplified.}$$

$$\sqrt[4]{5^2} = \sqrt{5} \text{ is simplified.}$$

Because square roots occur so frequently, the remainder of the examples will use only square root radicals.

Radicals that have the same index and the same radicand are like radicals. To add or subtract like radicals, combine their coefficients and write the result as the coefficient of the common radical factor. Indicate the sum or difference of unlike radicals.

$$5\sqrt{3} + 2\sqrt{3} = 7\sqrt{3}$$

You may have to simplify the radical expressions before combining them.

$$5\sqrt{3} + \sqrt{12} = 5\sqrt{3} + \sqrt{4 \cdot 3} = 5\sqrt{3} + 2\sqrt{3} = 7\sqrt{3}$$

To multiply radicals that have the same index, multiply their coefficients to find the coefficient of the product. Multiply the radicands to find the radicand of the product. Simplify the results.

$$5\sqrt{3} \cdot 2\sqrt{3} = 10 \cdot 3 = 30$$

For a sum or difference, treat the factors as you would binomials, being sure to simplify radicals after you multiply.

$$\left(2\sqrt{3} + 5\sqrt{7}\right)\left(\sqrt{3} - 3\sqrt{6}\right) = 2\sqrt{9} - 6\sqrt{18} + 5\sqrt{21} - 15\sqrt{42} =$$

$$2(3) - 6\sqrt{9 \cdot 2} + 5\sqrt{21} - 15\sqrt{42} = 6 - 18\sqrt{2} + 5\sqrt{21} - 15\sqrt{42}$$

$$\left(1 - \sqrt{3}\right)\left(1 + \sqrt{3}\right) = 1 + \sqrt{3} - \sqrt{3} - 3 = 1 - 3 = -2$$

The technique of rationalizing is used to remove radicals from the denominator (or numerator) of a fraction. For square root radicals, if the denominator (numerator) contains a single term, multiply the numerator and denominator by the smallest radical that will produce a perfect square in the denominator (numerator). Here is an example.

$$\frac{5}{\sqrt{3}} = \frac{5}{\sqrt{3}} \cdot \frac{\sqrt{3}}{\sqrt{3}} = \frac{5\sqrt{3}}{3}$$

If the denominator (numerator) contains a sum or difference of two terms involving square roots, multiply the numerator and denominator by the conjugate, which is obtained by changing the sign between the two terms. This action causes the middle terms to sum to 0 when you multiply. Here is an example.

$$\frac{5}{1-\sqrt{3}} = \frac{5}{\left(1-\sqrt{3}\right)}\frac{\left(1+\sqrt{3}\right)}{\left(1+\sqrt{3}\right)} = \frac{5\left(1+\sqrt{3}\right)}{1-3} = -\frac{5+5\sqrt{3}}{2}$$

# Appendix B

# Long Division of Polynomials and Synthetic Division

Here is an example of long division of polynomials.

$$\frac{4x^3 + 8x - 6x^2 + 1}{2x - 1} =$$

| | |
|---|---|
| $2x-1\overline{)4x^3 - 6x^2 + 8x + 1}$ | 1. Arrange the terms of both the dividend and divisor in descending powers of the variable $x$. |
| $\begin{array}{r} 2x^2 \phantom{ - 6x^2 + 8x + 1} \\ 2x-1\overline{)4x^3 - 6x^2 + 8x + 1} \end{array}$ | 2. Divide the first term of the dividend by the first term of the divisor, and write the answer as the first term of the quotient. |
| $\begin{array}{r} 2x^2 \phantom{ - 6x^2 + 8x + 1} \\ 2x-1\overline{)4x^3 - 6x^2 + 8x + 1} \\ 4x^3 - 2x^2 \phantom{ + 8x + 1} \end{array}$ | 3. Multiply $2x^2$ by $2x - 1$ and enter the product under the dividend. |
| $\begin{array}{r} 2x^2 \phantom{ - 6x^2 + 8x + 1} \\ 2x-1\overline{)4x^3 - 6x^2 + 8x + 1} \\ \underline{4x^3 - 2x^2} \phantom{ + 8x + 1} \\ -4x^2 \phantom{ + 8x + 1} \end{array}$ | 4. Subtract $4x^3 - 2x^2$ from the dividend, being sure to mentally change the signs of both terms. |
| $\begin{array}{r} 2x^2 - 2x \phantom{+ 1} \\ 2x-1\overline{)4x^3 - 6x^2 + 8x + 1} \\ \underline{4x^3 - 2x^2} \phantom{ + 8x + 1} \\ -4x^2 + 8x \phantom{+ 1} \\ -4x^2 + 2x \phantom{+ 1} \\ 6x \phantom{+ 1} \end{array}$ | 5. Bring down $8x$, the next term of the dividend, and repeat steps 2–4. |
| $\begin{array}{r} 2x^2 - 2x + 3 \\ 2x-1\overline{)4x^3 - 6x^2 + 8x + 1} \\ \underline{4x^3 - 2x^2} \phantom{ + 8x + 1} \\ -4x^2 + 8x \phantom{+ 1} \\ \underline{-4x^2 + 2x} \phantom{+ 1} \\ 6x + 1 \\ \underline{6x - 3} \\ 4 \end{array}$ | 6. Bring down 1, the last term of the dividend, and repeat steps 2–4. |
| $\dfrac{4x^3 + 8x - 6x^2 + 1}{2x - 1} = 2x^2 - 2x + 3 + \dfrac{4}{2x - 1}$ | 7. Write the answer as quotient $+ \dfrac{\text{remainder}}{\text{divisor}}$. |

Here is a completed example in which the divisor has the form $x - r$.

$$\frac{2x^3 + x^2 - 13x + 6}{x - 4} = \quad x - 4 \overline{) \begin{array}{l} 2x^2 + 9x + 23 \\ 2x^3 + x^2 - 13x + 6 \end{array}}$$

$$\begin{array}{r} \underline{2x^3 - 8x^2} \\ 9x^2 - 13x \\ \underline{9x^2 - 36x} \\ 23x + 6 \\ \underline{23x - 92} \\ 98 \end{array}$$

Thus, $\dfrac{2x^3 + x^2 - 13x + 6}{x - 4} = 2x^2 + 9x + 23 + \dfrac{98}{x - 4}$.

You can shorten the division process when the divisor has the form $x - r$ by using synthetic division.

Synthetic division is a shortcut method for dividing a polynomial by a binomial, $x - r$. You simplify the process by working only with $r$ and the coefficients of the polynomial—being careful to use 0 as a coefficient for missing powers of $x$. Here is an example of the previous problem using synthetic division steps to solve.

$$\frac{2x^3 + x^2 - 13x + 6}{x - 4} =$$

| | |
|---|---|
| $2x^3 + x^2 - 13x + 6$ | 1. Write the polynomial in descending powers of $x$, using a coefficient of 0 when a power of $x$ is missing, if needed. |
| 2  1  −13  6 | 2. Write only the coefficients as shown. |
| 4 \|2  1  −13  6 | 3. Write $r = 4$ as shown. |
| 4 \|2  1  −13  6 <br><br> 2 | 4. Bring down the first coefficient. |
| 4 \|2  1  −13  6 <br>    8 <br> 2  9 | 5. Multiply the first coefficient by $r = 4$, write the product under the second coefficient, and then add. |
| 4 \|2  1  −13  6 <br>    8  36 <br> 2  9  23 | 6. Multiply the sum by $r = 4$, write the product under the third coefficient, and then add. |
| 4 \|2  1  −13  6 <br>    8  36  92 <br> 2  9  23  98 | 7. Repeat step 6 until you use up all the coefficients in the polynomial. |
| 4 \|2  1  −13  6 <br>    8  36  92 <br> 2  9  23  98 | 8. Separate the final sum, which is the remainder, as shown. |
| $\dfrac{2x^3 + x^2 - 13x + 6}{x - 4} = 2x^2 + 9x + 23 + \dfrac{98}{x - 4}$ | 9. Write the quotient and remainder using the coefficients. |

# Common Formulas

## Temperature

$F$ (degrees Fahrenheit) $= \dfrac{9}{5}C + 32$; $C$ (degrees Celsius) $= \dfrac{5}{9}(F - 32)$

## Percentage

$P = RB$, where $P$ = percentage, $R$ = rate, and $B$ = base

## Business Formulas

### Simple Interest

$I = Prt$, where $I$ = simple interest accumulated, $P$ = principal invested or present value of a future amount $S$, $r$ = annual simple interest rate, and $t$ = time in years

$S = P(1 + rt)$ = maturity value of $P$

### Compound Interest

$S = P\left(1 + \dfrac{r}{m}\right)^{mt}$, where $S$ = maturity value, or the compound amount of $P$, $P$ = original principal or the present

value of $S$, $r$ = stated annual percentage rate, $m$ = number of compoundings per year, and $t$ = time in years

$S - P$ = compound interest accumulated

### Ordinary Simple Annuity

$S = R\left[\dfrac{(1+i)^n - 1}{i}\right]$, where $S$ = amount of the annuity, $R$ = periodic payment, $r$ = stated annual percentage rate,

$m$ = number of payments (compoundings) per year, $i = \dfrac{r}{m}$ = interest rate per compounding period, and $n$ = total number of payments

$Rn$ = total of payments

$S - Rn$ = interest earned

### Amortization

$A = R\left[\dfrac{1-(1+i)^{-n}}{i}\right]$, where $A$ = amount financed, $R$ = periodic payment, $r$ = stated annual percentage rate,

$m$ = number of payments (compoundings) per year, $i = \dfrac{r}{m}$ = interest rate per compounding period, and $n$ = total number of payments

$Rn$ = total of payments

$Rn - A$ = interest paid

## Distance Formula

$d = rt$, where $d$ = distance traveled, $r$ = (uniform) rate of speed, and $t$ = time

## Basic Trigonometry Formulas

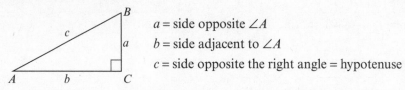

$a$ = side opposite $\angle A$

$b$ = side adjacent to $\angle A$

$c$ = side opposite the right angle = hypotenuse

The basic trigonometry formulas relative to $\angle A$ in right triangle $ABC$ are

$$\text{sine of } \angle A = \sin A = \frac{\text{side opposite}}{\text{hypotenuse}} = \frac{a}{c}$$

$$\text{cosine of } \angle A = \cos A = \frac{\text{side adjacent}}{\text{hypotenuse}} = \frac{b}{c}$$

$$\text{tangent of } \angle A = \tan A = \frac{\text{side opposite}}{\text{side adjacent}} = \frac{a}{b}$$

$$\text{cosecant of } \angle A = \csc A = \frac{\text{hypotenuse}}{\text{side opposite}} = \frac{c}{a}$$

$$\text{secant of } \angle A = \sec A = \frac{\text{hypotenuse}}{\text{side adjacent}} = \frac{c}{b}$$

$$\text{cotangent of } \angle A = \cot A = \frac{\text{side adjacent}}{\text{side opposite}} = \frac{b}{a}$$

## Formulas from Science

### Gas Laws

$$\frac{p_1 v_1}{T_1} = \frac{p_2 v_2}{T_2} \text{ (General)} \qquad \frac{v_1}{T_1} = \frac{v_2}{T_2} \text{ (Charles's Law)} \qquad \frac{p_1}{p_2} = \frac{v_2}{v_1} \text{ (Boyle's Law)}, \quad \text{where } v_1 = \text{volume at pressure } p_1$$

and temperature $T_1$, and $v_2$ = volume at pressure $p_2$ and temperature $T_2$

### Specific Gravity

$$\text{Specific gravity of substance} = \frac{\text{weight of given volume of substance}}{\text{weight of equal volume of water}}$$

### Lever

$$\frac{W_1}{W_2} = \frac{L_2}{L_1}, \text{ where } W_1 = \text{force at distance } L_1 \text{ from fulcrum, and } W_2 = \text{force at distance } L_2 \text{ from fulcrum}$$

### Pulley

$$\frac{R_1}{R_2} = \frac{d_2}{d_1}, \text{ where } R_1 = \text{revolutions per minute of pulley of diameter } d_1, \text{ and } R_2 = \text{revolutions per minute of pulley}$$

of diameter $d_2$

# Measurement Units and Conversions

| U.S. Customary Units | Conversion |
|---|---|
| **Length** | |
| Inch (in) | $1 \text{ in} = \dfrac{1}{12} \text{ ft}$ |
| Foot (ft) | $1 \text{ ft} = 12 \text{ in}$ <br> $1 \text{ ft} = \dfrac{1}{3} \text{ yd}$ |
| Yard (yd) | $1 \text{ yd} = 36 \text{ in}$ <br> $1 \text{ yd} = 3 \text{ ft}$ |
| Mile (mi) | $1 \text{ mi} = 5{,}280 \text{ ft}$ <br> $1 \text{ mi} = 1{,}760 \text{ yd}$ |
| **Weight** | |
| Pound (lb) | $1 \text{ lb} = 16 \text{ oz}$ |
| Ton (T) | $1 \text{ T} = 2{,}000 \text{ lb}$ |
| **Capacity** | |
| Fluid ounce (fl oz) | $1 \text{ fl oz} = \dfrac{1}{8} \text{ c}$ |
| Cup (c) | $1 \text{ c} = 8 \text{ fl oz}$ |
| Pint (pt) | $1 \text{ pt} = 2 \text{ c}$ |
| Quart (qt) | $1 \text{ qt} = 32 \text{ fl oz}$ <br> $1 \text{ qt} = 4 \text{ c}$ <br> $1 \text{ qt} = 2 \text{ pt}$ <br> $1 \text{ qt} = \dfrac{1}{4} \text{ gal}$ |
| Gallon (gal) | $1 \text{ gal} = 128 \text{ fl oz}$ <br> $1 \text{ gal} = 16 \text{ c}$ <br> $1 \text{ gal} = 8 \text{ pt}$ <br> $1 \text{ gal} = 4 \text{ qt}$ |

| Metric Units | Conversion |
|---|---|
| **Length** | |
| Millimeter (mm) | $1 \text{ mm} = 0.1 \text{ cm} = \dfrac{1}{10} \text{ cm}$ <br> $1 \text{ mm} = 0.001 \text{ m} = \dfrac{1}{1000} \text{ m}$ |
| Centimeter (cm) | $1 \text{ cm} = 10 \text{ mm}$ <br> $1 \text{ cm} = 0.01 \text{ m} = \dfrac{1}{100} \text{ m}$ |
| Meter (m) | $1 \text{ m} = 1000 \text{ mm}$ <br> $1 \text{ m} = 100 \text{ cm}$ <br> $1 \text{ m} = 0.001 \text{ km} = \dfrac{1}{1000} \text{ km}$ |
| Kilometer (km) | $1 \text{ km} = 1000 \text{ m}$ |

| Metric Units | Conversion |
|---|---|
| **Mass** | |
| Milligram (mg) | $1 \text{ mg} = 0.001 \text{ g} = \dfrac{1}{1000} \text{ g}$ |
| Gram (g) | $1 \text{ g} = 1000 \text{ mg}$ <br> $1 \text{ g} = 0.001 \text{ kg} = \dfrac{1}{1000} \text{ kg}$ |
| Kilogram (kg) | $1 \text{ kg} = 1000 \text{ g}$ |
| **Capacity** | |
| Milliliter (mL) | $1 \text{ mL} = 0.001 \text{ L} = \dfrac{1}{1000} \text{ L}$ |
| Liter (L) | $1 \text{ L} = 1000 \text{ mL}$ |

| Time | Conversion |
|---|---|
| Second (s) | $1 \text{ s} = \dfrac{1}{60} \text{ min}$ <br> $1 \text{ s} = \dfrac{1}{3,600} \text{ hr}$ |
| Minute (min) | $1 \text{ min} = 60 \text{ s}$ <br> $1 \text{ min} = \dfrac{1}{60} \text{ hr}$ |
| Hour (hr) | $1 \text{ hr} = 3,600 \text{ s}$ <br> $1 \text{ hr} = 60 \text{ min}$ <br> $1 \text{ hr} = \dfrac{1}{24} \text{ d}$ |
| Day (d) | $1 \text{ d} = 24 \text{ hr}$ |
| Week (wk) | $1 \text{ wk} = 7 \text{ d}$ |
| Year (yr) | $1 \text{ yr} = 365 \text{ d}$ <br> $1 \text{ yr} = 52 \text{ wk}$ |

## Approximate Equivalents

| English to Metric | Metric to English |
|---|---|
| 1 in = 2.54 cm (exactly) | $1 \text{ cm} \cong 0.3937 \text{ in}$ |
| $1 \text{ ft} \cong 30.48 \text{ cm}$ | $1 \text{ m} \cong 39.37 \text{ in}$ <br> $\cong 1.094 \text{ yd}$ |
| $1 \text{ yd} \cong 0.914 \text{ m}$ | $1 \text{ km} \cong 0.621 \text{ mi}$ |
| $1 \text{ mi} \cong 1.609 \text{ km}$ | |
| $1 \text{ oz} \cong 28.35 \text{ g}$ | $1 \text{ g} \cong 0.035 \text{ oz}$ |
| $1 \text{ lb} \cong 0.454 \text{ kg}$ | $1 \text{ kg} \cong 2.205 \text{ lb}$ |
| $1 \text{ T} \cong 907.18 \text{ kg}$ | $1000 \text{ kg} \cong 1.1 \text{ tons}$ |
| $1 \text{ fl oz} \cong 29.574 \text{ mL (cc)}$ | |
| $1 \text{ c} \cong 237 \text{ mL (cc)}$ | |
| $1 \text{ qt} \cong 0.946 \text{ L}$ | $1 \text{ L} \cong 1.057 \text{ qt}$ |